The Portuguese Massacre of Wiriyamu in Colonial Mozambique, 1964–2013

The Portuguese Massacre of Wiriyamu in Colonial Mozambique, 1964–2013

Mustafah Dhada

Bloomsbury Academic
An imprint of Bloomsbury Publishing Plc

B L O O M S B U R Y
LONDON · OXFORD · NEW YORK · NEW DELHI · SYDNEY

Bloomsbury Academic
An imprint of Bloomsbury Publishing Plc

50 Bedford Square
London
WC1B 3DP
UK

1385 Broadway
New York
NY 10018
USA

www.bloomsbury.com

BLOOMSBURY and the Diana logo are trademarks of Bloomsbury Publishing Plc

First published 2016
Paperback edition first published 2017

© Mustafah Dhada, 2016

Mustafah Dhada has asserted his right under the Copyright, Designs and Patents Act, 1988, to be identified as Author of this work.

All rights reserved. No part of this publication may be reproduced or transmitted in any form or by any means, electronic or mechanical, including photocopying, recording, or any information storage or retrieval system, without prior permission in writing from the publishers.

No responsibility for loss caused to any individual or organization acting on or refraining from action as a result of the material in this publication can be accepted by Bloomsbury or the author.

British Library Cataloguing-in-Publication Data
A catalogue record for this book is available from the British Library.

ISBN: HB: 978-1-4725-1198-0
PB: 978-1-3500-3680-2
ePDF: 978-1-4725-0622-1
ePub: 978-1-4725-1200-0

Library of Congress Cataloging-in-Publication Data
A catalog record for this book is available from the Library of Congress.

Typeset by RefineCatch Limited, Bungay, Suffolk

*To Those Who Perished at Wiriyamu,
I Hope They Find a Place to Rest Here*

Contents

Foreword *Peter Pringle*	x
Preface	xv
The road map	xv
The limits of this endeavor	xviii
Acknowledgments	xxi
List of Illustrations and Maps	xxiii
1. Introduction	1
Exile politics and diplomacy	1
The framing of the narrative	5
2. Literature Review	11
Written sources and their limits	13
The war and Wiriyamu in Portuguese sources	16
Church and other public records	18
Affirmative literature on the massacres	20
Wiriyamu from two perspectives	21
Texts on denial and doubts	23
Fictional narratives: Two works examined	26
3. Oral Research	31
The trial run	31
The false start	34
The work on site	37
Interviews off site	39
The final push	39
4. The Nationalist Struggle and the Colonial War in Mozambique	41
Geography, war, and Wiriyamu	41
Formative leadership	42
Nationalist diplomacy, internal dissent, and deaths	46
Portuguese counter-insurgency and the changing of the guard	52
The role of water in Tete's warfare	56
Wiriyamu at a point of no return	61

5. The Church in Tete 69
   Bishop Resende and the shortage of priests 72
   Portugalization and its impact on the Church 75
   Church–State relations in Unkanha 78
   The conflict over burials 80
   FRELIMO's courtship of priests 83

6. The Church and Mass Violence 87
   Missionaries and mass violence 87
   Parish responses to the liberation struggle 90
   The missionary protest against silence 93
   The Burgos priests and the massacre at Mucumbura 97
   Portuguese reprisals 102
   Mucumbura priests are sent to prison 106

7. The Wiriyamu Narrative: Genesis and Revelation 111
   The origins of the Wiriyamu story 111
   Wiriyamu travels overseas 118
   The labyrinth behind the publication 121

8. Portuguese Reaction to the Public Narrative 125
   Of denials and dismissals 125
   The response from *The London Times* and *The Sunday Times* group ... 129
   Understanding the Portuguese volte-face 134

9. Wiriyamu before the Massacre 139
   Wiriyamu and the destroyers 139
   The Wiriyamu triangle in structural perspective 141
   Creeks, rivers, and puddles 144
   The spirit world and the rainmakers 146
   Village life 148
   Cattle barons and the poor 151
   The final days 152

10. The Anatomy of the Wiriyamu Massacre 159
    Sadism and fire at Chaworha 162
    Juawu's swift disappearance 164
    Wiriyamu's demise and Melo's act of mercy 165
    Djemusse in flames before dark 166
    A tally of the numbers killed 169

11. Conclusion 173

Tables

1. Attesters to Wiriyamu — 179
2. Wiriyamu triangle, population census, 1970–2007 — 181
3. Djemusse population census, 1972 estimates — 182
4. Wiriyamu population census, 1972 estimates — 183
5. Juawu population census, 1972 estimates — 184
6. Riachu population census, 1972 estimates — 185
7. Chaworha population census, 1972 estimates — 186
8. List of the dead in Djemusse, December 16, 1972 — 190
9. List of the dead in Wiriyamu, December 16, 1972 — 191
10. List of the dead in Juawu, December 16, 1972 — 192
11. List of the dead in Chaworha, December 16, 1972 — 193
12. List of the dead in the triangle, unspecified locations, December 16, 1972 — 194

Bibliography — 197
- Portuguese manuscript collection: Torre do Tombo — 197
- British manuscript collection: Foreign and Commonwealth Office — 199
- FRELIMO ephemera and Maputo-based oral sources — 200
- Missionary ephemera, IEME: Instituto Español de Misiones Extranjeras, Madrid — 202
- Interviews, fieldnotes, and tape recordings — 203
- Articles, *The London Times* — 206
- Articles, *The London Sunday Times* — 211
- Articles, *Africa Report* — 212
- Books, miscellaneous articles, periodicals, and reports — 216

Index — 229

Foreword
Peter Pringle

In the chronicles of indiscriminate and brutal slaughter of human beings over the centuries, the story of the Wiriyamu massacre is not widely told. Under "events named massacres"—to distinguish them from genocide—Wikipedia lists more than one hundred and seventy, starting with the Romans killing Druids in Britain in the year 61, and ending with Sandy Hook Elementary School in the USA in 2012. Many of these atrocities from the last hundred years are well known: Amritsar, India, 1919; Guernica, Spain, 1937; Katym, Soviet Union, 1942; Sharpeville, South Africa, 1960; My Lai, Vietnam, 1968; Derry, Northern Ireland, 1972; Shabra and Shatila, Lebanon, 1982; Tiananmen Square, Beijing, 1989; Luxor, Egypt, 1997; Virginia Tech, USA, 2007; Houla, Syria, 2012.

The name of Wiriyamu, once a thriving African village of mud huts with straw roofs in west-central Mozambique, is not on the list. Yet on the morning of December 16, 1972, Portuguese colonial troops herded the inhabitants of Wiriyamu, including women and children, into the central square and ordered them to clap their hands and chant "goodbye." The troops then opened fire. Those who were not killed in the fusillade were blown to pieces by grenades. Shouting, "Kill them all," the soldiers continued the slaughter in four neighboring settlements near the banks of the Zambezi River where Mozambique juts into Zimbabwe (then Rhodesia), Zambia and Malawi, a region the Catholic missionaries knew as "the land God forgot." By the end of the day, almost four hundred villagers lay dead, their remains smoldering in funeral pyres made by the soldiers with straw from the roofs of their huts. A handful escaped to tell the story to local missionaries, who managed to smuggle lists of the dead to Europe, and eventually to London. Seven months later, on July 10, 1973, *The Times* published an account of the massacre by Father Adrian Hastings, a former British missionary in Africa. The single-column story with its restrained headline "Portuguese massacre reported by priests" reflected the uncorroborated nature of the report. The priests themselves had not witnessed the killing fields; no *Times* journalist had been to Mozambique to investigate them. Lisbon seized on this vulnerability and denied the report, calling the allegations "hearsay" and even claiming that a settlement named Wiriyamu simply did not exist.

This was an era before the Internet, before social media and Google Maps, a time when such reports from remote lands were filed without computers, or satellite phones, or the back-up of CNN. Journalists sent their stories, laboriously, via telex machines, if they could find one. The truth that four hundred Africans had been massacred emerged slowly. The priests had initially carried their reports to Rome, and only when that avenue produced no results had Father Hastings taken them to London.

The consequences of this revelation were huge. They triggered a mutiny by the young captains of the Portuguese colonial army who had long known that the African wars against the liberation movements were not winnable—despite proclamations from their generals about imminent victory. Nine months after *The Times* story, these young officers, with carnations instead of bullets in their rifle barrels, toppled the fifty-year-old fascist dictatorship in Lisbon. In that revolution, not a shot was fired.

Over the years, several authors—of articles, books, academic journal papers, two novels, and the makers of a documentary—have attempted to recreate what really happened. But the story of Wiriyamu has been hard to piece together. The records are sparse. Key official government documents have been lost, or deliberately destroyed, or never existed. The archives of the liberation movement, known as *Frente de Libertação de Moçambique* (Front for the Liberation of Mozambique, FRELIMO), were fragmentary. Access to witnesses always was and has remained a problem. Getting to the site that was Wiriyamu was an ordeal, and finding villagers willing to speak of that day has always been difficult, and, of course, the perpetrators of the crime, the young Portuguese soldiers and the Direcção-Geral de Segurança (General Directorate of Security) or DGS agents, were not ready to admit what they had done. Shortly after *The Times* report, FRELIMO fighters assassinated a key witness, the chief DGS undercover agent who had orchestrated the massacre.

Now, an author with credentials like no other for reconstructing the narrative has emerged to tell the story of Wiriyamu. A Mozambican-born son of a mechanic, Mustafah Dhada became a history professor. He grew up in central Mozambique, leaving only when the colonial war became unbearable for him and his family. For the last four decades, he has been putting together an archive documenting the massacre. His book is a unique insight into what happened.

As a British journalist based in London at the time, I played a small part in this drama by reporting on the massacre after the priests had revealed it. Within a few weeks in the summer of 1973, I encountered the complex backdrop to the massacre: the row over the first reports in London, the inevitability of the defeat of the Portuguese colonial masters in Africa, the cruelty of the secret police who kept Europe's last fascist regime in power, the fraught relations between the priests and the church hierarchy, the stunning courage of the young Catholic missionaries, and the rising power of the nationalist movements in Portugal's 400-year-old African colonies.

I met Mustafah Dhada in the summer of 1973. He was a 22-year-old researcher, working in the cramped offices of a tiny lobbying organization named the Committee for Freedom in Angola, Mozambique and Guinea. I was a journalist on *The Sunday Times* (*The Times*' sister paper) trying to verify Father Hastings' reports that caused such a rift in British politics.

The Times published the Wiriyamu story on the eve of a state visit to London by Portugal's then President, Marcello Caetano. The Tory government of Edward Heath rushed to the defense of Portugal, famously Britain's 600-year-old ally (and a North Atlantic Treaty Organization [NATO] member who provided the United States with important staging posts for its role as the world's policeman). Heath denounced *The Times* report as unsubstantiated propaganda. In a bitter House of Commons debate, Harold Wilson, the leader of the opposition Labour Party, called on Heath to cancel the visit, suggesting instead extending an invitation to the Prime Minister of New Zealand (whose government was protesting French nuclear tests in the Pacific). The Labour Party's objection was not connected with the massacre reports, Wilson asserted. Rather, it was "a condemnation of the whole life-style of Portuguese fascism at home and repressive colonialism abroad." But the Tory government went ahead with the visit.

Caetano arrived in London. A police cordon surrounded the Portuguese embassy and five thousand soaked demonstrators turned out to protest under the banner of the Committee for Freedom in Mozambique, Angola and Guinea. A few days later, in the Mozambique capital, Lourenço Marques, the Lisbon government organized a counter demonstration of tens of thousands protesting against *The Times* report and Harold Wilson's House of Commons speech. "May God deliver our English friends from Mr. Wilson," said one placard. The governor-general of Mozambique, Pimentel dos Santos, told the crowd, "We [Portugal] are the only country which has not yielded to the psychosis of abandonment [of our colonies] and continue silently devoted to the concept of a multiracial society, which is our reply to the problems of Africa and the world."

The *Sunday Times* sent me to Mozambique to investigate the massacre. Journalists for British daily newspapers had already arrived seeking the truth—and had left empty-handed. The *Daily Telegraph* correspondent (who was later found to be helping Lisbon counteract the reports) was promoting the official line that the settlement named Wiriyamu did not exist. The *Times* correspondent had been expelled from the country before he could complete his report.

Lisbon didn't want to give me a visa. A diplomat at the Portuguese embassy in London explained the delay: "We fear for the safety of any representative from the *Times* or the *Sunday Times*," he said. The people of Mozambique "are angry about the published reports," and "the places you want to visit are very small and people will know where you have come from and we cannot be sure of your safe passage. You are not likely to be shot, only really hindered."

A few days later, however, the visa was granted, and I was on my way. I stopped off in Madrid at the headquarters of the Burgos Fathers, the secular priests who had compiled the massacre report. They gave me a letter and a tape recording to play to the missionaries in Mozambique, asking them to help with my inquiries.

On arrival, the Portuguese authorities ignored all of my requests for assistance. In the capital, Lourenço Marques, the British consulate said they couldn't help either, and wished me luck. I flew to Tete, the nearest big town to the site, and checked in to the only place to stay, the Hotel Zambezi. The next morning, I walked the two miles through the bush to the small white-washed San Pedro mission where the priests lived and worked. I presented my tape recording from Madrid and they agreed to help. They showed me mission maps on which Wiriyamu was clearly marked. On the third day, the priests produced a fifteen-year-old boy, António Mixone, who had survived the December 16 massacre at one of the settlements named Chaworha. He had been shot in the shoulder. His parents and other relatives had been killed, but he and his four-year-old brother had escaped by running out of the funeral pyre.

Here was the first primary evidence, however slight and imperfect, that a massacre had indeed taken place. I took photographs of António with the priests, and the priests took photographs of him with me.

On the third day, as I was walking back to Tete, a burly DGS secret policeman arrested me. He insisted that I accompany him inside where Captain Joaquim Sabino, the local DGS chief, was waiting for me. Why had I been spending so much time with the priests? Sabino demanded. Other journalists had only spent a few hours at the mission. And what was I carrying in my satchel?

On his orders, I emptied the contents of the satchel onto his desk—notebooks, maps, the tape recorder, a copy of the Madrid letter to the priests, my camera and rolls of film. He was so absorbed with my notebook, which contained names and phone numbers supplied by human rights groups like Amnesty International, that I managed to take one of the rolls of film off his desk without him or his assistant noticing, and put it in my pocket.

Without further questions, Captain Sabino told me that I was being expelled, like my *Times* colleague before me, and I would be accompanied by an agent on the return flight to Lourenço Marques. I stayed there for several days, effectively under house arrest at the Hotel Polana. I tried to send a cable to the *Sunday Times* through the official cable office but was told no connection could be made. Later, I managed to send a cable via the hotel telex machine and the newspaper published my story. The DGS was angry that I had eluded their censorship. The next day, an agent arrived at the hotel and informed me that I must accompany him. We drove to a DGS safe house in a suburb of Lourenço Marques where another agent interrogated me. He claimed I had broken Portuguese law by publicly revealing the name of Captain Sabino. And he accused me of espionage. He claimed that rolls of film from my confiscated camera had showed that I had been taking photos of military installations and railway lines. He spread the photos on his desk. "That's nonsense," I said. "You know I didn't take those photos."

At that point, a very tall white man—so tall he could apparently not find trousers long enough to cover his calves—came into the room and sat down beside me. In a strong South African accent, he asked me several questions about my visit to the São Pedro mission. I assumed he was an agent of BOSS, the South African secret police, which was well known to have strong ties with the DGS. He suggested that we go together to the basement of the building, where there was a cafeteria, and have coffee. He told that I had been badly mistaken in believing anything the "lying" priests had told me, and that I was to be put on a plane immediately for Lisbon.

I arrived back in London without further incident, having concealed the roll of film from Captain Sabino's desk in my wash bag. It turned out that the film contained a photo I had taken of the massacre witness António at the São Pedro mission.

That weekend, August 5, 1973, the *Sunday Times* published my interview with António Mixone, which I had to recall from memory as my notebook was never returned. We agonized over whether to reveal his name, fearing there would be reprisals, but we also knew that Captain Sabino already knew his name from my notebook. The imperfect solution, we concluded, was to publish and take all possible steps to raise international alarm about his existence. The BBC immediately reported the story. We alerted British embassies and Amnesty International. I also gave evidence to the United Nations in New York. We contacted the Catholic Apostolic Delegation in London and they agreed to pass the information to the Vatican.

The evidence was still not enough for some readers of the *Sunday Times*. One letter to the editor said it was naïve to place any value on the evidence from a fifteen-year-old boy. "One would have preferred to see your resources and influence better deployed than in propagating sensationalism from what will prove to have been no more than a disgraceful canard."

In December 1974, two years after the massacre, the UN published its own report, concluding the atrocity had occurred. But Lisbon's vehement denials, its refusal to launch a thorough inquiry and its effective disinformation campaign, plus the international support for Lisbon by the United States, left a legacy of doubt over what had really happened at Wiriyamu.

In his meticulous reconstruction, Dhada has employed the crafts of an historian with the modern tools now available through cyberspace. Over the years, he has interviewed an impressive list of the players, many for the first time. He has traced the origins of the war between the colonial forces and the liberation movements. He has followed the evolution of relations between Lisbon and the Church, how the colonial conflict strained those relations and how the Church, through the missionaries, became an agency for social change. He has detailed the inner conflicts the priests experienced, as the Church hierarchy remained silent on the brutality of the secret police and the atrocities committed by the army. He has charted the break in this relationship when the priests started to record the names of those who were killed in atrocities, starting before Wiriyamu.

One interview, in particular, displays the priests' bravery and devotion: Padre José Sangalo of the Burgos Fathers was sitting in his mission, without electricity or running water, preparing to go to bed on the night of August 5, 1973, when the voice of the BBC newsreader crackled over his short-wave transistor radio, informing him that the story of António, the survivor from Chaworha, was now known to the world. Without regard for his own safety, he jumped on his moped, collected António from relatives, drove with him on the back through the bush to a FRELIMO base camp and handed over the boy, knowing he would now be safe. In the days that followed, the DGS interrogated and tortured Padre Sangalo trying to find out where António was, but each time Sangalo refused to tell them, and, in the end, he was expelled and put on a plane to Madrid. The Burgos priests were pleased to find him alive: the DGS had informed their headquarters that Sangalo had committed suicide by jumping out of the airplane.

Importantly, for the first time, Dhada has attempted what others have bypassed: a fascinating reconstruction of social and economic life in the five villages that made up the Wiriyamu region: who lived there, how they lived, and how they dealt with the increasing influence of the liberation fighters.

Finally, he describes how they died on December 16, 1972, with graphic descriptions of the atrocities they endured, and a tally of how many died. Not two hundred, as the official Portuguese report eventually conceded, but three hundred and eighty-five (all of them named), or approximately one-third of the one thousand, three hundred and fifty inhabitants of the five villages. It is not a story for the faint-hearted, but it is a complex, compelling and thorough narrative that finally, and unequivocally and firmly, puts Wiriyamu on the list of world "events named massacres."

Preface

The road map

Context-sensitive restorations are labor-intensive, mercifully never perfect—else they would be rendered 3D blueprints—and always messy. They entail examining where you stand, and where you ought to stand, before you begin the project. They also involve scanning the context of a given narrative, exposing and then evaluating its structural strengths and weaknesses, devising methods to procure evidentiary materials, locating these in written and oral repositories, and then restoring the narrative to nest in its appropriate historical space; all this before the actual narrative gets going.

This book's re-nesting of Wiriyamu is no exception. The first three chapters are a hard slog, and the slow pace may well discourage readers from continuing with the book, though these preliminaries are there to expose the problematic beams, reveal where the dry rot is in the literature, and explain the methods to be used to procure new written and oral evidence on the massacre. Readers lacking the patience to plough through these issues may well wish to plunge straight into the story with Chapter 4 as a starting point.

Readers will note that the section on literature review omits one minor work of fiction[1] and does not discuss photographs and films—for good reasons, their scarcity and value being two. Film rolls on the Mucumbura massacre that preceded Wiriyamu and that were sent by Tete's bishopric disappeared once they reached the colonial capital, where they are untraceable in the colonial archives that the Portuguese left behind. The whereabouts of Wiriyamu photos taken by Jorge Jardim, a supporter of the fascist dictator Salazar, are unclear. Photos by Dr dos Santos, a Portuguese medic, taken of the site visit, and publicly revealed in 2010 are now of poor image quality, though they do clearly display evidence of a massacre. Dos Santos junior, his son, is presumed to have these in his collection. The remainder, taken by Peter Pringle and the *London Times* and *Sunday Times*, are easily accessible through the papers' electronic archives. Of these, the most valuable depicts António Mixone, a survivor of the massacre, with a wounded shoulder, and this picture is included in the book. Obtaining copyright approval for the other image proved difficult. Felícia Cabrita, a Portuguese journalist, and her team took the remaining series of fourteen images.[2] These are invaluable as they depict survivors nineteen years after the massacre.

---

[1] António Lobo Antunes, *Os Cus de Judas* (Lisbon: Objetiva, 1979).
[2] Felícia Cabrita, "Os Mortos Não Sofrem," *Revista Expresso*, December 5, 1992; Felícia Cabrita, "Wiriyamu, Viagem ao Fundo do Terror," *Revista Expresso*, November 21, 1998; and Felícia Cabrita, *Massacres em África* (Lisbon: Esfera dos Livros, 2008).

Three maps grace the book: one of of twenty-five Church mission parishes in the Tete diocese. The map surrounds these with place names deemed important and cited in the book. One map shows the approximate boundaries of the Wiriyamu triangle's three chieftaincies. The last map identifies the massacre sites and the surrounding area, which were etched by rivers, creeks, mountains, and neighboring villages.

The book has nine images. I took all but two. Of these, six are portraits of leading figures in the Wiriyamu narrative: Domingo Kansande, who documented the events still warm to the touch on the night of the massacre; Padre Domingo Ferrão, who carefully tallied the dead; Padre José Sangalo, who helped the journalist Peter Pringle collect the qualitative evidence and saved Mixone from the jaws of certain death from the Portuguese secret police; Father Adrian Hastings, the intrepid priest who brought the story to light via *The London Times*; Peter Pringle, the lanky journalist who affirmed the revealed narrative, filing his story from memory, having been stripped of evidence collected from survivors; and António Mixone, who alerted the hospital about his ordeal. Peter Pringle took the last two pictures in 1973. The next two images were taken on site in 1995: one identifies exactly the spot where the massacre began, when Johnny Kongorhogondo, a Portuguese agent, shot dead his nemesis Consembera; the other pinpoints where the massacre ended, when villagers in Djemusse lined up to run a Portuguese gauntlet blocked at the other end by a set of burning huts. The image on the front cover frames the Wiriyamu memorial constructed approximately thirty feet from a large hut packed with people that was set alight by exploding grenades.

Of the several films about the massacre, two are documentaries and one is a work of fiction. One film records the return of Antonino Melo, the commander leading the carnage, to face survivors of the massacre,[3] which the author Robert Stocks analyses in depth in a seminal text in an edited volume on memories and reconciliation.[4] The other documents the massacre using synthetic footage as part of a larger text on Portugal's colonial wars.[5] A third film, based on a book of fiction,[6] elicited much discussion and a master's thesis, but it skirts around the anatomy of the massacre itself, and therefore is omitted from this book.[7]

The literature review on primary sources on Mozambique's freedom struggle relies on ephemera and oral interviews—a collection of one hundred artifacts in total. Of the set of documents culled from the Portuguese secret police archives, only forty-two proved reliable to inform the text, of which a handful brace the foundation for the

---

[3] Felícia Cabrita and Paulo Camacho, *Regresso a Wiriyamu* (Portugal: Sociedade Independente de Comunicação, 1998).
[4] Robert Stock, "Apologising for Colonial Violence: The Documentary Film *Regresso a Wriyamu*, Transitional Justice, and Portuguese-Mozambican Decolonization," in Brigit Schwelling (ed.), *Reconciliation, Civil Society, and the Politics of Memory: Transnational Initiatives in the 20th and 21st Century* (Bielefeld: Verlag, 2012), 239–276.
[5] Rádio e Televisão de Portugal, RTP, aired such a narrative on the Portuguese colonial wars. Joaquim Furtado, *A Guerra Colonial do Ultramar de Libertação* (Lisbon: Rádio e Televisão de Portugal, RTP, 2012).
[6] Margarida Cardoso, *A Costa dos Murmúrios*, DVD (Lisbon: Filmes do Tejo, 2004).
[7] Susana Maria Correia Poças de Carvalho, "Dois olhares sobre uma guerra: A Costa dos Murmúrios" (MA thesis, Open University, Lisbon, 2008).

colonial war narrative. The remainder has been used to evaluate Portugal's state of knowledge and its take on the colonial war in the district surrounding Wiriyamu. This evaluation is to be found in the review of the literature on Portuguese primary sources.

Apropos Portuguese archival documents, these are identified in the footnotes only by their classification, sufficient to track them down in the archives. The Bibliography provides a more complete citation of each artifact either used in or consulted for the book.

The collection of articles outlined in the Bibliography serves two purposes. One set of ninety-six items scooped from *Africa Report*, augmented by a few from *Jeune Afrique*, *Africa Today*, *Presénce Africaine*, and *Lusotopie*, helped lay the groundwork for the text in the nationalist war before 1970, which is presented here with very few footnotes to allow the narrative to flow. The collection of two hundred and twenty articles from *The London Times* and *The Sunday London Times* aided by a stack of thirty primary sources from the British Foreign and Commonwealth Office went to chisel the narrative on the revelation and its Portuguese denial. Titles of news bulletins and articles from *Africa Report* are omitted in the footnotes, but they are recorded in the Bibliography under a separate heading, sufficient for cross-referencing.

Electronically accessible sources are cumbersome word-hoggers. They appear once in the footnotes; the Bibliography omits them, unless they are viewed as crucial to the text. To save valuable footprint, inordinately long URLs (Uniform Resource Locators) have been contracted using *TinyURL.com* online software. One table on Tete's demographics proved too lengthy to include and appears posted at http://tinyurl.com/q4yn52t.

The Bibliography gives details on the eighteen tape-recorded interviews and ninety-six recorded fieldnotes, but excludes one hundred and two data sources recorded in annotated fragments during fieldwork. Two hundred and sixteen carefully curated respondents supplied data for the twelve tables wedged between the text and the Bibliography, while qualitative data for the study came from an additional pool of thirty informants.

Tape-recorded oral sources are quoted fully in the footnotes once, and thereafter shortened to last name, interview, and date held. Of the oral sources culled, fifteen undergird the narrative on Wiriyamu's military context in Tete. The anatomy of that day's massacre was pieced together from details provided by twenty-four respondents, supported by a group of fact-checkers who worked closely with the two hundred and sixteen affected families already mentioned. One hundred and seven of these respondents came from Chaworha, thirty from Wiriyamu, thirty from Juawu, fourteen from Riachu, and thirty-five from Djemusse.

Data on the Church in Tete between 1970 and 1974 and its role in the story came from two sources: thirty documents of synthetic value lodged in the Burgos archives, and oral evidence provided by missionaries and others involved in Wiriyamu's trajectory as it reached the pages of *The Times of London*.[8]

---

[8] They were Miguel Buendia, António Cachavi, José Capela, Padre Alberto Fonte Castellã, António Chuva, Enrique Ferrando, Padre Domingo Ferrão, Father Adrian Hastings, Kalifornia Kaniveti, Domingo Kansande, Abidu Karimu, Padre Vicente Berenguer, Sister Irmã Lúcia Saez de Ugarte, Alfonso Valverde de Lion, Antonino Melo, António Mixone, Podista Mchenga, Peter Pringle, Cantineiro Raul, Padre José Sangalo, Enéria Tenente Valeta, Vasco Tenente Valeta, João Xavier, and Bulachu Pensadu Zambezi.

The limits of this endeavor

Military operations before 1970 directly unrelated to this narrative on the massacre are missing from the ensuing pages. Works by Mondlane, Munslow and Isaacman cover these from the nationalist perspective,[9] while several others evaluate the same critically, and occasionally from a pro-Portuguese perspective.[10] Additionally, studies by Jundanian, Cruz e Silva and João Cabrita are useful to those seeking a detailed analysis of insurgent leadership during the nationalist and post-independence period.[11]

In addition, for reasons of space, and perhaps in a haste to reach Tete, the chapter on the nationalist struggle and the Portuguese colonial war truncates the blow-by-blow account of the military strategies at play, the role of diplomacy and the contribution that foreign aid made during the initial phase of the war. The subject of diplomacy and foreign aid deserves a separate treatment in its own right—perhaps as a seminal article similar to one on Guinea-Bissau's liberation diplomacy.[12]

While oral data culled from interviews with military commanders, priests and grass-root respondents inform the book's discussion on the colonial war after 1970, it does not cover aspects unrelated to Wiriyamu proper. Readers seeking a broader perspective on the character of the war, and the war in Tete in particular, are urged to consult Sayaka Funada-Classen and João Paulo Coelho, the Mozambican historian and novelist.[13]

The text discusses the Church in Tete and its role in exposing Wiriyamu, but it fails to provide an omniscient narrative on the White Fathers and their missionary work in Tete specifically, though it covers their last stand before their departure from Mozambique. Now that the archives of the White Fathers in Rome are open, a deeper treatment on the subject will be warranted as a stand-alone study. Also to be noted is the text's limited treatment of the Burgos priests, which is confined to two aspects of the story: personnel involved in Wiriyamu and Church–State relations materially connected to it.

---

[9] Eduardo Mondlane, *The Struggle For Mozambique* (Harmondsworth: Penguin Books, 1970); *Panaf Great Lives, Eduardo Mondlane* (London: Panaf, 1972); H. Shore, in E. Mondlane, *The Struggle for Mozambique* (London: Zed Press, 1983), pp. xii–xxxi; Barry Munslow, *Mozambique: The Revolution and Its Origins* (Harlow: Longman, 1983), 62, 66, 69, 81, 89, 98–104, 105, 107, 110, 111, 114–115, 119, and 139; Allen Isaacman and Barbara Isaacman, *Mozambique: From Colonialism to Revolution, 1900–1982* (Boulder: Westview Press, 1983); and John Paul, *Mozambique: Memoirs of a Revolution* (Harmondsworth: Penguin Books, 1975).

[10] Thomas H. Henriksen, *Revolution and Counterrevolution, 1964–1974* (Westport, Connecticut: Greenwood Press, 1983); and João M. Cabrita, *Mozambique: The Tortuous Road to Democracy* (Basingstoke: Palgrave Macmillan, 2001).

[11] Brendan F. Jundanian, "Resettlement Programs: Counterinsurgency in Mozambique," *Comparative Politics*, 6 (1974): 519–540; Teresa Cruz e Silva, *Protestant Churches and the Formation of Political Consciousness in Southern Mozambique (1930–1974)* (Basil: P. Schletwein, 2001); and João Cabrita, *Mozambique: The Tortuous Road to Democracy*.

[12] Mustafah Dhada, "Guinea's Liberation Diplomacy," *Portuguese Studies Review*, 4, 1 (Spring–Summer 1995): 20–40.

[13] Sayaka Funada-Classen, *The Origins of War in Mozambique* (Somerset West: African Minds, 2013); and João Paulo Borges Coelho, *O Início da Luta Armada Em Tete, 1968–1969* (Maputo: Archivo Histórico de Moçambique, 1989).

Readers will note unfilled gaps in this book, which is silent on a specific aspect of the massacre related to a small area below the village of Wiriyamu, named Riachu. The tentative nature of the data collected on its erasure proved too weak to speak about it with authenticity. What is available lies buried in Padre Domingo Ferrão's list of the dead, and perhaps in the hearts and memories of commandos involved in Riachu during the military operation dubbed Marosca "Entrapment."

In addition, we know next to nothing about the three-day manhunt for survivors after the massacre. The little that we know is discussed in the text. That section of the book, while bringing the triangle to life, has two sets of details missing: one is on the chief of Kongorhogondo who played a role before Wiriyamu was laid to waste. His whereabouts and the fate of one of his two sons are uncertain. The other son's post-massacre identity and location are known to this author but omitted here to protect his life and in the hope that one day the truth of his role will be placed on archival record.

The portrait of life in Wiriyamu is a diptych, one statistical and the other qualitative. The statistical one is hard on the eyes, and viewers will be sorely tempted to gloss over it. It appears as is for two reasons: one to bear witness to restoration, the giving back to history what Wiriyamu was in raw numbers, and the other to settle once and for all the claim made recently by two Portuguese authors[14] that Wiriyamu was a cluster of transient dwellings too insignificant to be noted in colonial maps.

The qualitative panel is a complex triple-layered jigsaw puzzle. The basic layer comprises micro-data from eyewitnesses and informants. Too numerous to annotate individually, they can be gleaned from the list of interviews in the Bibliography. While one eyewitness could tell where the yard of a family was, several others could recall the range of a tree's shade at noon, the color of a certain pregnant goat, the number of goats a family had, who was married to whom, a person's gait, nicknames by which some individuals were known, or the pace of a victim's walk just before they fell. Some information was deliberately left under-explored for reasons of sensitivity, such as the height of the pyre under which informants fell.

The second layer draws from a considerable body of literature[15] now developed in the field of traditional authorities, spirit mediums, witchcraft and sorcery. This body cumulatively informs the canvas' discussion on the chieftaincies of Wiriyamu, and their religious practices.

The third layer is restorative. Inspired by Collingwood's "historical imagination" thesis,[16] it connects the dots between disparate data to bring to light village life in Wiriyamu. In the process, vague chronological references have been left as they were given and as they would appear in a naive portrait, while every attempt was made to re-create the site founded soon after the Tawara rebellion at the turn of the last century.

---

[14] Bruno C. Reis and Pedro A. Oliveira, "Cutting Heads or Winning Hearts: Late Colonial Portuguese Counterinsurgency and the Wiriyamu Massacre of 1972," *Civil Wars*, 14, 1 (2012): 80–103.
[15] Authors consulted included works by Lars Buur, Fernando Florêncio, Christian Geffray, Alcinda Honwana, Victor Igreja, Paolo Israel, Helene Maria Kyed, Christy Schuetze, Leroy Vail and Landeg White, and Harry G. West. See Bibliography for details.
[16] Robin George Collingwood, *The Idea of History* (Oxford: Oxford University Press, 1994).

The final section of the book warrants additional remarks. It does not cover life in the triangle *after* the massacre—that trajectory, best studied under the rubric of trauma and healing, proved beyond the scope of this book, as did resilience strategies adopted by survivors and their families to heal trauma.

Finally, ethno-historians and linguists will note two anomalies in the book. Wiriyamu shared a common cosmology in the region, in which the spirit of the lion plays an important role in rainmaking. Studies in neighboring Wiriyamu refer to this spirit as *mhondoro*. Informants in the Wiriyamu triangle called it *mphondorho*, which this book elects to use out of respect for the dead, as the spirit was said to have been active in the final days before the massacre. Similarly, the spelling of Chaworha has been left as I heard it phonetically, and not Chawora, as reported during the massacre revelation. On the other hand, informants referred to chiefs sometimes as "*mfumus*," and at other times as "*chefe*." This text elects the use of "chiefs" for the sake of consistency.

These, then, are some of the limits of this endeavor.

Acknowledgments

This book has one objective: restore Wiriyamu to its nest. As such, it is a labor of many. Herman Lujan, President Emeritus of the University of Northern Colorado (UNC), supported my leave of absence for a Maputo-bound Fulbright for field research. António Sopa, archivist at Mozambique's national repository in Maputo, located documents worked on by earlier scholars, notably Teresa Cruz e Silva, João Borges Coelho, Gulam Taju, Tony Hedges, and Yussuf Adam. Jeanne Penvenne shared her knowhow on archival research in Maputo-based repositories. Kristi Ehrig-Burgess, head of the Library, Archives and Digitization at the Mingei, procured documents needed for this book after fieldwork. Felícia Cabrita tracked down the commander responsible for the carnage and facilitated a meeting that led to interviews.

Abidu Karimu trained to collect data on mass violence and deal with fallouts from continued exposure to mass violence and trauma-filled narratives. Among the military informants on the nationalist side, three are worthy of note: General Hama Tai, General António Bonifácio Grouveta, and Mariano de Araújo Matsinha. All three agreed to talk openly on the armed struggle in Tete before and after the Wiriyamu massacre. General Hama Tai cancelled several meetings to accommodate the needs of this project as we both pored on all fours over maps documenting the nationalist movements in Tete after 1970.

Four additional informants deserve a mention. António Cachavi, brother of Chico, the secret police agent who led the charge to leave no one alive at Chaworha talked about his late brother, risking reprisals against his family. The second informant is Antonino Melo, the commander who led the colonial troops to "clean up" Wiriyamu. While following orders, he appeared to have shown flashes of compassionate courage, once by plucking a child and her mother out of a hut set on fire by soldiers upon his orders, and once by protecting an adult female from sexual predators among troops under his command.

The third respondent is the late Father Adrian Hastings who granted access to his papers and diaries that inform this text but are not included here, while his sister fed me when I needed sustenance the most! Peter Pringle, *The Sunday Times* investigative journalist, deserves two mentions, once because he managed to retrieve a roll of film from under the nose of the secret police agents, which he took to London to back up Father Hastings' revelations.

Marc Aramian restored re-magnetized cassettes, which were transcribed by my student assistant, Leandro Simões. Another student, Jeff Provencher, shared his findings on nationalist diplomacy and foreign aid during Mozambique's colonial struggle and helped me digitize my collection of documents on Wiriyamu. Nichole Villanueva, my undergraduate research intern, checked and re-checked some of the text's citations, and compiled data on nationalist military operations and diplomacy that inform, but are not included in, this text.

One exceptionally talented colleague has made a mark on this work. Brett Schmoll read the work from start to finish, and his handiwork looms larger than he suspects. Also, I could not have had a better Departmental Chair in Jeanne Harrie and her successor Clíona Murphy. My thanks also goes to Bill Grantham, a fellow Catz scholar and alumnus, who piloted smoothly my landing as a faculty among colleagues. Blind reviewers and editors at *Civil War*, *History In Africa*, and *The American Historical Review* helped sharpen the focus of parts of this narrative as did Rosemary Galli, who read earlier drafts of this work. Blind reviewers at Bloomsbury Academic made a compelling case for re-framing the book, which they thought needed a "bold" introduction and a fuller portrait of Wiriyamu before its demise. Their wishes are partly filled here, I think.

The text went through numerous edits, the last one at the capable hands of Paula Devine and Tara Grover Smith. Every attempt has been made to address errors, factual omissions, and their interpretation. Where possible I have sought to tone down stylistic infelicities, which native English speakers would find idiomatically too jarring to read. Three individuals at Bloomsbury nurtured this work to safe delivery: Rhodri Mogford, Commissioning Editor in History, who nudged the project along when most needed and in the right direction; Emma Goode, Senior Editorial Assistant, who ensured everyone connected with it met submission deadlines; and Merv Honeywood at RefineCatch, whose unfailing patience in undertaking repeated edits at the page proof stage eliminated numerous errors festering the text.

Peter Pringle penned the Foreword, which neatly ties this book in a bow. Finally, my thanks go to Dr Elizabeth Kaback, MD, who brought me back from the brink of my own heartless extinction. Needless to add, none mentioned above is responsible for the limited nature of this endeavor. I am.

Mustafah Dhada
dhada@mindspring.com

List of Illustrations and Maps

Illustrations

Cover image: the Wiriyamu monument, erected at the behest of Padre Berenguer soon after Mozambique's independence. Photo taken by author, © 1995.

1	António Mixone, Chaworha survivor. Photo taken by Peter Pringle, © 1973. Used with permission.	6
2	Padre José Sangalo, Madrid. Photo taken by author, © 1995.	89
3	Domingo Kansande, Cantina Raul. Photo taken by author, © 1995.	112
4	Padre Domingo Ferrão, Tete. Photo taken by author, © 1995.	113
5	Peter Pringle, Tete. Photo taken by Peter Pringle, © 1973. Used with permission.	130
6	The reconstruction of the Chaworha massacre with Mixone showing where he stood as he watched Consembera, the first victim of the massacre, fall where Abidu Karimu stands in the image. Photo taken by author, © 1995.	163
7	Reconstruction of the final gauntlet that faced the people of Charowha, with Abidu Karimu leading the discussion. Photo taken by author, © 1995.	167
8	Father Adrian Hastings, Leeds. Photo taken by author, © 1996.	176

Maps

1	Church missions and place names in Tete	2
2	Chieftaincies of the Wiriyamu triangle	155
3	The Wiriyamu triangle	160

1

Introduction

Exile politics and diplomacy

Life in exile slams you against a wall of dreadful silence. In a sense, exile is worse than death. You are gone. At home they whimper at your loss. The land below you vanishes and you are left hugging memories fractured by distance. You are never the same again. Trauma envelops your view, filtering the world in layered gauzes. The uncertainty of where you are shape-shifts to form the new you. Your landless past then freezes your old identity. You have tons to say but your tongue is dry-iced.

It is not easy to re-craft a life in exile, though. I should know. I shall never forget the afternoon of August 16, 1972. I had arrived at London's Heathrow airport from Mozambique via Zambia with a one-way ticket and fifteen hundred pounds sterling in my pocket—and very little English. The little English I had, had been "picked off the pavements"[1]—to quote Amílcar Lopes Cabral, the Cape Verdian agronomist then leading the fight to free Guinea and the adjacent Cape Verde Islands from Portuguese colonial rule in West Africa. He was alive then and had six more months to live.

I remember the English sun most vividly. It was tired and mellow, crafted to fit an empire in decline; not a fireball fit to roast your back and shelter others under your shadow. But I was not alone. Others before me had gone through the exile mill. Some had survived to tell the tale. Others had turned adversity into a weapon of choice to fight the power of silence over the past.[2]

Several who fought back come to mind as I write this. Cabral was one.[3] Another was Agostinho Neto, then leading the fight to oust the Portuguese in Angola via the MPLA—the Popular Movement for the Liberation of Angola.[4] Yet another was

---

[1] Oral remark made by Cabral during his 1972 visit to the United States at a speech at Lincoln University.
[2] The phrase is Michel-Rolph Toruillot's from the title of a book examining the West's failure to acknowledge rebellion, slaughter and mass violence, and thereby exercising its power in the making and recording of history. Michel-Rolph Toruillot, *Silencing the Past: Power and the Production of History* (Boston: Beacon Press, 1995).
[3] For Cabral's life in exile, see Patrick Chabal, "Cabral as Revolutionary Leader" (PhD dissertation, University of Cambridge, 1980). A synopsis is also given in Mustafah Dhada, *Warriors at Work, How Guinea Was Really Set Free* (Niwot: University Press of Colorado, 1993), 139–148.
[4] For details of Neto's formative years, see "Bishop R. E. Dodge, António Agostinho Neto. Some Biographic Notes" (Kitwe, Zambia: Mozambique, Angola, Guinea-Bissau Information Centre, MAGIC, Repository, 1967), 1–2.

CHURCH MISSIONS & PLACE NAMES IN TETE

✝ ◯ CHURCH MISSIONS

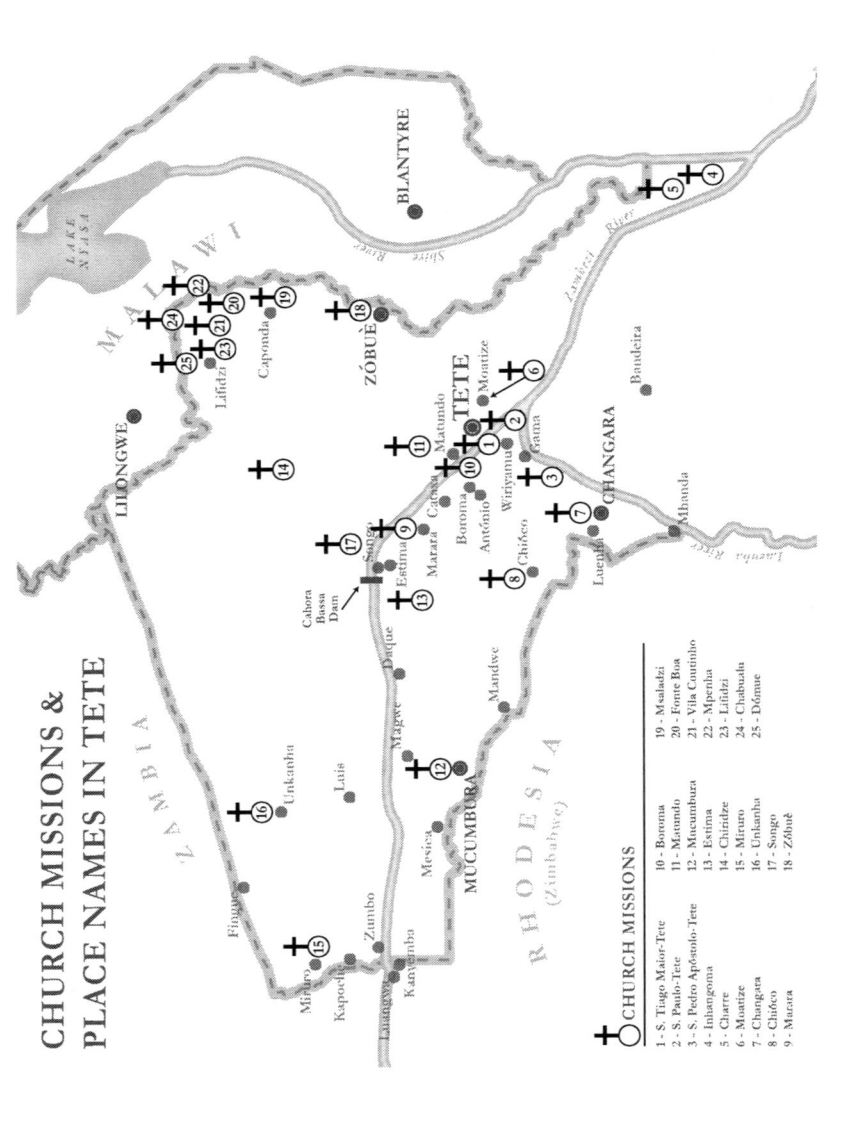

1 - S. Tiago Maior-Tete
2 - S. Paulo-Tete
3 - S. Pedro Apóstolo-Tete
4 - Inhangoma
5 - Charre
6 - Moatize
7 - Changara
8 - Chiôco
9 - Mucata
10 - Boroma
11 - Matundo
12 - Mucumbura
13 - Estima
14 - Chiridzi
15 - Miruro
16 - Unkanha
17 - Songo
18 - Zóbuè
19 - Msaladzi
20 - Fonte Boa
21 - Vila Coutinho
22 - Mpenha
23 - Lifidzi
24 - Chabualo
25 - Dómuè

Map 1 Church missions and place names in Tete

Eduardo Mondlane, by then dead, but who had led FRELIMO until 1969. Whereas Cabral sought the re-crafting of the self through a strategy of "re-Africanization" as a relational matrix on which the nurturing of identity and culture could rest,[5] Neto had opted for a different route.

Cabral had stressed the vitality of liberation diplomacy in the global context to educate the host of others on Luso-Africa.[6] Neto, on the other hand, focused on poetry as a vehicle for healing from within and Marxism as a strategy for liberating the Angolan collective wounded by colonialism.[7] Mondlane had taken a very intricate and perhaps too delicate approach resting on charismatic pluralism. He was to deploy the force of his personality and his considerable persuasive skills to bring disparate nationalist forces to co-exist and thence work together towards one aim—a free Mozambique.[8]

But Cabral et al. were beings fueled by intellects on fire. Some of them were analytically agile. Others were swift to apply normative matrices to transcend the purely personal by transforming it into a utilizable strategy of liberation for mainland Luso-Africa—Guinea-Bissau, Mozambique and Angola. For lesser mortals of my ilk, the perspective was much narrower and the existential and intellectual handicaps more difficult to overcome.

The West stood disengaged, in epistemological silence, watching the armed struggle unravel before their eyes. Their bread was buttered on the Portuguese side. They helped shore up its military capabilities with arm supplies, and training in counter-insurgent combat, while supporting Lisbon's diplomacy at the United Nations, which viewed its colonial holdings as a visceral mission worth fighting for to save Western civilization.[9] Ultimately, Luso-Africa fought free of imperial Portugal during the late 1950s, the 1960s, and the early 1970s despite the West's indifference.

This is not to say there were not periodic rumbles here and there. No. There were. A report or two on labor conditions; obtuse debates in the General Assembly of the United Nations; and articles in leading newspapers—more of that later—did appear only to fade into a distant memory. On the whole, though, Luso-Africa inhabited the margins of the West's conscience as a political fakir. As Trouillot's meditation on similar cases suggests, this response was not surprising given the West's powerful refusal to engage Portugal's adversaries as partners in the production of non-European history.[10]

---

[5] For the root source of this perspective, see Etudiants d'Afriques Portugaise, "Situation des Etudiants Noirs Dans le Monde," *Presénce Africaine*, 13 (1952): 236.
[6] As early as 1965, Cabral had already realized the importance of diplomacy in liberation. In an interview with the South African journalist Frene Ginwala of *The New African*, he said, "In this time of our struggle it is more important for us to get economic help than even weapons." "Liberating Portuguese Guinea from Within," *The New African*, 4, 4 (1965): 85. Cabral's actual diplomacy is documented in Dhada, "Guinea's Liberation Diplomacy."
[7] Mário de Andrade, "Literature and Nationalism in Angola," *Presénce Africaine*, 13, 41 (1962): 115–122; and Mário de Andrade, "Poesia Africana de Expressão Portuguesa, Breve Notas Explicativas," *Presénce Africaine*, 80, 58 (1966): 433–500.
[8] Mondlane, *The Struggle for Mozambique*, 122–138.
[9] The earliest and the best treatment on this subject of arms and ammunition from the West still remains that by William Minter, *Portuguese Africa and the West* (New York: Monthly Review Press, 1972).
[10] Trouillot, *Silencing the Past*.

The problem of lack of global consciousness in matters Luso-African was real. Cabral and his fellow leaders had repeatedly addressed this issue by establishing solidarity committees in major European capitals with a view to affecting a change of policy towards Portugal's African colonies. Cabral, perhaps more than any other, understood the importance of public and private diplomacy to free Luso-Africa. In this, he was an unparalleled master and a consummate practitioner. Between 1960 and 1973, he traveled to over twenty countries clocking up over eighty visits—visits that yielded new friends and donors for the cause, and which neutralized several enemies from various quarters.[11]

Nothing had worked—and for good reason. Evidence provided by liberation movements on Portugal's misconduct was seen by the Western powers as suspect at best and attacked as a lie. Portuguese missions abroad had the upper hand here given their diplomatic heft, financial prowess, and support garnered from the West in return for the use of the Azores, strategically important for NATO security. This is not to suggest that the solidarity committees did nothing for liberation. They did. They strengthened ties among liberation sympathizers, which led to new converts, facilitating the flow of much-needed humanitarian aid for Luso-African liberation.[12]

However, these committees had failed to persuade Portugal's allies to view history as a non-imperial narrative, one justly deserving their engaged partnership, by stemming the flow of arms running through Portugal's imperial jugular. An incision was needed to open that jugular, a credible strategy of information diplomacy, for lack of a better term. For such a strategy to work, it had to be collected by a disinterested third party and handled by a respectable media with a broad readership outside the converted. In short, a publicity drive involving the press had to be handled by a paper with clout —a thunderer, a trustworthy gatekeeper of truth striking at the heart of the Western establishment.

In the end, two entities split open Portugal's imperial jugular. One was the Vatican, then undergoing major doctrinal revisions under the Vatican II Council, which invited Luso-African leaders in their capacity as Christians to a Papal audience. In the eyes of the Portuguese, however, this invitation tacitly acknowledged the legitimacy of the Luso-African fight, bringing the Vatican into open diplomatic conflict with Caetano's Lisbon, while leading to an increase of state-level humanitarian aid for the liberation struggle.[13]

The other entity was Catholic priests who revealed Wiriyamu to the world, a story untouched by Luso-African nationalists and published by a major newspaper, a story powerful enough to rattle Portugal's imperial cage and unnerve its allies. Portugal's conscript army had encircled Wiriyamu, located 267 miles as the crow flies from where da Gama had originally landed. They were convinced they would find insurgents embedded among civilians. They found none. There ensued Wiriyamu's massacre.

---

[11] See Tables 2 through 5, Appendix C, in Dhada, *Warriors at Work*, 172–181.
[12] Reuter, "Sweden to double its aid to Frelimo," *The Times*, July 16, 1973, 1d; and Reuter, "Sweden triples its aid to Frelimo fighters," *The Times*, March 26, 1974, 5c.
[13] Details to be found in Dhada, "Guinea's Liberation Diplomacy," 20–40.

Once revealed, Portugal denied the story; its propaganda offensive however, failed to stop the flood of revelations that followed.[14]

The framing of the narrative

I heard of the Wiriyamu massacre on Tuesday, July 10, 1973, at 9:30 in the morning, when a classmate handed me that morning's *London Times*. It had "Portuguese massacre reported by priests" on its front page. Father Adrian Hastings, a White Father, member of the Society of the Missionaries of Africa and a prolific scholar of African Christianity, had bylined the report 206 days after it had happened, and had given the details to *The Times* for publication. An accomplished historian, Father Hastings was particularly sensitive to issues of human rights and self-determination in Africa and was keenly aware of the need for scholars to listen to the voices of the colonized from the canyons below and to incorporate these in historical works. To him, the voiceless at the margins of authority and power mattered: "I came from an old liberal tradition in Britain. Social justice was a cornerstone of my upbringing."[15]

I sat down to read the rest of the massacre story. On December 16, 1972, at noon, the Portuguese colonial army surrounded Wiriyamu and Chaworha; killed their inhabitants; set fire to the thatched huts and holding pens for cattle, goats, and chickens; camped nearby for three days "to finish off fleeing survivors"; packed up their gear, and left. The complex fell silent, except for the burning field of cadavers covering the area in smoke.

In subsequent stories, one photograph depicted a victim with bullet wounds traversing his shoulder blades. Nearly four hundred people died on that Saturday, as several villages perished during the killing spree between noon and sunset,[16] one man bellowing the final directive, "Aphane Wense!"—"Kill Them All," followed by "Leave No One Alive. Those Are Our Orders."[17] Some of the soldiers returned weeks later to burn and bury the bloating dead.[18]

Wiriyamu sat crouched, as it were, protected by boulders on the southwest central banks of the River Zambezi, at 16°18'6.55"S, and 33°38'50.47"E, in a triangle 351 miles northwest of Búzi, the village of my birth.[19] Both villages had rivers running nearby: the mighty Zambezi and the Búzi river.[20] Both were near a colonial district capital (Beira and Tete respectively). Like Wiriyamu, Búzi had no electricity, running water or a sewerage system. Unlike Wiriyamu, Búzi had neither tarred roads nearby, nor public

---

[14] The earliest compilation of the story is in a book by Adrian Hastings, *Wiriyamu: My Lai in Mozambique* (London: Search Press, 1974).
[15] Father Adrian Hastings, interviews by author, Oxford, London, and Leeds, 1977, 1978, 1979, 1981, 1995, 1996. For Hastings' biography, see "Adrian Hastings," *The London Telegraph*, June 26, 2001.
[16] The five villages were: Chaworha, Wiriyamu, Juawu, Riacho, and Djemusse.
[17] Eyewitness accounts on site during 1994–1995 fieldwork.
[18] Antonino Melo, interview by author, near Lisbon, Portugal, 1995 and 2014.
[19] Map coordinates: 20° 7' 29" south, 34° 35' 10" west.
[20] For a biography of the Zambezi river, see "Zambezi, River of Life (Episode 4)," accessed February 3, 2013, http://www.youtube.com/watch?v=UX3RH82E5Eg.

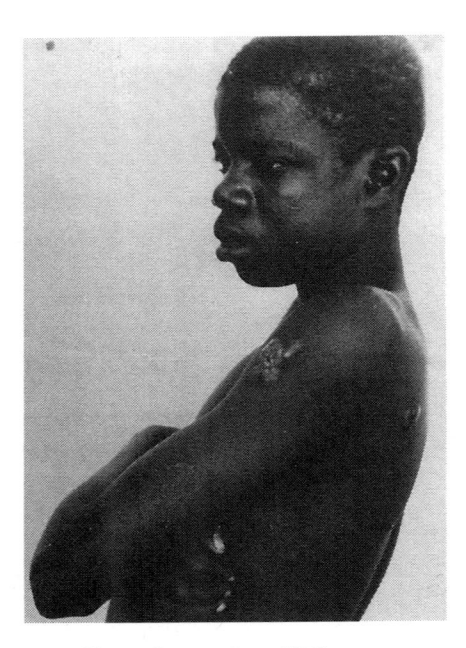

Photo 1 António Mixone, Chaworha survivor, 1973

transport buses. Wiriyamu and Búzi both hugged a riverbank abundant in toads, crocodiles, mambas, hippopotamuses, turtles and iguanas.

I knew from contacts in the region that the colonial war was heading southbound towards Mozambique's narrowest girth, diagonal from my village. Grief overwhelmed me. The thought of a similar tragedy striking at or near the place of my birth threatened my sense of belonging. Memories of Búzi welled up, and memories were all I had far away from home.

In Búzi, the nights of my childhood were as filled with sounds as Wiriyamu's. Toads would belch and croak. A mamba slithered amidst tall grass on its way to eat. Occasionally, its muscular vise snapped shut and the toad ceased to be. A brief mourning would ensue, then the war on life would resume. On hot and humid summer nights, Búzi, like Wiriyamu, filled with rhythmic beats from *batuques*, beating drums draped in goatskin. Strange as it may sound in the case of my village, they appeared to originate from the sky, depending on the breeze on a given night. Occasionally, these sounds were laced with peals of laughter from men on a binge, killing the pain of want or worse, numbing the blows of forced labor, which denied them the right to ache.

Whispers and soft talk in the house meant "*os gentes estavam falar assuntos e coisas*," the people were discussing matters, "things," that kept everyone safe and protected. We were a patriarchy. My father's tones were predictable, regular, and reassuringly consistent. My mother's nuzzle-wrapped his words firmly in a cupped bundle. On those nights, neither the mambas and the crocodiles, nor the mythical lions on the prowl opposite the house, could touch the warmth within. They reassured me of my place in the universe. Young ones must have found similar nights in the dark reassuring in Wiriyamu before it was erased.

Wiriyamu reawakened memories of life in colonial Mozambique, of which one was the sight of convicts in shackles heading to prison in the meat-roasting midday sun. The other was of witnessing forced laborers waiting to have their wounds triaged at the clinic, its walls oozing with the blood of unhealed wounds. By the time I left Mozambique, we had already heard of labor unrest 800 miles to the north of Búzi in Mueda, reportedly put down with deadly force.[21]

But perhaps the most hurtful of all were memories of micro-aggression,[22] predators lying in wait as you stood in line to buy a cheese bun in the school cafeteria. Such attacks intensified after the nationalist war began in 1964, particularly attacks against ethnic minorities.[23] For that cheese bun, we were willing to put up with slurs and eat isolated from predators near the gulch abuzz with mosquitoes. At thirteen, such indignities eviscerated your guts into balls of adolescent trauma. All I could think of then was to escape from that hell. It later transpired I was not alone in praying for deliverance.[24]

The Wiriyamu massacre was not a surprise to those who had lived in the belly of the beast. Mozambique was not alone in incurring massacres. Angola witnessed similar violence with the Luanda uprisings, which then spread into the countryside.[25] Vigilante groups sprang up overnight to protect civilians. Lisbon's failure to supply weapons to colonial troops compounded the problem, leading to the gruesome slaughter of UPA-led Angolans (União das Populações de Angola). In one instance, eight hundred were listed dead.[26] Guinea-Bissau too had its share of violence, though not as gruesome as Wiriyamu's. Similar reports of violence circulated among political activists and refugees from Cape Verde to São Tomé and Príncipe.[27]

---

[21] "Quantos Morreram Em Mueda," *Macua.org*, accessed December 16, 2011, http://www.Macua. Org/Quantos_Morreram_Em_Mueda.Htm; "Reunião de indígenas perturbada por agitadores estrangeiros que f–oram repelidos," *O Século*, June 19, 1960; Alberto Joaquim Chipande, "The massacre of Mueda," *Mozambique Revolution*, 43 (1970): 12–14; "Mueda evocada em Portugal," *Notícias*, June 13, 1981; "Mueda: memórias de um massacre," *Tempo*, 609, June 13, 1982, 24; *Notícias*, June 19, 1982. Yussuf Adam and Hilário Alumasse Dyuti, "Entrevista: o massacre de Mueda—falam testemunhas," *Arquivo*, 14 (1993): 117–128; and Guilherme Almor De Alpoím Calvão, Comandante da Marinha reformado e ex-combatente na Guerra Colonial, "Quantos Morreram em Mueda?" *Jornal Público*, June 16, 2002.

[22] María Eugénia Mata, "Interracial Marriage in the Last Portuguese Colonial Empire," *E-Journal of Portuguese History*, 5, 1 (2007): 19; Tony Simões da Silva, "Raced Encounters, Sexed Transactions: 'Luso-tropicalism' and the Portuguese Colonial Empire, Pretexts," *Literary and Cultural Studies*, 11, 1 (2002): 27–39. See also João Filipe Marques, "Les Racistes, C'est Les Autres," *Lusotopie*, 14, 1 (2007): 88, for a counter-narrative.

[23] Susana Pereira Bastos, "Ambivalence and Phantasm in the Portuguese Colonial Discursive Production on Indians (Mozambique)," *Lusotopie*, 15, 1 (2008): 77–95.

[24] Rosa Cabecinhas and João Feijó, "Collective Memories of Portuguese Colonial Action in Africa: Representations of the Colonial Past Among Mozambicans and Portuguese Youths," *International Journal of Conflict and Violence*, 4, 1 (2010): 28–44.

[25] John Marcum, *The Angolan Revolution, Volume I* (Cambridge: MIT Press, 1969) and John Marcum, *The Angolan Revolution, Volume II* (Cambridge: MIT Press, 1978).

[26] Furtado, *A Guerra Colonial*.

[27] See Dhada, *Warrior at Work* on Pigiguiti riots; Cabrita, *Massacres em África*; Lucinda Canelas and Esabel Salema, "Relatório Militar revela que tropas portuguesas participaram em decapitações," *O Público*, December 16, 2012, 4; and Nuno Tiago Pinto, *Dias de Coragem e de Amizade: 50 Histórias Sobre A Guerra Colonial* (Lisbon: A Esfera dos Livros, 2011).

As a colonial empire in Africa, Portugal was in stellar company. The French too acted with armed cruelty in Algeria during their "savage war of peace,"[28] as did the South Africans before and during apartheid,[29] the British in Kenya, and the Belgians in the Congo.[30] Perhaps the most noteworthy case of mass violence was von Trotha's near annihilation of the Herero, whose army nearly matched Hideyoshi's for cruelty. In Wiriyamu, though, it was the cry commanding soldiers to "Aphani Wense!"—kill them all, "leave no one alive"—that proved the most chilling. In other words, the Wiriyamu massacre typified the anatomical morphology of slaughters in colonial pacification wars.

Marcelino dos Santos, a leading nationalist, viewed Wiriyamu in an equally broad context:

> The atrocities committed by the Portuguese army, despite their horror and barbarism, express the true nature of the Portuguese fascist colonial regime, just as the gas chambers of the Nazi camps, the massacre at Lidice in Czechoslovakia... expressed the true nature of Hitler and Nazism; just as Sharpeville expressed the true nature of the regime in South Africa; just as Sajiet Sidi Youssef expressed the true nature of French colonialism in Algeria... just as Guernica in Spain showed the nature of Franco fascism; just as My Lai expressed the true nature of American imperialism in Viet-Nam. Each colonial war, each racist war, each Nazi war, each imperialist war includes a Mueda, a Sharpeville, a Pidgiguiti, an Lcolo Bengo, a My Lai... Therefore, let us try to understand these facts, this reality, in that manner.[31]

Wiriyamu's demise was therefore a significant event in advancing the nationalist narrative *and* helping Portugal disengage from Mozambique. Furthermore, Portuguese denial of the story was equally significant as a genre in the phenomenology of erasures. Wiriyamu therefore justly deserved an appropriately framed discourse.

Several texts helped construct this frame. Geoffrey Barraclough's texts on scientific methods in history were among them. These argued that,[32] if properly treated, history can presage future social realities. This perspective of directional causality, if you will,

---

[28] Alistair Horne, *A Savage War of Peace: Algeria 1954–1962* (New York: New York Review of Books, 2006); and Martin Thomas, *The French Colonial Mind, Volume 2: Violence, Military Encounters, and Colonialism* (Lincoln: University of Nebraska Press, 2012).

[29] Tom Lodge, *Sharpville: An Apartheid Massacre and Its Consequences* (Oxford: Oxford University Press, 2011); and Mohamed Adhikari, *Anatomy of a South African Genocide: The Examination of the Cape San Peoples* (Ohio: Ohio University Press, 2011).

[30] David Anderson, *Histories of the Hanged: The Dirty War in Kenya and the End of the Empire* (New York: W. W. Norton, 2005); and Adam Hochschild, *King Leopold's Ghost* (Boston: Houghton Mifflin, 1998).

[31] "Marcelino dos Santos, Vice President Frelimo, testifying before the Committee of 24 of the United Nations, 20 July, 1973," *ACOA Fact Sheets* (August 1973).

[32] Geoffrey Barraclough, "The Social Dimensions of Crisis," in *Germany 1919–1932: The Weimar Culture, Social Research*, 39, 2 (1972): 341–359; Geoffrey Barraclough, "Scientific Method and the Work of the Historian," *Studies in Logic and the Foundations of Mathematics*, 44 (1966): 584–594; and Geoffrey Barraclough, "History, Morals and Politics," *International Affairs*, 34, 1 (1958): 1–15.

helped me view the Wiriyamu massacre as a two-sided coin, one historical and the other powerfully prophetic.[33] One side therefore nested its past, the seed of its epistemic genesis. The other helped frame Portugal's imperial demise once its military entrapment was outed as an act of pure evil, for entrapment is what Portugal's commanders in Tete called the operation that devastated Wiriyamu—*Operação Marosca*, Operation Entrapment.[34]

E. H. Carr's works also argued against historical omniscience.[35] "The historian is necessarily selective. The belief in a hard core of historical facts existing objectively and independently of the interpretation of the historian is a preposterous fallacy, but one which it is hard to eradicate."[36] Historians, argued Carr, assigned prominence to selective facts they deemed important to reveal new incremental insights, insights that could be superseded by new findings and new perspectives. In other words, omniscient history did not exist. It was a fetish, or in the words of Dominick LaCapra, "a totalized object that pretends to closure."[37]

What I heard in effect was a whisper inspired by Carr et al.—call into question the text, the facts presented therein, and the iconography used to convey the meaning behind the text, which in this instance was directed towards socially progressive action. In other words, both texts and facts, or narrative language and narrative meaning, to borrow Frank Ankersmit's terms,[38] were dialogically suspect; as were two other aspects of the narrative: the tonal silhouettes through which the hermeneutic symbols, in the Ricouerian sense,[39] conveyed meaning when narrating the events; and the latter's textual erasure with weapons of denials. Put differently, the Wiriyamu text as revealed had driven the selection of the facts to tell the Wiriyamu story as a binary. Digging into Portugal's attempts to silence the narrative and the silent iconography lacing it was as important, therefore, as the discovery of new facts behind Wiriyamu.

As a binary narrative, Wiriyamu was framed by the dynamics of counter-insurgency,[40] in which Portugal was a key player on a demonic stage. Insurgents were like Wayang puppets lurking in the shadows of terror and as fleeting references, as were

---

[33] Paul Ricouer, "The Model of the Text: Meaningful Action Considered as Text," in *From Text to Action* (Evanston: Northwestern University Press, 2007), 140–164.
[34] Marosca's etymological origins are obscure, but the word means deceiving someone with a fraudulent act, ranging from *arriosca*, trap; to *trapaça*, trickery; *burla*, swindle; to *enredo*, entanglement. *Dicionário da Língua Portuguesa da Porto Editora—com Acordo Ortográfico* (Porto: Editora, 2012).
[35] E. H. Carr, *What Is History?* (London: Vintage, 1967).
[36] Carr, *What is History?*, accessed July 31, 2013, http://vidyardhi.org/Resources/books/historycarr.pdf.
[37] Dominick LaCapra, *Writing History, Writing Trauma* (Baltimore: The Johns Hopkins University Press, 2001), 11.
[38] Frank Ankersmit, "Reply to Professor Zagorin," *History and Theory*, xxix (1990): 275–296.
[39] Paul Ricouer, "The Model of the Text: Meaningful Action Considered as Text," in *From Text to Action* (Evanston: Northwestern University Press, 2007), 140–164.
[40] Hastings, *Wiriyamu*; Adrian Hastings, "Reflections upon the War in Mozambique," *African Affairs*, 292 (1974): 263–276; Kevin Parker, "Wiriyamu and the War in Tete, 1971–1974" (MA thesis, University of York, 1982).

the dead, objectified, their lives before the massacre left untold.[41] The Wiriyamu narrative had therefore silenced several entities in the story. Included among them were voices of data-gatherers and their transmitters, victims before their erasure, survivors, massacre perpetrators and priests all of whom, given the opportunity,[42] had much to contribute to the Wiriyamu narrative.

---

[41] Cabrita, "Os Mortos Não Sofrem"; Cabrita, "Wiriyamu, Viagem ao Fundo do Terror"; and Cabrita, *Massacres em África*.

[42] Amnesty International, *Annual Report 1973–1974* (London: Amnesty International, 1974), 63–64; and The International Defense and Aid Fund (IDAF), *Terror in Tete: A Documentary Report of Portuguese Atrocities in Tete District, Mozambique, 1971–1972* (London: IDAF, 1973).

2

Literature Review

Three factors made Wiriyamu difficult to study: the emerging historiography in the field; the paucity of written sources on Wiriyamu; and the impact that this paucity had in shaping the secondary literature.

The 1974 April coup that toppled Caetano's regime in Portugal set a new pace in the production of nationalist and colonial history. Uncritical use of written sources, though, encouraged binaries, which in the case of nationalist history viewed the Portuguese as an object for defeat, some local authorities as their enablers, and FRELIMO as a revolutionary vanguard marching towards a Hegelian victory. I could see the need for such a bias, partly to place Portugal on the defensive,[1] and partly "to establish a radical discontinuity with the colonial regime by eradicating alleged enemies from society and imposing a national revolutionary consciousness."[2] The problem was that this type of binary narrative assumed a scholarly life all its own after colonial independence, which two astute scholars identified as early as 1988 as damaging to the nationalist narrative.[3] Teleology distorted the early stages of Mozambique's liberation historiography, which under-reported the role of revolutionary violence, within the party and against the traditional grass-roots leadership.[4]

A similar fissure opened on the Portuguese side of the equation, as the gap between history as memory[5] and professional history-making closed once access was granted

---

[1] Mustafah Dhada, "Contesting Terrains over a Massacre: The Case of Wiriyamu," in *Contesting Terrains and Constructed Categories: Critical Issues in Contemporary Africa* (Boulder: Westview Press, 2001), 259–277.

[2] Victor Igreja, "Frelimo's Political Ruling through Violence and Memory in Postcolonial Mozambique," *Journal of Southern African Studies*, 36, 4 (Dec. 2010): 781.

[3] Aquino de Bragança and Jacques Depelchin, "From Idealization of Frelimo to the Understanding of Mozambique Recent History," *Review (Fernand Braudel Center)* 11, 1 (1988): 95–117.

[4] Allen F. Isaacman and Barbara Isaacman, *Mozambique: From Colonialism to Revolution, 1900–1982* (Boulder: Westview Press, 1983); Mondlane, *The Struggle for Mozambique*; Barry Munslow, *Mozambique, the Revolution and Its Origins* (Harlow: Longman, 1983); Barry Munslow, *Samora Machel: An African Revolutionary* (London: Zed Books, 1985); Malyn Newitt, *A History of Mozambique* (London: Hurst, 1995); and John Saul, *Socialist Ideology and the Struggle for Southern Africa* (Trenton, New Jersey: Africa World Press, 1990) are but highly selective examples of the genre. For a critical overview of the problematic in the post-colonial period, consult M. Anne Pitcher, "Forgetting from Above and Memory from Below: Strategies of Legitimation and Struggle in Postsocialist Mozambique," *Africa: Journal of the International African Institute*, 76, 1 (2006), 88–122.

[5] For the politics of memory and erasure, see Paulo de Medeiros, "Hauntings, Memory, Fiction and the Portuguese Wars," in Timothy G. Ashplant (ed.), *The Politics of War Memory and Commemoration* (London: Routledge, 2000), 209–210.

to diplomatic military, national and police archives. By the early 1980s, the production of history on Portugal's colonial wars exploded,[6] as did exclusive reliance on written sources during the *Estado Novo* period. Unaided by field research in Portugal's former colonies, these works divided the field into camps. One elected to remain woundingly silent on Portugal's violent past during the wars of liberation,[7] while another minimized mass violence in colonial wars,[8] or worse, proved reluctant to visit such a past, as if an act of erasure through silence, "*oubli de réserve*," or "back-up forgetting," to quote Paul Ricouer.[9] A few sought a more realistic assessment of the *Estado Novo*'s colonialist period under Caetano through film media,[10] while others used the colonial archives with prosaic care.[11] One person reluctant to look back was none other than the President of the Republic. When questioned whether Portugal would apologize for the Wiriyamu massacre, he chose "*oubli de réserve*":

> People make history every day, with all its defects and virtues. Regarding history, I try to identify the positive facts, because, if we keep looking back at the past, we will lose the future.[12]

As a result, Wiriyamu's rightful place in early nationalist and colonial historiography disappeared, as did a more nuanced approach to early nationalist history, one that would strip ideology and fiction from ascertainable facts with which to study change as a culture of evidence. There were exceptions on both sides of the divide; these proved successful precisely because they triangulated with great finesse archival materials alongside rigorously curated oral evidence.[13]

---

[6] For a synopsis of what is available on Portuguese colonial wars in terms of books, films, veterans' associations, memorials, public monuments, social networks, and discussion groups, visit the home page of *Guerra Colonial Portuguesa*, accessed October 11, 2013, http://guerracolonial.home.sapo.pt. A bibiliography of emerging works in the field is given in *Portuguese Studies* 29, 2 (2013). Available at: www.jstor.org/stable/10.5699/portstudies.29.issue-2. See also, Stewart Lloyd-Jones and António Costa Pinto (eds.), *The Last Empire: Thirty Years of Portuguese Decolonization* (Bristol: Intellect Books, 2003).

[7] Comissão para o Estado das Campanhas de África, *Resenha histórico-militar da Campanhas de África: Dispositivo das nossas forças: Moçambique* (Lisbon: Estado-Maior do Exército, 1989); and José Freire Antunes, *A Guera de África, 1961–1974, Volume I and Volume II* (Lisbon: Temas e Debates, 1996).

[8] Reis and Oliveira, "Cutting Heads or Winning Hearts," *Civil Wars*, 14, 1 (2012): 80–103.

[9] Paul Ricouer, *Memory, History, Forgetting* (Translated by K. Blamey and D. Pellauer) (Chicago: Chicago University Press, 2006), 414.

[10] Furtado, *A Guerra Colonial*.

[11] Dalila Cabrita Mateus, *A Luta pala Independência: A Formação das Elites Fundadoras de* FRELIMO, MPLA *e* PAIGC (Mira-Sintra: Editorial Inquérito, 1999).

[12] Aníbal Cavaco Silva, quoted in Robert Stock, "Apologising for Colonial Violence: The Documentary Film *Regresso a Wriyamu*, Transitional Justice, and Portuguese-Mozambican Decolonization," in Brigit Schwelling (ed.), *Reconciliation, Civil Society, and the Politics of Memory: Transnational Initiatives in the 20th and 21st Century* (Bielefeld: Verlag, 2012), 239.

[13] Adam and Dyuti, "Entrevista: o massacre de Mueda—falam testemunhas": 117–128; Sayaka Funada-Classen, *The Origins of War in Mozambique* (Somerset West: African Minds, 2013); Borges Coelho, *O Início da Luta Armada*, and Furtado, *A Guerra Colonial*. A succinct summary of this debate is given in Paolo Israel, "A Loosening Grip: The Liberation Script in Mozambican History," *Kronos*, 39, 1 (Jan. 2013): 1–9.

Written sources and their limits

The second factor were gaps in quality of written sources on both sides, which reinforced the divide between teleology and empiricism. FRELIMO ephemera and oral records in *Mozambique Revolution, Voz da Revolução*, the Chilcote-curated nationalist texts, and Samora Machel interviews[14] are critical to consider here, as these shaped the early thinking in historical research for this book, which was to view propaganda materials, news clippings, posters, banners, photographs, comic strips, and cartoons, images, and films as legitimate sources to examine the war around Wiriyamu. The challenge was to find an appropriate methodology to data mine Wiriyamu in two contexts: the national liberation struggle, and the armed conflict in Tete. This I found after 12 months' professional training at the University of Sussex's School of African and Asian Studies (AFRAS) under the guidance of two scholars, the late Bruce Graham, an Australian-born political scientist,[15] and F. G. Bailey.[16]

The AFRAS common room was abuzz with discussions on the importance of visibility and positionalities, although they were not referred to as such. The question we argued over then, and I dare say with some ferocity, was how visible are the subjugated and where do they stand, not as objects, but as people in the hierarchy of power in colonial and post-colonial archives. Ranajit Guha was the resident historian in subaltern studies,[17] and his seminars added fuel to our fiery discussions on this problem of memory erasure, objectification and the self in printed nationalist and colonial archives.

With this newfound awareness, I went back to strip-mine data from the nationalist materials I had gathered, organizing them for ease of analysis later. The results suggested Graham's methodology to be exceptionally well suited to extract data elements from ephemera. It now remained for me to assess this data to tackle some of the queries framing this book.

FRELIMO materials viewed the Portuguese as objects of defeat in a struggle on three fronts: military, state-building, and diplomacy. The Wiriyamu massacre fit two of the three fronts: the military, which led to Wiriyamu's destruction, and the diplomatic, which led to its resurrection as a critique of Portugal's conduct of war.[18]

---

[14] Details are given in the enclosed Bibliography.
[15] B. D. Graham, *Representation and Party Politics: A Comparative Perspective* (Oxford: Blackwell, 1993) is pertinent here. Graham's political studies on Australian, Indian and French electoral history are easy to trace with Google Scholar. A short biography is posted here, "Bruce Graham, Research Professor of Politics, died suddenly on 3 October from a heart attack," *University of Sussex*, November 2, 2007, accessed July 30, 2013, http://www.sussex.ac.uk/internal/bulletin/archive/02nov07/article12.shtml.
[16] F. G. Bailey, *Stratagems and Spoils* (Boulder: Westview Press, 2001). Twenty years after his departure from Sussex, he penned his thinking on deeds and rhetoric in the context of truth and political action in another seminal study, F. G. Bailey, *The Prevalence of Deceit* (New York: Cornell University Press, 1991).
[17] Ranajit Guha urged historians to see the importance of delving into the narratives of the colonized from the canyons below. For details, see *Subaltern Studies: A Bibliography of Articles and Reviews*, accessed February 20, 2015, http://tinyurl.com/o7hq6u8. See also, Ranajit Guha, *History at the Limits of World-History* (New York: Columbia University Press, 2003).
[18] The analysis used two sets of FRELIMO publications: the Portuguese-language *A Voz da Revolução* produced for the party's internal use and *Mozambique Revolution* (titled *Mozambican Revolution* until 1966), which began publication in December 1965, ceasing in June 1975.

Graham's methodology, however, did little to improve the quality of the data, which proved woefully inadequate to explain the causes of the Wiriyamu massacre. Data on public pressure diplomacy and foreign aid was often difficult to date—though less so after the Portuguese secret police files were opened for review.[19] Data on cadres in the field, their popular base and support were sparse. Where generalities abounded, teleology infected the data. The resulting texts, to no one's surprise, reinforced formulaic narratives, and twisted history to serve a normative purpose. Incidentally, Portugal shared a similar teleological fate under *Estado Novo*, which was most pronounced in literary historical narratives.[20]

The little there was of empirical value suggested that FRELIMO had undertaken mobilization campaigns in the two northern fronts before engaging the Portuguese militarily.[21] By tapping successfully into local dissents, the party accelerated its hold in northern Mozambique—and evidence drawn from documents penned by FRELIMO's nationalist counterparts elsewhere tells us why. An effective mobilization strategy implied asking the colonized social apex to commit cultural suicide while the disfranchised social sector engaged in a similar transformational self-discovery. To this end, FRELIMO materials suggested, a variety of self-empowering tools were deployed, ranging from performance theater, to story-telling, art, music and dance,[22] all striving to create *O Homem Novo*, a new post-colonial citizen.

However, liberation also showed two self-destructive practices kept firmly under wraps from transparent disclosure, and only revealed in public jousting matches between FRELIMO and the *Resistência Nacional Moçambicana* (Renamo), the Mozambican National Resistance,[23] after the end of the civil war in 1992: one was ideologically designed to instill political rectitude in cadres, using teach-ins, mini-conferences, and, it is now revealed, intimidation and repression; the other was violent, aimed at solidifying the culture of emergent nationalism through the use of group confessionals, show trials, and summary executions, which continued in the post-independence period under the

---

[19] Samples of foreign aid files worthy of note for the post-1970 period are Direcção-Geral de Arquivos, Arquivo Nacional da Torre do Tombo, Pastas de Moçambique, PT/TT/PIDE/D-F/001/00023; PT/TT/PIDE/D-F/001/00024; and, PT/TT/PIDE/D-A/1/2826-11.

[20] See Ingemai Larsen, "Silenced Voices: Colonial and Anti-Colonial Literature in Portuguese Literary History," *Lusotopie* 13, 2 (2006): 59–69.

[21] For a graphic illustration of mobilization dynamics in Mueda, northern Mozambique, see Harry G. West, "Sorcery of Construction and Socialist Modernization: Ways of Understanding Power in Postcolonial Mozambique," *American Ethnologist*, 28, 1 (Feb. 2001): 128–130.

[22] For a pithy study on forms of resistance in songs, see Leroy Vail and Landeg White, "Forms of Resistance: Songs and Perceptions of Power in Colonial Mozambique," *American Historical Review*, 88, 4 (1983): 883–919; Paolo Israel, "The Formulaic Revolution: Song and the 'Popular Memory' of the Mozambican Liberation Struggle," *Cahiers d'Études africaines*, L 1, 197 (2010): 181–216; and Paolo Israel, *In Step with the Times: Mapiko Masquerades of Mozambique* (Athens: Ohio University Press, 2014).

[23] The literature on Renamo is extensive and, according to Baxter Tavuyanago, divided into two camps. One views it as a counter-insurgency serving Rhodesian interests by proxy. The other places Renamo as a broadly based regional force fighting communism in Southern Africa. See bibliography succinctly provided by this author in "Renamo: From Military Confrontation to Peaceful Democratic Engagement, 1976-2009," *African Journal of Political Science and International Relations*, 4, 1 (2011): 42–51.

guise of revolutionary justice.[24] Here, official papers are silent on the details of both, reinforcing the march to liberation thesis in early literature. One such understudied session of institutionally driven violence began with the "Mocuba Plan" to round up suspected collaborators to face a show trial. It culminated in the formation of re-education camps leading to the "Meeting of the Compromised" in 1982, which proved particularly counter-productive in advancing FRELIMO's *O Homem Novo* project.[25]

Written records remained equally silent on FRELIMO's actual relationship with the grassroots in Tete itself, and more specifically near Wiriyamu.[26] Unraveling the cause of this silence was important for two reasons: to clarify how FRELIMO managed to advance so rapidly in Tete, and then falter once they reached Mozambique's central midriff after liberation; and to determine the role of the party, if any, in attracting Wiriyamu's terminal entrapment.

Several texts outside FRELIMO give us a clue here. One set is Church-related. Discussed below, it suggests the Church's central role in developing, without an intent to do so, sympathies for FRELIMO among parishioners and their families living near the missions. The other set of texts are post-colonial, which examine FRELIMO's take on traditional authorities,[27] as a colonial agency, worthy of derisive dismissal.[28] According to Christian Geffray,[29] this measure rapidly galvanized internal local resistance, feeding into externally aided dissent headed by Renamo.[30] Fieldwork in and

---

[24] A catalog of these practices is given in several works. Yussuf Adam, "Samora Machel e o desenvolvimento de Moçambique," in António Soupa (ed.), *Samora: Homem em Povo* (Maputo: Maguezo Editores, 2001), 41. J. Leguèbe, "Mozambique Under Frelimo Rule," in W. Veenhoven and W. Ewing (eds.), *Case Studies on Human Rights and Fundamental Freedoms* (The Hague: Martinus Nijhoff, 1976), 3–28; Margaret Hall and Tom Young, *Confronting Leviathan: Mozambique since Independence* (Athens: Ohio University Press, 1997), 47; John Saul and C. Leys, "Lubango and After," *Journal of South African Studies*, 29, 2 (2003): 334–353; and João Cabrita, *Mozambique: The Tortuous Road to Democracy*, 82–83.

[25] The understudied nature of this subject is in itself reflective of binaries in the selective use of memory to produce historical knowledge on the Samora Machel period. The pro-FRELIMO texts are covered in Ian Christie, *Samora Machel: A Biography* (London: Zed Press, 1989); Joseph Hanlon, *Mozambique: The Revolution Under Fire* (London: Zed Books, 1984); and John Saul (ed.), *A Difficult Raod: The Transition to Socialism in Mozambique* (New York: Monthly Review Press, 1985). See also João Coelho, "Sa Violência Ordenada à Ordem Pós-Colonial Violenta," *Lusotopie* (2003): 175–193, and Igreja, "Frelimo's Political Ruling through Violence," 781–799.

[26] This is not to suggest that oral history would not uncover evidence of such works in the Tete region.

[27] Harry G. West, "'This Neighbor is not my Uncle!': Changing Relations of Power and Authority on the Mueda Plateau," *Journal of Southern African Studies*, 24, 1 (1998): 141–160; and Harry G. West, *Kupilikula: Governance and the Invisible Ream in Mozambique* (Chicago: Chicago University Press, 2005), 164–179.

[28] Harry G. West and Scott Kloeck-Jenson, "Betwixt and Between: 'Traditional Authority' and Democratic Decentralization in Post-War Mozambique," *African Affairs*, 98, 393 (Oct. 1988): 455–484.

[29] Christian Geffray, *La cause des Armes: Anthropologie de la guerre civile au Mozambique* (Paris: Karthala, 1990). For critiques of his work, see A. Dinerman, *Revolution, Counter-Revolution and Revisionism in Postcolonial Africa: The Case of Mozambique, 1974–1994* (London: Routledge, 2006); and C. Serra, *Novos Combates Pela Mentalidade Sociológica* (Maputo: Livraria Universitaria, UEM, 1997).

[30] The literature on traditional authorities is now extensive. For southern Mozambique, see Euclides Gonçalves, "Finding the Chief: Political Decentralisation and Traditional Authority in Mocumbi, Southern Mozambique," *Africa Insight*, 35, 3 (Sept. 2005): 64–70. Additional references are given in this book's Bibliography.

around Unkanha, Mucumbura and the Wiriyamu triangle confirmed Geffray's thesis, as we shall see a bit later. "What can we say? We first had war '*com os colonos*', with the colonials. And we then fought with our own people. War, war, war. That is all we have seen," said two informants during an interview in Wiriyamu.[31]

Written FRELIMO materials remained resoundingly silent on three additional aspects of the war: the massacre itself; the society, culture and politics surrounding Wiriyamu; and Wiriyamu's response to FRELIMO overtures to attract popular support for the war in Tete—responses that may or may not have resulted in Wiriyamu's destruction.

Sometime later, a FRELIMO commander explained the reasons behind the poor quality of this data in terms of their communications strategy in Tete. Wherever possible, instructions were given orally to foil enemy detection. Military imperatives therefore dictated dispensing with record-keeping in Tete,[32] and may well have taken precedence over everything else. This assertion by FRELIMO, if true, helps to explain the rigidly Marxist rhetoric suffusing FRELIMO texts after Mondlane's assassination in 1969. Ideological rigidity therefore essentialized data on political, military and diplomatic campaigns in Tete, with nothing of primary value to offer on the biography of Wiriyamu and on the anatomy of its demise.[33]

The war and Wiriyamu in Portuguese sources

Portuguese archives,[34] though richer in depth and detail, came embedded with limits too. Several factors compromised the integrity of documents reviewed for this work, which included the following: Portuguese secret police reports,[35] intelligence data on FRELIMO and on specific military operations, surveillance memoranda on priests and Church personnel during the war in Tete,[36] the propaganda campaign to discredit Wiriyamu's public outing, specific colonial responses to journalists visiting Tete during the Wiriyamu crisis, and various geographic coordinates materially important to the story.

One such factor was Portugal's propensity to objectify the colony, to be protected from, or exploited to fight a communist-inspired insurgency. This perspective filtered data collection, analysis and dissemination. Much was lost in this process,

---

[31] Abidu Karimu, interview by author, Tete, 1995; and Bulachu Pentad Zambezi, interview by author, Wiriyamu, 1995.
[32] General Hama Tai, interview by author, Maputo, 1994 and 1995.
[33] Thomas H. Henriksen discusses this aspect of the history in his work: Thomas H. Henriksen, *Revolution and Counterrevolution: Mozambique's War of Independence, 1964–1974* (Westport, Connecticut: Greenwood Press, 1983).
[34] For a first-hand recorded experience of said archives, see Paul Bjerk, "African Files in Portuguese Archives," *History in Africa*, 31 (2004): 463–468.
[35] A selection of documents consulted to inform the flow of this narrative is given in the Bibliography.
[36] See, for instance, Arquivo Nacional da Torre do Tombo, Polícia Internacional e de Defesa do Estado; Direcção Geral de Segurança, *Actividades políticas dos padres Alfonso Valverde de Lion e Martin Hernandez Robles*, Direcção-Geral de Arquivos, PT/TT/D-F/001/00005.

marginalizing and at times erasing complex experiences from the grassroots, making it virtually impossible "to demonstrate in any depth the part played by African perceptions in the unfolding events. With the thoughts of the actors largely unregarded," observed Leroy Vail and Landeg White when reflecting on their text of resistance to colonialism.[37]

Sitting in Lisbon in the institutional archives the view was from top down, the humanity on the ground objectified as part of the anti-imperial matrix. You could be forgiven from viewing the affairs of the empire through rarified lenses and assume the records reflect both imperial rule and grassroots reality. Ergo, if the name of a place did not appear on a colonial map, it did not exist—nay could not exist! What survived was presented in the reports either as local resistance or as failures of policy worthy of derisive finger-pointing at the agency responsible. Efforts were indeed made to use ethnographic surveys and rapid-response appraisals to rectify this data so overwhelmingly contaminated with ideology.[38]

However, Portugal's authoritarian colonialism had little room for this type of data gathering with which to affect a dramatic change in colonial policy. Such a shift would have required the Salazarist "apparatchik" to commit hara-kiri *en masse*, that is, question their very *raison d'être* in Mozambique, an ideological fight to defeat FRELIMO. This lack of empiricism explains Portugal's tenacious grip on its imagined landscape, Lusotropicalism, a fiction aimed at rationalizing its hold on colonies, particularly in Africa, long after all others had given up theirs.[39]

Portugal's tenuous footprint on Mozambique's borderlands compounded the problem of a data-starved culture of authenticity, which resulted in poor intelligence on human traffic along the frontiers, particularly along the Zambian border. The problem was exacerbated once protected villages sought to contain conflict in Tete, disrupting the three-tiered administrative structure in place. Thereafter, where the Portuguese presence proved strongest, in cities and in specific zones of conflict, the Portuguese secret police dominated or sought to dominate the intelligence narrative.[40] As we shall see, this narrative was crafted with data that was sometimes obtained through pre-emptive terror and torture.[41]

A third factor was the impact that conflicts between the armed forces and the secret police, personal score-settling among agents in the lower ranks, and inter-agency rivalries had in underscoring official reports.

---

[37] Vail and White, "Forms of Resistance," 886.
[38] Jorge Borges Coelho, "Protected Villages and Communal Villages in the Mozambican Province of Tete, 1968–1982" (PhD thesis, University of Bradford, 1993).
[39] For a critique, see José Luís Cabaço, *Moçambique: Identidade, Colonialismo e Libertação*, preface by Omar Ribeiro Tomaz (São Paulo: Editora Unesp/ANPOCS, 2009). See also Gerald J. Bender, *Angola Under the Portuguese: The Myth and the Reality* (Berkeley: University of California Press, 1978).
[40] Portuguese intelligence reports on the case, such as they are, fail to provide an accurate narrative as these appear to have been crafted seven months after the event. Direcção-Geral de Arquivos, Arquivo Nacional da Torre do Tombo, Pastas de Moçambique, PT/TT/PIDE/D-F/001/00021. This work has not mined the publicly accessible archives of *Arquivo Histórico Militar*. For an inventory of its materials accessed on April 22, 2014, see, http://arqhist.exercito.pt/details?id=140738.
[41] A graphic text illustrating the use of torture and its impact on villagers in northern Mozambique is given in Harry G. West, "Voices Twice Silenced: Betrayal and Mourning at Colonialism's End in Mozambique," *Anthropological Theory*, 3, 3 (2003): 343–365.

Turning to Wiriyamu proper, the Portuguese papers tell us next to nothing, at any rate nothing new, on the role of the Church, Wiriyamu's collective prosopography, and the anatomy of the massacre itself. All three issues are crucial for understanding Wiriyamu as a narrative, a living community and a terminal event. Without them, Wiriyamu's existence could easily be denied, which, as we shall see, is what Portugal did in its clashing responses to the revelation.

However, the little there is on the Church that was examined for this work, vilifies the priests and nuns reportedly engaged in collecting data on the dead, but misses crucial subterranean actors central to the story.

The archives's near-total silence on Wiriyamu's collective prosopography was driven by the nature of its intelligence in the area. The majority of the local agents and their stringers assigned to gather rural intelligence were illiterate, and crudely trained as data extractors and analysts. In most cases, they appeared, as we shall see, too ready to torture prospective informants when seeking intelligence, and were well known for extortion and general abuse of power.

This is not to suggest that once sanitized with oral fieldwork this data could not further our general understanding of secret police methods in Portuguese counter-insurgency. They could, to a point, witness a recent article that makes use of such materials without oral input.[42] Such an enterprise, however justly deserving of a general study on violence and everyday micro-aggression, could not help us to de-objectify Wiriyamu. Without this de-objectification, Wiriyamu's visibility and the historiographical positionalities of its people disappeared. This is exactly what the archives structurally do: respond with silence to questions such as who lived in Wiriyamu before they died, where did they *have* to stand in the conflict and why, and how were they killed?

In addition, because of Portugal's obduracy to investigate Wiriyamu with primary data and do so in a timely manner as a serious case of mass violence, documentation on the anatomy of the massacre under *Operação Marosca*,[43] are practically non-existent. Instead, secret police reports viewed by this author, cursory though they are, rely on the list of the dead collected by the Church, and affirm the core of the narrative as revealed in the *London Times*. The commandos engaged in the operation viewed it as "small potatoes," one of many carried out during their stay in Tete—indeed military logs support this claim[44]—except that in this case it proved fatal for the Portuguese Empire.

Church and other public records

The Catholic Institute of International Relations (CIIR) generated a body of materials on Wiriyamu. Included among them were British newspaper clippings on Wiriyamu

---

[42] Filipe Ribeiro de Meneses, "Parallel Diplomacy, Parallel War: The PIDE/DGS's Dealings with Rhodesia and South Africa, 1961–74," *Journal of Contemporary History*, 49, 2 (2014): 366–389.
[43] Melo, interview, 1995 and 2014.
[44] ibid.

and the colonial wars,[45] and UN reports on the massacre based on public hearings held in New York. Photocopies of Father Hastings' private diary entries supplemented background materials held at the Burgos mission headquarters in Madrid and public access materials held in the libraries of various religious orders operating in Mozambique.

Combined, they corroborate publicly revealed evidence on Wiriyamu, while shedding some light on the priests' handling of the massacre. Perhaps more importantly, when read in conjunction with oral evidence, they suggest the Church's strong hand in fomenting a culturally sensitive civil society in Tete.[46]

Here, FRELIMO and the Church shared, somewhat inadvertently, the same goal— self-determination. The former stressed, in theory at least, the rediscovery of a new self as a precondition for liberation; while the Church cultivated a sentient Christian identity among its faithful.[47] In Tete, missionary priests were engaged in exactly the kind of transformational work that FRELIMO would have had to undertake unaided by the Church, and with the same degree of intensity that its counterparts in Portuguese Guinea had undertaken to initiate their armed insurgency.[48] That is why FRELIMO texts had nothing of cultural and contextual value directly related to Wiriyamu before its disappearance, but the Church documents and their ephemera did—up to a point.

But even here, it is remarkable how much the voices of the parishioners materially relevant for this study have been muffled. These texts fail to discuss the anatomy of mass violence before and after Wiriyamu. Church congregants and acolytes spoke through intermediaries, namely priests in missionary society bulletins,[49] leaving survivors and informants, priests and nurses, silent as they volunteered themselves into unwritten memory. Consequently, we learn nothing of how they gathered the data for Wiriyamu, checked and cross-checked these, if indeed they did so, who exactly wrote the text, and if more than one author, did they revise it, how they transported the story out of Mozambique, whether the priests acted as a group or individually to protect their sources and how they safeguarded the various components of the story.

This paucity of sources split secondary literature on Wiriyamu into three groups. Some of this secondary literature was scholarly,[50] some journalistic,[51] some fictional;[52]

---

[45] The Bibliography gives a selection of newspaper articles published in the *The Times* and *The Sunday Times*.
[46] Father Joseph, White Father, formerly of Zóbuè Seminary, interview by author, Seminário Maior, Maputo, 1994 and 1995.
[47] Padre Vicente Berenguer, interview by author, Maputo, 1994 and 1995. For a review of Padre Berenguer's recent work reflective of Burgos' fathers approach to transformational change in missionary work, see segments 33: 33 to 39: 29 in Creemos 13TV, *Misioneros por el Mundo, Misión Mozambique,* accessed June 1, 2013, http://www.youtube.com/watch?v=BXbt5pY8Mug.
[48] Dhada, *Warrirors at Work*, 9–12, 56, 67, 132–133, 210–215, 222–227, and 231–232.
[49] See Enrique Ferrando Piedra, *Bullentim de Mucumbura*. Periodic series lodged at IEME, Instituto Español de Misiones Extranjeras' manuscript holdings in Madrid, Spain. Details are in the book's Bibliography.
[50] Hastings, *Wiriyamu*; Hastings, "Reflections," 263–276; Dhada, "Contesting Terrains," 259–277; and Parker, "Wiriyamu and the War in Tete."
[51] Cabrita, "Os Mortos Não Sofrem"; Cabrita, "Wiriyamu"; and Cabrita, *Massacres*.
[52] Williams Sassine, *Wirriyamu* (London: Heinemann, 1980); Farida Karodia, *A Shattering of Silence* (Oxford: Heinemann, 1993); Ricardo de Saavedra, *Os Dias Do Fim* (Lisbon: Editorial Notícias, 1995); Lídia Jorge, *A Costa dos Murmúrios* (Lisbon: Publicações Dom Quixote, 2008); and José Rodrigues

others were digital: blog entries,[53] YouTube videos,[54] films,[55] scanned newspaper postings,[56] and undergraduate research papers in PDF format.[57]

Affirmative literature on the massacres

The first group pitched for the narrative integrity of the massacre as published despite gaps in evidence.[58] Works here identify Portugal's armed forces and the secret police as the decision-makers, actors, and organizers behind the killings. A handful provided details on the victims, drawn from quantitative and qualitative data gathered from witnesses and survivors almost immediately after the event, and memories recorded or told orally to researchers, twenty to thirty-six years after the event.[59]

Of the several works in this group, two are worthy of special attention because of their seminal appearance synthesizing the Wiriyamu narrative as revealed, the IDAF and the Hastings' monographs. The London-based International Defense and Aid Fund for Southern Africa (IDAF), an organization established in 1952 for not-for-profit work, produced one of the earliest reports on the massacre.[60] Comprising forty-eight pages of English text, it appeared in 1973, six months after the story came out. The report introduced the war with a special emphasis on the use of fortified villages, described the geographic location of the massacre on a map, and then discussed the

---

dos Santos, *O Anjo Branco* (Lisbon: Gravida, 2010). For a general survey of fictions on colonial war, see Isabel Moutinho, *The Colonial Wars in Contemporary Portuguese Fiction* (Suffolk, UK: Tamesis Books, 2008).

[53] See entries under Wiriyamu in *Choppertech Blog*, accessed June 15, 2012, http://choppertech.blogspot.com/; "Wiriyamu e Outras Polemicas" in, Macua Blogs, 10 June 2012, http://macua.blogs.com/; *The Delgoa Bay Blog*, accessed June 13, 2012, http://delagoabayword.wordpress.com/; "Wiryamu...o que foi?" *Cuamba Blog*, accessed November 17, 2012, http://cuamba.blogspot.com/2010/01/wiriyamu-o-que-foi.html.

[54] See, for instance, "massacre de Wiriyamu (01 de 07)" (no web title), accessed June 15, 2012, http://preview.tinyurl.com/pvvve8a.

[55] For feature films inspired by Wiriyamu, see Margarita Cardoso, *A Costa dos Murmúrios*, DVD (Lisbon: Filmes do Tejo, 2004), which examines the story in the context of Portugal's colonial wars. The film is given academic treatment in Poças de Carvalho, "Dois olhares sobre uma guerra." The fictional text that sought to tackle the colonial war more broadly was António Lobo Antunes, *Os Cus de Judas* (Lisbon: Objetiva, 1979), also translated in English as *The Land at the End of the World* (New York: W. W. Norton, 2012). For a broader discussion of how films sought to represent discourses affirming or questioning hegemonic power in Portuguese colonial narratives, see Carolin Overhoff Ferreira, "Decolonizing the Mind? The Representation of the African Colonial War in Portuguese Cinema," *Studies in European Cinema*, 2, 3 (2005): 227–239.

[56] "Atrocities and Massacres, 1960–1977: Wiriyamu, Mueda and Others, Dossier MZ-0354," *Mozambique History Net*, accessed July 15, 2012, http://www.mozambiquehistory.net/massacres.html.

[57] A sample of these in the author's possession include two sets of research papers, one submitted at California State University Bakersfield (CSUB) in partial fulfillment for the BA HIST 418; and the other set submitted at Bard College, Master of Arts in Teaching Program, Delano Campus, California, in partial fulfillment for History 501.

[58] Hastings, *Wiriyamu*; Hastings, "Reflections," 263–276; Dhada, "Contesting Terrains," 259–277; and Parker, "Wiriyamu and the War in Tete."

[59] Cabrita, "Os Mortos Não Sofrem"; Cabrita, "Wiriyamu"; and Cabrita, *Massacres*.

[60] IDAF, *Terror in Tete: A Documentary Report of Portuguese Atrocities in Tete District, Mozambique, 1971–1972* (London: IDAF, 1973).

challenges faced by the Church in the colony, the massacres before Wiriyamu, and the Wiriyamu massacre itself, in which four hundred are identified as dead, 177 by name and 223 as Jane and John Does. It ended with a discussion on the events surrounding the publication of the carnage appended to a detailed chronology of Portugal's denial. The report has seven short narrative appendices on mass violence penned by priests from several Catholic denominations in Mozambique. Adrian Hastings provided the majority of this material to IDAF.

Six months later, Adrian Hastings wrote a monograph, highlighting three causes for the massacre: Portugal's systemic colonial brutality, its historical past, and its military strategy in Tete. Hastings followed this with a reflective piece, which reviewed his findings, reaffirming his earlier conclusion holding Portugal wholly responsible for the massacre.[61] Two seminal works handed to him by the Burgos Fathers buttressed his theses, one of which was on an earlier massacre at Mucumbura. Generally, Portugal's colonial history in Africa, Hastings argued, had always been repressive and violent, but it had progressively worsened, becoming more systematic and brutal once the colonial war gathered momentum in the early 1960s. It reached its zenith in the early 1970s with the frequent use of incarceration and interrogations of priests and foreign-born missionaries.[62]

Hastings' texts placed Wiriyamu as a victim of Portugal's war. In laying the blame at Portugal's door, Hastings was clearly aiming to hold it accountable. The downside to this approach is that very little was revealed of what life was like in that triangle complex. Understanding Wiriyamu outside victimhood, however, would have required a broader narrative, which Hastings could not undertake, even if he wanted to, given Portugal's obduracy in the matter. Such a discussion would have entailed not only examining the local structural and social determinants behind the massacre, but also delving into Wiriyamu as a complex community. In the absence of such a narrative, Wiriyamu remained as portrayed—the victim of a violent demise.

Further, the focus on victimhood framed the massacre in terms of Portuguese counter-insurgency, leaving out of the narrative the dynamics of insurgency led by FRELIMO. Why were the Portuguese at war in the first place, and what impact did this story have on subsequent events in Portuguese imperial history? Having played a key role in bringing the story to light, he elected not to tackle the latter question. "It was for others," he said to me, "to review the impact of Wiriyamu on Portugal's future as an empire."[63]

Wiriyamu from two perspectives

Kevin Parker, then a young scholar from York University, thought this approach too narrow to understand Wiriyamu and crafted "Wiriyamu and the War in Tete 1971–1974" eight years after the publication of Hastings' texts. The monograph utilized sixty-nine sources, of which four were related to the Wiriyamu massacre. One detailed the massacre that followed Wiriyamu in a place called Inhaminga, located south of

---

[61] Hastings, "Reflections."
[62] Hastings, *Wiriyamu;* and Hastings, "Reflections."
[63] Hastings, interviews, 1977, 1978, 1979, 1981, 1995, 1996.

Changara. One source discussed the Mucumbura atrocities originally covered in the Hastings' document; one report discussed the killings at Kateme—material left untouched by Hastings.

The four sources on the Wiriyamu case included the official Portuguese rebuttal denying Wiriyamu's very existence and its bloody disappearance.[64] In addition, Parker's monograph mined published sources: Adrian Hastings' own collection of papers, typescripts, and monographs now deposited at the Borthwick Institute for Archives; and "Facts and Reports," orange-colored mimeographs on Portugal's colonial wars from both sides of the divide collated by an anti-colonial activist center in Holland.

Parker's text broadened the discussion by examining the massacre in two contexts: the nationalist and the colonial. The dynamics of armed nationalism were, he suggests, as much a factor in the massacre as Portuguese counter-insurgency. Initially, Portugal had fought the war unsuccessfully, until 1970 when overwhelming firepower and armed men stalemated the nationalists in northern Mozambique, who in turn opened a new front in Tete to gain tactical advantage over the colonial army.

The massacre at Wiriyamu, concludes the manuscript, was a gift to FRELIMO, which it could not have foreseen. Ultimately, with the coup in Portugal in April 1974, Mozambique's accelerated independence marched ahead of FRELIMO's political ability to deepen its roots south of Tete where it was at its weakest politically.[65] Ultimately, Wiriyamu emerges from Parker's text unchanged from Hastings' treatment recognizing its destruction, while leaving unquestioned the perception advanced in the *London Times* report of the victims and survivors as passive recipients of colonial mass violence—and understandably so.

Whereas the purpose of Hastings' text was to talk truth to power, Parker's objective was to view the massacre from the perspective of both players in the colonial war. Questioning the role of the victims in this mass violence therefore fell outside the limits of their respective objectives. In the final analysis, Parker's text also omits to examine the role that the people in the Wiriyamu triangle may have played or had to play in their own destruction.

One writer who sought to uncover the anatomy of the bloodshed at Wiriyamu was Felícia Cabrita, a Portuguese journalist and investigative social commentator, biographer, and critic of the Portuguese Catholic Church. Cabrita originally carried out her field research in 1991 and followed up by another investigative visit to Tete in 1997/8. Both trips were short, and both entailed interviews with seven survivors and nine soldiers involved in the carnage at Chaworha and at various locations in the Wiriyamu complex. Cabrita produced two articles, which included fourteen informative images of survivors taken on site. Cabrita reworked the original articles for a book. Published in 2008, it incorporated two long italicized prefaces, one of which narrated the difficulties encountered in returning to the site as a comedy of ideological errors. The other described Antonino Melo's highly dramatic return to the scene as a former commander of the Portuguese soldiers involved in the deadly mission.[66]

---

[64] Parker, "Wiriyamu and the War in Tete."
[65] ibid.
[66] Cabrita, "Os Mortos Não Sofrem," Cabrita, "Wiriyamu, Viagem ao Fundo do Terror," and Cabrita, *Massacres em África*.

In theory, Cabrita's texts had the necessary field research to further our understanding of what happened that afternoon and during the next three days. In reality, they did not—and logically so. Cabrita was sent by a newspaper to pursue a viable story on an empire at colonial war. She achieved her objective.

The evidence collected from the victims in such a tight timeframe could only do so much. The survivors' recollections were published as synaptic pulses as they fled the scene. The story of the soldiers fared no better, for their tales proved to be as jagged as their victims. "You have to understand we were there not standing still but moving. I was responsible for my men, and their safety. We used grenades to save on bullets as we shoved them into huts," said the commander during a two-day interview with this author at an undisclosed location in Portugal in 1995.[67] Put differently, neither Antonino Melo nor his men at arms had or could afford an overview in that carnal theater from noon until sunset; at least, that is what Cabrita's text portrays. Further, when asked for her fieldnotes and records in 1995, Cabrita intimated she had not kept these after her first article was published.[68]

Nevertheless, Cabrita's work did advance the narrative somewhat with an impressionistic portrayal of victims facing the certainty of death. What we did not have is the full anatomy of the killings. How did the massacre happen at Wiriyamu? How was it planned and staged? Answers to these questions would have helped fill in the remaining gaps in the narrative. In the absence of such answers, the field was left open to denials, and speculation.

Texts on denial and doubts

There are two sets of writings in the second group: one of outright denial and one questioning the authenticity of affirmative narratives. Texts of denial were authored by three agencies: the Portuguese Ministry of Foreign Affairs,[69] pro-Portuguese journalists, and Bruce Loudon, a Lisbon-based stringer financed by Portugal to write for the *Daily Telegraph*.[70] All three sought to dispute the revelations with photographs and counter-testimonies aimed to prove Wiriyamu to be a mare's nest, a non-event in a place that did not exist.[71]

The last text in this group was penned by two Portuguese academics, Reis and Oliveira. It was published 14,424 days after Wiriyamu's destruction.[72] It did not deny the massacre, but questioned its narrative integrity in the affirmative literature.

---

[67] Melo, interview, 1995 and 2014.
[68] Felícia Cabrita, phone interview by the author, Lisbon, 1995.
[69] "*Wiriyamu*" or a Mare's Nest (Lisbon: Ministry of Foreign Affairs, 1973); Reis and Oliveira, "Cutting Heads," 80–103.
[70] James Sanders, *South Africa and the International Media 1972–1979, A Struggle for Representation* (New York: Routledge, 2011), 11–12.
[71] Bruce Loudon, "No Massacres, Say Tete Tribesmen," *The London Daily Telegraph*, July 13, 1973; Bruce Loudon, "Priests Do Not Know of Massacre," *The London Daily Telegraph*, July 14, 1973. For the impact that this type of reporting had on "weakening" the case, see James J. Kilpatric, "The Portuguese Atrocity that Didn't Happen," *National Review*, May 10, 1974, 525–527.
[72] Reis and Oliveira, "Cutting Heads."

Three data sets buttress the text's anti-affirmative arguments: one draws on "various missionary reports that were widely (but only partially) publicized in the media in 1973"; FRELIMO reports; and literature that appeared in the aftermath of the scandal. The nature of materials in the second set is unclear, as is the data drawn from it, except that both involve unspecified evidence from "recent media coverage; and some historical and memorialistic literature."[73] The third data set relies on diplomatic documents from the British and Portuguese archives; "official Portuguese documents;" and a short reference from an unseen report authored by Dr Rodrigues dos Santos, the father of the author of *The White Angel*, a work of fiction discussed below.

Data from these sources brace the text's coverage, leading to the following findings: the "exact location, even the existence of Wiriyamu ... remain contentious."[74] "Wiriyamu, with that name, did not officially exist," since such "relatively improvised rural dwellings" "were not big enough or even stable enough to be registered in most maps."[75] What can be stated with certainty is, "killings of large numbers of people with great cruelty *probably* [my italics] took place not in one location but in several, *probably* [my italics] three closely adjoining locations..." in which "a company of Portuguese commandos" tortured and summarily executed inhabitants during operation Marosca.

The preponderance of evidence in the first data set does not support the text's thesis questioning the location of the massacre, the magnitude of the death toll, and the known. They do, however, support the points raised about the unknowable facts. Of the actual materials consulted, the article utilizes approximately twenty-five sources, twenty of which were secondary and five primary, including works by Hastings,[76] Bertulli,[77] and Cabrita,[78] articles by journalists in British papers, notably *The Times* of London,[79] and a text by Sousa Ribeiro.[80]

A review of these works tells us this: The Hastings and IDAF texts put the death toll at 400, identify the locations of the massacre, list the names of some of the dead, and indicate where some of them died and how they perished. Bertulli's text, secondary in nature, is tangentially related to Wiriyamu. It focuses in the main on the White Fathers and the Church amidst conflict in Tete. The 1974 Sousa Ribeiro book is a Portuguese translation of the IDAF report published a year before Hastings' monograph and used a Spanish source authored by missionaries stationed in Mucumbura, southern Tete.

The Cabrita texts not only provide the precise location of the massacre verified on site with photographs, but also suggest the carnage to have been a theater of chaos. As we saw earlier, FRELIMO had nothing materially significant on Wiriyamu—except

---

[73] ibid.
[74] ibid.
[75] ibid.
[76] Adrian Hastings, *Wiriyamu: My Lai in Mozambique* (London: Search Press, 1974).
[77] Cesare Bertulli, *A Cruz e a Espada em Moçambique* (Lisbon: Portugália Editora, 1974).
[78] Cabrita, "Os Mortos Não Sofrem"; Cabrita, "Wiriyamu, Viagem ao Fundo do Terror"; and Cabrita, *Massacres em África*.
[79] The text does not indicate the extent of the research undertaken in *The Times of London* archives. See *The Times Annual Index* for a complete set of articles related to the case between 1973 and 1975.
[80] António Sousa Ribeiro, *Terror em Tete: Relato Documental das Atrocidades dos Portugueses no Distrito de Tete, Moçambique, 1971–1972* (Porto: A Regra do Jogo, 1974).

for an article of a survivor's recollection of her father's blood-soaked death during the massacre south of Mucumbura. In fact, FRELIMO had relied on the Church for their knowledge on Wiriyamu, which they had acquired much, much later, after the London outing.

These sources in the first data set therefore affirm without a doubt the veracity of all four aspects of the Wiriyamu narrative except one—a blow-by-blow account of the massacre. Here the article is correct: given the materials in print "it is impossible to know with certainty many of the details of the events," although it is incorrect when adding that "all the parties involved in this bloody event had conflicting interests that made it likely that they would tell different stories about the atrocities—and indeed they did..." With the result that it is "... difficult to establish with accuracy the events that took place around 16 December 1972."[81]

In fact, it is quite the contrary! The Hastings and IDAF monographs, despite the shortcomings, exhibit no contradictions in telling us what happened. They lay a framework for Cabrita to plug the missing holes. Neither does Cabrita's work, in lending a voice to the Portuguese commando in his telling of Wiriyamu's destruction. Further, there were only two parties to Wiriyamu's outing: Portugal, its paid journalists, and public relations firms on one side; and its victims and their immediate and primary spokesmen, who were virtually all priests and who acted in unison, on the other. In the face of Portugal's public relations campaign they had to erase the narrative. No one else had a dog in this fight. So the text's allusion to clashes in memory recall as a result of conflict of interests at the time of the revelation is mystifying—indeed, to paraphrase the authors in a different context, it does beggar belief![82]

Does the second data set help undergird the text's stance on Wiriyamu? This question is difficult to answer. The annotations for the sources, namely the "recent media coverage; and some historical and memorialistic literature," are too vague to evaluate their qualitative strength.

That leaves us with the third data set: diplomatic sources. To the best of this author's knowledge, Britain did not officially investigate the massacre independently of the Church and the Portuguese authorities. However, the British must have utilized Church-based narratives and Portuguese counter-narratives to guide their bilateral diplomacy—and this could easily be verified by a quick review of the British index of materials related to this event. One journalistic source suggests the British Foreign and Commonwealth Office generally sought not to place Britain's wider economic and strategic interests at risk by becoming embroiled in the Wiriyamu story.[83]

This leaves us to question whether the text's thesis can be held together with the two remaining sources: Portuguese official materials and Dr dos Santos' report, which the authors did not see first hand since it "remained unpublished and unaccounted for to date, but is cited in various accounts." Presumably, the authors had access to the medic's son, dos Santos the journalist-writer, and if so, may have seen the two photographs of the massacre site proving Wiriyamu's existence and location.

[81] Reis and Oliveira, "Cutting Heads," 80–103.
[82] Bruno C. Reis and Pedro A. Oliveira, "Reply to Mustafah Dhada," *Civil Wars*, 14, 4 (2013): 559–562.
[83] Peter Pringle, interview by author, New York, 2013. See also A. M. Rendel, "Whitehall Plays it by Ear in Africa," *The Times*, July 19, 1973.

In other words, the two sources here, Portuguese materials and dos Santos' figures, do indeed lend strong support to the text's thesis, but they also ring alarm bells. Why would the text select Portuguese official materials bereft of solid data on the massacre to build its case, materials that the authors recognized as anemic? To whit, "Portuguese authorities, both before and after the military coup of 25 April 1974 did not authorize an *independent enquiry* [my italics] into Operation Marosca," in part because Portugal proved "incapable of prevailing over the imposing personality of the politically powerful commander-in-chief general Kaúlza de Arriaga." For months, therefore, "there was no sign of such an inquiry."[84]

For that matter, what methodological and ethical criteria governed the choice of the figure of 200 dead, which Dr dos Santos estimated from an aerial investigation some time after the massacre, over its rival estimate of 400 dead? The latter was given credence in IDAF and Hastings' monographs precisely because they came from cross-indexed data spearheaded by priests and their assistants on the very night of the massacre. These were meticulous and conscientious priests passionately concerned with the truth.

There are no easy answers here. Was this article intentionally revisionist? The authors claim it was not.[85] If not, then are we to conclude that the text fell victim to poor methodology?[86] Perhaps so, given its failure to triangulate nationalist and colonial sources with oral evidence. However, its choice of ideologically suspect sources appears, to this author, too uncomfortably close to support a *denial of the narrative* in affirmative literature.[87]

Fictional narratives: Two works examined

In the third group stands a body of fiction[88] which bridges the gap in evidence with imagined texts. Of the several, one by Sassine focused on the anatomy of the massacre, one by Karodia portrayed the life of a survivor after a massacre, and one by dos Santos dealt with the complexities of the war surrounding the carnage.

Of these, two justly deserve attention here because they cover the ground left untouched in the affirmative literature, and because they deal directly with the thematic queries to be addressed in this book. The earliest work was published in 1976 by the Paris-based *Présence Africaine*, a quarterly journal founded in the 1940s by Alioune Diop, the polyglot Paris-based Senegalese scholar of the classics and a man of letters.[89]

---

[84] Reis and Oliveira, "Cutting Heads," 83.
[85] Reis and Oliveira, "Reply to Mustafah Dhada."
[86] Vail and White refer to this problematic as the social historians' "difficulty of transcending the particular" by not looking "at the creations of the people themselves, the forms in which their own major concerns are expressed." Vail and White, "Forms of Resistance," 886.
[87] David William Cohen discusses a quasi-similar case in his essay on Dr Ouko, "In a Nation of White Cars ... One White-Car, or 'A White Car,' Becomes a Truth," in Luise White, Stephan F. Meischer, and David William Cohen (eds.), *African Words, African Voices: Critical Practices in Oral History* (Bloomington: Indiana University Press, 2001), 264–280.
[88] Sassine, *Wiriyamu*; Karodia, *A Shattering of Silence*; Saavedra, *Os Dias Do Fim*; Jorge, *A Costa dos Murmúrios*; and dos Santos, *O Anjo Branco*.
[89] Alioune Diop, "Niam n'qoura ou les raisons d'être de Présence Africaine," *Présence Africaine*, I (1947), accessed July 11, 2011, http://preview.tinyurl.com/n9fsmrq.

The novel developed an imagined anatomy of collective murder at Wiriyamu as a three-day character-intensive carnage, laid out in spliced chunks of text, each headed by an hourly timeline. The narrative is emotively charged. The villains, victims and a poet, all with Portuguese-sounding names, appear inexorably drawn towards death and damage.

As fiction, *Wirriyamu* is eminently readable and at times poetic. As a novel, tenuously based on facts, however, it fails to fill in the gaps left blank by Felícia Cabrita. The novel's characters lack strong fictional flesh and bone to drive either the imagined narrative or the factual story. At times, it appears to use a tragedy to produce poetry and fiction. The scenes, the plot, and the events could have occurred anywhere in Africa; but perhaps that is the point that the novel wants to convey.

The narrative suggests at the end that the events at Wiriyamu had a role to play in the liberation of Southern Africa—and here Sassine is on the mark. The story in *The Times of London* would appear to have weakened Portugal's tenure in Mozambique, which when set free, strengthened the resolve for others to liberate the rest of southern Africa. Sassine's book conveys this idea through Kabalango, a Byronesque poet, who realizes at the end of the book that "Wirriyamu" can only carry meaning if it is avenged with a call to arms to liberate the region, "walking the talk" as it were. In Kabalango's view, that is the only way to end the colonial violence, suppressing the subjugated voices in Southern Africa.

Unlike Sassine's fiction, dos Santos' "O Anjo Branco," *The White Angel*, forms part of a larger national trend in fictional nostalgia festering Portugal's imperial and colonial past and covers the intricacies of Mozambique's colonial war, Tete as a place, and the anatomy of the massacre at Wiriyamu. It features a Portuguese medical doctor, José Branco, an unfortunate name for a main character given the racial undertones of the conflict, modeled after the author's father, dos Santos senior. He had fallen out of favor of the Portuguese officialdom who sent him to the "white men's hell": they referred to Tete as "a cemetery for whites."[90]

Colonial authorities hoped his exile would send him into oblivion. Instead, he found a new lease of life. The medical challenges facing the province were gargantuan, and the resources close to non-existent. He created an aerial medical service, flying in a small plane to remote locations, tending to the sick and the frail impeccably dressed in medical whites.

The novel follows the life story of this medic against the background of war, politics, torture, and conviviality between races and social classes. The author's declared aim was to offer a highly nuanced treatment of the war. Eschewing condemnation of the colonial power and their nationalist opponents, the novel rejects a simplistic view of the Portuguese presence in Tete. Instead, it argues for a more sophisticated narrative in which the Portuguese secret police and colonial administrators, and FRELIMO and its wounded, acknowledged each others' periodical, and at times clandestine presence in the same space, allowing for mutual coexistence without condoning each other's legitimacy to engage in warfare.

---

[90] Berenguer, interview, 1994 and 1995.

Unlike Sassine, dos Santos succeeds in advancing the notion that perhaps the war in Tete was more complex and morally uncertain than is made out to be; and that perhaps Wiriyamu too may well merit a second review. The latter point is not explicit in his book, though the message to this effect is clearly implied by the author's own political and personal perspectives on the war.

Two aspects of this novel are troubling. One relates to its perspective and the other to the inaugural events that launched the book. The novel promotes an image of conviviality in Tete between the colonial hierarchy and its opponents of both persuasions, FRELIMO supporters, and guerrilla fighters in Tete. As several who lived in that district during the war can attest, this is way off the mark. The conviviality was minuscule, if not negligible. If it existed as a widely practiced norm, it did so virtually, in the author's imagined world of consorting enemies engaged in a bitter cat-and-mouse game over liberty.

Further, by my reckoning, the author would have been around eight years old during his father's medical ministry in Tete. Oral research in Tete could easily have informed the narrative better in this regard. Granted, the work is fictional; still, given the claims by the author of having carried out intense "fact-based" research, this perspective of complex coexistence between enemies drawn to kill becomes difficult to overlook.

The second aspect of the work is perhaps ethically troubling if not ghoulish. We now know that the author's father had photographed the outer edge of Wiriyamu nearest to the main road weeks after the carnage, giving us an indicative view of what had transpired on the day.

According to an eyewitness, Lisbon's Geographic Society displayed unsuccessfully, two of these images at the inaugural launch of the book in 2010, which this author did not see. Adrian Hastings was proven right, after all these years! Here was photographic evidence that the massacre had occurred. The tragedy is that this independent body of photographic evidence has come to light fully nine years after Hastings' death, twenty-eight years after he helped reveal the massacre. Sadly, Hastings went to his grave not knowing where this photographic evidence lay buried. A second body of photographic evidence had been taken, reportedly by Jorge Jardim, and this is now easily accessible on the internet.

Santos Senior and Santos Junior sat on the images for thirty-eight years while some of us searched for them. Their continued burial is truly painful, particularly since Portugal's colonial wars in Africa had ended, its fascist regime had been toppled, and the country was now fully democratic and a member of the European Union. Unearthed earlier than 2010, the evidence would have buried once and for all any doubts of Wiriyamu as a visually verifiable certainty. More troubling is the photographic outing of Wiriyamu to coincide with the inauguration of a fictional work depicting a Portuguese "Albert Schweitzer" dressed in whites dispensing medical healing to Tete's needy.

The review of the literature above sent clear messages for this work. The re-nesting of Wiriyamu would require triangulated research entailing vigorously curated oral evidence. On their own, written sources could only do so much. *Hansard* records of proceedings in the British House of Commons and declassified materials from the British Foreign and Commonwealth Office could, for instance, help to address two additional aspects of the Wiriyamu crisis: Anglo-Portuguese relations, and how and why the story broke the way it did in *The Times*. But that is it!

To do full justice to even these two aspects of the story would have taken the study away from its main focus and would have required mining two disparate sets of primary materials: declassified documents in American[91] and South African archives; and the appropriate archives in London,[92] Warwick,[93] and Cambridge.[94]

Until someone undertook this kind of research, Wiriyamu would continue to fuel fictional works, attract deniers and skeptics, and haunt the sentient with questions: Why did Wiriyamu happen? How did the Church get involved and why? How was the narrative constructed and revealed? How and why did Portugal deny, recant the denial, and then justify its conduct? What was life like in Wiriyamu, and how did it come to an end?

Bluntly put, the struggle against Portuguese colonialism was not over yet. Of course, the ten-year armed struggle had helped operationalize Mozambique's constitutional independence,[95] but it had not completely erased the imperial mindset. It was the fight *after* constitutional independence that mattered now. That struggle was against epistemological imperialism claiming ownership of production of knowledge with tools of doubt and erasure. This fight had to be two-pronged, one actively opposing the demonizing, ridiculing, or erasing from consciousness the memory of former oppressors, while the other fought for legitimacy for us, to have a say in the colonial narrative. Until then, the massacres at Wiriyamu and similar mass violence narratives in Africa would atrophy in exile as marginalia in the history of colonial wars. We have seen from Cavaco Silva's statement that the prospect of Portugal continuing to silence this past remained real. After all, Portugal had objectified us with their colonizing of our past with imagined landscapes under Lusotropicalism. It was quite capable of doing so moving forward, this time by remaining silent on colonial mass violence as if it never happened.

---

[91] National Archives, RG 59, "Transcripts of Secretary of State Kissinger's Staff Meetings, 1973–1977, Entry 5177, Box 1, Secretary's Analytical Staff Meetings." Secret. National Archives, RG 59, Central Files 1970–1973, POL 19 PORT-GUIN. Confidential; No Foreign Dissem; Controlled Dissem. Drafted by Heyniger, cleared by Summ, and released by Mark.

[92] Two archives are pertinent here: The BLNR, which housed hard copies of London-based papers including *The Times* and *The Sunday Times*; and the Bourne and Hinsley Papers at Westminster Diocesan Archives, which are perhaps less central to this text but give information on Cardinal Hinsley's vision behind the formation of the CIIR's predecessor organ to fight fascism and totalitarian regimes trammeling basic human rights in Europe. Articles consulted in the BLNR are given in the Bibliography.

[93] Warwick has materials on the unionized printers and typesetters who affected the timing of the Wiriyamu outing. See *National Society of Operative Printers, Graphical and Media Personnel* (MSS.39/NAT), Modern Records Centre, University of Warwick.

[94] The papers of Sir William John Haley, 1901–1987, Knight, Journalist, Churchill Archives Centre, Churchill College, Cambridge, GBR/0014/HALY, HALY 15, 1955–1969, 11 folders and volumes. While peripheral to the main story, Haley proved instrumental in nurturing the one key player, Louis Heren, responsible for the outing of Wiriyamu on the front page of *The Times of London*.

[95] V. I. Lenin, *Imperialism: The Highest Stage of Capitalism* (Sydney: Resistance Books, 1999).

3

Oral Research

The search for answers in the Wiriyamu massacre began in earnest in 1994. The trajectory of the search in written records entailed consulting repositories in various locations. Britain, Spain, Mozambique and the United States have already been mentioned. In Britain, access to Hastings' private diaries pinpointed the day he had received the text from Madrid, while the collection of his papers at Northwick, York University, helped to flesh out the details of the White Fathers' exit from Tete. The Madrid collection of Burgos public records were useful to a point, in illuminating how they viewed their work in Tete.

The trial run

The trajectory of oral research proved less straightforward. It developed in several distinct phases, some of which were dictated by unforeseen exigencies. The first phase began by considering oral historical methods.

Here, several seminal texts made a mark: works by the founder of the Oral History Society (OHS)[1] Paul Thompson,[2] aided by that of Jan Vansena on oral traditions as history[3] and a growing literature on mass violence, trauma, and social suffering narratives[4] helped develop methodological tools to test, through simulation, the conditions to be found in Wiriyamu: respondents without a secure livelihood, some homeless, and all ruptured by violence. The simulation's respondents were former Cowley autoworkers who had lost their jobs, their homes, and while not subject to mass violence, acknowledged their rupture as sufficiently traumatic, even though they were now gainfully employed as stewards in colleges.[5] Significantly, the simulation project did not engage in trauma studies, since its aim was forensic history and as such did not tap secondary memories of family members of respondents to compare factual

---

[1] See *Oral History Society*, accessed October 11, 2013, http://www.ohs.org.uk. See also "Paul Thompson," *Pioneers of Qualitative Research*, accessed October 11, 2013, http://preview.tinyurl.com/nq78ouw.
[2] Paul Thompson, *The Voice of the Past* (Oxford: Oxford University Press, 1988).
[3] Jan M. Vansena, *Oral Tradition as History* (Madison: The University of Wisconsin Press, 1985).
[4] Social suffering literature is extensive. For a quick overview, see Arthur Kleinman, Veena Das, and Margaret M. Lock, *Social Suffering* (Berkeley: University of California Press, 1997).
[5] Mustafah Dhada, "Murmurs Under the Stairwell: What Butlers, Stewards, and Servants Do in an Oxford College" (unpublished paper, St Catherine's College, 1980).

dissonance between vicarious narratives and primary source data. Awareness of these flaws of the project proved instrumental later to identify and recover very quickly from a flood of meme narratives, discussed below.

The project encouraged the view of potential informants as an oral archive of human fonds. As such, they posed two challenges, one related to retrieval methods and the other to refractions in collected data. While print-media repositories remained static, that is to say, virtually unaffected by how data were organized, retrieved, and used for nurturing cultures of evidence, oral data in this field behaved differently. They place-shifted data and shape-shifted their interpretative textures in response to complex factors, interacting dynamically with methods of retrieval to produce a variety of narratives. Put differently, they invited

> us to see historical knowledge as fully engaged with broader social intelligence, known, experienced, and manipulated, of which our redactions of testimonies... [would prove]...narrow, selected, privileged pieces.[6]

Of these, three types of testimony proved useful for this study: triage, data-anchored, and meme. In triage testimonies, first-time respondents spoke primarily to heal themselves.[7] Data were presented in fractured nodes, their jagged edges held together with emotive tissues. Data-retrieval objectives here had to take a back seat to allow space for informants to grieve, a process later codified in the literature as social suffering.[8] When re-telling the same narrative, respondents appeared to depart from triage narratives.

Data-anchored testimonies affected frequently retrieved data from memory. In such instances mnemonics anchored such oft-repeated oral texts. Furthermore, such narratives exhibited authenticity of voice similar to written sources. It was later discovered that normative questioning during data retrieval could easily corrupt this type of narrative, rendering them a teleology.

Lastly, meme testimonies elasticated hearsay beyond verifiable credulity and normally undergirded vicarious evidence, particularly those several steps removed from memory of a lived experience.

In light of these discoveries, I took several measures to reduce my data retrieval footprint and minimize its refractive impact on the data collected. One such measure was to enter the site by myself with an icebreaker, in this case a 1973 photo of a survivor with Peter Pringle. My hope was to remain engaged but self-effacing, gauzy if not transparent. I hoped to encourage respondents to retrieve their data without stirring trauma episodes, while I scooped these as they bubbled up from the human fonds. I realize here there was a fine line between treating respondents holistically and viewing them primarily as data-objects in human clothing. In the end, it was a question of

---

[6] David William Cohen, "The Undefining of Oral Traditions," *Ethnohistory*, 36, 1 (Winter 1986): 9–18.
[7] For a comparative study on memory and healing in neighboring Zimbabwe, see Heike Schmidt, "Healing the Wounds of War: Memories of Violence and the Making of History in Zimbabwe's Most Recent Past," *Journal of Southern African Studies*, 23, 2 (June 1997): 301–310.
[8] Kleinman, Das, and Lock, *Social Suffering*.

intentional alignment, between external transparency and internal authenticity of purpose. Given appropriate sensitivity, awareness, and practice I felt confident that I could achieve this balance over time.

Additional measures put in place aimed to be as light-footed on the human fonds as possible. Before departing for Tete, micro-cassettes and the clothes to be worn during the interviews were muted in color to tone down visual dissonance during interviews, aided by the minimal use of cameras, recording equipment and their carry-ons. The intention, which proved largely successful in the end, was to leave the interview process visually free of the "learned tools of the trade"—pen, paper, et al. Where needed, these could be bought locally. This way, respondents would be free to focus on their testimonies, preferably in a place of their choosing, almost free of icons of imported modernity.

With this preparation in place, the project entered a new phase, interviews with FRELIMO military commanders in Maputo to cull data on their presence in the triangle that led to the Wiriyamu massacre,[9] followed by similar interviews in various locations with Church personnel. These interviews sought data on Wiriyamu's trajectory to London[10] and the Church in Tete.[11]

After a quick dip into both the national archives in Maputo, and the collection at the Centro de Estudos Africanos, Eduardo Mondlane University, the project moved to Tete—its third phase. Here, it hit upon a snag. Given the site's national importance, the local office of national heritage controlled the site and would dictate what we could see and who we could interview. Would showing the project proposal and keeping them in the loop satisfy them to grant unfettered access to the site? Not really: "Why do you want to wake up the dead?" "But the project was designed to be least disruptive," I pleaded. "Its overall objective was to complete the affirmative narratives and restore Wiriyamu to its nest." "Yes, but you cannot go there and dig things we do not want you to see. We must protect our dignity, our heritage, our national security," said the official refusing to identity himself. They had a point. Any archivist would have insisted on conditional terms of access given that the events were less than thirty years old. There was little else I could do to convince them of the project's transparent intentions. Theirs, on the other hand, were muddied, perhaps mixed with a desire to filter out data on FRELIMO's role, if any, in the Wiriyamu tragedy.

Returning to Maputo to get approval from a higher authority would have set the project back several months. My predicament reached a pair of sympathetic ears, a relative of a classmate now deceased with whom I had shared cheese sandwiches in the gulch on many occasions. He went to bat for my project. This boulder was eventually removed after intricate negotiations with the heritage office. When asked to reveal how he had won approval, he declined to say, "Some things my dear Essufo (my Búzi name) are best kept buried but I told them you were a native son and moved to do this work

[9] They were General Hama Tai, General António Bonifácio Grouveta, interview by author, Maputo, 1994 and 1995; and Mariano de Araújo Matsinha, interview by author, Maputo, 1994 and 1995.
[10] White Father missionaries at the Seminário Maior in Maputo, Irmã Lúcia, Miguel Buendia, Padre Vicente Berenguer, and last but not least, Padre José Sangalo.
[11] José Capela, nephew of Bishop Soares Resende, Father Joseph, Padre Alfonso Valverde de Lion, Padre Alberto Fonte Castellã, and Padre Enrique Ferrando.

by the power of our ancestors." "But that is a lie!" "You see, I told you not to ask questions." In return, I had to guarantee I would respect the site and not turn it into a "spectacle," alluding here presumably to how the site may well have been accessed in the past. By then, word was out: "Um gordão Americano," a fat American, was in town to investigate Wiriyamu.

That night, someone was at the door of my one-bedroom rental with a message. Isaías Marrão, proprietor of Pensão Univendas, competitors to Hotel Zambezia where Peter Pringle had stayed before his expulsion from Tete, was keen to help and would welcome a visit, which I paid the next day, first thing in the morning.[12] Once there, I was in a time-warp. The living room was studded with hunting trophies and guns mounted high up along the walls. Sepia photographs of safari exploits and meetings with high-ranking officials jostled cheek by jowl in mahogany frames to catch you at eye level across the two couches facing each other.

Animated voices filled the room from a crowd below. There Marrão stood, crystal decanter in hand, pouring a dram of single malt in a cut glass. He approached to say he had gathered informants downstairs to help get the project started post-haste. Was this a set-up? It transpired later, he had his reasons. By providing informants and hosting interviews, he and one retailer opposite his establishment had a captive pool of customers to sell goods to respondents, who expected to be paid in exchange for information. The larger the pool, the larger the profit margin!

The false start

I sprinted downstairs and flung open the door to the room jam-packed with people. Over 100 would-be informants held their precious cargo tightly to their chest in this confined space, all claiming to know Wiriyamu, all expecting to be paid. Primary source respondents commingled with individuals desperate to sell synthetic data and memes for surplus cash to buy food. The pilot project had ill-equipped me to tackle such an avalanche of human fonds. Marrão's "generosity" threatened to drown the project in memes and hearsay. I had to act, and fast, to steer the project decisively away from such a potentially damaging start. This is not how I had imagined my point of entry into Wiriyamu oral fonds.

However, such a large pool was an opportunity, to gather statistical data on the triangle, separate primary from secondary fonds, tag the former for prosopographic interviews later, evaluate these for supportive evidence, select candidates to train as team leaders and co-informants in data collection, trauma triage, vicarious trauma avoidance,[13] and put in place other protocols for minimally invasive data retrieval.

---

[12] For Isaías Marrão's short biography, see "fazem-se Casas e Casas, Sem Ruas: Isaías Marrão, um home, uma história," *Jornal Calowera* (March 22, 2010): 18–19.
[13] Post-traumatic stress disorder (PTSD) literature is extensive. Among works that informed the text here include Hanna Kienzler, "Debating War Trauma and Post-Traumatic Stress Disorder (PTSD) in an Interdisciplinary Arena," *Social Science and Medicine*, 67(2008): 218–227.

Two informants[14] chosen as prospective team leaders for their local knowledge, language skills in Portuguese and Nyungwe, and literacy were left in charge while I secured from Marrão's shop below pen and paper on which to format data tables for culling genealogical, economic and casualty figures. Their instructions were to place the crowd in four massacre groups, one for Chaworha, one for Juawu, one for Wiriyamu and one for locations not yet identified in public records, with each group split into primary and secondary data carriers. A quick conference with the two informants followed once the task of separating preliminary primary source data from the rest finished. The two informants, now emerging as team leaders, aided by primary source informants in each group, put together a list of qualified volunteers who, given training, could help facilitate the interview process, help cross-check narrative and qualitative data, and track down informants willing to come forward to share in the project's data collection work.

That is how that day chez Marrão went. It ended with a communal meal for all, and spare food for them to take home, while the team leaders convened afterwards for several days of training. While imparting best practices in oral history methods proved relatively easy, trauma recognition and avoidance training proved most difficult, in part because I too was relatively new to the field. Details notwithstanding, this training entailed two modules: symptom recognition and preventive best practices for those involved in fieldwork. Subsequently, eight key best practices in resilience strategies were highlighted and adhered to, by and large. These ranged from self-care, daily reflection, physical exercise, close social and family engagements, frequent breaks during workdays, religious practice for those so inclined, team work and conscious adherence to democratic decision-making.[15]

Of the two, Abidu Karimu handled the task with great ease, in part because of a solid family support system, and a social life, which he evenly balanced with his weekly religious observance at the local mosque, to which I too was invited, given my knowledge of his faith, but elected not to accept. Generally, Karimu helped with fact-checking, logistics, provisions, lodgings, water and fuel supplies, and structured time-management. He also brought several other assets to the table: some knowledge of important local customs and mores to facilitate access to informants; negotiating skills to navigate local politics in the triangle, which kept the research timetable on target; an extensive social network in Tete city with which to negotiate access to informants from the local church and business community; and contacts with missionaries willing to be interviewed in Changara, Moatize, Matundo, Zóbuè, Unkanha, and Mucumbura.

Senhor Elídio's taciturn disposition and past encounters with the secret police and torture victims dictated a stricter adherence to preventative measures to mitigate

---

[14] Abidu Karimu, interview by author, Tete, 1995; and Senhor Elídio, interview by author, Wiriyamu, Chaworha, Cantina Raul, and Matundo, Tete, 1995.
[15] Sandra L. Bloom, "Caring for the Caregiver: Avoiding and Treating Vicarious Traumatization," in A. Giardino, E. Datner, and J. Asher (eds.), *In Sexual Assault, Victimization Across the Lifespan* (Missouri: G. W. Medical Publishing, 2003), 459–470. A full list of relevant publications is given on this site, http://www.sanctuaryweb.com/bloom.php.

vicarious trauma. Senhor Elídio's instinct for self-preservation kept him in check by not overextending, which in the end served the project well. His analytical skills, however, ensured the economic and demographic data included in this book remained free of obvious internal contradictions. His deeply reflective demeanor, on the other hand, helped him remain calm during emotionally charged narratives.

Once the two team leaders completed their training, the training of co-informants got underway, but on the fly, and on site, in part to accelerate the pace of fieldwork. Of the several co-informants trained this way, Enéria Tenente Valeta and Vasco Tenente Valeta, siblings who survived the massacre at Wiriyamu, proved instrumental in initiating conversations with fellow survivors at the center of the Wiriyamu village. In addition to the two Valetas, the following played an equally important role in the culling of data: Bulachu Pensadu Zambezi, a goat-herd closely connected with the events days before and after the massacre; Vasco Xavier, living in the gulch below Wiriyamu, whose knowledge of Riachu's economy helped the text flesh out that area's importance to Wiryamu's governance structure; Kalifornia Kaniveti, master brewer and butcher and the one adult male survivor available for interview from the village of Juawu; and António Mixone, well-known eyewitness survivor of the massacre at Chaworha.

One last session of team leaders and co-informants was then held on site before the project moved into its Wiriyamu-based final phase. Its objectives were two-fold: go over the topics and best practices, which included the need to listen more and be less preoccupied with extracting information from respondents. An engaged and active self-effacement, it was stressed during this session, would allow respondents a dominant role in sharing the data from within as part of what later came to be known as social suffering narratives, in which "the texture of the dire affliction...[was]...best felt in the rough details of biography."[16] For social suffering, Kienzler explained, "one must embed individual biography in the larger matrix of culture, history, and political economy..."[17] The other purpose of the final session was to discuss the project's central objectives while on site, construct a biography of Wiriyamu, and the anatomy of its demise.

Following a lengthy discussion, I was designated to tackle triage testimonies, interview first-time informants among survivors and witnesses. Team leaders would deal with data-anchored narratives, the re-telling of oral texts informants had crafted for a different audience. Co-informants were assigned to fill the gaps in data on demography, animal husbandry, homes, agricultural plots, grain silos, and geographical markers, and to team leaders as and when they were needed. It was understood that while this division of labor would keep the project moving, it would be subject to immediate change to reduce emotional fatigue or meet unforeseen situations.

---

[16] Paul Farmer, "On Suffering and Structural Violence: A View from Below," *Daedalus*, 125, 1 (1996): 263.
[17] Kienzler, "Debating War Trauma," 225. A good example of one such study on Croatia is Michaela Schäuble, "'Imagined Suicide': Self-Sacrifice and the Making of Heroes in Post-War Croatia," *Anthropology Matters Journal*, 8, 1 (2006): 1–14.

The work on site

With this final preparation over, fieldwork began. A short pre-selection process was held to identify and interview eyewitnesses placing on hold respondents with stories based on hearsay. Generally, the interviews went well, where interview protocols were followed. One important example of a successful protocol was the care taken to strip evocative bias in oral evidence by exploring inferences from the facts presented. The story of a young herder carrying a goat in his arms could imply affectionate care. Subsequent probes exploring context revealed they were protecting pregnant goats about to deliver. The loss of a kid would have meant the loss of a potential forty escudos at the local market.

Similarly, where informants felt comfortable with their surroundings, the data collected proved instrumental in fleshing out the anatomy of the massacre. The majority of the respondents here chose their place of interview. The foot of a baobab tree on the massacre site at Wiriyamu proved most popular. Those interviewed at adjoining massacre sites either chose a spot near a chapel or a water well. Survivors interviewed in Djemusse selected a larger baobab tree to lean against "because it saw and could hear what we are saying."[18]

In the same vein, the formats of several interviews were varied to fit in with the needs and the pace of respondents. Some preferred constant prodding. Others invited didactic probes, and here the help of companions was sought to cross-check facts on memory recall. Group discussions and palavers were used frequently for collecting and cross-checking data on lineage, demography, poultry, pigs, goats, and cattle.

Not all interviews were successful from the get-go. Of these, at least four cases are worth noting here to illustrate the role that contextual flexibility played in data collection. Respondents in two of these cases initially withheld what they knew, perhaps afraid of reawakening the trauma of their ordeal. In both cases, the interviews took unprecedented turns once respondents had internally processed a safe zone. One reconstructed on site how he escaped from the inferno enveloping him and his family. The other relived with eerie precision the process used to collect the list of the dead on the night of the massacre. Both felt they had accomplished something by choosing to relive the day. In doing so, they uprooted, as a tsunami would, the interview protocols carefully put in place to facilitate data gathering.

The third respondent, who became blind from an undisclosed ailment following the massacre, proved equally reluctant to talk until he asked to be taken to the spot where his home once stood. There, he re-lived the trajectory of his escape from the carnage. The final respondent worthy of note here was from Juawu. He opened up once he took the team to his brewery. Aided by fellow respondents, he narrated vividly Juawu's demise.

The least challenging aspect of the fieldwork was the gathering of quantitative data on vital commodities and resources, perhaps because these related to life in a village before its end. Such data ran the gamut: points of reference pegged to specific boulders

---

[18] Kalifornia Kaniveti, interview by author, Wiriyamu and Juawu, Mozambique, 1995.

and land and water marks; sources of, and proximity to, water; location of homes, their shapes, and their social significance; the making and selling of woven baskets, *batuques*, coal, and artisanal goods; the slaughtering of meat for personal use, for social events, and for generating income; the construction of distilleries of local beer and spirits; rainmaking rituals; location of football fields and courtship rituals; trading in animal husbandry; hunting rats and fishing; approximate location of sacred forests; stories of wild life; and arboreal genealogies.

Two aspects of the fieldwork proved challenging and left unresolved, one related to memes and one dealt with data recovery on gender-related issues. Respondents during a group interview told of children pounded to death with pestles in wood-carved mortars. Yet armed men in particular, did not handle mortar and pestle, viewing it as a woman's job. If the Portuguese colonial forces did engage in beating children to a pulp with mortars, then they must have had ample time to devote to this task, thereby delaying their mission's objective, to clean up Wiriyamu quickly before they set up camp for the night in a "relatively safe zone." This is not to suggest that rape, pillage, and the taking of women as trophies did not occur. They did, at least in two cases. However, reliable eyewitnesses were not forthcoming to prove the pounding of infants to a pulp as a norm during the Wiriyamu massacre.[19]

One conclusion to be drawn from this is that in the heat of the storytelling, someone may well have gestured pestle when they meant the butt of a gun. This was very likely to have happened since the Portuguese shortage of arms and ammunition dictated alternative killing methods. "We used grenades instead. They killed more people than a bullet," attested the commander of the operation to me when interviewed later for this work.[20]

Unless respondents volunteered detail on rape and genderized violence, the project eschewed culling such data to minimize the emotional footprint on female respondents unaccompanied by the only female fieldworker on the team. In all these gender-related instances, care was taken to avoid triggering post-traumatic stress disorder (PTSD) episodes. Such a precaution to obviate dissociative behavior was important for sustaining productivity in agriculture,[21] and mitigating the effects of trauma on parenting.[22] In the face of such episodes (and there were not many), data-gathering stopped as protocol demanded and was replaced with empathy and motionless silence, bearing witness to the social suffering, which allowed respondents an uninterrupted space to mourn the events until their memories dissipated safely and securely. Such interviews were terminated straight away. Respondents and fieldworkers were asked to take a break to relieve stress and consider a change in the seating arrangements for subsequent sessions. Further, fieldworkers were asked to be particularly vigilant to

---

[19] Melo, interview, 1995 and 2014.
[20] ibid.
[21] Victor Igreja, Wim Kleijn, Beatrice Dias-Lambranca, Clara Calero, and Annemick Richters, "Agricultural Cycle and the Prevalence of Post-Traumatic Stress Disorder: A Longitudinal Community Study in Postwar Mozambique," *Journal of Traumatic Stress*, 22, 3 (June 2009): 172–179.
[22] Victor Igreja, 'The Effects of Traumatic Experiences on the Infant–Mother Relationship in the Former War Zones of Central Mozambique: The Case of Madzawe in Gorongoza," *Infant Mental Health Journal*, 24, 5 (2003): 469–494.

keep sessions on data collection distinctly separate from their other forms of social interaction among respondents.

In the case of this author, Abidu Karimu was asked to stand by, particularly during certain triage narratives, to monitor boundary maintenance during the interviews. He checked daily for signs of premature vicarious trauma from continuous exposure to massacre testimonies. Fieldwork protocols advised mandatory sabbaticals in case of suspected vicarious trauma injury. I took two, one to share preliminary findings with scholars at the Center of African Studies, Eduardo Mondlane University, Maputo; the other at Ponta d'Oro, a beach resort, to sculpt two pieces, one *mphondorho*, depicting the lion-spirit, and the other named "Eve Ascending," memorializing Podista Mchenga, a survivor at Wiriyamu.

Interviews off site

Interviews in Tete outside the triangle, Maputo, Matola, Madrid, Lisbon, London, Leeds and New York, followed a similar protocol—except in a handful of cases. One such case entailed Padre José Sangalo, a Burgos priest, son of a bullfighter, whose interview was held in a sanatorium in Madrid as he performed three chores assigned to him, as a rooftop gardener, pigeon breeder, and assistant to a priest in the local medical therapy program. Some of the interviews were conducted walking during lunchtime as he headed to the parish church. Attached to microphones linked to an analog micro tape recorder we remained appropriately tethered as we dodged Madrid's pedestrian traffic. The interviews on the rooftop among pigeons proved trickier—it was difficult to mitigate the sounds of flapping wings and cooing, which threatened to drown the recordings of his data-strewn narrative.

Several interviews had to be held in hotel lobbies, army barracks, luggage store rooms, private dining clubs, hotel rooms, a bar, a coffee house, a yacht club, a seminary, a church, and over restaurant meals. Interviewing respondents in these places proved challenging, without the aid of team leaders to ensure boundary maintenance. Consequently, such interviews required frequent stops and starts to fill gaps in the data covered. Despite these challenges, two interviews recorded under these conditions yielded a set of multi-layered and richly textured texts. Of the two, the most noteworthy was the interview with Peter Pringle, *The Sunday Times of London* journalist, which lasted for twelve hours straight, during which he confirmed the veracity of the massacre. The other was with Antonino Melo, the commander heading the operation at Wiriyamu.

The final push

The project went dark in 1997 for two reasons: loss of data and vicarious trauma. The inordinately low pH content of note-papers bought locally deteriorated rapidly under humid conditions, smudging data records. In addition, the filaments in some of the ferric oxide tapes magnetized, which digital sound engineers re-constructed to salvage data contained in a few of these tapes. Regrettably, the rest was lost.

During fieldwork, I had remained consciously detached from all aspects of the research, the interviewing process, the data, and persons interviewed. I cannot say the same about my inner state after processing the information I had uncovered. Put differently, the historical had come to devour the personal within. The horror of the evidence collected would traumatize anyone.[23] Failure to have professionals in the field address the matter in a timely manner did not help;[24] neither did my "grin and bear it" attitude. In the meantime, two texts on my preliminary findings sought to advance the project into print. One examined Portugal's denial of the massacre,[25] the other, published bereft of footnotes in compliance with the journal's publishing guidelines, exposed Portugal's culpability in the affair.[26]

The final push to consolidate the research came in 2010 after retreating to full faculty status, which led to two additional texts. One offered a critique of the article in *Civil Wars*, discussed earlier,[27] and the other[28] gave a skeletal outline of the Wiriyamu massacre.

This is the final text on Wiriyamu's terminal entrapment. It tackles its context, its erasure, its resurrection as a publicly outed narrative, and its afterlife on real and contested terrains. A companion volume on mediated testimonial narratives on Wiriyamu for instructional purposes will hopefully follow this work in the future.

---

[23] Literature on PTSD and STS among Portuguese war veterans is covered in Angela Maia, Teresa McIntyre, M. Graça Pereira, and Eugénia Ribeiro, "War Exposure and Post-Traumatic Stress as Predictors of Portuguese Colonial War Veterans' Physical Health," *Anxiety, Stress, and Coping*, 24, 3 (May 2011): 309–325; M. Graça Pereira and Susana Pedras, "Vitimização Secundária nos Filhos Adultos de Veteranos da Guerra Colonial Portuguesa," *Psicologia: Reflexão e Crítica*, 24, 4 (2011): 702–709; and M. Graça Pereira, Susana Pedras, and Cristina Lopes, "Post-Traumatic Stress, Psychological Morbidity, Psychopathology, Family Functioning, and Quality of Life in Portuguese War Veterans," *Traumatology*, 18 (2013): 49–58.

[24] Literature on vicarious trauma and trauma prevention in the post-narrative phase is extensive. See John Barnhill, *DSM-5 Clinical Cases* (Arlington, Virginia: American Psychiatric Association, 2013). For secondary literature, consult Peter Glick and Elizabeth Levy Paluck, "The Aftermath of Genocide: History as a Proximal Cause," *Journal of Social Issues*, 69, 1 (March 2013): 200–208; and Jessica Johnson, "Agency-Level Interventions for Preventing and Treating Trauma: A Qualitative Study," Master of Social Work Clinical Research Papers, Paper 41, accessed December 12, 2014, http://sophia.stkate.edu/msw_papers/41.

[25] Dhada, "Contesting Terrains Over a Massacre," 413–455.

[26] Mustafah Dhada, "Frankly My Dear, We Should Give a Damn!" *Peace Review*, 12: 3 (2000): 457–462.

[27] Mustafah Dhada, "The Wiriyamu Massacre of 1972: Response to Reis and Oliveira," *Civil Wars*, 15, 4 (2103): 551–558.

[28] Mustafah Dhada, "The Wiriyamu Massacre of 1972: Its Context, Genesis, and Revelation," *History in Africa* (June 2013): 1–31.

4

The Nationalist Struggle and the Colonial War in Mozambique

Geography, war, and Wiriyamu

Mozambique is a 309,495-square-mile oblong territory shaped like a sling bone in southeast Africa, wedged between South Africa and Tanzania. It faces Madagascar, across the shark-infested waters of the Indian Ocean forming the Mozambique Channel. The district of Tete, colonial Mozambique's westernmost arm, extends deep into neighboring Malawi, Zambia and Zimbabwe. The River Zambezi cuts Tete in half along its midriff as it engorges at the Cahora Bassa dam, swelling the western half of the district with flooded plains abundant in tiger fish, crocodiles, and hippopotamuses. The Zambezi trundles southeast for 254 nautical miles after Cahora Bassa near the township of Marara. Here, it ends in a birds' paradise, formed by a huge cobwebbed triangle filled with islands and waterways that stretch south of Chinde, close to the Marromeu National Reserve.

Portugal discovered Mozambique on Thursday, January 25, 1498, when a group of Portuguese sailors and translators beached near the coast of Quelimane 56 miles north of the mouth of the Zambezi. That coastline was sprinkled with Arab traders and mini-sultanates.[1] Vasco da Gama led the travelers, dressed as a Muslim from Morocco to elicit a friendly local reception. Thereafter, Portugal stayed in Mozambique for 477 years, and left in 1975 after fighting an armed insurgency for ten years.

The insurgency itself began in 1964 with nationalists demanding outright independence, which Portugal refused to grant on several grounds, one of which was its view of the war, an ideological conspiracy cooked up by communists advancing Cold War politics in the region. In the face of this challenge, Portugal had to defend, in its view, its historic mission, to promote and bring Western civilization and Christian values to the colonies. As an empire, therefore, it had to draw the line somewhere. Besides, with Mozambique as a colony, one of many in its possession, Portugal was a great European empire, the longest surviving, rivaling its peers, Britain, France and

---

[1] Sanjay Subrahmanyam, *The Career and Legend of Vasco da Gama* (Cambridge: Cambridge University Press, 1998), and Nigel Cliff, *Holy War: How Vasco da Gama's Epic Voyages Turned the Tide in a Centuries-Old Clash of Civilizations* (New York: Harper, 2011).

Belgium. Without the colonies, Portugal was an underdeveloped European state tucked snugly in Spain's peninsular shadow.[2]

The colonial war developed in two distinct phases. The first lasted for six years and ended with major changes in leadership on both sides of the divide. The second phase began in 1970 with a dramatic shift in military and diplomatic strategies. The military strategy lasted until Portugal's own armed forces toppled the Lisbon regime in 1974, two years after the massacres at Wiriyamu.

Adrian Hastings and Kevin Parker have tackled the causes of Wiriyamu massacre in their respective texts discussed earlier. This chapter picks up the story where they left off, by exploring in greater depth questions untouched or under-explored by them. Briefly, Parker's work recognizes FRELIMO's successful strategy before 1969, despite dissent devouring its political innards. This chapter examines this dissent within FRELIMO, which was every bit as real as the success of its military strategy after 1970.

In addition, both works address the role that changes in leadership played in reshaping the colonial war after 1970. In doing so, they raise an additional question: How did the change in leadership come about and what effect did it have on military strategy in Tete, which included Wiriyamu?

Formative leadership

The colonial war in Mozambique began in September 1964, reportedly after 1,000 FRELIMO fighters returned from training in Algeria ready to launch the northern front.[3] Before this date, several regionally based nationalist organizations, urban literary guilds, and ethnic self-help groups had agitated to negotiate better wages and living conditions with the Portuguese, who retaliated with torture, killings and incarcerations, accusing them of sedition of Mozambique, which Portugal considered a legally binding overseas province as of 1951.

The case of Mueda on June 16, 1960 is appropriate here; as are two similar unrests in central and in southern Mozambique. Their agitations demanding productive self-sustainable cooperatives met with slaughter, though it now transpires not in the magnitude reported in the current literature.[4] Many aspiring nationalists felt they had no choice but to resort to armed resistance, since the Salazar-led empire would not allow representative governance or pluralism in politics.[5] Two years later, three highly dissimilar nationalist groups—dissimilar in ideology, educational formation, religious affiliation, and points of origin and ethnicity—were brought together to become

---

[2] In the early 1970s, Portugal's Human Development Education Index was less than 0.5, among the lowest in Europe. United Nations Development Program, *International Human Development Indicators*, accessed November 26, 2013, http://hdrstats.undp.org/en/tables/.

[3] *Africa Report*, 1 (1965): 29; and *Africa Report*, 4 (1965): 32.

[4] "Quantos Morreram Em Mueda"; "Reunião de indígenas perturbada por agitadores estrangeiros que foram repelidos"; Chipande, "The Massacre of Mueda," 12–14; "Mueda evocada em Portugal"; "Mueda: memórias de um massacre"; Adam and Dyuti, "Entrevista: o massacre de Mueda," 117–128; and Calvão, "Quantos Morreram em Mueda?"

[5] Centro de Estudos Africanos (CEA), Universidade Eduardo Mondlane, Pasta 967.5 25/I.

FRELIMO,[6] to be headed by Eduardo Mondlane who was elected a year later aided by a team of key players from a base in exile in neighboring Tanganyika.[7]

FRELIMO's team included Marcelino dos Santos, the Reverend Uria Simango, Pascoal Mocumbi, Filipe Magaia, José Mungwambe, and several others. Together, they balanced the vested interests of FRELIMO's legacy members with a mixture of other factors related to demographics, geography and experience that each member of the team brought to kickstart the party's liberation strategy. As a southerner, Mondlane had a clear grasp of rural, urban and ethnic politics south of Beira and could exploit to FRELIMO's advantage his contacts and his networks among community organizers in the colony's capital, South Africa and Swaziland.

He also brought to the table enviable qualifications as an academic and practicing sociologist, as a consensus-driven leader and diplomat, and as someone with work experience in matters of diversity and multiculturalism. Having lived and studied in South Africa, Portugal and the United States, and having served in one of the agencies of the United Nations dealing with decolonization and self-governance for South West Africa, Mondlane had garnered a veritable portfolio of other skills pertinent for the job as FRELIMO's founding leader: an intimate knowledge of apartheid politics and Salazarist ideology; an appreciation for pluralism in discourse, interest-aggregated governance, and the role of education in nation-state building and human capacity development; a gift for winning over skeptics to isolate Portugal; and marketing skills to attract prospective donors of humanitarian aid, and military assistance to train FRELIMO cadres in guerilla warfare.[8]

Marcelino dos Santos was a northerner from Lumbo, a small town of 5,000 people south of Nacala on the eastern edge of the Makonde plateau across from the Island of Mozambique.[9] A gifted polemicist[10] and poet, he brought several assets to the table: an uncanny ability to detect subversion within the ranks, analytical skills at dissecting the structure of Portuguese empire in a comparative context, and contacts with clandestine anti-colonial organizations and political activists in North Africa and Europe. In the

---

[6] CEA Pasta 967.5 25/I. The groups were the Mozambican African National Union (MANU), the National Democratic Union of Mozambique (UDENAMO), and the National African Union of Independent Mozambique (UNAMI).

[7] Background on Mondlane is to be found in: *Panaf Great Lives, Eduardo Mondlane* (London: Panaf, 1972); Herbert Shore, "Resistance and Revolution in the Life of Eduardo Mondlane," in E. Mondlane, *The Struggle for Mozambique* (London: Zed Press, 1983), xii–xxxi; Barry Munslow, *Mozambique: The Revolution and Its Origins* (Harlow: Longman, 1983), 62, 66, 69, 81, 89, 98–104, 105, 107, 110, 111, 114–115, 119, and 139; and Livio Sansone, "Eduardo Mondlane and the Social Sciences," *Vibrant: Virtual Brazilian Anthropology*, 10, 2 (July–December 2013): 73–111. Archival materials on Mondlane consulted in the Herbert Shore Collection, Oberlin College, included: Series 1. "Biographical Files, 1950s–2003," and Series 4, 1952–1966. Subseries 1, "Writings by Eduardo Mondlane, 1952–1968, n.d.," Box 1. Catalog of materials in the collection accessed December 16, 2012 can be viewed at http://tinyurl.com/l4kgxm3.

[8] On the subject of pluralism and conflicts at the apex of leadership, see Walter C. Opello, Jr., "Pluralism and Elite Conflict in an Independence Movement: FRELIMO in the 1960s," *Journal of Southern African Studies*, 2, 1 (October 1975): 66–82.

[9] Latitude 15° 02' 48" S; Longitude 40° 38' 02" E. Location of Lumbo in *The Times Comprehensive Atlas of the World* is plate 89 J11.

[10] See Marcelino dos Santos, "Discurso: Proferido, Primeiro Congresso," CEA Pasta 967.5 25/I (Dar es Salam, 1962), 6–7.

past, he had successfully foiled surveillance by the notorious secret police during his student days in Lisbon, whence he had fled to study in Paris. Here, he proved instrumental in establishing Movimento Anti-Colonial (MAC) in 1957, and four years later became an overseas member of the União Democrática Nacional de Moçambique (UDENAMO) which later joined FRELIMO.[11]

Paris's left bank was a haven for exiled intellectuals and activists plotting the overthrow of African and South-East Asian colonial rules, and Marcelino benefited from these discussions, chiseling his thinking and quill to eliminate Portuguese rule in Africa. He found his métier in FRELIMO as its head of external affairs, helping FRELIMO's nascent ideological core from contumacy within its ranks. He also facilitated the procurement of foreign aid while staving off external threats by the Portuguese secret agents eager to exploit dissension in FRELIMO leadership. His role as keeper of state secrets after 1975, however, proved less savory, particularly in justifying summary executions of leading dissenters as a necessity in post-colonial Mozambique.[12]

The 26-year-old Reverend Uria Simango, made Vice President of the party, was a second-generation Presbyterian pastor from Beira, a port capital of nearly half a million inhabitants,[13] and brought into the leadership a five-year track record as an organizer of the Mozambican community in Salisbury, Rhodesia; an intimate knowledge of Manica-e-Sofala, the district at Mozambique's narrowest midriff; and a willingness to negotiate with former adversaries during crisis to preserve the interests of the greater whole. Temperamentally, Simango was fiercely opposed to doctrinarian Marxism, and appeared to have shared Mondlane's view of political pluralism, but perhaps not his tact and diplomacy—a trait that in the end cost him his leadership position in FRELIMO and ultimately life itself.[14]

Besides these three, Lourenço Mutaca, originally from the Zambêzia region north of Beira, served as FRELIMO's treasurer, financial secretary and economics "minister" in charge of state reconstruction behind the frontline; while Lázaro Kavandame, a sixty-year-old community activist and organizer, was brought into FRELIMO's fold to continue his mobilization effort among an estimated 800,000 Maconde inhabiting the plateau in the northeast corner of Mozambique. Pascoal Mocumbi was placed as Secretary for Information and Propaganda, aided by dos Santos, while João Mungwane was sent to Algiers as a FRELIMO's point person to facilitate military training and procure arms.[15]

---

[11] Dos Santos' biography remains to be written. His speeches and poems, which he penned under the pseudonyms Kalungano and Lilinho Micai, are to be found scattered in several collections which are noted in two succinct paragraphs in his *Gale Encyclopedia of Biography* entry, accessed August 18, 2013, http://www.answers.com/topic/marcelino-dos-santos.

[12] See Marcelino dos Santos, "Nós não estamos arrependidos," Canal de Moçambique, May 17, 2006 broadcast, accessed August 18, 2013, http://preview.tinyurl.com/mfkemz7.

[13] Latitude 19° 50' 18" S; Longitude 34° 52' 31" E. Location of Beira in *The Times Comprehensive Atlas of the World* is plate 89 G13.

[14] *Africa Report*, 11 (November 1967): 9–21. Several recent works tackle his life's work and death. Barnabé Lucas Ncomo, *Uria Simango: Um Homem, Uma Causa* (Maputo: Uma Causa Edições Novafrica, 2004).

[15] FRELIMO, *Mozambique Revolution*, 2 (January 1964): n.p.

Three personalities added their talent to this mix. One was Janet Mondlane, whose skills at getting aid underpinned the early success of FRELIMO's education strategy at the Mozambican Institute; the other was Padre Mateus Pinho Gwenjere. Gwenjere had fled the dreaded secret police from the Muraça Catholic mission headed by the White Fathers, and had brought with him several young followers to join the Mozambique Institute, strengthening its initial cohort of students expecting to be trained as post-colonial administrators. The influence of the White Fathers and that of Soares de Rezende, his titular bishop in Beira, had molded Gwenjere to embrace a progressive view of Christianity, which he preached as a gravitational force for self-determination. Padre Gwenjere added passion to the mix. He was spellbinding, charismatic, but fiercely didactic, with strong views on formative pedagogy for the oppressed in Mozambique, which ultimately contributed to his undoing in the party.[16]

The appointment of Leo Clington Aldridge, Jr., alias Leo Milos, alias Seifal Aziz, a young intellectual with a Masters in Romance languages from the University of Southern California, was perhaps the most enigmatic—and to this day remains a mystery in FRELIMO's early history. Milos was reportedly put in charge of training new militants for guerrilla warfare—a position that required method and cautious discipline, an eye for detail in pedagogy, patience in inspiring cadres to excel under adversity, and stamina to impart instruction under self-sustaining conditions. Milos had a few of these qualities but was greatly hampered by his lack of ability as a team player. He loved conflict. His sheer presence and personality appeared to have been a source of constant contumacy among peers and tutees, as were his declamations of Mondlane-leadership as too pro-American. One clue that may explain this appointment transpired after his expulsion from FRELIMO in 1965.[17] The FRELIMO leadership may well have hoped to tap into his self-proclaimed contacts behind the "bamboo curtain" to procure arms and secure training for FRELIMO cadres at the prestigious Beijing Military Academy.[18]

The formation of a Central Committee earmarked FRELIMO's formative period. Additional members joined this committee much later, notable among them Jorges Rebelo, originally from the colonial capital, who quit his law studies at Coimbra University; and a military trio, Filipe Samuel Magaia, Samora Machel, and Joaquim Chissano—all three later played a key role in the party. To ensure political supremacy over military affairs two measures were adopted: monthly meetings presided by Mondlane, Simango, dos Santos or his designee, with the secretary of defense briefing the central committee on military operations.

By 1966, the geographic scope of the war extended over a vast territory, propelling Mondlane to take one other measure, to split the theater into a dozen regions under a military commander reporting to a twelve-member war council, formed after the death of Samuel Filipe Magaia during a battle with Portuguese forces. Samora Moises

---

[16] "Joaquim Chissano: Há gente com tendência para desprezar e deturpar a história" (Saturday, August 18, 2012), accessed August 18, 2013, http://tinyurl.com/mbowufg.
[17] *Africa Report*, 1 (Jan. 1965): 29.
[18] *Africa Report*, 11 (Nov. 1967): 9–21.

Machel headed this war council and reported its activity as its titular head to the central committee,[19] which deliberated on all matters. Decisions were made by a simple majority vote, secret ballot or consensus through palavers.

Nationalist diplomacy, internal dissent, and deaths

Once appointed leader, Mondlane, his partner the American-born and educated Janet Mondlane, and a few in leadership positions prepared FRELIMO for war. Internally, Mondlane sought, with mixed results, to keep the coalition of disparate nationalist groups united under FRELIMO, which he justified as a strategic necessity to defeat Portugal.[20] Externally, he focused his energies on two diplomatic fronts. One laid the groundwork for isolating Portugal internationally by exploiting his former professional contacts established during his brief association with the United Nations; while the other sought help from Algeria and Egypt to train the party's cadres for guerrilla combat.

Diplomatic efforts to publicize the plight of the colonized in Mozambique had began as early as 1962, four months before the formation of FRELIMO, during the United Nations' seven-member fact-finding mission to Dar es Salam. FRELIMO's legacy members sought to attain two objectives here: to disabuse the mission of their view that the Portuguese were peace-loving and trustworthy colonizers, and to seek their help in isolating Portugal from its global armament networks fueling counter-insurgency.

Earlier, Portugal had enlisted the help of Konrad Adenauer's government to send an envoy to Mozambique, who having been given a highly mannered tour of the colony returned to confirm what Portugal had claimed all along—that it was a constructively engaged imperial ruler of Mozambique. Portugal subsequently used this affirmation at the UN to chip away at its nationalist detractors, particularly among some members of the mission in Dar es Salam susceptible to pressure and propaganda.[21] FRELIMO countered with specific citations demonstrating racially biased three-tiered social structures that ultimately ensured segregation and unequal access to medical and educational facilities.[22]

The objective of breaking the armament supply chain proved much harder to achieve—and here the legacy members opted for an evidence-based strategy: serial numbers, photographs and details of dates and places of manufacture of weapons used during that year and earlier, as evidence to argue their case against Portugal. While this approach seeded doubts among members susceptible to Portuguese propaganda, it failed in the short run to isolate Portugal as it was intended to do, until the Wiriyamu revelations achieved this for FRELIMO.[23]

---

[19] ibid.
[20] "Ancien professeur de l'université de Syracuse (USA)," *Jeune Afrique*, Numero Special Annuel (1970): 558–559.
[21] *Mozambican Revolution*, 1 (December 1963): n.p.
[22] *Mozambican Revolution*, 3 (February 1964): 8
[23] *Mozambican Revolution*, 1 (December 1963): n.p.

Arms procurement, on the other hand, proved a success. A few years later Mondlane acknowledged his party's debt to Algeria as the first country "to bother with the training of our military units."[24] His partner Janet, in the meantime, had secured aid from the Ford Foundation to develop the Mozambique Institute mentioned earlier, FRELIMO's premier school for developing human capacity needed to fuel the war and the reconstruction of the liberated zones behind the front lines. Janet led the institute, aided by Padre Mateus Gwenjere.[25]

By late 1964, Mondlane felt sufficiently confident that his party would have both trained cadres to lead an armed revolt in October, and a blueprint for a guerrilla strategy would then follow. He viewed Algeria's Front de Libération Nationale (FLN) struggle as the ideal model to emulate, with an outbreak of insurgency "in all parts of the territory."[26] But not before the end of the rainy season in October, Mondlane added, to avoid "pointless slaughter."[27] With this strategy in place, his party expected to free Mozambique from Portuguese colonial rule by 1969.[28] With that said, Mondlane prepared for a three-week tour of Western and Eastern Europe, to publicize FRELIMO's planned offensive and its need for additional aid to sustain the war effort over the long term.[29]

However, dissident elements within the party disagreed with the leadership over timing and launched a series of unauthorized strikes. The first of these occurred on August 21, 1964, when insurgents nominally affiliated to FRELIMO under the general command of Filipe Samuel Magaia attacked an area patrolled by the Portuguese Armed Battalion 588 in Cabo Delgado. Similar armed assaults on Portuguese assets followed in two locations: Chai in Cabo Delgado and Xilama. Both locations were in the north, right across the border from Tanganyika, which five months earlier had joined with Zanzibar to become a bi-territorial unified republic of Tanzania.

On Friday, September 25, 1964, FRELIMO cadres then launched simultaneous attacks on ten military outposts "covering a vast area of the country," according to the *Mozambican*, FRELIMO's military bulletin issued from the Dar es Salam office. Two additional attacks followed, one against military outposts in the district of Zambezia, and one in an unspecified location to disrupt the flow of military convoys.[30]

A year later, the war in the district of Niassa deepened once a two-year mobilization effort in that region came to a successful end. Subsequently, Niassa acquired a military

---

[24] *Africa Report*, 5 (May 1967): 29.
[25] Janet Modlane, "Mozambique Institute: Ray of Hope for Refugees," *Toward Freedom*, 14, 11 (1965): n.p.; and "Ancien professeur de l'université de Syracuse (USA)," *Jeune Afrique*, Numero Special Annuel (1970): 558–559.
[26] Party documents seem to indicate a nuanced change in Mondlane's thinking on the Algerian FLN model for FRELIMO after a visit to China as a guest of Beijing's Institute of Foreign Affairs at the end of 1964. "He left China convinced that the historical struggle of the Chinese people has relevance to the present struggle of the people." While this does not imply rejection of the FLN model, it does suggest that China's mobilization of the peasantry to sustain the March had much to offer to FRELIMO's own rural campaign for popular support to win the colonial war. Archivo Histórico de Moçambique, AHM, PP565, *Mozambican Revolution*, 2 (January 1964): n.p.
[27] *Africa Report*, 5 (May 1964): 5.
[28] *Africa Report*, 9 (October 1964): 26.
[29] *Africa Report*, 12 (December 1964): 23.
[30] ibid., 23.

camp with provisions to train a female fighting force.[31] Given the abundance of forageable food, weak intelligence, and an even weaker Portuguese presence in Cabo Delgado and Niassa, FRELIMO rapidly advanced in this part of northern Mozambique, sustaining itself without the need to establish a supply food chain from across the border, which would have been vulnerable to Portuguese aerial attack.

In 1965, FRELIMO forces, said to have been 7,000-strong, opened a new front in Tete using Malawi as a point of entry to reach the district of Manica-e-Sofala, south of the mighty Zambezi.[32] That attempt failed. On July 6, 1964, a year after the dissolution of the Federation of Rhodesia and Nyasaland, Nyasaland became Malawi, under the leadership of Kamuzu Banda, an Edinburgh-trained medic. From the outset, Banda clearly outlined his foreign policy "of blunt pragmatism" with neighboring states, which ultimately prevented FRELIMO from penetrating Tete from across Malawi.[33]

Banda had publicly opposed armed nationalism in the region, singling out Joshua Nkomo's party for disapproval and by extension siding with the Rhodesian white-dominated government a year before its Unilateral Declaration of Independence (UDI), in 1965. He then did away with import duties of Southern Rhodesian goods in exchange for $120 million to secure the flow of trade established during the federation period.[34] In addition, he established friendly relations with Portugal right away—and here Banda was propelled by sound reasoning in his view. As a landlocked territory, Malawi's survival depended on an open access to the port of Beira, located in Mozambique's narrowest midriff; airport links with Maputo, Johannesburg and Salisbury; and railway links to Beira, and the port of Nacala across Lake Niassa.[35]

> I have to be realistic. Colonial geography and history are against us. We cannot boycott South Africa, Rhodesia, or Portuguese Mozambique—that would mean the breakdown of Malawi's economy. I do not approve of [the] South African apartheid policy, but South Africa is there with her army and her policy... Boycotting South Africa....is apartheid in reverse on our part. If discrimination is bad when practiced by white on black, is it good when practiced by black on white? This is why I have refused to boycott South Africa, Rhodesia, or Mozambique.[36]

---

[31] *Africa Report*, 21 (September 1965): 23.
[32] ibid., 7.
[33] David Hedges, "Apontamento Sobre as Relações Entre Malawi e Moçambique, 1961–1987," *Cadernos de Historia*, 6 (1987): 5–28; R. Henderson, "Relations of Neighbourliness: Malawi and Portugal, 1964–74," *Journal of Modern African Studies*, 15, 3 (1977): 425–455; N. Patel and R. Hajat, "Foreign Policy and International Relations," in *Government and Politics in Malawi*, eds. N. Patel and L. Svasand (Zomba, Malawi: Kachere, 2007), 375–406; and Mukuse Daniel Sagawa, "Power Politics or Personality? Re-Visiting Malawi's Foreign Policy Conception and Strategy under Kamuzu Banda, 1964–1994," *Forum for Development Studies*, 38, 2 (June 2011): 131–156.
[34] *Africa Report*, 10 (November 1964): 12–16.
[35] *Africa Report*, 8 (August 1964): 8–11, 20. See also Central Office of Information, *Malawi*, RFP 5659 (April 1964), Griff Jones, *Britain and Nyasaland: A Story of Inattention. Fitful Care, and Political Vacillation* (London: Allen and Unwin, 1964); and Roy Welensky, *Four Thousand Days* (London: Collins, 1964) on the history of the Federation leading to Malawi's independence.
[36] *Africa Report*, 12 (1966): 26; and *Africa Report*, 1 (1967): 30.

Given Malawi's strategic needs, Banda staunchly opposed FRELIMO, whose leaders and their armed struggle he considered communist. Banda had one other reason to deny FRELIMO free access to Malawi—Henry Chipembere, who having been ousted as Banda's education minister was now leading the charge against him for democratic change in the country, and could therefore form an alliance with FRELIMO to usurp Banda from the presidency.[37]

Portugal exploited Banda's position by strengthening its diplomatic ties with Malawi appointing Jorge Jardim, a Mozambique-based pro-Salazarist cement industrialist, as its special envoy and ambassador-at-large.

With this diplomatic blockade in place, FRELIMO retreated from Tete until 1968. By then, Kenneth Kaunda had become President of the newly independent republic of Zambia, formerly Northern Rhodesia, a territory abutting Tete's snout above the Zambezi near Luangwa.[38] With Kaunda seated and his blessing secured, FRELIMO resumed its penetrative offensive in Tete near Unkanha.

In that same year, FRELIMO underwent a near-total self-destruction, which began with a leadership crisis initiated by Father Gwenjere at the Mozambique Institute. Within a year of his arrival in Dar es Salam, Gwenjere had risen rapidly in the ranks earning Mondlane's confidence in his public speaking abilities to present the FRELIMO case at a special session of the United Nation in New York. According to one source, his speech was an "atomic bombshell," said Mondlane, propelling the Portuguese delegate at the UN session to walk out. Gwenjere's charismatic personality easily won him friends and valuable allies for the party, among them Robert Kennedy, who, according to the same source, invited him to emigrate to the United States; he declined, preferring to serve his people and share in their suffering as they fought for Mozambique's independence.

Gwenjere's charisma *à la Dead Poets Society* had proved an asset for FRELIMO's Mozambique Institute where he continued to inspire young minds to bring change for the world ahead. However he also expected moral consistency in FRELIMO leadership. Further, he was temperamentally impatient, driven by quick results. It was only a matter of time before this combination of charisma and impatience brought him in direct conflict with Mondlane's leadership, who was equally charismatic, but an empirically inclined pragmatist prone to phlegmatic compromises.[39] "He moves too slowly and speaks too softly," complained Gwenjere.[40]

In December of the previous year, Mondlane had informed the party faithful during the Christmas party that they faced a long war ahead. Mondlane's assessment was tempered by a number of factors, ranging from FRELIMO's logistical difficulties in penetrating the border from Malawi and Zambia, competition from emerging rivals who could pose a threat to FRELIMO's nascent hegemony in insurgent politics, to Portugal's aggressive strategy to shape-shift the region's economic map with the help of

---

[37] *Africa Report*, 1(1967): 30.
[38] General Grouveta, interview, 1994 and 1995. For details on the opening of the 1968/9 front, see Borges Coelho, *O Início da Luta Armada*.
[39] Lawe Laweki alias João Baptista Truzão, "A Outra Face dos Acontecimentos: Uma Resposta a Janet Mondlane," accessed August 12, 2013, http://macua.blogs.com/moambique_para_todos/2011/10/a-outra-face-dos-acontecimentos.html.
[40] *Africa Report*, 10 (1968): 41.

its allies, Malawi, Rhodesia, South Africa, and infrastructure investment procured from international multinational capital.

Gwenjere, in the audience, was shocked by what he heard. In his view, Mondlane had sold them a fictitious bill of goods having promised a quick march to victory for Mozambique. "You are a traitor," he was heard to say. Mondlane said he very much respected Padre Gwenjere, but found him abrasive and contentious, and his unbridled ambition to occupy a more prominent leadership position in the party while encouraging dissent among his acolytes was damaging the party's objectives for the greater good. Put differently, Mondlane saw him to be a real threat to stability in FRELIMO and its leadership. He and his loyalists at the Mozambique Institute had to go.[41]

Gwenjere-inspired agitation then followed at the Institute which was shutdown in March 1968. The Tanzanian authority and the Liberation Committee of the Organization of African Unity (OAU) set up a commission to study the case, which confirmed the role of Padre Gwenjere in inciting unrest at the Institute. Gwenjere was not about to give in so easily.

On May 9, 1968, a Tanzanian Field Force arrived to quell a disturbance at the Mozambique Institute, the second of its kind, during which twenty students, all Gwenjere loyalists, armed with pangas and clubs barged into FRELIMO headquarters demanding an immediate change in the leadership and an accelerated pace in the party's liberation strategy. Three members of staff were injured and taken to hospital, one of whom later died.

Mondlane was away on a fact-finding mission in Mozambique. Following an investigation upon his return, he identified Padre Mateus Pinho Gwenjere as the key instigator behind the Mozambique Insitute unrests. The matter came to a head two months later at FRELIMO's Second Congress held in July, at which prominent leaders accused each other of Byzantine skullduggery. Mondlane accused Reverend Uria Simango of being too close to Beijing and actively conspiring to assassinate him. Uria Simango, in turn, suggested Mondlane to be an American stooge. Both Mondlane and Simango on the other hand, accused Gwenjere of treason, bent on destroying the party.[42]

In the end, Mondlane's assassination brought the matter to a head. On February 3, 1969, a parcel addressed to him exploded as he opened it. It reportedly contained a book on Hegel he had ordered.[43] There were three possible culprits. One was Silvério Nungo, FRELIMO's treasurer, whose ideas for the future of the party as well as his own political ambitions were sources of both jealousy and discontent among certain political ideologues, who for lack of a better term, were "von Clausewitz Marxists," and

---

[41] "Em lamentação um dia Mondlane disse a mim e a outros que estiveram a comer comigo numa mesa: "eu respeito muito o padre Gwenjere. É um homem muito educado, mas não gosto da maneira como age." "Joaquim Chissano: Há gente com tendência para desprezar e deturpar a história" (Saturday, August 18, 2012), accessed August 18, 2013, http://ambicanos.blogspot.com/2012/08/joaquim-chissano-ha-gente-com-tendencia.html. See also, John Saul, "FRELIMO and the Mozambique Revolution," *Monthly Review*, 24, 10 (1973): 22–52; and Eduardo Mondlane, "FRELIMO White Paper," *African Historical Studies*, 2, 2 (1969): 321.

[42] "Ancien professeur de l'université de Syracuse (USA)," *Jeune Afrique*, Numero Special Annuel (1970): 558–559.

[43] Oberlin Alumni Notes and News, "In Memory of Eduardo Chivambo Mondlane '53 1920–1969, to be Honored at May Reunion," *Oberlin.edu*, accessed June 1, 2010, http://www.oberlin.edu/alummag/oampast/oam_spring98/Alum_n_n/eduardo.html.

viewed the war principally as a politically transformative struggle, albeit armed, for achieving an equitable just order.

Lázaro Kavandame, the second suspect, was an obvious target because he had quite openly opposed Mondlane's conciliatory overtures towards contending factions within the party. He felt the party needed to accelerate the pace of the fight, which he could help lead, with the strong backing of the Makonde ethnic group whose respect he commanded.

The third suspect was the PIDE—Polícia Internacional e de Defesa do Estado, International and State Defense Police. Its strong links with pro-colonial and international pro-fascist forces suggested its involvement. Soon after this "success by associated proxy," the PIDE was restructured to incorporate into its *modus operandi* such and other similar "best practices" in anti-nationalist intelligence. In this, they were inspired by the Buro vir Staatsveiligheid, the South African Bureau for State Security organization, which subsequently served as a template for the PIDE. PIDE itself was then renamed DGS.

On July 18, 1969, according to eyewitness accounts, Silvério Nungo was bludgeoned to death. Kavandame surmized his position in the party to be hopelessly weakened. He was outnumbered and politically outgunned by the newly formed triumvirate that was composed of the Presbyterian reverend Uria Timoteo Simango, the Paris-trained left-wing ideologue Marcelino dos Santos, and Samora Machel, a battle-hardened ideologically dogmatic commander, originally from Gaza in southern Mozambique, who had joined the party in 1962 and returned to fight and lead FRELIMO units after extensive training in several African countries during 1963. Rather than risk an uncertain future in FRELIMO, Kavandame defected to the Portuguese in April of that year.

The triumvirate then assumed FRELIMO's full leadership— though not for long. In the intervening months between Kavandame's defection and Nungo's painful death, Reverend Simango grew increasingly uneasy of the party's swift march to the extreme left and what he saw as its unraveling, a dramatic break from its ideological, tactical and consensus-driven past—a hallmark of Mondlane's leadership, under whom pluralism had flourished. Simango had served as deputy leader. On November 4, 1969, Uria Simango published a thirteen-page document accusing the other two members of the triumvirate of plotting to kill him. He also advocated the expulsion of Janet Mondlane to purge the party of agents of American imperialism.[44]

In the end, the good reverend was stripped of his leadership in the triumvirate and expelled from the party, as Gwenjere had been earlier. Simango's vocal tussles among peers and his party apparatchiks proved untenable for the remaining duo, who felt the urgent need to consolidate their reign over the party, which they saw as eminently vulnerable to Portuguese counter-insurgent infiltration.

Thus ended Mondlane's pluralist leadership and coalition-building, which had been FRELIMO's governing hallmark. With Machel at the helm, and dos Santos and Pascoal Mucumbi as the party ideologues, FRELIMO leaders turned avowedly monist—and this turn to the left was inevitable. The new leaders were forged in the everyday reality of the armed struggle and trained to view the people's power as a struggle for a new social order fought through force of arms. This march to the left accelerated the flow of

[44] "Ancien professeur de l'université de Syracuse (USA)," 558–559.

much-needed military aid from the Soviets, the Chinese, the Eastern bloc states, Cuba, and African countries to launch sophisticated attacks on the colonial army and its defenses. The change of leadership also attracted several state-supported, non-governmental, and non-profit agencies who provided free access to political and social networks, allowing FRELIMO delegates to network with fellow nationalists from Angola, Guinea-Bissau, São Tomé and Príncipe, and Cabo Verde. They subsequently received aid through these channels, including humanitarian help from the non-profit sector to reconstruct territories under its influence. With the tragic and brutal bloodletting behind it, FRELIMO was ready to take the fight to a new level in late 1969 to early 1970.

Portuguese counter-insurgency and the changing of the guard

Portugal had started preparing for FRELIMO-led insurgency in Mozambique as early as 1962, which it saw as a "communist-inspired rebellion threatening to unravel five hundred years of its work in bringing Western civilization to its colonies in Africa";[45] Portugal had already stationed nearly 66,000 troops to this end, of which 20,000 were assigned specifically to combat FRELIMO in "defense of the sacred integrity of the territory of our motherland."[46]

> There is no choice for Portugal but to continue as hitherto the insurgent defense of the integrity of the motherland wherever attempts be made to attack it... We are convinced that as we fight for the sacred integrity of the territory of our motherland, we are also fighting for the remnants of Western civilization which 500 years ago we took to Africa and the East. With our fight, which should not be only ours, we have lost precious lives and immense assets, which could well have other uses.

The defense budget subsequently climbed to $200 million, which was further augmented to an unspecified amount to cover military exigencies in the "overseas" territories. Initially, the bulk of the troops in the first phase of the rebellion in the north in the Cabo Delgado region were white, with the police force aiding intelligence units headed by white police officers.[47] Fearing this measure insufficient, Salazar dispatched Portugal's President Américo de Deus Rodrigues Tomás for a fifteen-day fact-finding visit to Mozambique in 1964.[48] Subsequently, additional troops arrived to bolster Mozambique's defenses in the north,[49] and the colony was granted access to a special

---

[45] *Africa Report*, 2 (1966): 30.
[46] ibid.
[47] *Africa Report*, 1 (January 1964): 16.
[48] A propaganda film on the visit can be viewed at "Américo Tomás Em Moçambique, 1964," accessed December 11, 2013, https://www.youtube.com/watch?v=9rS46Ptd0Z0.
[49] *Africa Report*, 9 (October 1964): 26; and *Africa Report*, 12 (December 1964): 23. Portugal's Defense Ministry denied newspaper reports circulating at the time of the presence of 35,000 troops and 10,000 police force as an "appreciable exaggeration." *Africa Report*, 3 (1965): 38.

line of credit of over $33 million established to underwrite the "extraordinary" military expenditure for the defense of Portugal's "overseas provinces."[50]

By October 11, the pace of Portugal's clampdown on insurgent discontent accelerated. By May 1965, Mozambique's only independent voice, *Diário de Moçambique*, was ordered to shut down. An article commemorating the twenty-fifth anniversary of the missionary agreement, which the Bishop of Beira had penned, was deemed too subversive, arguing as it did for a rapid march to development in the colony. "We have to repair the past gloriously..." averred the Bishop.[51] Months later, the Portuguese police swooped suspects behind the front lines, culling over 2,000 reported activists and intellectuals while apprehending three of five insurgent groups during a massive hunt which spread throughout the territory, including Mueda, the site of the original rebellion.

Portugal's overwhelming use of force however, failed to rout out these insurgents bringing in its wake an influx of nearly 5,000 refugees into Tanganyika across the Ruvuma River. Two thousand of these were reported to have crossed on the weekend of the 4th of October, bringing in their wake a smallpox epidemic in refugee camps set up by the Tanganyika government.[52] Similar numbers of refugees flooded Malawi's Likoma Island from neighboring Niassa district causing severe food shortages in Lake Malawi. Such influx while taxing the resources of the host governments proved to be to FRELIMO's advantage as an added demographic source to recruit cadres much needed to fuel the insurgency.[53]

In the summer of 1968, the Portuguese leadership suffered a similar major blow. António de Oliveira Salazar, Portugal's longest serving premier, suffered a stroke. On September 27, Américo Tomás, the President of the Portuguese Republic, called upon Marcello Caetano to take over from Salazar, who died two years later, on July 27, 1970.

Though a Salazarist to the core, Caetano proved more amenable to considering some changes in war policies, which, once enacted, proved too little too late. In the meantime, the Portuguese had examined their performance for the last five years and had concluded they needed to revamp their strategy to stem the tide of FRELIMO-led nationalism. As part of that strategy, they began with General Francisco da Costa Gomes, who had assumed control of military operations in 1964.

Gomes had advocated using an African army fighting in tandem with the Portuguese military, since a Mozambique-born and preferably highly localized force could fast track Portuguese military strategy familiar with local conditions. In addition, given FRELIMO's dependence on exile bases, Gomes supported Salazarist diplomacy with Banda and military collaboration with neighboring colonies, principally Southern Rhodesia, which was willing to engage in intelligence sharing, and coordinated hot pursuit across borders.

However, Gomes' hands were tied behind his back preventing him from orchestrating a bold counter-insurgency. In addition, he had no stomach for internecine politics, failing in the process to outmaneuver fellow commanders demanding

---

[50] *Africa Report*, 8 (August 1965): 36.
[51] *Africa Report*, 19 (June 1965): 6–9.
[52] *Africa Report*, 12 (December 1964): 23.
[53] *Africa Report*, 8 (August 1965): 28.

much-needed resources from Salazar and his successor. Further, paucity of materiel festered his men at arms, who fought with vintage equipment dating back to the Second World War. The air force flew in planes tactically ill-equipped for lightening aerial bombardment and for supporting combat operations on the fly, which later proved so crucial for disrupting logistic supply lines. This did not imply Portugal could not procure war materials directly from suppliers or from its networks via NATO. It did, but they went largely to bolster defenses of the metropolis.

In addition, Portugal's best experts, trainers, and personnel in counter-insurgency institutes had yet to venture willingly overseas to replicate their training of locals in modern guerrilla warfare so urgently needed for an effective counter-insurgency in Mozambique.

Portugal's failure to stem the tide of nationalism reflected both its failure to appreciate the gravity as well as the fast pace of the unfolding war, which threatened its imperial hold on Mozambique and Salazar's own provincial predilections. In fact, Salazar himself hated flying and had never set foot on African soil, let alone visited Portugal's African colonies, which were and remained to his dying days abstracts populated with imagined subalterns steeped in Lusotropicalism. His knowledge of Luso-Africa was at best second-hand, or at worse adduced from returning high-ranking officials promoting agendas of their own.

In addition, Salazar was an extreme fiscal conservative—and that outlook colored the initial stages of the colonial war. He believed the nation should live within its means, balance its books to maintain social stability, and not go back to the political chaos Portugal had experienced at the beginning of the twentieth century. He was said to have little use for education for social progress, at home or in the colonies.

While Salazar's extreme frugality had helped Portugal build enormous surplus reserves with which to initiate the economic boom of the mid-1960s, it had come at a price: high illiteracy; a deeply dysfunctional corporatist economy; poor industrial infrastructure for national productivity and revenue; and above all, repression of unrest in the colonies.

His successors took a different view of the war, and replaced General Gomes with General Kaúlza de Arriaga, a high-ranking military general with an engineering background, who was also a prolific author with a track record in military politics and military training. At face value, he appeared weak as he had little if any combat experience, but he came with a trifecta. He had the right credentials in the eyes of the new regime, the right connections to execute a campaign of his own making, and an up-to-date knowledge of Lisbon's new thinking to buttress the war through economic and infrastructure initiatives, of which the Cahora Bassa Dam in Tete was about to become a centerpiece.

In addition, de Arriaga was steeped in the discipline of counter-insurgency. He had designed programs in the field, taught, supervised, managed and mentored young cadres and specialists in Lisbon's military school for such elites. He had a global understanding of emerging doctrines, particularly American thinking in Vietnam. He had met General Westmoreland as one peer to another via the NATO network, which convinced him that FRELIMO could be trounced in a properly funded aggressive war of attrition.[54]

---

[54] William Minter, "Propaganda and Reality in Mozambique," *Africa Today*, 16, 2 (1969): 3.

Unlike Westmoreland, he did not have to contend with the court of domestic public opinion. Neither Portugal nor the overseas provinces were democracies. Nor did he have to worry about fallouts from excessive use of force and collateral damage of innocent civilians, as the Americans had to during the Tet Offensive in January 1968 leading up to the My Lai Massacre three months later.[55] Here in Mozambique, de Arriaga had a *carte blanche* to execute his strategy.

Upon arrival in Mozambique, he assembled 35,000 armed men for combat. It was one of the most formidable concentrations of forces aimed at weakening FRELIMO in the north. Then, on June 10, 1970, he ordered Operação Nó Górdio, Operation Gordian Knot, a coordinated offensive involving paratroopers, commando, naval, and specialist units. The Portuguese Air Force provided cover, reconnaissance, and strategic bombardment to soften enemy units, bases, field clinics, and training and mobile camps. At the end of the operation, General de Arriaga declared the offensive an unmitigated success, earning him, among officers under his command the sobriquet, the Pink Panther, a nimble architect of enemy entrapment. His critics thought differently.[56] In a strict military sense, he was right. FRELIMO was considerably weakened, having been deprived of a network of 165 camps affiliated to sixty-one bases and supplied with over forty tons of war materiel, much of which had been obtained from African, communist and Eastern bloc states.[57]

Operation Gordian Knot proved expensive, politically ineffective, and, according to one source,[58] left FRELIMO free to retreat, regroup, and re-engineer itself to come back to the battlefield from the western flank, as it were, while still keeping colonial forces engaged in Niassa and Cabo Delgado. De Arriaga followed Operation Gordian Knot with a set of three American-inspired containment initiatives that the British had successfully deployed earlier in Malaya against the Malayan National Liberation Army under the Briggs Plan.[59] To this end, they built strategic hamlets to starve FRELIMO of its popular support;[60] deployed scorched-earth tactics to extend fire-free zones aimed at paralyzing FRELIMO's logistics and food supplies; carried out pre-emptive hit-and-run strikes to weed out areas suspected or proven to have FRELIMO bases and or party activists; encouraged dissidence within FRELIMO; and nurtured FRELIMO rival organizations, some of which coalesced a bit later to form Renamo.

---

[55] J. R. Bullington, "Assessing Pacification in Vietnam: We Won the Counterinsurgency War!" *Small Wars Journal*, March 23, 2012. For a sobering analysis comparing the two approaches to unconventional war, see John Nagle, *Counterinsurgency Lessons from Malaya and Vietnam: Learning to Eat Soup with a Knife* (Santa Barbara, CA: Praeger, 2002).

[56] Herb Shore, "Mondlane, Machel and Mozambique: From Rebellion to Revolution," *Africa Today*, 21, 1 (1974): 3–12.

[57] General Kaúlza de Arriaga, *História das Tropas Pára-quedistas Portuguesas*, vol. III, BCP 21, CTP.1, accessed January 1, 2010, http://preview.tinyurl.com/qzeovqb.

[58] Walter C. Opello, Jr., "Guerrilla War in Portuguese Africa: An Assessment of the Balance of Forces in Mozambique," *Issue: A Journal of Opinion*, 4, 2 (1974): 29–37.

[59] Karl Hack, "British Intelligence and Counter-Insurgency in the Era of Decolonisation: The Example of Malaya," *Intelligence and National Security*, 14, 2 (1999): 124–155.

[60] Brendan F. Jundanian, "Resettlement Programs: Counterinsurgency in Mozambique," *Comparative Politics*, 6 (1974): 519–540.

De Arriaga's strategy remained effectively unchanged until 1974. Reasonably straightforward to execute in the Niassa and Cabo Delgado, it proved less effective in Tete.

The role of water in Tete's warfare

Portugal's one objective in Tete was to prevent FRELIMO from reaching the districts of Manica-e-Sofala and thus threatening the security of Beira. Beira was an important gateway for two Portuguese landlocked allies, Ian Smith-led Rhodesia, and Banda's Malawi, on whom Portugal relied for its strategic needs to fight FRELIMO.

On the other hand, Tete's geography posed a challenge for FRELIMO.[61] Tete is cleft asunder horizontally by the Zambezi River, with several crossing points. One west of Unkanha was near the Zambian border. The other in Tete city's southwest, was near the Zambezi River at a narrow bend allowing foot traffic to cross during the dry season. The bend occurs just north of the Luenha tributary, south of Wiriyamu near Changara. The Luenha tributary spread, as did the Zambezi, into several creeks. Wiriyamu sat astride one of these creeks protected by deep ravines. The third crossing point was in the north just off Zóbuè, near the Malawi border.

The Portuguese sought to plug the points of entry in the north with pre-emptive strikes, which were coordinated between various elements of the armed, naval and air force, militia units and the DGS. A string of strategic hamlets were then constructed, leaving areas outside these as fire-free zones. By early 1972, Tete had 109 such villages, with twenty-seven under construction. Seventy more were planned, at a total cost of 41,875,00 escudos, placing 84,458 people under Portuguese control. One such strategic hamlet that played a role in the events leading up to the Wiriyamu massacre was P'adwe, named by the locals M'Pharhamadwe, "Goat-Pen," so-called because of the barbed-wire fences, cramped and unsanitary conditions, poor schools, unreliable water supply, and insecure access to horticultural plots, all of which the Portuguese authorities secretly acknowledged as true.[62]

These measures left two crossing points open to FRELIMO penetration and these were to be plugged with the construction of the Cahora Bassa dam, which envisaged flooding the area west of Sungo to form a huge lake, the "Albuferas."[63] Once accomplished, the lake formed an inverse triangle pointing towards Mucumbura. Strategic hamlets eventually encircled the large lake, which formed a buffer between the dam and FRELIMO fighters.

The Cahora Bassa project had one other important aspect to it: the international financial involvement in Portugal's defense needs in Tete. South Africa was one key player in this regard. The dam was envisaged as a major project in Africa generating electrical power to meet the needs of neighboring Southern states. Portugal viewed the project regionally integrating the Euro-African territories in Southern Africa, a

---

[61] PT/TT/D-F/001/00001, January 1, 1970, and, May 29, 1970.
[62] PT/TT/D-F/001/00001, May 28, 1971, PT-TT-PIDE-D-F-001-00006, February 28, 1972, and, PT/TT/PIDE/D-F/001/00025, October 4, 1973.
[63] PT/TT/PIDE/D-F/001/00015, February 17, 1973.

collaborative force to defeat a communist conspiracy seeking to usurp capitalist Western values.[64]

In political terms, the dam afforded Portugal an added opportunity to break out of its isolation in the international arena. The fight to brand Portugal a pariah state was most ferocious at the United Nations, where members of the OAU had joined forces with other non-Western states to criticize Portugal's colonial policies in Africa. In this, FRELIMO's representatives and representatives of the liberation movements in Angola and Guinea-Bissau added their own respective weight as they sought help from the UN to support self-determination in Portuguese-dominated Africa.

Cahora Bassa, therefore, was Portugal's last chance for a strategic comeback—an opportunity to counter with international financial backing what it considered to be a legitimate fight against Afro-Asian encroachment on her "internal affairs" in the overseas territories, for that is what Mozambique was legally considered by Lisbon following constitutional reforms in the 1950s when the colonies were declared Portuguese overseas provinces.[65]

Faced with the prospects of a blockage to the south of the Zambezi River through the Albuferas,[66] FRELIMO sought to reach the south as fast they could; they did so by stealth and by focusing their energies on Zóbuè. The strategy was an odd one to select. The region was heavily armed, relatively close to Tete, and logistically easy to defend. Further, Malawi had taken a resolutely pro-Portuguese stand in the conflict across the border, with the result that FRELIMO found its covert activities within the territory severely curtailed by constant arrests and deportations.

FRELIMO leaders in Tanzania and two FRELIMO operatives in Malawi and Zambia, General Bonifácio Grouveta and Mariano de Araújo Matsinha, thought differently, as did General Hama Tai. The objective of the Zóbuè focus in their eyes was to draw Portuguese firepower in this corner away from the Zambian border, allowing FRELIMO to penetrate Maravia and Unkanha.[67] They chose this area for two reasons: poor Portuguese presence and the prevailing anti-colonial climate in the

---

[64] By far the best, though dated, narrative on Cahora Bassa is Keith Middlemas, *Cabora Bassa: Politics and Engineering in Southern Africa* (London: Weidenfeld and Nicolson, 1975). See also Allen Isaacman and Chris Sneddon, "Towards a Social and Environmental History of the Building of Cahora Bassa Dam," *Journal of Southern Africa Studies*, 26, 4 (2000): 597–632; W. Nussey, "The War in Tete, a Threat to All in Southern Africa," *Johannesburg Star*, July 1, 1972; Allen Isaacman and Barbara Isaacman, "Cahora Bassa: Extending South Africa's Tentacles of Empire" (paper presented at the Agrarian Seminar, Yale University, September 20, 2013): 1–41; and Allen F. Isaacman, *Dams, Displacement and the Delusion of Development: Cahora Bassa and Its Legacies in Mozambique, 1965–2007* (Ohio: Ohio University Press, 2013). This book excludes Keith Middlemas' oral interviews on Cahora Bassa Dam lodged at the Hoover Institution at Stanford, materials that Thomas H. Henriksen exploited in his text on Mozambique's revolution and counter-revolution.

[65] South African and Rhodesian collaboration with Portugal and their involvement in the colonial war was covered in secondary literature and news media at the time. See Michael Morris, *Terrorism: The First Full Account in Detail of Terrorism and Insurgency in Southern Africa* (Capetown: Howard Timmins, 1971), 173; *Rand Daily Mail*, September 7, 1971. The British Foreign and Commonwealth Office archives contain some references on the dam, details can be tapped electronically at the National Archives, UK.

[66] PT/TT/PIDE/D-F/001/00015, February 17, 1973.

[67] PT-TT-PIDE-D-F-001-00006, March 15, 1972.

area.[68] This penetration, once achieved, strained relations between the mission staff in the region, the Portuguese military personnel and FRELIMO activists, details on which are given in the following chapter dealing with State–Church relations in Unkanha.

FRELIMO presence in and west of Unkanha had alarmed Tete's Portuguese commanders. Intelligence-gatherers sent to assess the depth of the "FRELIMO contagion" prompted them to institute bicycle patrols in this section of the border and move the entire population of Unkanha to Mucumbura, south of the river. This move, using army vehicles and personnel, emptied the zone of people, thereby making it easier and more cost-effective for the Portuguese to patrol the area, search for and destroy enemy targets with minimum collateral damage in an exchange of fire.

FRELIMO, on the other hand, loaded its activists on the military trucks disguised as Unkanha residents and parishioners, thus gaining in a fell swoop a political foothold near Lundo, Buxo and Mucumbura, where they regrouped to politicize the local population. Ultimately, once their logistics and food supplies were securely in place, FRELIMO initiated attacks on the colonial army in southern Tete.[69] By December 1971, the Portuguese political intelligence estimated, FRELIMO had under its influence half of Tete's population.[70]

Subsequent military activities in the region suggest that the colonial army may well have been untroubled by the Unkanha relocation. Confident that their subsequent strategy for the south would work, de Arriaga's commanders ordered their troops guarding the borders with Zambia to move to the south, enlisting Rhodesian troops to defend southern Tete right up to Zumbo. To this end, the Rhodesian armed men were authorized by de Arriaga's ground troop commanders to hot pursuit east of Mucumbura, despite objections from the Portuguese Air Force.[71] De Arriaga then placed Colonel Armindo Martins Videira to succeed Rocha Simões.[72] Videira, one of the earliest Green Beret graduates of the Portuguese military academy and a veteran of Gordian Knot, was de Arriaga's handpicked choice—and in his view, the right choice to succeed Simões, which he did in early 1972 as head of Tete's military affairs.[73]

Unlike Simões who believed in some form of restraint in combatting FRELIMO,[74] Videira viewed the war as winnable—all you needed was to have your wits about you, be on high alert at all times, unbridled force, and an arsenal of weapons at your beck and call! He had a real distaste for taking prisoners, though perhaps not as strong a distaste as von Throta during Germany's campaign against the Herero. Further, Videira

---

[68] Padre Alberto Font Castellà, interview by author, Changara, Tete, 1995.
[69] ibid.
[70] PT/TT/D-F/001/00004, December 15, 1971.
[71] PT/TT/D-F/001/00003, October 20, 1971.
[72] *The Guardian*, July 28, 1971.
[73] A brief biography on Brigadier Videira is to be found in *Operacional: Defesa, Forças Armadas de Segurança*, accessed June 13, 2012, http://preview.tinyurl.com/l7jdxrv; and Gen. Kaúlza de Arriaga, *História das Tropas Pára-quedistas Portuguesas* vol. III, BCP 21, CTP.1, accessed January 1, 2010, http://preview.tinyurl.com/m8bfh94. Additional information can be gleaned from two blog sites, both catering to the military alumni, accessed November 18, 2011, http://preview.tinyurl.com/kpgcds4; and, http://estrolabio.blogs.sapo.pt/2011/02/07/.
[74] This observation is based on exchanges between the Burgos Fathers' delegation, Tete's Bishop and Rocha Simões over the Mucumbura massacres.

was an experienced counter-insurgency commander with a Cartesian appetite for frighteningly fast strikes. He understood with clarity and depth how and when to deploy his men to eliminate hostile targets and their supporters. War had no place for human emotions—or acts of charity, which to him weakened resolve in winning combats.[75]

Five months of continuous attacks from Chioco however, failed to rid the area of FRELIMO. Videira blamed it on dated intelligence generated by the DGS, while the DGS defended its record at an emergency meeting presided over by de Arriaga.[76] In the meantime, FRELIMO consolidated its presence south of Changara and began targeting the army and its valuable military assets. Videira's men were immediately dispatched to sweep the area, which they did at the cost of civilian casualties, some of whom were parishioners of the local church staffed by two young Burgos priests. As a result of this onslaught, FRELIMO temporarily froze in its tracks. With food burnt, cattle dispersed, and foliage exposed to the elements and air surveillance, FRELIMO commanders and their fighters faced renewed challenges threatening their survival south of the Zambezi.[77]

Apart from the food supply,[78] one additional challenge proved most pressing: a reliable supply line of arms and ammunition protected from Videira's men and their birds of prey. To address both needs, commanders moved nearer food-producing and cattle-raising areas, on both margins of the Luenha tributary and raided retailers and trucks supplying domestic goods to commercial vendors.[79]

As for logistics, FRELIMO used three arms supply routes at its disposal, though none proved easy to navigate. One was the eastbound trail from Zambia to Tete above the flooded margins of the Zambezi, past Cahora Bassa and Sungo and then down along the banks of the Zambezi. This route was heavily armed with Portuguese soldiers on direct orders to protect the dam at all costs.

The second route descended southbound from Malawi. This crossing remained difficult as ever, more so after late 1971. Banda had not changed his views on FRELIMO as communists, and continued to obstruct them on all fronts. The Portuguese saw to it that Malawi was kept in the loop on suspected FRELIMO border crossings. The problem of logistics here lasted until June 1973, after which FRELIMO's heavy arms transportation accelerated to sustain the new front in Manica-e-Sofala.[80]

The third route was below Zumbo at the narrowest point of entry from Zambia into Zambezi, located between Kanyemba and Kapoche along route D145. This route had perhaps two of the best quadrangles of wilderness in which to hide arms and

---

[75] This Videira composite was glued together from a variety of sources including intelligence analysis provided during an interview with General Hama Tai who had closely studied Videira and de Arriaga in the Tete theater of war. General Hama Tai, interview, 1994 and 1995.
[76] PT/TT/D-F/001/00001, April 27, 1971.
[77] General Hama Tai, interview, 1994 and 1995; General Grouveta, 1994 and 1995; and Matsinha, interview, 1994 and 1995. Information also provided by Enrique Ferrando, Miguel Buendia, and, Alfonso Valverde de Lion.
[78] PT/TT/PIDE/D-F/001/00008, July 3, 1972.
[79] PT/TT/PIDE/D-F/001/00008, June 17, 1972.
[80] PT/TT/PIDE/D-A/1/2826-10, June 11, 1973.

ammunition for subsequent distribution. Each was split by a narrow gauntlet formed by a rectangular appendix of water jutting from the Zambezi near Bandeira and Mesica.

By the middle of 1971, FRELIMO commanders concluded at a regional meeting held at an undisclosed location in Tete that now that they had resolved their three-tiered logistics thereby consolidating their military gains,[81] they needed to focus on two priorities. One was the dam—not sabotage it but slow down its construction, using the Wiriyamu triangle as a launching pad. The other was to prepare for war on Mozambique's midriff. To these ends, FRELIMO reorganized its theater of war into four sectors, two on each side of the River Zambezi. The largest sector between Capoche and the Tete to Zubue road had twenty-three bases. West of it lay the first sector, which had twelve bases with one field hospital. One of the two southern sectors covered southeast of Tete with three bases, while the fourth sector south of the River Zambezi had seven bases surrounding a training camp specifically for preparing cadres to open FRELIMO's fifth front in Manica-e-Sofala.[82] Portuguese intelligence initially reported FRELIMO had in total a force of 1,850, which included a contingent of 200 female cadres.[83] The political organization too was changed, with José Moiane holding the portfolio for defense under the leadership of the party secretary António Almeida.[84]

Wiriyamu's strategic proximity to Cahora Bassa Dam aside, the triangle proved ideal for FRELIMO's continuing logistic and food supply needs. It was across from the main road leading to Cahora Bassa—an ideal target with which to rattle Portugal's military cage. Wiriyamu's back curled up against a crop of elevated rocks abutting the Zambezi at one of its many narrow points south of Tete—an ideal location to transport arms and men across the river from the northern and eastern supply lines. The triangle itself was densely populated and was rich in cattle and food crops.[85] Subject to rains, local cooperation, and good harvest, it could supply much needed fresh recruits and provide food for an entrenched guerrilla force to supplement its own horticultural plots in the region.[86] Tete city itself was twenty-five miles north along a well-tarred road. Attacks against the colonial army from this proximity made eminent sense to unsettle the strategic nerves of the colonial army, the presiding military governor, and his chief executive strategist, Videira.

FRELIMO operations were led by Raimundo Dalepa, a Makonde warrior who had gained a hagiographic status among insurgents and civilian supporters, having earned the popular soubriquet Kadembo, "the Stinker." "We knew when he was around, we

---

[81] FRELIMO claimed in its regular bulletin that between June 1970 and July 1971, its armed insurgents had killed 1,603 enemy soldiers, destroyed 277 military vehicles, four trains, seventeen bridges, and had shot down two airplanes and one helicopter. *Standard of Tanzania* (September 16, 1917).
[82] PT/TT/D-F/001/00001, April 7, 1971.
[83] PT-TT-PIDE-D-F-001-00006, February 28, 1972. The estimate was revised in November to suggest 2,570 armed FRELIMO combatants: 1,050 in sector one, 750 in sector two, 50 in sector three and 220 in sector four. Of the total, 500 were undergoing training to open a new front south of the River Zambezi. By November of the following year, the estimate had climbed to a force of 6,100. PT/TT/D-F/001/00004, November 2, 1971; and, PT/TT/PIDE/D-F/001/00027, November 16, 1973.
[84] PT/TT/PIDE/D-A/1/2826-5, June 19, 1971.
[85] PT/TT/PIDE/D-A/1/2826-9, March 10, 1973.
[86] PT/TT/PIDE/D-F/001/00012, November 11, 1972.

could smell him... he left a trail wherever he went... his enemies never caught him."[87] Raimundo had "a magnetic personality," testified Sangalo, with a commanding presence and highly skilled in insurgency.[88] "The air made way for him before he entered a room."[89] He was charming, and was remembered after the war almost as a mythic figure.[90] He "could disarm his enemies without moving a finger," said one informant.[91] Highly respected by FRELIMO fighters under his command and by fellow commanders stationed in Tete, Raimundo proved Videira's most worthy opponent.

Wiriyamu at a point of no return

Raimundo reorganized his bases in the triangle first,[92] imported heavy artillery, and then sent a young cadre to test the political waters in and around Wiriyamu. Bulachu Pensadu Zambezi picks up the story from here. "It was in early October when they came." He can't recall exactly what date. All he knows is that he had to be up early on that day. "It was around six thirty." How did he know it was six thirty and not seven? "I know because the sun was up there," pointing at a spot between the branches of the tamarind tree in the east still standing at the site where Wiriyamu had stood once before the massacre, and where he, Bulachu, stood now as he recalled the events of that morning. "Besides, the taste of the sun was different later in the morning."[93]

"My parents were already gone when I got up." The night before, Pensadu senior had told him to take the animals to graze first thing in the morning. "Your (step) mother and I are going to take your brother to the *curandeiro*." Pensadu senior was worried. His newborn son by his younger second wife was ill. At first blush, Bulachu could not recall if the *curendeiro* was Senhor Soda—the village sorcerer who lived not very far from Wiriyamu. "No, it could not have been (near the village). This *curendeiro* lived there, far away. That is why they had to get up so early."

Pensadu's decision to visit the *curendeiro* did not make sense at face value because he could just as easily have gone to the hospital in Tete, which would have been quicker to reach by bus and which was staffed by missionary nurses headed by Irmã Lúcia Saez de Ugarte, a Consolata nun well known in the community and familiar with Wiriyamu. In addition, Pensadu senior would have received a friendly reception and be seen promptly, given that his contact, chief Wiriyamu's son-in-law, was well known at the hospital.

Pensadu felt differently. He wanted a treatment he could understand. To take the bus, he would have had to pay for the ride, wait by the tarred road connecting Tete and Cahora Bassa dam, now under construction post-haste, and be at the mercy of military traffic, which lately appeared to be permanently congested along the Changara–Tete

---

[87] Elídio, interview, 1995.
[88] Padre José Sangalo, interview by author, Madrid, Spain, 1995.
[89] Irmã Lúcia Saez de Ugarte, interview by author, Tete, 1995.
[90] Berenguer, interview, 1994 and 1995.
[91] Bulachu Pensadu Zambezi, interview by author, Tete and Wiriyamu, 1995.
[92] PT/TT/PIDE/D-A/1/2826-6, June 28, 1972.
[93] Zambezi, interview, 1995; Vasco Valeta, interview, 1995.

route because of ambushes. Using foot-tracks well before dawn when the soldiers were still in their barracks or in makeshift tents in the *mato* (bush) meant he could avoid strangers, and soldiers unfamiliar with backroads.[94]

Further, the *curendeiro* was familiar "with our people's way. He was no stranger to us and he lived in the sacred forest between Mazoe and Cuiro, south of the village. Also my father preferred the *curendeiro*'s herbs," said Bulachu. He was particularly good with children. Pensadu's decision reflected his and his peers' approach to health and healing—a faith in traditional medicine strengthened by anxieties of having to deal with *mzungus*, the hospital staff, and military patrols on the open roads "*dos colonos que controlavam as estradas.*"

Bulachu junior got out to stretch, holding on to the gnarled beam propping up the roof of his parents' hut. He took a few paces forward nearer the tamarind tree—a favorite spot where he sat, played and talked with friends. He looked up. The sunrays that morning were clear and bright. It had rained the night before and the air smelled of freshly watered earth ready to be baked by the sun. He then turned to his left towards his neighbors, the Tenente Valetas, to look at his family's corral. Just as he did that, he spotted a young man walking towards him. He and his cohorts had waited patiently for someone to rise in Wiriyamu, perched as it was on an elevated plateau encircled on all sides but the southwest by ravines and creeks.

He had come out of hiding behind large boulders diagonally across from Bulachu's tree nearer another larger tamarind tree to the north, facing the entrance of chief Wiriyamu's compound. The boulders formed a forty-five-degree incline at the edge of a dry creek which had once yielded much needed water. The young man was in military uniform. He had come from one of the four bases near the mountains abutting River Luenha.[95] He was gangly. He had an AK-47 strapped to his chest. "That is how he approached me."

The stranger appeared to be a Portuguese soldier. He was about to run away but he froze. The young man's army fatigues were threadbare; he wore canvas shoes and not boots. Also, "There was something strange about the rifle." It was not normal issue, now that he knows a thing or two about rifles. The cap was ill-fitting on his head, and the style "*dum revolucionário*"—of a revolutionary. Above all, he came out alone. Portuguese soldiers on patrol went in tandem and back-to-back. They would never have risked to come alone. Unless of course, he was "a son of the village" or married to someone in the village, then yes, he could come and go as he pleased, added Bulachu. "And such things did happen, you know." Marriages did occur, in one case, that of chief Wiriyamu's daughter Nonika who married Tai Kongorhogondo—a soldier in the militia force stationed in Tete.

The young man had taken due precautions before approaching Bulachu. The group he had left behind had lain in wait behind the boulders in the deep ravine and was truly protected on all sides from enemy detection. They had also studied the goings on in the village to establish its lack of defenses by the militia before they approached Bulachu.

---

[94] PT-TT-PIDE-D-F-001-00006, February 9, 1972, and, PT/TT/PIDE/D-F/001/00007, May 11, 1972.
[95] PT/TT/D-F/001/00003, October 20, 1971.

That hour in the morning, it was unlikely that the Portuguese soldiers on patrol would have ventured this far so early in the day.

The young man was soft-spoken and "was very polite. He greeted me and then said 'where is the chief of the village?' I took him to Wiriyamu's place." The young man greeted the chief. He was invited in. He had a talk with Wiriyamu the substance of which is unknown. The cadre in question could not be found to further our understanding of FRELIMO's recruitment strategy. Wiriyamu himself died soon after this meeting, taking with him the details of their conversation.

Bulachu maintains that he heard the man explain that he was FRELIMO. He invited Wiriyamu to gather some people and come with him to "*lá no mato*," there in the bush, where he and his men were camped to hear more about what they were all about, who they were, why they were there, and why they were fighting for "our people, our land." The young man did not reveal the location of the base. Nor did he take his eyes off the chief. To keep matters discreet, Wiriyamu was asked to gather the people by word of mouth and not to beat the *batuque*—the village drum. Wiriyamu agreed. He gathered a trusted few and accompanied FRELIMO fighters to the base. Balachu went with them, as did Wiriyamu's own two sons.

> The trek took several hours to reach the base. We met FRELIMO leaders. Some wore military uniform. Others looked like me, ordinary, in normal (civilian) clothes. I cannot exactly remember what they said. All I know is that they were there to free us, liberate us from "*os colonos*"—the colonials—*e os mzungos que estavam dar a nos tantos dor de cabeça*—the whites giving us so much headache. They talked, talked and talked. We listened. Then time came to eat. We got food and cooked. We all shared. The next day many of us joined the party. I was one of them. Even one of the sons of Wiriyamu joined.

There is little direct evidence that villagers near Wiriyamu had joined the movement that day; in the months ahead, a handful did. It is hard to imagine the contrary. Wiriyamu and the satellite villages of Djemusse, Juawu, and Riachu were closely spaced, their inhabitants in close contact and communication with each other. Wiriyamu itself was within eyesight of FRELIMO's arms supply route. According to several informants, Chaworha had not participated in either supplying recruits or helping FRELIMO with its logistic needs.[96]

Furthermore, according to the surviving members of the Bulachu, Tenente Valeta, and Mixone households, the five villages in the triangle affected by the massacre did not have insurgents embedded among them. Once recruited, said Bulachu, cadres left the villages permanently to join mobile base camps dotted along the Luenha estuary.

It is clear from this episode that, on that day, Wiriyamu took a historically significant decision to "side" with FRELIMO. But why? He may well have been politically naive and a poor visionary strategist, and as such may well have shared the view expressed by some informants in the village about the colonial war as "something out there and not at our doorsteps." "Yes we heard of the war of the colonials but we were naive. We never

---

[96] Zambezi, interview, 1995.

thought that it would come to us." "These people came to us for help and they came to help us. The massacre bit us hard like a spirit from the *m'phondorho*"—an evil unleashed from a lion-spirit that normally remained self-chained, explained several informants intimately knowledgeable on the matter.[97]

On the other hand, he could not have acted differently. Wiriyamu chose to deal with knowns. For unknowns, he relied on others, notably Senhor Soda, whose roles, among many, were to invoke the spirit of the *mphondorho* to bring down the rains and to tackle knotty issues beyond his control.

Furthermore, resistance to FRELIMO would have proved fatal, as it would either have signaled neutrality or a pro-Portuguese disposition, which would have sealed Wiriyamu's fate and that of his people sooner than December 1972. That is what had happened to chiefs in Mucumbura, Buxo, Chiutse, Campulussa, and Foya, who died, victims to revolutionary justice.[98] Given frequent migration to and from the triangle to Rhodesia and the South African mines, news of such killings traveled fast into the triangle—and its lessons would not have been lost on Wiriyamu.

The Portuguese first got wind of FRELIMO's presence in the triangle in June.[99] After their arrival, FRELIMO commanders accelerated the pace of gathering arms from the north into the triangle,[100] declared Changara to be theirs, and unleashed attacks in and around the area to paralyze road traffic along the Tete corridor connecting Blantyre and Salisbury.[101] Similar attacks followed to paralyze Tete railways used for coal exports, the significance of which the Portuguese embassy in Pretoria sought to minimize.[102] Confident of the local support and the protection offered by the ravines below Wiriyamu, FRELIMO commanders in charge of the Zóbuè-Changara logistics dispensed with military scouts. This move proved fatal for the triangle. Arms transporters could now be spotted by unexpected visitors.[103]

One such visitor was none other than Wiriyamu's son-in-law Tai, who was enlisted in the Portuguese militia. He arrived in the village unannounced, looking for his wife, Nonika, who had sought refuge from repeated domestic violence to be with her parents. Wiriyamu and his first wife had welcomed their daughter, assuring her a safe haven until the matter of spousal abuse could be resolved.

Tai himself was the son of chief Kongorhogondo and was betrothed to Nonika, a marriage aimed at diffusing mounting animosity between the two chieftaincies. But Tai had been brought up in a deeply restrictive environment and shared the same values as his father and older brother. Both brothers were "dark, moody, and like their father, mercurial. Chief Kongorhogondo was deeply afflicted by darkness, no I would say

---

[97] Senhor Elídio, interview, 1995; Zambezi, interview, 1995; Abidu Karimu, interview by author, Wiriyamu, Tete, 1995; and António Chuva, interview by author, Wiriyamu, Tete, 1995.
[98] PT/TT/D-F/001/00001, April 7, 1971, and May 11, 1971; PT-TT-PIDE-D-F-001-00006, February 9, 1970; and PT/TT/D-F/001/00004, November 10, 1971.
[99] PT/TT/PIDE/D-F/001/00008, June 17, 1972.
[100] ibid.
[101] PT/TT/PIDE/D-F/001/00008, June 13, and June 24, 1972; and, PT/TT/PIDE/D-F/001/00008, May 3, 1972, and June 13, 1972.
[102] PT/TT/PIDE/D-A/1/2826-8, November 16, 1972.
[103] Zambezi, interview, 1995; and Elídio, interview, 1995.

surrounded by a cloud of evil spirits."[104] He viewed Wiriyamu and his people to be a "mixed breed of lower social status" and not a true native son.[105]

Wiriyamu's progressive tendencies troubled Kongorhogondo, as did his economic success and his readiness to welcome non-Portuguese "foreigners" and their religion. Kongorhogondo was socially conservative, authoritarian, and an advocate of traditional medicine. Worship of ancestors and the practice of sacrifices to the spirits inhabiting the sacred forests were important to him. Missionaries and their enterprise were corrosive, stripping the Nhungwe of their true nativity, their culture and ultimately their identity. Wiriyamu was therefore a traitor to the Portuguese in his eyes—a native son seduced by modernity: Portuguese trading and commerce, and Catholic values and ways of life.

Chief Kongorhogondo, however, appeared untroubled by his son's career as a Portuguese militia, a choice that furthered Portuguese interests as Tete's colonial occupiers. To him, this choice posed little, if any, contradiction since he, this son, and his sibling then serving in the Portuguese secret police, were in essence enemy infiltrators, sort of cultural double agents. The earning power and the access to information from Portuguese intelligence networks enabled that chieftain to target Wiriyamu, and his neighbor to the north, the chief of Chaworha.

Upon climbing the crops of rocks on which Wiriyamu stood, Tai spotted a caravan of heads bobbing up and down carrying guns and ammunition. According to three informants familiar with the incident, Tai alerted the Portuguese about FRELIMO arms supply route. Although Tai was unavailable to confirm the information provided for this narrative, it is safe to assume that he could not have hidden this security breach from his superiors in the militia, all the more so given the animosities between Wiriyamu and his father and given Wiriyamu's refusal to release his daughter to him.

Soon after this incident, a Portuguese veterinarian came to the village unannounced to help chief Wiriyamu vaccinate his cattle. He stood with his back to the chief's compound, staring at the tamarind tree on the western edge of the village. He turned around as his name was called to be told that Wiriyamu was not home but that he would come to see him to rearrange a date to convene a meeting between the two. At that moment, the vet spied a caravan of recumbent guns on padded heads bobbing up and down heading south towards the Mazoe River. He pretended not to have seen the trail and made a hasty retreat to alert the authorities in Tete. The vet was a white Portuguese colonial civil servant with a side business as cattle trader, and a close friend of the chief of secret police in Tete city.

The triangle's most dramatic encounter between FRELIMO and the outside world occurred in early December. It was related to food supply and logistics and illustrated not only Wiriyamu's careful handling of the newcomers but also the strain that FRELIMO was placing on the supply of food for the FRELIMO soldiers in the triangle, which was under severe drought. True to character, the chief of Wiriyamu

---

[104] Sangalo, interview, 1995.
[105] Zambezi, interview, 1995; Padre Domingo Ferrão, interview by author, Tete Diocese, 1995; Vasco Tenente Valeta, interview by author, Wiriyamu, Tete, 1995; and António Mixone, interview by author, Tete and Chaworha, 1995.

remained tactfully silent in the face of this added demand for food from his people. Instead, he sought an increase in food production by commissioning two diviners specializing in rainmaking. Neither was successful, which led him to call Senhor Soda, a specialist with a track record, who successfully induced the first rains in October, the night after the young FRELIMO activist met chief Wiriyamu to invite him over to visit Dalepa's camp a few hours' walk from the village.

In the meantime, the food shortage deepened, as did the need to feed the fighters nearby. "We were chewing on leaves from the baobab tree and harvesting its hard-shelled fruits just to survive."[106] FRELIMO cadres too suffered the shortage of provisions, as DGS archives note when annotating repeated food raids on retailers.[107] "One day before [...] December," FRELIMO cadres were returning from a food-scouting trip near Wiriyamu when they spotted a Portuguese cattle trader in the triangle. Normally, cattle traders came every Thursday on market days held on the edge of a football field a short distance north of Juawu. This trader had appeared on a day off. Given the triangle's need for cash to buy food and essentials, he came to buy cattle hopefully below market price. Before he could get out of the truck, though, he was surrounded by FRELIMO cadres, blindfolded, taken to a make-shift base nearby, where he was interrogated for hours; then stripped to his underwear, divested of his shoes, socks, and clothes, taken half-way back and released to find his way home. To add insult to injured dignity, he was instructed to come back to a specific location with a long list of food, medical supplies, and articles of clothing.

"It was hot that day, too hot to walk for us (let alone for) a fat *mzungu* cattle-trader."[108] He eventually reached chief Wiriyamu's compound, where he rested under the shade of a tamarind tree. At sunset, he got in his truck and went home. A few days later, he arrived with the goods as promised, but this time he was accompanied by an army intelligence officer who asked around if they had spotted FRELIMO cadres. They were met with silence. "Tell them if you see them that I came with the goods as promised."[109]

Alarmed by FRELIMO's presence in the triangle, the Portuguese sent Johnny Kongorhogondo[110] and his supervisor, Chico Cachavi, two agents familiar with the area to confirm FRELIMO's presence in the triangle. We have no record of what they reported to their DGS superiors in Tete, but we can easily surmise what they must have said judging from their subsequent actions in the triangle—the place was contaminated and needed to be cleaned up.[111]

Both agents were well known in the triangle, but were poor intelligence-gatherers, for both had agendas of their own to pursue. Given the drought, Cachavi's profiteering had taken a tumble, prompting him to ratchet up his demands for a bigger slice of his cut from sales in domestic animals. In addition, because of his philandering, he had fallen foul of several prominent leaders in the villages.[112]

---

[106] Kaniveti, interview, 1995.
[107] PT/TT/PIDE/D-F/001/00028, December 19, 1973.
[108] Zambezi, interview, 1995.
[109] ibid.
[110] He was also known as Tomás among the DGS.
[111] Mixone, interview, 1995.
[112] Zambezi, interview, 1995; Mixone, interview, 1995; and Elídio, interview, 1995.

Nationalist Struggle and Colonial War 67

With the departure of the two agents from the triangle, FRELIMO was truly outed—and it was a matter of time before the Portuguese initiated an offensive. We do not know how Dalepa reacted once informed of how FRELIMO units had so brazenly exposed their logistic routes in the triangle. What is clear is that FRELIMO's sudden exposure in the triangle forced Raimundo's hand. He elected to ignore the dire need to supply food for his combatant units and the even greater need for a stronger cache of arms to initiate guerrilla operations on Videira's nerve center in Tete. Instead he asked his units to initiate attacks on Portuguese military assets protecting the construction of the Cahora Bassa dam.

Of the several assaults after June 1972, three are worthy of note. The first occurred in late November, the second two days before the Wiriyamu wipeout, when a civilian aircraft flying from Beira to Tete was hit, resulting in a forced landing at Tete Airport. Its occupant, reported to have been a Portuguese entrepreneur of some pull, and confirmed by one uncorroborated source to be Jorge Jardim, complained to the military authorities and the chief of secret police about the incident,[113] who subsequently determined the location of the anti-aerial attack to be at or near the Wiriyamu complex. Clearly, from the Portuguese viewpoint, the *turras* had contaminated Wiriyamu. It had to be cleaned up.[114]

The final and third operation was an ambush on a unit of heavily armed commandos, which suffered severe casualties. The surviving commandos swore to avenge the fallen. The two DGS agents Johnny and Chico joined the chorus advocating retribution.[115]

The reality, of course, was far more nuanced. Wiriyamu and its chief were dictated by survival and collective self-interest. They had no choice but to allow FRELIMO access to its ravines for arms transportation and recruitment in the triangle. Nor did Wiriyamu have any power to restrict FRELIMO's troop movement in the triangle as they readied to attack Portuguese military assets. However, chief Wiriyamu had made sure that neither FRELIMO cadres nor Wiriyamu inhabitants were engaging in anti-colonial warfare as prospective FRELIMO members were living in the village. Most important of all, according to informants, the village of Chaworha had no contacts with FRELIMO, nor did it supply FRELIMO with cadres to fight the Portuguese.[116]

The Portuguese view of the triangle as an infected zone was simplistic. They failed to understand how pluralist decision-making, devolution, compromises, marriage alliances, diplomacy and tact had built a prosperous living community under a tutored and reasonably self-trained village elder. In fact, Wiriyamu offered the agents of the empire an opportunity to question their own narrative as colonial subjugators. Instead of seeing themselves as victims of their own deception, they viewed the triangle as a binary fight between the "communist"-inspired FRELIMO and their supporters. The tragedy is that they destroyed Wiriyamu with a lethal cocktail of faulty intelligence, prejudice, rage, and dated information, shaken with convulsive revenge!

---

[113] Ferrão, interview, 1995.
[114] PT/TT/PIDE/D-F/001/00008, June 17, 1972.
[115] Hastings, interviews, 1977, 1978, 1979, 1981, 1995, 1996.
[116] Mixone, interview, 1995; Zambezi, interview, 1995; Vasco Valeta, interview, 1995, and Kaniveti, interview, 1995.

On December 16, they struck but failed to eradicate Raimundo Dalepa and his bases. He, on the other hand, simply moved his operation south, nearer the margins of the Luenha River. By late afternoon, the triangle fell silent. Five villages ceased to exist. A narrative—the Portuguese massacre of Wiriyamu in colonial Mozambique—replaced them.

5

The Church in Tete

On Tuesday, May 7, 1940, Salazar and Pius XII signed a concordat laying down the precise terms for the Church to operate in the Portuguese dominion.[1] The encyclical *Saeculo Exeunte Octavo* that resulted from this concordat gave Salazar full control over education to sponsor state ideology, while granting the Portuguese Catholic hierarchy the sole responsibility for proselytizing in the colonies.[2] Embedded in the concordat were two provisions that proved crucial for this narrative on Wiriyamu. One allowed Portugal to approve candidates nominated by the Vatican to fill vacancies in the hierarchy from a pool of appropriately qualified Portuguese nationals. Portugal's Church hierarchy, therefore, was to be constituted wholly of Portuguese subjects free of alien influences. The other provision allowed Portugal to import qualified foreigners to meet its missionary needs, should these go unfilled by Portuguese-born priests and nuns. With these provisions in place, Salazar controlled the Church and could now use its assets and expertise to serve and further the interest of the empire—or so he thought![3]

The concordat left out two issues: how Portugal would respond to doctrinal shifts in the Church and what specific protocols would Portugal follow to resolve conflicts between Church and State. Lack of provision on how to deal with these two issues effectively shaped the narrative history of the Church during Mozambique's colonial war.

However, the state of literature in this field remains fractured. No comprehensive and substantively analytic text exists on the history of the Church during the colonial war in Portuguese Mozambique,[4] though a recent work does tackle Church–State

---

[1] For the life of the dictator, see Filipe Ribeiro de Meneses, *Salazar: A Political Biography* (New York: Enigma Books, 2009).

[2] A more complex narrative on this is explored in António Costa Pinto and Maria Inácia Rezola, "Political Catholicism, Crisis of Democracy and Salazar's New State in Portugal," *Totalitarian Movements and Political Religions*, 8, 2 (June 2007): 353–368.

[3] Pius XII, "Saeculo Exeunte Octavo, Encyclical of Pope Pius XII on the Eighth Centenary of the Independence of Portugal to the Venerable Brother, the Patriarch of Lisbon, the Archbishops, Bishops and Other Ordinaries of Portugal and Its Overseas Possessions, in Peace and Communion with the Apostolic See," *Vatican.va*, accessed December 23, 2011, http://preview.tinyurl.com/qy8asol.

[4] Luis B. Serapião, "The Preaching of Portuguese Colonialism and the Protest of the White Fathers," *Issues: A Quarterly Journal of Africanist Opinion*, 2, 1 (Spring 1972): 34–41; Luis B. Serapião, "The Influence of the Catholic Church on Portuguese Colonial Policy," *Current Bibliography on African Affairs*, 7, 2 (Spring 1974): 138–155; Luis B. Serapião, "The Roman Catholic Church and the Principle of Self-Determination: A Case Study of Mozambique," *Journal of Church and State*, 23, 2 (Spring

relations in Portugal and by extension the empire.[5] Several scholarly works have sought to advance this narrative—some more successfully than others. De Sousa and Cruz Correia attempt the impossible: 500 years of Portuguese evangelical work in Moçambique in 224 pages.[6] Michel Cahen's work is more measured, thorough in places, and less ambitious in methodically assessing the Church in Moçambique between 1930 and 1974.[7] Ramos Brandão partly covers the ground trodden by Cahen and advances the narrative from the point of view of Church and State relations using PIDE/DGS archives.[8]

The remainder splits into thematic sets. One such set tackles Protestant colonial history and its role in raising social consciousness in southern Moçambique while nurturing the formation of some of the most prominent leaders in early nationalism.[9] Another comprises narrowly defined histories of Catholic congregations, of which there were reportedly fifteen[10] during the colonial war.[11] One additional set assesses specific

---

1981): 323–355; J. Luzia, "A Igreja das Palhotas: Genese da Igreja em Moçambique, Entre o Colonialismo e a Independencia," *Cadernos de Estudos Africanos*, 4 (1989): 127; and Luis B. Serapião, "Mozambique Liberation Front (Frelimo) and Religion in Mozambique, 1962–1988," *Africa, Revista trimestrale di studi e documentazione dell'Instituto italiano per l'Africa e l'Oriente*, 48, 1 (March 1993): 110–124.

[5] Duncan A. H. Simpson, *A Igreja Católica e o Estado Novo Salazarista* (Lisbon: Edições Almedina, 2014).

[6] José Augusto Alves de Sousa and Francisco Augusto da Cuz Correia, *500 Anos de Evangelização em Moçambique (11 de Março de 1948 to 1 de Março de 1998)* (Maputo/Braga: Paulinas/Livraria A.I., 1998).

[7] Michel Cahen, "L'État Nouveau e la Diversification Religieuse au Mozambique, 1930–1974. I. Le Résistible essor de la Portugalisation Catholique (1930–1961)," *Cahiers d'Études Africaine*, xl-2 (2000): 309–349; and Michel Cahen, "L'État Nouveau e la Diversification Religieuse au Mozambique, 1930–1974. II. La Portugalisation Désespérée (1959–1974)," *Cahiers d'Études Africaine*, xl-3 (2000): 551–592.

[8] Pedro Ramos Brandão, *A Igreja Católica e o Estado Novo em Moçambique, 1960/1974* (Lisbon: Editorial Notícias, 2004): 261 pp.; and Pedro Ramos Brandão, "A Igreja Católica e o Estado Novo em Moçambique, 1960/1974," *Latitudes*, 27 (September 2006): 87–91.

[9] Alf Helgesson, *Church, State and People in Mozambique: A Historical Study with Special Emphasis on Methodist Developments in the Inhambane Region* (Uppsala: Studia Missionalia Upsaliensia, 1994), 442; Teresa Cruz Silva, "Igrejas Protestantes no Sul de Moçambique e nacionalismo: O Caso da 'Missão Suiça' (1940–1974)," *Estudos Moçambicanos*, 10 (1992): 19–39; and Teresa Cruz Silva, *Protestant Churches and the Formation of Political Consciousness in Southern Mozambique (1930–1974)* (Basel: P. Schlettwein Publishing, 2001).

[10] Eric Morier-Genoud, "The Catholic Church, Religious Orders and the Making of Politics in Colonial Mozambique: The Case of the Diocese of Beira, 1940–1974" (PhD Dissertation, State University of New York, 2005).

[11] Work on the Comboniani fathers is covered in Arnaldo Baritussio, *Mozambique, 50 anni id persons die missionary combonian* (Bologna: Editrice Missionaria Italiana, 1997). Materials on the Franciscans are given in Carlos Azevedo, Manuel Marques Novo, José A. Correia Pereira, and America Montes Moreira, *Franciscanos em Mozambique, cem anos de missão, 1898–1998* (Braga: Editorial Franciscana, 1974); M. Alves Correia, *Missões Franciscanas Portuguesas de Mozambique e da Guiné* (Braga: Typography das Missões Franciscanas, 1934); Félix Lopes, *Missões Franciscanas em Moçambique, 1898–1970* (Braga: Editorial Franciscana, 1970); and Ernesto Gonçalves Costa, *A Obra Missionária em Moçambique e o Poder Político* (Braga: Editorial Franciscana, 1996). The Jesuit congregation's work is given in José Augusto Alves de Sousa, *Os Jesuítas em Moçambique, 1541–1991*. *No Cinquentenário do Quarto Período da Nossa Missão* (Braga: Livraria Apostolado da Imprensa, 1991); and Zélia Pereira, "Les Jésuites et la formation d'élites au Mozambique, 1961–1974," LFM, *Social Sciences and Missions*, 14 (July 2004): 75–116. The best work on the White Fathers pertinent here is by Cesar Bernoulli, *A Cruz e a Espada em Moçambique* (Lisbon: Portugalia Editora, 1974).

dioceses, while the last set of works are biographies on two Portuguese-born prelates who served Mozambique, Dom Sebastião Resende, Bishop of Beira,[12] and Dom Manuel Vieira Pinto, Bishop and later Archbishop of Nampula.[13]

Of the works cited here, Morier-Genoud's doctoral dissertation advances the narrative covered by Cahen and others[14] by focusing on the diocese of Beira as a case study typifying the history of the Church between 1940 and 1974. The text uses archives and synthetic literature buttressed by oral data culled from forty-six Church-related informants, which explore the diocese's formative stage, its first bishop, and his role in creating and then leading a genuinely vibrant church.

This church, as the text argues, was staffed by missionaries from diverse backgrounds, some possessing rigorous religious training in the Jesuit tradition, others boasting a track record in effective missionary experience from other parts of Africa. How this church—and by inference the Portuguese Church in Mozambique—negotiated Church–State relations forms part of the text's penultimate treatment. Following the death of its bishop, the Beira diocese underwent a crisis of leadership from which it never quite recovered during the colonial war period. His successor Dom Altino Ribeiro de Santana lasted only a year, dying of a heart attack due to pressure from the turmoil enveloping his diocese.[15] The text tackles this aspect of the story and discusses the role of the Church in advancing the nationalist narrative from the viewpoint of the diocese of Beira before it was split to form two dioceses: Beira and Tete.

The dissertation does not address in great depth the history of the Church in Tete before and during the colonial war, which gives us an opportunity to do so here. Tete's church evolved through several complex periods. Between 1962 and the onset of the war, it underwent a transformative change, moving away from "Portugalization" to become an agency for social change. The colonial war plunged the Church in conflict with several entities: the State, FRELIMO, and the hierarchy, which stood resoundingly silent over Portugal's conduct of war. Missionaries serving Tete finally broke that silence. While one group elected to protest against the hierarchy's silence with mass resignation, another sought to work within the hierarchy and the Church to confront Portugal over its military conduct. In the end, neither group succeeded in their respective objectives, prompting one of the two groups to take the fight overseas. The Wiriyamu massacre was, in essence, that Church group's final stand against collective mass violence in Portugal's imperial Africa.

---

[12] A. Carlos Lima, *Aspectos da Liberdade Religiosa. Caso do Bispo da Beira* (Lisbon/Braga: Diário do Minho, 1970); Gulamo Tajú, "Dom Sebastião Soares de Resende, Primeiro Bispo da Beira: Notas Para Uma Cronologia," *Archivo, Boletim do Arquivo Histórico de Moçambique* (October 1989): 149–176; Carlos A. Moreira Azevedo, "Perfil biográfico de D. Sebastião Soares de Resende," *Lusitania Sacra*, 2, 6 (1994): 391–415; and Carlos Lima, *Caso do Bispo da Beira, Documentos* (Porto: Civilização, 1990).

[13] Anselmo Borges (ed.), *D. Manuel Vieira Pinto, Arcebispo de Nampula. Cristianismo: Política e Mística* (Lisbon: Edições ASA, 1992). His views on the massacre are given in "Massacres de Wiriyamu e visita de Marcello Caetano a Londres," *Gerracolonial.org*, accessed January 10, 2014, http://www.guerracolonial.org/index.php?content=2087.

[14] Morier-Genoud, "The Catholic Church."

[15] Arquivo Histórico Diplomático, D. Altino Ribeiro Santana, *Bispo da Beira*, 1973–1974, PT/AHD/MU/GM/GNP/RNP/0456/07052.

Bishop Resende and the shortage of priests

The story of how the Church became an agency for social change in Tete merits a reflective pause here. Individuals shaped key events in Tete's religious history by breaking forcefully the tensions between personal action and structures of State oppression, a break that ultimately determined the future tenor of Tete's Church. In addition, Tete's Church illustrates how Salazar's fascist dictatorship nearly succeeded in eradicating the will of the Church as an epistemic force in society, by seeking to eradicate pluralism out of national and imperial polity. One key factor stood in the way of this success. As a multidimensional and multicultural global entity, the Church was undergoing changes in doctrinal perspectives on social and developmental issues.[16] The Church in Tete was thus caught in a triangulated conflict between the broader Church, which acted as a global force for change, the State, which played the role of the Church's authoritarian overlord and paymaster, and the colony's progressively minded priests, who attempted to realign the hierarchy and the State with new doctrinal thinking under Vatican II. The majority of the prelates in the empire remained staunchly entrenched in religious conservatism until the end of the colonial war.[17]

Until 1962, Tete formed part of the Beira diocese. Three years into the concordat, Beira received its founding bishop, Dom Sebastião Soares de Resende. With the concordat in place, Mozambique's non-Catholic missionaries were gradually withdrawn, paving the way for the bishoprics to replace these with Catholic missions. A few Protestant missions were left alone in the colony, one below the Limpopo River and one near the Niassa district.[18] In theory, this move was designed to yield a Portugalized Church, with prelates and priests working in tandem to serve Christ *and* Country.

Two factors derailed this project. One was Resende himself, who, once seated as bishop, underwent his own internal transformation.[19] Highly conservative on his arrival in Beira, he came to view the Church in Mozambique as a faith-based force for cultivating grace, civic-mindedness, and human capacity. Resende was a thinking man's bishop, intense and passionate, with an enormous capacity for hard work. He was also gifted with an epistolary quill, which he wielded with analytical precision to dissect the social reality of the "indígena," unassimilated Africans. What he saw troubled him.[20]

Colonial Beira of the 1950s to early 1960s wasn't a Shangri-La. Income disparities between the rich and the white and other minorities effectively segregated the city,

---

[16] Documents of the II Vatican Council are electronically available in Vatican archives at www.vatican.va/archive/hist_councils/ii_vatican_council/.
[17] For a useful take on the role of the Church in advancing Mozambican nationalism, see Francisco Miguel Gouveia Pinto Proença Garcia, "Análise global de uma guerra (Moçambique 1964–1974)" (PhD Dissertation, Universidade Portucalense, 2001).
[18] The biography and subsequent withdrawal of one such non-Catholic mission in the north is given in John Paul, *Mozambique: Memoirs of a Revolution* (Harmondsworth: Penguin, 1975).
[19] Morier-Genoud, "The Catholic Church," 77–157.
[20] José Capela, interview by author, Maputo, 1994 and 1995.

with the majority, black and poor, living in sprawling shanty towns bereft of basic utilities, sewerage, electricity and running water.[21] Yet here was a church in service of Portugal's civilizing mission in Africa doing its work from the top down, impervious to "suffering," that is to say, impervious to the social conditions glaring at its crucifix. The church was, in his eyes, perhaps not meeting the true spirit of *imitatio christi*— addressing the needs of the poor regardless of color.[22]

Cleft between God and government, Resende's solution typified the soul of a reflective pragmatist, according to his nephew, the late José Capela, alias José Soares Martins.[23] His first port of attack here was to establish *Diário de Moçambique* as a vehicle for open discourse—as open as the regime would allow. During its last days of circulation as an independent paper, the *Diário* achieved fame as a voice of conscience on social justice issues during its coverage of the trial of priests accused of treason.[24]

In this thinking, Resende was a patrician, not a rebel by any means.[25] He was unwilling to confront the Portuguese establishment but felt he would do all he could to invigorate the Church as a meaningful, tangible, constructive and highly accessible social force for everyone—a mission of hope and deliverance. He sought justice and peace for his flock through Christ as a lived experience. His immersion in Vatican II deliberations in Rome consolidated this view of the Church as a global social narrative transcending parochial State-centric interests. That was Resende, in essence. "If these are the political objectives of the country let us really put them to work for the betterment of all...and let us make the church truly what it purports to be—a message of hope, reconciliation, an instiller of family values and Christian life," said his nephew quoting Resende.[26]

The second factor was the shortage of priests in Mozambique, which continued to trouble the Church hierarchy during the period under review. Portugal itself had a shortage of its own largely as a result of the purges of the Jesuits during the Pombalist era, from which it never recovered.[27]

---

[21] Studies on the labor force and conditions in and around Beira are now proliferating. An indicative bibliography can be gleaned from Corrado Tonimbeni, "The State, Labour Migration and the Transnational Discourse: A Historical Perspective from Mozambique," *Stichproben. Wiener Zeitschrift fur kritische Africastudien*, 8 (2005): 5, accessed December 18, 2013, http://preview.tinyurl.com/l2hv7og. Consult also Eric Allina, *Slavery by Any Other Name: African Life under Company Rule in Colonial Mozambique* (Charlottesville: University of Virginia Press, 2012).

[22] These observations are abstracted from his writings. See, in particular, Sebastião Soares de Resende, *Os Grandes Relativos Humanos em Moçambique* (Porto: Livraria Nelita Editora, 1957); Sebastião Soares de Resende, *Responsibilidades dos Leigos* (Porto: Oficinas Gráficas da Sociedade de Papelaria, 1957); and Sebastião Soares de Resende, *Problemas do Ensino Missionário* (Beira: Tip. E.A.O., 1962); and Sebastião Soares de Resende, *Um Moçambique Melhor* (Lisboa: Livraria Morais Editora, 1963).

[23] Capela, interview, 1994 and 1995.

[24] José Capela, "Para a História do Diário de Moçambique," *Arquivo. Boletim do Arquivo Histórico de Moçambique*, 6 (1989): 177–180.

[25] Capela, interview, 1994 and 1995.

[26] ibid.

[27] Adrian Hastings, *The Church in Africa: 1450–1950* (Oxford: Clarendon Press, 1994), 82; and C. R. Boxer, *The Church Militant and Iberian Expansion: 1440–1770* (Baltimore: Johns Hopkins University Press, 1978), 4.

This shortage was acutely felt in Tete, seen by Portuguese missionaries eligible to serve overseas as a hardship post,[28] "the white man's grave, the land that even God forgot."[29] Before Resende assumed his responsibility in 1943, four churches had served Tete since 1562, two established in the nineteenth century, both in the Songo region, one in Boroma and one in Miruro, and one mission located in Angonia, in Lifidzi, formed in 1909. This network of four covering 6,135 square miles was headed by Tete city's cathedral church, established fifty-four years after da Gama's landing on the coast.

To resolve the shortage, Resende invited Comboniani, Pipcus, White Father, and Burgos missionary societies to work in his diocese.[30] By the late 1950s, he had successfully recruited the priests he needed for this part of the world, which enabled him to separate Tete from Beira to function as a diocese in its own right under its own founding bishop, Félix Niza Ribeiro.[31] By 1962, Tete had acquired a well-established missionary network comprising of one seminary at Zóbuè, which was directly accessible by route 103 northeast of Tete bordering Malawi, and ten missions and attendant parishes. By 1972, this network had grown by another nine missions, increasing the area of episcopal coverage by 29,081 square miles,[32] staffed by 600 foreign missionaries.[33]

Tete then could boast a network of twenty-five missions parishes, and 4,237 missionary schools attended by half a million students, aided by 141 community and social activity centers (see Map 1). In addition, its 202 health centers cared for one and a half million patients, while numerous associations and clubs for cultural and youth activity supported the Church's enterprise in human capacity development.[34]

Of these missions, the most pertinent to this narrative were Unkanha, Mucumbura, Changara, Moatize, and Tete city. Unkanha, established in 1956, covered 6,357 square miles of territory and sat perched along the margins of the river bearing the same name. Mucumbura, which had been established in 1960, nestled south of the River Zambezi near the border with Ian Smith's Rhodesia. The Changara mission formed in 1965 (16° 50' 11" South, 33° 16' 26" East) sat astride two highways, one leading to Beira and the other to Salisbury then, now Harare. Moatize (16° 7' 0" S, 33° 44' 0" E), located past Tete Airport near a coal-mining town twenty-five miles directly northeast

---

[28] PT/TT/D-F/001/00002, January 1, 1971.
[29] Sangalo, interview, 1995.
[30] This section of the chapter has greatly benefited from materials in Morier-Genoud's text; interviews with José Capela, alias Bishop Resende's nephew, during 1994 and 1995; discourses with former Jesuit seminarians, Professors Mario Azevedo and Luis B. Serapião, 1995 and 1996; oral discourses with António Sopa; and informal exchanges with resident historians at the Regional House at the Juniorate for the Society of Jesus, Maputo, 1994–1995.
[31] In February of 1972, Bishop Augusto César Alves Ferreira da Silva was appointed to succeed Bishop Ribeiro. *Diocese de Tete*, accessed December 23, 2013, http://www.diocesedetete.org.mz/diocese/features.html.
[32] ibid.
[33] Reportedly included among them were 146 priests, fifty-five monks and 450 nuns.
[34] Piero Gheddo, "Una chiesa nuova nasce dalla persecuzione," *Mondo e missione*, 22, November 15, 1979.

from the colonial army regional headquarters in Tete, was founded in 1958 and served a population of nearly 100,000 spread over 5,559 square miles. Tete city housed the bishopric itself, the São Pedro mission complex, comprising a day and boarding school, a parish center frequented by Burgos priests and missionaries on travel, and a nearby mission hospital.[35]

Portugalization and its impact on the Church

Resende had chosen his men with great care. Among them were White Fathers and Burgos priests. The White Fathers mirrored his own views on what a forward-thinking Church should look like. Their work in Uganda and territories neighboring Mozambique bore witness to that fact, as did their ministry of socially progressive Christianity. Once in place, the seminary at Zóbuè and the missions encircling it came to stand as a testament to the type of missionary work Resende wanted to see in action.[36]

Unlike the White Fathers, the Burgos were first and foremost secular priests on secondment to Tete by their dioceses in Spain. The congregation was founded in 1922, and by the early 1970s had grown to 300 members.[37] As a secular order of priests, they were *de facto* free agents, reporting to two authorities but effectively supervised by neither. Although once in Tete they reported to the local bishopric as a courtesy, their allegiance was to the decanal authority some thousands of miles away in Spain who paid their monthly salaries regardless of performance, since for cost-prohibitive reasons the Spanish hierarchy rarely saw them, let alone managed and guided their ecclesiastical work.[38]

Moreover, they were a diverse group of priests, experienced in missionary work with a strong presence in Rhodesia, Gambia, Rwanda and Burundi. They were thus eminently suited to work in Tete, work that called for a deeply felt compassion for the poor. Their work in Japan and in South and Latin America, especially in Peru, Brazil, Colombia, Guatemala, and Costa Rica, equipped the Burgos to engage in this kind of transformative ministry in a multi-cultural setting.[39] In addition, most Burgos priests chosen for Tete had worked among the poor in Spain and were thus operationally inclined to execute Resende's episcopal as well as doctrinal vision for the new Tete diocese.[40]

"Besides," said one Burgos priest referring to Tete, "no one wanted to come to a remote hell hole which even time had forgotten."[41] "We spoke Spanish, very similar to

---

[35] ibid.
[36] Hastings, interviews, 1977, 1978, 1979, 1981, 1995, 1996.
[37] "Mozambique in London," *The Tablet Archives*, accessed December 24, 2013, http://preview.tinyurl.com/o99ctgj
[38] Miguel Buendia, interview by author, Maputo, 1994 and 1995.
[39] "Mozambique in London."
[40] Berenguer, interview, 1994 and 1995.
[41] Sangalo, interview, 1995.

Portuguese, you know. And it was easier for us than for others from non-Latin-speaking countries to come to Lisbon to study the Portuguese language for one year and then undergo the required acculturation process," added another Burgos Father interviewee. "Also our national situation in Spain was similar to Portugal's."[42] Both countries had long-surviving dictators in place, were predominantly Catholic, and had been historically twinned.

With the Burgos, the White Fathers and other foreign nationals, the Tete diocese moved firmly away from Portugalization towards a socially transformative ministry. The impact of the missionary work in the diocese was felt most acutely in mission schools and the parishes. Aware of how important it was not to alienate the Portuguese state, the Tete clergy assiduously worked to comply with Portugal's three most important dictates: teach in schools "História, Língua e Pátria"—Portuguese History, Language and Civics; allow activities of the Mocidade Portuguesa—a sort of Scouts Club designed to instill patriotism for the Salazarist state—and preach the gospel in Portuguese.[43]

But "we also did other things too."[44] The History, Language and Civics classes were taught in a critical comparative context to help students and seminarists alike to self-determine where they fit as individuals in the community, society, and beyond.[45] Above all, students in the parish schools were given a stake in their future through decentralized student-centered governance, which encouraged debates and discussion on current critical issues.[46]

"We did not encourage political sedition," however, said Father Joseph, formerly of the Zóbuè seminary. "We did not encourage subversion of the state, disrespect of the flag or rebellion against Portuguese rule in Africa." Rather, the new missions provided a nurturing environment for personal and educational growth, a collegial atmosphere where everyone felt comfortable to ask daring questions: "Other countries have Presidents, Senhor Padre, how come we don't?" "Padre, is it right for them to take our women '*no mato*' in the bush at night '*para juntar com elas*' to be joined with them (carnally)?" "Padre, how come you are not married? You must have a woman '*escondida no qualquer lugar*' hidden somewhere, haha." "How would Christ feel about independence, to rule our lives ourselves?"[47]

As consciousness-raisers among parishioners, the Spanish Burgos, in particular those who had worked among the poorest of the poor in the Basque region, sought to

---

[42] Enrique Ferrando, interview by author, Madrid, Spain, 1995.
[43] The role of the Church in the production of a new cultural matrix to serve the interests of the state is far more complex than suggested here, and entailed a web of entities. These included literary institutions, political and religious movements, publishing houses and the book-buying public. For a good introduction to the literary side of the story, see Chapters 2 and 4 of Margarida Rendeiro, *The Literary Institution in Portugal since the Thirties: An Analysis Under Special Consideration of Publishing Market* (Bern: Peter Lang AG, 2010), 35–55 and 89–119.
[44] Father Joseph, White Father, formerly of Zóbuè Seminary, interview by author, Seminário Maior, Maputo, 1994 and 1995.
[45] Father Joseph, White Father, formerly of Zóbuè Seminary, interview by author, Seminário Maior, Maputo, 1994 and 1995; and Berenguer, interview, 1994 and 1995.
[46] Father Joseph, interview, 1994 and 1995.
[47] Berenguer, interview, 1994 and 1995; Ferrando, interview, 1995; and Buendia, interview, 1994 and 1995.

balance compliance with state mandates and creative missionary practices that encouraged critical thinking on civics. They gained proficiency in the local languages to deepen missionary roots in the parish. Preaching in the local languages then followed after 1965, which coincided with the implementation of Vatican II encyclicals. The subject matter tackled in public discourses broadened thereafter to cover social issues and Christian responses to these. "Our sermons changed. We no longer focused on identifying a good Christian with patriotism and loyalty to the Portuguese state and the empire," said one priest.[48]

Most missionaries treated their parishioners as equals, exposing them to the joys of self-empowerment. Parishioners exposed to this way of viewing Christ as a concerned human and social reformer attained new perspectives, both as subalterns in a colony and as Christians steeped in post-coloniality. "What would Christ do or say in the face of an invitation to free one's shackles albeit to better one's life as a Christian?" some argued, said a Burgos Father.[49]

This consciousness spread in the broader local community surrounding the missions, particularly those near the borders, namely Zóbuè, Unkanha and south Mucumbura, where Portuguese administrative presence was weakest. Here missionaries worked without administrative restraints or oversight and their work had the greatest impact, "we were not (there) to civilize Tete's downtrodden for the Portuguese fatherland." They were foreign agents of change, "neither loyal to the Portuguese state nor supporters of Salazar, his 'Francoista' ideology and their military debacle in Mozambique. We were loyal to Christ..." and therefore committed to evangelize his message in a broader socially conscious way.[50]

By 1969, the people in and around Tete missions were fully "*consciencizado*," socialized to evaluate critically where they stood under Portuguese colonial cultural values and rule. The impact of the Church's work in border regions was tellingly predictable, leading to an increase in migration into neighboring countries. Seminarists at Zóbuè deserted in periodic waves to Tanzania to join FRELIMO, leaving behind prospects of priesthood and a better life as Mozambique's future assimilated.[51] A similar political climate prevailed near Unkanha exacerbating tensions between the Portuguese and the local chiefs and villagers, prompting a border chief to move his people in a mass exodus across to Zambia.[52]

Missionary work in Tete proved to FRELIMO's advantage, prompting its leaders to capitalize on these "socially softened" areas—by penetrating Tete from Malawi near the Zóbuè seminary headed by the White Fathers. The objective behind this move was two-fold: draw firepower away from the remote northwestern frontier of Tete in Maravia and the Unkanha region; strengthen FRELIMO's logistic capacity, by recruiting prospective activists in this area associated with the Zóbuè seminary and the surrounding parishes, who were encouraged to stay put and help FRELIMO's

---

[48] Castellã, interview, 1995.
[49] Berenguer, interview, 1994 and 1995.
[50] Sangalo, interview, 1995.
[51] Luis B. Serapião, "Mozambique Liberation Front (Frelimo) and Religion in Mozambique," 110–124.
[52] Personal exchange with João Paulo Borges Coelho.

logistics and enemy intelligence network by moving nearer heavily fortified Portuguese areas.[53]

With this measure firmly in place, FRELIMO acquired a ready source of supply of men, contacts, and topographical information to penetrate Tete from the west near the Zambian border. Once inside Tete, its cadres sought to gain a political foothold as they prepared to deepen the colonial war. With specific reference to Unkanha, they could not have hoped for a better climate to resume their accelerated mobilization drive abandoned since 1965. Parishioners near the Unkanha missions received FRELIMO's political messages favorably. It is not surprising, therefore, that FRELIMO should have moved so swiftly once inside Tete. Nor is it a coincidence that the two-pronged race to reach south of the Zambezi should have commenced in areas of missionary presence.[54]

Church–State relations in Unkanha

The colonial conflict strained Church-State relations in Tete to a near breaking point. It started with the Unkanha mission, which experienced the first wave of mass violence in northwest Tete. Unkanha therefore is justly deserving attention here to examine the challenges the Church faced in managing conflict to survive as a mission for the poor, and attempt to do so under the most adverse conditions. Moreover, Unkanha proved historically important to both sides, enabling FRELIMO to traverse the Zambezi and damning the Portuguese to engage in Tete's first independently documented massacre, the one at Mucumbura—precursor to Wiriyamu.

FRELIMO had selected Unkanha to fast-track its march in Tete and then head towards Mozambique's midriff. Unkanha's mission was headed by Padre Alberto Font Castellá, a 38-year-old Burgos missionary from Barcelona, a popular, intense, gregarious, witty, forthright priest and forgiving of foibles among his parishioners, but fearlessly defiant of authority, ecclesiastical or of the state, with an ever-present sense of wonder about him. Simple pleasures moved him to reflect on Christ: a chilled glass of water in the hot midday sun, a crucifix chiseled from local woods given to him as gifts to adorn the mission church, a simple meal at night with the sounds of cicadas in the background.[55]

Padre Castellá was isolated in Unkanha, with little contact with either the bishop in Tete to whom he had to report or his home bishop of Gerona in Spain, under whose ecclesiastical authority he fell and to whom he reported as a secular priest. He also claims to have been out of touch with Vatican II proceedings, though he was "aware of what they were thinking. But then I was doing all that in my work in Unkanha,"

---

[53] General Hama Tai, interview, 1994 and 1995; General Grouveta, interview, 1994 and 1995; and Matsinha, interview, 1994 and 1995.
[54] These observations are drawn from discussions with General Hama Tai et al., and the Burgos Fathers.
[55] This composite image is drawn from personal observations and interviews with his colleagues and former students. Included among them were Padre Sangalo, Enrique Ferrando, Padre Berenguer, Karimu, Senhor Elídio, Irmã Lúcia, and Padre Ferrão.

he said.[56] Isolation from the world and the Church outside liberated him, giving him considerable autonomy in the day-to-day running of his mission and the adjoining parish, leaving him free to push to the limits the envelope of missionary work.[57]

Intense and a workaholic, Padre Castellá threw himself into his missionary work, "that is all I had to live for, to serve Christ in Unkanha." Isolation and his own temperament therefore brought him closer to his parish community: its hopes, its fears, its future, its hard times during food shortages, and its celebrations of marriages, deaths, births, and baptisms. He grew much closer to the people of his parish than his colleagues elsewhere in similar isolation in rural Tete. In this aspect, he was unique. If Resende was the thinking man's bishop, Padre Castellá was the priest of the people: focused, driven, and devoted.

Cautious but unafraid of death, he was, however, afraid of losing his mission—the *raison d'être* of his existence. When fighting north of Unkanha intensified, he found his parish work curtailed, his parishioners unwilling to participate in activities. Should he abandon his mission, as the White Fathers were about to do? Should he seek the protection of the Portuguese? Should he wait until FRELIMO contacts him? Or should he open dialogue with them? Abandoning the mission made little sense to him. "I will not," he said. Christ did not forsake his mission in trial. "Why should I?" This was his trial *for* Him.

Seeking the protection of the Portuguese was not an option, he said. It was a death sentence. Death, though, did not bother him, he said. However, Portuguese protection would have alienated him from his parish, particularly among FRELIMO sympathizers and those neutral in the conflict. In any case, "they are all God's children, to me it made no difference. They are all people." Further, siding with the Portuguese would have signaled to FRELIMO that he had sided with the Portuguese in this conflict.[58]

Padre Castellá however, felt uncomfortable about waiting for FRELIMO to approach him. He was a man of action—he hated events to dictate him and the fate of his parish. In this instance, however, the initiative was in FRELIMO's hands. All he could do was to force the issue. Should he or should he not initiate contact? He agonized for days. How should he approach FRELIMO? If so, what should he say? "I prayed for guidance and sought Him" and "I got it." One evening he sat by the paraffin lamp to compose a letter to FRELIMO. "It was dark outside but I was aware of FRELIMO presence '*lá no mato*' —there in the bush". He wrote, asking them what role he should play as a priest *not* as someone wedged between partisanship and the Portuguese.[59] He reckoned that by framing the letter as he did, he would know whether he had to leave his mission, or stay put and continue to work for Him.

> I then let the local chief know that I was interested in meeting with them and gave them a letter I had written. A few days later, one of our girls in our boarding school who had not returned from the Easter weekend knocked on my window at night and said "Padre, some men want to talk to you." I went out. The fighters were hidden

[56] Castellá, interview, 1995.
[57] Sangalo, interview, 1995.
[58] Castellá, interview, 1995.
[59] ibid.

in the bush. They were armed. When I met them, I greeted them. They said, "Padre, we have your letter here. You ask what is the role of a priest in Unkanha. Should he stay put or ought he to leave. You see we are at war with the Portuguese. We have nothing against you. We are very grateful that you are here working for the people. More than that, we have not found anyone who spoke badly of you. You have our complete support." I said, "I am glad you support our work. Please remember that as priests we are not political. Nor are we the Portuguese. We do not fear the dangers of war. But it is difficult not to be nervous at the sound of frequent bullets too near the mission, and at night." I then added, "We now fear the Portuguese even more. It is they who are going to be more bothersome, now that I know that you are in support of us." "What can we do to help you, Padre?" they asked.[60]

A deal was struck. Padre Castellã was granted his wish—or so he thought. In reality, he had merely bought time to remain in Unkanha a bit longer.

In the meantime, he could come and go as he pleased, travel to and from Unkanha with FRELIMO providing for his safety, warning him beforehand where the mines were laid and when and which road to take for travel outside the mission. Occasionally, he would meet them *no mato*. They knew who he was, and he who they were. They would exchange greetings and go their separate ways. "In return, I helped them now and then by sending young men, equipping them with a map to head for Malawi. There, the FRELIMO secretariat helped them reach Tanzania."

The military commander near Unkanha[61] thought Padre Castellã had sold out even though he was ignorant of the precise nature of his relationship with FRELIMO. It was enough for him to suspect it to be strong and frequent—and that irked him. "How come I could travel by car everywhere despite the mines and yet be safe?" he and his soldiers would repeat.

The conflict over burials

One day, Padre Castellã had to go to Salisbury, "to buy things and had to go through the war zone. I went. I departed early morning taking the road to Zumbo and then reached Salisbury. I returned to Unkanha a bit late." The military commander was visibly rattled. How dare he go into the thick of war and come back unscathed? The next morning, the commander was at Padre Castellã's door. "He was really angry, more so than usual. 'Padre, you do things at night that we cannot even do during daytime, and he was not implying anything sexual.' He really hated me and he wanted me out of Unkanha. I had to leave the scene I was so disgusted with him."[62]

He was interrogated by the DGS, whose agents grilled him for hours. He was accused of having maintained contacts with the *turras*, the terrorists. "Technically it was true," added Padre Castellã. But he refused to answer questions or reveal particulars.

---

[60] ibid.
[61] Actual name withheld according to the wishes of Padre Castellã.
[62] Castellã, interview, 1995.

"Yes," he said, "I live in the bush. That is where my church is. When I am in the bush I meet them frequently." "But where exactly did you meet them?" they asked. "I am sorry. I am not the police. My mission was religious. For me all are brothers. All Mozambicans are equal. Their quarrel they said was with you, the Portuguese, and I have nothing to do with it."[63]

Here the commander was at a disadvantage and could not go beyond interrogation. "You see I was his priest too! He attended mass at my church and took Holy Communion from me. Also, I was a white foreign priest," Padre Castellã said. He said he would have been dealt with differently had he been from Unkanha. "I would not have survived torture from the DGS." The commander also knew Padre Castellã had recourse to his bishop in Tete, Félix Niza Ribeiro, who could intervene as a last resort. That is exactly what happened. The bishop of Tete intervened, and Padre Castellã was released. The military commander was bitterly disappointed—he had to let go of his prey, the only source of reliable information that could lead him to the *turras*, the terrorists. This was the only recorded evidence of Niza Ribeiro's active intervention on behalf of activist ministry for the church. As the conflict in Tete deepened, Niza Ribeiro took a more "Portugalized" stance in the conflict.

Thereafter, Padre Castellã's life was not his own. A contest of wits and will ensued between him and the military commander; the former resolutely refusing to give in to the latter's taunts and jeering. The matter came to a head in a dramatic turn of events that brought to an end the Unkanha mission Padre Castellã had loved and worked to build "in the middle of nowhere, mind you," he added.

In the meantime, the war had intensified after Operation Gordian Knot, and the commander had yet to nail down the *turras* or discover their points of verified penetration. In the meantime, his soldiers patrolling the area continued to submit false reports of their day's work, preferring instead "to shade from the sun and play cards all day long," said Padre Castellã. In the end, Tete's high command intervened. The local commander was informed of an impending visit from Tete's governor to assess the military situation in Unkanha. He was to be accompanied by the bishop of Tete. Would he, the commander, gather people in the village for a meeting and inform Padre Castellã that he attend the session? He duly did, but informed Padre Castellã at the last minute.[64]

Padre Castellã panicked. "Suddenly I saw what could happen if FRELIMO spotted the plane with the bishop on board and they fired at it with anti-aircraft guns."[65] He broke off from the meeting and dashed "*lá no mato*" to inform FRELIMO fighters of the bishop's impending visit. The last thing he wanted on his priestly conscience was a dead bishop.

The bishop and the governor arrived and headed the meeting, in which "the villagers, the mission staff, and that included me," were accused of being "nothing more than traitors." "They mingle and eat with them, the terrorists." I said, but they consider them as brothers, why should they not? Even today and near here, you may well find them

---

[63] ibid.
[64] ibid.
[65] ibid.

intermingled with the population. "But where?" The military commander asked me without a beat. The provincial governor stood there attentive but silent.[66]

> *Excuse me*, I am a priest and not a military man. I cannot denounce them. Ask your men to find out who they are. If you suspect something, then go there and find out for yourselves. Let me tell you something, though. I have your soldiers staying very near my mission. They sleep the whole day or play cards. They don't work at all. They make no effort to meet people. Actually they seem quite afraid of the bush. As conscripts they should do bush patrol. Instead they get to the nearest village, settle down, read and play cards. At night they fill out their report. We went here and there and we found nothing. How do you expect to catch anyone this way?[67] I said, and this time I spoke firmly and quite openly. The Portuguese still had some respect for the Church and men of the cloth. They had not begun imprisoning and torturing missionaries.[68]

This revelation of military incompetence in front of the governor was a mortal blow to the local commander. "He was now revealed for what he was—incompetent." What followed then was predictable. Three weeks after the meeting, the Portuguese changed personnel and tactics. They instituted patrol units on bicycles and began an intense series of search and destroy operations to unearth *turras*—the terrorists.

Ironically, Padre Castellã's revelations at the meeting were now to turn into a Pyrrhic victory for him. With the onset of destruction of "lives and property," the "people began leaving, heading for Zambia. They left behind burnt huts and livestock." Padre Castellã was not about to give up yet. "I made a cassette film of this" depicting "the burning huts in a village near Unkanha in the direction of Fingue… including shots of mines exploding… (and) of burning huts as people fled for their lives. How I managed to film… I do not know now."[69] Padre Castellã wanted evidence of what he had seen in case the authorities challenged him in a court of law.

However, what churned him inside out, and perhaps led him to risk his life and that of his parishioners, was Portuguese callousness in the treatment of their own dead; *that* ultimately made him seriously think "of packing up." One such incident in question entailed the death of one bicycle patrol unit:

> They (had) sent soldiers on bicycle patrol. One such patrol was asked to stop by the guerrillas but didn't and several in the unit were killed. The pastor of the nearby village in my parish came to notify me. "Padre, there are two soldiers dead there." I went to the military barrack. I got there and said, "Listen, you have two of your soldiers dead near that village." "Many many thanks Padre. Many thanks," they said genuinely grateful.[70]

---

[66] ibid.
[67] A DGS report backs Padre Castellã's contention of non-commissioned soldiers falling short as soldiers. PT/TT/PIDE/D-F/001/00026, November 3, 1973.
[68] Castellã, interview, 1995.
[69] ibid.
[70] ibid.

A day passed. Two days passed. Nothing happened. The pastor from the village returned to see Padre Castellã. "Padre, the dead bodies are still there and they are beginning to bloat." He went to the military barrack and this time began haranguing them. He said, "If they had been white they would now be in Portugal. Because they are black they are there rotting in the bush." "Padre you know, the bodies could be booby trapped. It is dangerous." "They are dangerous because they are Africans. Is that not true? Very well then, they are no danger to me. Why don't you let *me* bury them?" "With great pleasure, Padre." "In that case," I said, "put it in writing."[71] They did and on headed notepaper.

Armed this way, I went to the villagers near the dead. The people said, "Padre, they will kill us if we try to bury the dead." "No, they will not. I have here written permission to bury them. Let us go and do that. We left. I was in a truck. I loaded shovels and a villager in the back of the truck. We started. I went ahead and the villagers followed behind. We got there. We could not handle the bodies. What with the sun, they were bloated and nearly cooked. They fell, ripping apart as we sought to lift them up. We began digging a hole nearby. We took turns. It was our turn. I and a parishoner were in the hole when someone tapped on my shoulders asking me to look up. I did. I saw heads with guns pointing. I said, "hey, don't shoot, don't shoot. Brothers, I am Padre Alberto."[72]

"You are not the enemy?" they asked. "No, we are not." The armed men blurted back, "Then get out of the hole." Evidently they had waited, hoping for the Portuguese to come to bury the bodies and kill them in the act.[73]

Padre Castellã was now serious about leaving. He voiced his thoughts to his parishioners. Word was out that "the Padre" was thinking of leaving. The Portuguese military command breathed a sigh of relief. Finally, they faced the prospect of a region free of Padre Castellã and could now pursue an aggressive defense strategy, with no holds barred.

FRELIMO's courtship of priests

FRELIMO, on the other hand, was truly concerned. As an icon of fairness and justice, Padre Castellã offered a dramatic contrast for all to see between his conduct as a Catholic priest and that of the Portuguese military and administration in Unkanha. As such, Padre Castellã's presence alone had helped raise consciousness among parishioners by sheer force of example, making FRELIMO's task to mobilize the villagers that much easier. Further, Padre Castellã's departure would end a ready supply of potential cadres in the future. As far as Portuguese counter-insurgency was concerned, with Padre Castellã's departure FRELIMO faced the prospect of confronting an area

[71] ibid.
[72] ibid.
[73] ibid.

saturated with a defense network difficult for the fighters to penetrate southern Tete. FRELIMO had to act—and fast—or stood to lose everything: Padre Castellá himself, the foothold they had gained in the region, and the strategic initiative to head south.[74]

Would Padre Castellá contemplate helping FRELIMO more directly, they pondered? They had good historical reasons to think this way. FRELIMO did have priests working actively and directly with its educational programs at party headquarters in Tanzania.[75] Padre Castellá too might consider working for them. They had but to ask which they did through intermediaries. "FRELIMO let me know they wanted to meet me to discuss this. At the meeting, they said they wanted me to go with them to Tanzania with the boys and girls in the fourth grade from our boarding school..." They wanted him to move immediately and that alarmed Padre Castellá. FRELIMO negotiators failed to appreciate the fact that Padre Castellá's could not decide on his own. He had to consider his position as a priest, his flock, the hierarchy in Tete, and his titular bishop in Spain if he were to remain active as a missionary.

FRELIMO negotiators, on the other hand, were uninterested in Padre Castellá as a priest. As a pedagogue, though, he was invaluable since he had under him a school full of young men and women ready for plucking. The negotiators could have been more sensitive to his position as a priest, having witnessed, if covertly, his dealings with his parishioners as well as the Portuguese. Granted, his relations with the Portuguese had soured, but only in the context of Christian justice and peace. He was not, as he repeatedly reminded himself, a freedom fighter. He was fighting for his church. For FRELIMO leaders to have expected more was not only shortsighted but belied their lack of sophisticated thinking in assessing the extent to which priests of Padre Castellá's ilk could act in matters affecting the Church politically without jeopardizing the interests of the Church as a collective.

Padre Castellá listened in silence and then said, "Look! I cannot give you a reply right away." FRELIMO negotiators sensed then Padre Castellá would not budge without meditative reflection. They played the only card they had at hand to force a decision on him on the spot. They let him know in a roundabout way that he may soon not have a church to fight for, "because we are about to intensify the war in the region with the appointment of a new commander, Raimundo Dalepa." In short, Padre Castellá was being informed that he may have to leave, as he was now likely to be in FRELIMO's way. In their eyes, the question for Padre Castellá was which side to choose. Padre Castellá returned to consider his options.[76]

FRELIMO, however, were not about to give up. Their tactics perhaps differed from Padre Castellá's when dealing with difficult issues, but both were resilient and tenacious when faced with difficulties impeding strategic objectives. A short time later, FRELIMO

---

[74] This observation has benefited from discussions with General Hama Tai. General Hama Tai, interview, 1994 and 1995.
[75] Uria Simango and Mateus Gwenjere were two such priests who had played a prominent role in FRELIMO's early formative history. Simango's biography is given in Barnabé Lucas Ncomo, *Uria Simango: Um homem, Uma causa* (Maputo: Edições Novafrica, 2003).
[76] Castellá, interview, 1995.

sent their two important people from Tanzania's central committee, one João Pelembe and the other, one called Biafra, it may well have been a bush name (*nom de guerre*). They came there to see me. They were dressed in ministerial style, jackets, and ties and with briefcases! They called me to come in the middle of nowhere in the bush. I was surprised as I saw them dressed like this in the bush. "Are they ministers or what, and dressed like this in the middle of all this. They must have something important to say," I said to myself. They had come armed with a letter from President Samora Machel inviting me to come to Tanzania with the boys and girls from the boarding school. The war was about to intensify even further the letter said.[77]

"I thought a lot about it but in the end (however) I felt it was not prudent of me to leave Mozambique at the time because the bishop of Tete would have suffered a backlash." Padre Castellá felt the decision required the bishop's input, and he wrote for advice. "I asked him what to do, to stay or to leave. Since the parish was dwindling so rapidly, there was nothing to do I said. The bishop too thought as I did, that I ought to leave." The bishop, however, counseled him to go to the mission of Mucumbura until its designated missionary could return to take over the reins.[78]

Padre Castellá complied. FRELIMO had lost this round—or had they? Other events conspired in FRELIMO's favor. Padre Castellá's subsequent decision was to shake his ever-dwindling parish community by its roots. He himself agonized as to what to do for them before his departure. He could not abandon them without making provisions for their safety and future. Many had remained neutral. Others, according to Padre Castellá, may well have been active in FRELIMO.

Some had opted to work for the Portuguese as informants and in the DGS. The parishioners who saw no future without Padre Castellá and under war conditions contemplated either fleeing to safety to Zambia or possibly joining him. Would Padre Castellá consider taking them with him? He was approached to consider their request. Padre Castellá listened and realized he could not, not without permission from the Portuguese, who after all were still the legal authority in the area. The chances of the Portuguese acceding to this request were, in his view, slim. No government official would have granted permission to export a contingent from an area "contaminated" by insurgency to the peaceful south where insurgency had yet to begin.

Padre Castellá, though, was undeterred by his personal misgivings. He broached the subject with the Portuguese. Astonishingly, the Portuguese said yes. They could now be rid of Padre Castellá and his flock. "So they do not want to be left with the terrorists, hem! Very well then. We will give you military trucks to take you and these people to Mucumbura." Overnight, 200–300 people gathered to move to the south.[79]

From the point of view of counter-insurgency, the Portuguese move proved disastrous. By transporting the Uncanha parish, they opened the floodgates for political activism in the south. What more could FRELIMO ask? Neither the commander nor the administrator vetted the people gathered to move south. No interrogations were

[77] ibid.
[78] ibid.
[79] ibid.

carried out by the DGS to weed out potential and/or real *turras*; nor were records kept of the people gathered for the Mucumbura authorities to monitor their activities as potential activists and fighters. On the other hand, the authorities may well have felt confident that the move placed the threat of insurgency away from Cahora Bassa, soon to be isolated by a lake. With the installation of a new military commander as governor in the field, aggressive counter-insurgency combined with a program of fortified villages would resolve the terrorist "menace" south of the Zambezi. Events were about to prove them wrong.

For FRELIMO, of course, Padre Castellá's march was an act of Hegelian providence. The Portuguese move could not have failed to raise a jubilant chuckle among FRELIMO leaders on the ground.

Padre Castellá then had a final meeting with FRELIMO to say good-bye. By this time, in early or mid-1970, a new commanding officer, Raimundo Dalepa, had taken the reins of FRELIMO strategy. They talked; Padre Castellá cannot recall the exact details. At the end of the meeting, Padre Castellá got up to say good-bye. Dalepa shot back with prophetic prescience: "We will shortly be there... and will come to visit you." That meeting spelled an end to Unkanha as a mission, and a new beginning for FRELIMO's insurgency south of the Zambezi, in Mucumbura.

6

The Church and Mass Violence

Missionaries and mass violence

Mucumbura had a Catholic mission headed by the Burgos Fathers, with a formidable presence in the region. It was founded in 1960 by Enrique Ferrando, also known as Quique, a Spanish Burgos Father, originally from Valencia, Spain, whose love of the underdog had deep roots in his family's past. His mother had passed away when he was young. His father had been tortured during the Spanish Civil War and young Quique admired his capacity to forgive his tormentors. He grew into a sensitive man, a searcher for truth, and poured his soul into writing his reflections as a missionary. He became adept at public relations and became a journalist of sorts, skills that he later employed to solicit donations as well as attract prospective candidates for the ministry.

Ferrando was promoted and left Mucumbura for Beira in "June or perhaps July" of 1969 where he stayed until June 1972, at which point he departed for Spain to study journalism. He intended to return to Mozambique to serve the order with his newly acquired skills as a Burgos priest, which he did in Mucumbura, again for a very brief period in April and June 1972.[1] Several Burgos Fathers had served the mission in the interim, Padre Sangalo, Padre Castellá and Padre Berenguer, to name but three.

The mission started as a small mud hut. By 1964, the entire complex was complete, personally built by Ferrando and his colleagues with bricks and cement blocks manufactured on site to ensure consistency in measurements and standards. The complex had a health center with housing for its staff, a chapel that could hold 100 people, and a hut for the local medic. "The father's house and ours was built last." The boarding school could accommodate twenty-five boys and girls, and the school of two large classrooms could accommodate fifty to sixty students each. They were charged eighty escudos a month for tuition. Since the mission did not have extensive agricultural plots, namely *machambas*, to grow food, the school fees went into groceries and supplies to keep the mission schools and other units running.[2]

The mission had several other schools for students in the area, of which two led the pack performance-wise: They were headed by Apostle Daniel Conga at Daque and Avelino

---

[1] Ferrando, interview, 1995.
[2] ibid.

at Zambeze.[3] Both principals were well trained. Conga, known for his level-headedness and hospitality, portrayed an air of stability around him. His community admired and respected his work ethic and his consciousness-raising efforts for the ministry. Zambeze was a gifted teacher, but prone to long bouts of melancholy. He later took to the bottle, which threatened to undo the school's mission-centric work in raising civic consciousness, leading the Burgos Fathers to counsel him on the matter. Zambeze took heed and, according to Ferrando, mended his ways. While Conga had a wife and a son, Zambeze's family details are unknown. Both of these details proved relevant later. Apostle Conga was to die during the Mucumbura massacre while attempting to save his family.

By 1969, Mucumbura extended its missionary reach to include locations uncharted on colonial maps but worthy of note here, namely Beremo, Catonda, Chadereca, Changara, Changwa, Chioco, Daque, Deretode, Estima, Guse, Kapinga, Magwe, Matambu, Mandwe, M(a)handa, Muterese, Mvuze, Xagua, Xangura, and Zambeze. Daque and Zambeze were mentioned earlier. Chioco, located seventy-five miles away, was later absorbed into neighboring Changara, once it got a mission of its own. António was located slightly east of Mucumbura and had a majority of the region's Christians. Catonda, wedged between Magwe and Mucumbura, was a strong trading area with a local retail store and a school that served all three locations, Catonda, Magwe and Daque. Buxo, located between Mucumbura and António, proved fatally important, as we shall see in a moment.

Mission staff paid frequent visits on motorbikes and jeeps to initiate, maintain and deepen faith-based social networks. Given the lack of tarred roads, visits were most frequent during the dry season between May and October. At other times, visits dropped precipitously once the Calue and the António Rivers flooded near Mucumbura.

Mucumbura was close to another mission managed by the Burgos Fathers on the other side of the border in Ian Smith's Rhodesia. Mucumbura Burgos visited this mission regularly for fraternal reasons and to bring back much-needed supplies not available locally. Once the colonial war got underway, these trips landed the Mucumbura priests in jail as suspects engaged in illegal activities. Ferrando was one such victim. PIDE interrogated him for hours and released him only after intervention from the newly appointed bishop of Tete. A similar incident in 1972 involving Enrique Ferrando's successors, Alfonso Valverde de Lion and Martin Hernandez Robles, landed them in jail for two years on charges of sedition.

FRELIMO's arrival south of Zambezi changed Mucumbura's landscape, bringing in its wake renewed tensions between the Church, the State and FRELIMO. Portugal's counter-insurgency added a lethal dose of volatility to this mix, much to the detriment of the mission.

In Unkanha, the Church had managed its conflicts with the State, allowing mutual survival to dictate its interaction with FRELIMO. FRELIMO protected the mission and some of the parishes that supported the cause with advanced military intelligence in return for the Church's active neutrality, and with the understanding that it would offer the State little in the way of intelligence on FRELIMO.

[3] Father Adrian Hastings, interviews by author, Oxford, London, and Leeds, 1977, 1978, 1979, 1981, and 1996; Ferrando, interview, 1995; Miguel Buendia, interview by author, Maputo, 1994 and 1995; and Sangalo, interview, 1995.

Photo 2 Padre José Sangalo, Madrid, 1995

In addition, FRELIMO had garnered a near-universal support among parishioners in Unkanha, largely because of the Burgos' progressive missionary work. Both Padre Castellá and his predecessor Padre Sangalo sought to demonstrate, somewhat successfully, that the people in this zone mattered and were equal to the "*mzungos*," the whites. In sharp contrast, Portuguese administrative behavior was often racist, demeaning or marginalizing of the local culture, thereby creating an ideal mirror for people on which to reflect the merits of a political switchover.[4] Once Zambia became independent in 1964 the prospect of migration increased, as stated earlier, if only to escape this under-developed region of Tete's economy. Border villagers could, in this way, avoid the "objectified otherness" that some administrators appeared prone to display.[5]

Mucumbura was different. The region was more complex in terms of geography, social development, history and religion. Mucumbura was near Ian Smith's Rhodesia to begin with. White rule there was alarmed at the prospect of black power fast approaching its border, ultimately threatening what Salazarists saw as the Southern

---

[4] Padre Sangalo, interview, 1995.
[5] This section has greatly benefited from discussions with Padre Sangalo, Padre Berenguer, Father Joseph, Miguel Buendia, and Enrique Ferrando. Additional reflections were sought from Padre Domingo Ferrão.

Euro-Africa. To address this wind of change, Smith had already set two cooperative agreements with Portugal: one for his troops to engage in hot pursuit into Tete, which we covered earlier, and the other was for intelligence and military collaboration with the DGS over repatriation of suspects crossing the borders.

In addition, Mucumburans were far savvier politically that their counterparts elsewhere in Tete, said Padre Sangalo. "They were sharp, reliable, and sophisticated," with long memories of resistance to Portuguese rule.[6] The beneficial proximity to the colonial economy along the north–south trading corridor near Mucumbura, however, complicated FRELIMO's recruitment strategy, while chieftaincies aligned with the Church in Mucumbura rendered Portuguese intelligence and military strategy somewhat ineffective. Missionary work here had socially softened the parishes to new ideas and thinking on self-determination as a Christian narrative, with varying degrees of success.

Parish responses to the liberation struggle

Because of these complex factors, Mucumbura's initial response to FRELIMO was asymmetric. The four chieftaincies of António, Lundo, Matambu and Buxo illustrate the point here. According to Enrique Ferrando and Miguel Buendia, two of these chiefs came out as pro-FRELIMO, strengthening FRELIMO politically overnight, enabling its insurgents in the process to march in two simultaneous directions—Beira and Tete's northeast underbelly.

The predominantly Christian communities near António were equally supportive of FRELIMO. Clearly sensitized to view Christianity as a force for social change, many received FRELIMO as an integral part of the new gospel advocating self-determination. Some elements of the Church in António in fact thought the Church missionaries too slow in recognizing FRELIMO as a force for social change working outside the Church. Was the Church on the side of full emancipation for its congregation? Or was it just talk, they wondered? In one recorded incident, they deemed the Church deficient, threating the lives of the Burgos priests, during a meeting in which they had come to warn the parishioners of an impending Portuguese attack. Their lives were spared after FRELIMO successfully intervened to assure the people of António of the priests' commitment to social justice.[7]

The chief of Lundo reacted differently. He was torn inside "because of the pressure from both sides. FRELIMO did not threaten him, but they insisted that he take a position. He could not remain neutral and play both sides."[8] On the other hand, Lundo had a great deal to lose. He depended on the Portuguese for access to sell agricultural goods, domestic animals, and surplus artisan products. The relatively better-developed economy in the neighboring British ex-colony, and easy access to roads leading to it and to Mozambique's southern midriff, strengthened the stability of his trading networks.

---

[6] Padre Sangalo, interview, 1995.
[7] Alfonso Valverde de Lion, interview by author, Madrid, 1995; Berenguer, interview, 1994 and 1995; Miguel Buendia, interview by author, Maputo, 1994 and 1995, Padre José Sangalo, interview by author, Madrid, Spain, 1995; and Ferrando, interview, 1995.
[8] Buendia, interview, 1994 and 1995.

Further, he had cultivated with great care his relationship with the Burgos, placing the people under his chieftaincy at an advantage to receive missionary education, which in the end increased the prospect of an assimilated, "civilized" life for his people.

But Lundo was a sensitive soul, a loner prone to introspection, unable or perhaps unwilling to lean on others for advice and help, and with a visceral distaste for confrontation. He mulled over his dilemma, and dreaded the day he would be visited again by a FRELIMO delegation seeking an answer. That day arrived. Four FRELIMO cadres "went to talk to the chief," who received them politely and begged for a postponement. "Let us wait a bit. I will get something to eat and we can then talk." He never came back. "The guerrillas thought he had gone to the Portuguese to denounce them. So they left," only to see his daughter on her way home. They told her, "Tell your father he likes to walk a lot. We are going to come back, and he won't walk again."[9] Unbeknown to his daughter, Lundo had not gone out to lunch but to commit suicide. His people got the message. They joined the newcomers—presumably reluctantly.

Chief Matambu's response to the newcomers on the other hand, was driven by ambition and tactical exigency. He was willing to form an alliance with the newcomers without ceding the power of his chieftaincy. Matambu was young, well respected, and proud. "He lost no opportunity to flex his muscle when he came to the mission," said Ferrando. After all, he was married with four wives, and as he said, he was wealthy enough to afford four. He collaborated readily with foreign missionaries and with the Portuguese on occasions, not only because it made good business sense but also because it demonstrated to chiefs more powerful than him that he, Matambu, was as sophisticated as them. He, too, could deal with the "*mzungos*" and their white ways and therefore was their equal. Given this perspective, he viewed the newcomers as yet another set of players in the Mucumbura mix. All he had to do was to switch patrons. Besides, FRELIMO offered limitless possibilities. They were African players and here to stay. By aligning himself with FRELIMO he had one fewer indeterminate variable to contend with. Portugal's future on the other hand, was proving to be increasingly uncertain.

By late December to early January of 1970–1971, FRELIMO initiated military action, having consolidated its political hold on the entire region except for two parishes, a small area surrounding the mission north of Mucumbura headed by a minor chief, and territories under the Buxo chieftaincy. The region north of Mucumbura was strategically important for a march towards Tete. Burgos Fathers interviewed here couldn't name the minor chief—"memory fails me here," said Miguel Buendia.[10]

FRELIMO took matters in hand, and went straight for the chief's jugular. They kidnapped his two children at the boarding school at the Mucumbura mission to force his hand. "Wasn't this a bit extreme? Why did they not try to mobilize him more aggressively?" I asked. "Oh, I think they were a rogue element . . ." "But it appears they

---

[9] ibid. Corroborating evidence provided by Padre Berenguer and Padre Sangalo.
[10] Padre José Sangalo, interview by author, Madrid, Spain, 1995; Ferrando, interview, 1995; Alfonso Valverde de Lion, interview by author, Madrid, 1995; Berenguer, interview, 1994 and 1995; and Buendia, interview, 1994 and 1995.

did the same thing elsewhere in Mucumbura. Could it be that they generally viewed the chieftaincies as suspect?" I inquired. My priestly informants chose to say nothing.

Subsequent literature in the field suggests a different take on this. Right from its inception, FRELIMO leadership considered chieftaincies as ideologically suspect, a colonial agency doing Portugal's bidding by collecting taxes, supplying forced labor, and enforcing cotton cultivation. This perspective remained unchanged even after independence until the new constitutional decree fifteen of 2000 recognized local authorities through which community engagement would ensue in a controlled setting to be driven by an agenda set by the government from above, as it were.[11]

Padre Berenguer was at the mission when he heard of the kidnapping. "He was livid." The children were in his charge and were his responsibility. Their parents had trusted him and his colleagues at the mission and vouched for their safety. Having maintained neutrality at Mucumbura while supporting the non-violent aspect of self-determination, FRELIMO had overstepped their bounds, he thought. He took four of his colleagues with him and headed straight to FRELIMO base to retrieve his charges. He was held up at gunpoint near the gates. "Don't shoot, don't shoot. It is me with my colleagues," he said, identifying himself. He had to stay at the base camp overnight as he negotiated their release. "I was really very uncomfortable having to spend the night there."[12] In the end, this proved Padre Berenguer's undoing. The DGS used the incident as a categorical proof enough to expel him from the colony.

Current oral literature essentializes Buxo as a supine Lear spurning what was good for him, namely, to switch sides and join FRELIMO.[13] However, Buxo shared Lundo's temperament to a point, loathe to lose what he had built over decades. His wealth was indeed a colonial micro-dependency and that alone should have proved enough for him to support "*os colonos*." Buxo, however, was profoundly spiritual, "not necessarily Christian but spiritual,"[14] and cherished his ties with the Burgos, who were a great solace to him. FRELIMO, on the other hand, could neither protect him from the colonial army's wrath nor nurture his religious dialectics.

On the contrary, FRELIMO were asking him to sacrifice all he had for a greater cause—national liberation. Opting to support the Portuguese, he thought, somewhat naively, made eminent sense under the circumstances. By doing so, he signed his own death warrant. FRELIMO commanders viewed his decision as grounds to terminate him. He was given three warnings to switch sides—to no avail. The house of Buxo now stood in the way of FRELIMO's strategy, namely to march northeast while protecting

---

[11] Lars Buur and Helene Maria Kyed, "Contested Sources of Authority: Re-Claiming State Sovereignty by Formalizing Traditional Authority in Mozambique," *Development and Change*, 37, 4 (2006): 847–869; Helene Maria Kyed and Lars Buur, "New Sites of Citizenship: Recognition of Traditional Authority and Group-Based Citizenship in Mozambique," *Journal of Southern African Studies*, 32, 3 (September 2006): 563–581; Fernando Florêncio, "Autoridads tradicionais vandal de Moçambique: o regress do indirect rule ou uma espécie de nep-direct rule?" *Análise Social*, 43, 187 (2008): 369–391.
[12] Miguel Buendia, interview by author, Maputo, 1994 and 1995; Berenguer, interview, 1994 and 1995; and Sangalo, interview, 1995.
[13] Miguel Buendia described him as a person of "extraordinary religious interest but was manipulated, politically very naive and easily manipulated by others. Guileless. Easily seduced by power and impressed by colonial authority and docile in temperament."
[14] Buendia, interview, 1994 and 1995.

its southern flank from Rhodesian forces operating inside Tete. Buxo was killed. His replacement shared the same fate.[15] Their deaths ushered in the first independently recorded case of Portuguese mass violence in southern Tete, at Mucumbura.[16]

The missionary protest against silence

In the meantime, Portugal's own Church began to question the colonial wars.[17] Buckling under renewed pressure from within the Church, Portugal's episcopacy underwent changes. In May 1971, António II Ribeiro, a cardinal widely recognized as a savvy compromiser on matters non-canonical, replaced Cardinal Manuel Gonçalves Cerejeira, Salazar's friend from university days in Coimbra. In addition, António Ferreira Gomes, bishop of Oporto, an opponent of fascist Lisbon, was allowed to return from overseas, where he had languished in exile at Salazar's behest until 1969.[18] He returned, however, unrepentant, unbowed as a prelate for the poor, unchanged in temperament, still a fierce advocate for a free press, and a painful thorn in the regime's authoritarian flesh.[19]

Portugal's relations with the Vatican in the meantime deteriorated, largely because of doctrinal shifts in the Church, which prompted Pope Paul VI to grant an audience to Luso-African liberation leaders as advocates of justice.[20] Portugal viewed the audience held on July 1, 1970 as an affront to its national integrity, an intentional aiding and abetting "rebellion against an established Government which maintains centuries-old relations with the Holy See ..." Two days later, Lisbon recalled the Ambassador to the Holy See. In response, the Papal office declared that the meeting was of no political significance since the three leaders were received as Roman Catholics and not as liberators. Perhaps satisfied with this explanation, Portugal duly returned its diplomat to the Vatican. However, lest Portugal assumed all matters fully resolved, the Papal office welcomed the diplomat back with a not-so-subtle rejoinder. In the interest of furthering peace and justice, the Vatican averred, Portugal might reconsider its pacification wars in the colonies. "Pacification, or liberation by force of arms—according to which side one takes—is a source of misery and death [...] May Angola, Guinea and Mozambique at last achieve peace in Justice."[21]

In Mozambique itself, tectonic shifts developed deep within the Church over the hierarchy's silence on the colony's mass violence, which affected in particular the White

---

[15] PT/TT/D-F/001/00001, May 11, 1971.
[16] Ferrando, interview, 1995; Alfonso Valverde de Lion, interview by author, Madrid, 1995; and Sangalo, interview, 1995.
[17] Thomas C. Bruneau, "Church and State in Portugal: The Crisis of Cross and Sword," *Journal of Church and State*, 18, 3 (1976): 471.
[18] The DGS archives contain detailed materials on the bishop in two hefty folders. Direcção-Geral de Arquivos, Arquivo Nacional da Torre do Tombo, 2878/58 SR and 3953-CI.
[19] See *Informations catholiques internationales*, nos. 341–342, August 1969, 15.
[20] *1970 Pope Paul VI grants an audience to Amílcar Cabral, ...*, accessed April 15, 2014, https://www.youtube.com/watch?v=vVvCTv8vHXc&noredirect=1.
[21] "Dispute with Vatican after Pope's Reception of Rebel Leaders from Portuguese Africa ...," *Keesing's Contemporary Archives*, xvii (1970): 24147.

Fathers who ran the Zóbuè seminary and missions associated with it. In terms of numbers, the White Fathers, the bulk of whom served the diocese of Beira, constituted a minority, only 2 percent, of the total and 6 percent of the total non-Portuguese missionary priests in Mozambique. However, their influence in the colony, particularly in Tete, was considerable, largely because of the transformative nature of their ministry, which the colony's bishop recognized as noteworthy, a "remarkable spiritual and material work carried out for the benefit of the Church in Mozambique throughout twenty-five years of continuous and praiseworthy toil."[22] According to one other independent observer, the White Fathers "had proved effective in raising social consciousness among its acolytes, students, and seminarians," inadvertently preparing them for a sentient civil society actively engaged in self-determination. "From FRELIMO's perspective, they were indeed ideal candidates for membership in the party," added a Burgos Father.[23]

However, the White Fathers were not Burgos, experienced in ministries forged under conflicts in a variety of settings across three continents, Latin America, Africa, and Europe, Spain to be more specific. Unkanha was a stellar example of their work, where they had demonstrated how the Church could survive surrounded by war and do so with pre-emptive transparency, while obviating needless confrontation with colonial authorities.

To the White Fathers, this silence by the hierarchy was troublesome. "The Church was becoming identified with Portuguese rule and the local hierarchy would not take a stand over 'police brutalities.'" They also complained that, while it was understandable that the Portuguese viewed the Church's promotion of "true social justice" as subversive,[24] the hierarchy's silence effectively suggested a collusion of sorts with Portugal's war policies, and that in their view was problematic.[25] "As missionaries," said Father Theodore van Asten, the White Father's Superior General, "we consider it our task to help to establish a church really incarnated in the life and culture of the African people. It also meant to preach the gospel and its integrity . . . we therefore stood behind the legitimate rights and dignity of the African as human beings."[26]

Put differently, the hierarchy in Mozambique had failed to recognize the core values of the White Fathers' mission in Tete, by remaining silent, despite repeated requests "that it take a definite stand in order to dispel this ambiguous attitude over injustice and police brutality. Baffled by the persistent silence," they now felt that "in conscience we have not the right to allow ourselves to be accounted the accomplices of the official support which the bishops appear to be giving to a regime which uses the Church to consolidate an anachronistic situation within the African 'continent.'"[27]

---

[22] "Fact and Fiction in Mozambique: The Bishops' Communique," *The Tablet Archives*, accessed December 24, 2013, http://archive.thetablet.co.uk/article/26th-june-1971/19/documentation.
[23] Buendia, interview, 1994 and 1995.
[24] "White Fathers 'backed the rebels,'" *Catholic Herald UK*, June 11, 1971, 2.
[25] "End of a Mission: Why the White Fathers Left Mozambique in Despair," *Mozambique Revolution*, 48 (1971): 19–20.
[26] Father Theodore van Asten, "Notes" (December 1974): 1–2, Father Adrian Hastings Archive, Borthwick Institute, Box WIR2: B4/1.
[27] "Fact and Fiction in Mozambique: The Bishops' Communique."

The hierarchy stood silent and still. It ignored the requests to reconsider its position. In February 1971, van Asten took the matter to the next level, first with the colony's Bishops' Conference and then with the Papal Nuncio in Lisbon, who was subsequently informed that unless Mozambique's episcopacy broke its silence, they would consider withdrawing from the colony. Would the Nuncio consider putting pressure on Mozambique's hierarchy to make a stand? To no avail. Even if such a pressure were to emerge, Portugal had no reason to buckle under, since it financed the hierarchy's salary-related expenses. Van Asten then tried a more direct approach by meeting with Portugal's Foreign Minister as well as the Minister for Overseas Provinces. With the state thus involved and, it later transpired, fully supportive of the hierarchy's Portugalized stance in the colony, van Asten felt he had exhausted all avenues to dislodge the episcopacy from its speechless perch.

A "meeting to take a decision on the matter (of staying or leaving) was held in Mozambique of the 37 White Fathers there and the Superior General." The minutes of that meeting suggest thirty-three voted to leave and four to remain, "not out of sympathy with the situation in Mozambique but because they wanted to confront it more vigorously," a decision that van Asten considered at the time, "an unrealistic resolve which could only have ended in their expulsion."[28] To protect the reputation of the Order and continue to remain patently transparent in governance, van Asten informed first the 4,000 men serving the order in Africa in a letter about the vote taken and the reasons behind the decision to leave Mozambique.

On May 18, 1971, three days after this letter, he personally delivered a similar text to the Vicar General of Beira, announcing their intention to depart by July 1, 1971. They had no option but to pull out altogether from the colony, said van Asten. He then added that they understood that history would see their action differently.[29] So be it. Indeed, the hierarchy did see their actions as politically motivated and said so in a written response signed by all the bishops in the colony, including Bishop Vieira, who was known to be exceptionally critical of the Portuguese state. In this instance, Vieira had sided with the episcopal majority.[30]

Eight days later, Lisbon announced it was expelling the White Fathers, charging them with vandalism of church property at the Barue mission. They had forty-eight hours to pack their bags and go. They left in four separate groups on May 28, 29, 30, and 31, 1971. The charges were vigorously denied by the White Fathers and, following an investigation, their denial was backed by fellow missionaries, who prepared an eight-point statement sympathizing with the White Fathers' decision to withdraw. The Dean of Beira's Cathedral added his voice to this statement at a service, broadcast on the radio.[31]

In expelling the White Fathers, the empire had followed an earlier precedence set in 1965 when it had forced thirteen Montfort priests to abandon their missions in a contested zone over trust issues.[32] This time, however, the expulsion proved

---

[28] ibid.
[29] "White Fathers Backed the Rebels," *Catholic Herald UK*, June 11, 1971, 2.
[30] ibid.
[31] ibid.
[32] Joseph C. McKenna, S. J., *Finding a Social Voice: The Church and Marxism in Africa* (New York: Fordham University Press, 1997), 83.

disingenuous. "The White Fathers (had) left Barue mission in January. The Foreign Minister's press conference was on 28 May." The Foreign Ministry had taken four months to discover the putative damages, a claim that lacked credibility given that Barue was teeming with secret agents and informants.[33]

The expulsion had far-reaching consequences for Portugal, which up to now had kept critics in the dark about its conduct in the African colonial wars.[34] The Vatican then got directly involved. It sent a delegation of three priests headed by Monseigneur Pio Gasparri on a fact-finding mission, which confirmed the White Fathers' version of events in its report to the Pope, which is yet to be revealed.[35] Portugal's critics could now tap into first-hand accounts on Lisbon's wars. These revelations Portugal could hardly afford. The case of the bishop of Oporto had already demonstrated that expulsion had only strengthened his voice of social conscience for the poor. Expulsion of the White Fathers was about to achieve a similar result, allowing them unfettered access to an international audience to publicize Portugal's use of mass violence in the colonies.

De Arriaga, Tete's colonial administrators, and even the Tete's resident bishop, considered by the DGS a politically neutral prelate,[36] thought differently. They breathed a sigh of relief at the departure of the White Fathers from Zóbuè, which they considered a training ground for FRELIMO cadres, namely, a place for producing literate "indígena" critical of Portugal's colonial presence in Mozambique. With their departure, the seminary was entrusted to a "safer" pair of hands—Portuguese Jesuits, who were seen as filially loyal to Portugal, willing to promote the wishes of the pro-Salazarist hierarchy. The new priests turned the ministry to its advantage and were observed by fellow priests using the missionary establishments and schools as recruiting grounds for the DGS.[37] With Zóbuè pro-Portugalized, FRELIMO lost a friend in court, so to speak, and with that loss also went much-needed intelligence from pro-FRELIMO seminarians and help with arms storage from sympathizers neighboring the mission.[38]

After the White Fathers' sudden departure, the Mozambique Church's disquiet over the colonial war deepened. With a supportively silent hierarchy, however, Portugal had nothing to fear from its detractors in the colonial Church, and therefore had little incentive to restrain its military in Tete. In addition, Portugal had, by and large, respected the inviolacy of the colony's foreign missionaries, leaving them relatively free to engage in their ministry, barring occasional incarcerations on minor infractions. Portuguese-born missionaries and Mozambican priests were another matter. Their fate was intricately entwined with the appropriate laws of sedition for metropolitan citizens and colonial subjects of the empire.[39]

---

[33] "White Fathers Backed the Rebels," *Catholic Herald UK*, June 11, 1971, 2.
[34] A detailed narrative on the history of diplomacy and foreign aid during Mozambique's war of liberation proved beyond the scope of this study. A shorter study is in the offing.
[35] Jose da Fonseca, "Wiriyamu, Rome's Duty," *Sunday Times*, August 12, 1973, 13.
[36] The reference to political neutrality is taken from Pedro Ramos Brandão, *A Igreja Católica e o Estado Novo em Moçambique, 1960/1974* (Lisbon: Editorial Notícias, 2004), 176.
[37] Buendia, interview, 1994 and 1995.
[38] Father Joseph, interview, 1994 and 1995.
[39] Ferrão, interview, 1995.

Foreign missionaries inside Mozambique pondered whether to respond to Portugal's armed conduct from within the walls of the Church or resort to outside agencies. Tete's missionaries discussed this issue extensively among themselves.[40] The real problem here was that up until 1971, missionaries had not presented the hierarchy with eyewitness accounts systematically documenting mass violence—in part, because none were to be had, unless one considered texts by FRELIMO, which lacked independent verification.[41] Until such an account presented itself, the hierarchy's silence supported the contention that some human rights abuses were inevitable given the dynamics of counter-insurgency in Tete. That was the Tete bishop's view according to several informants, and the view of the Archbishop in Lourenço Marques who had drafted a succinct memorandum of guiding principles for State–Church relations to be followed by priests and missionaries. The hierarchy therefore deserved the benefit of the doubt in the meantime, argued a priestly minority at the Bishops' conference in Beira.[42]

The Mucumbura massacres, however, removed that doubt, somewhat painfully.

The Burgos priests and the massacre at Mucumbura

The Mucumbura massacre is well documented. Its genesis as a narrative began almost immediately after the first phase of the killings on April 27, 1971. The massacres themselves lasted until the first week of November, during which Valverde de Lion and Hernandez Robles penned four texts on what they and others had seen. The first such text was a letter by Valverde de Lion to Padre Castellá. "You cannot imagine what we have been through and seen," he said.[43] By late June to early July, the letter was fleshed out "in a second edition" to incorporate additional details as the massacres evolved. The White Fathers were the principal handlers of this edition. How they acquired the report given their expulsion in May remains a mystery—Valverde de Lion could not be reached to clarify it. Father Cesare Bertulli, Regional Superior of the White Fathers' Congregation in Mozambique, used it subsequently to inform the text of his statement on the colonial conflict in an Italian newspaper, *La Veritas*. Someone in the White Fathers' congregation sent a copy of this same second edition to a sister congregation of missionaries in Tanzania, who forwarded a copy to FRELIMO, which published it in a redacted format in its regular bulletin on September 30. FRELIMO's information and propaganda office then forwarded a copy of the same as a press release to the local *Standard* newspaper, which published the text in its entirety.[44]

---

[40] Buendia, interview, 1994 and 1995.
[41] Father Joseph, interview, 1994 and 1995. Texts on collective mass violence authored by FRELIMO were by definition tainted as politically motivated to advance the liberation narrative.
[42] Buendia, interview, 1994 and 1995.
[43] As recollected by Padre Castellá. See also Brandão, *A Igreja Católica*.
[44] "The White Fathers' Testimony," *Mozambique Revolution*, 48 (July–September 1971): 21–22; and *Standard of Tanzania*, September 20, 1971, quoted in "Portugal's Rule by Violence Exposed: Massacre in Mozambique," *ACOA Fact Sheet* (August 1973): 3–4. See also "Priests 'give details of massacre,'" *The Catholic Herald*, October 8, 1971.

In early November, the report, which began as a personal letter underwent its fourth iteration. This time it was framed in the context of human rights violation, bearing the title "Mucumbura 1971 and Human Rights Recognized by Portugal at the United Nations,"[45] and was backed with supporting evidence drawn from eyewitnesses.

While the details of the massacre are covered thoroughly elsewhere,[46] some of these deserve repeating here on two grounds: one to underscore that the massacre was not, as Tete's military governor Rocha Simões suggested,[47] an aberration, nor was it an unauthorized undertaking by a rogue police agent, as the PIDE/DGS archives indicate.[48] Rather, this was how Portugal conducted its counter-insurgency in Africa, as a norm, which entailed widespread use of mass violence in Portugal's colonial Africa—as eyewitness accounts elsewhere attest.[49]

One further reason to repeat the details here is to highlight how those working on Wiriyamu emulated the methodology used to produce the Mucumbura report. These included ways to collect data; verify the provenance of primary and secondary sources; record Portuguese methods of torture; and catalog enhanced killing methods to execute swift clean-ups of FRELIMO-influenced zones.

PIDE archives suggest the Portuguese had a network of informants embedded in Mucumbura, among whom was Buxo a well-placed chief at Mucumbura's social apex mentioned earlier in this text.[50] He and his social network of informants supplied FRELIMO-related information. As long as he remained in power, FRELIMO was open to lightening strikes from both the colonial army in the northeast and the Rhodesian forces crossing the border in the south. On April 27, 1971, FRELIMO commanders eliminated Buxo as we noted earlier,[51] inviting the Portuguese authorities to replace him with Guse, an even more pliant chief, overtly pro-Portuguese. FRELIMO beheaded him too. With southern Mucumbura cleared of Portuguese intelligence by proxy in this way, FRELIMO mined roads near the southern border to obstruct Rhodesian units from aiding Portuguese counter-insurgency. One such set of mines exploded, killing three Rhodesian soldiers and wounding several.[52]

These two episodes set off systematic reprisals which began on May 4, 1971, when following an extended interrogation session several villagers acknowledged having seen FRELIMO in the areas where they lived. Two, however, came forward with specifics. One admitted he had a son in FRELIMO and the other confessed he knew a certain Aroni had a nephew among the "*turras.*" Once apprehended and tortured,

---

[45] Alfonso Valverde de Lion and Martin Hernandez Robles, "Mucumbura 1971 and Human Rights Recognized by Portugal at the United Nations," Mss. Father Hastings Personal Archives. A copy of the same text appears as Adrian Hastings, "Wiriyamu: Mucumbura 1971 by Alfonso Valverde de Lion and Martin Hernandez" in the Borthwick Institute for Archives, University of York, Adrian Hastings Collection. Hastings, *Wiriyamu,* 31–47 reproduces a revised version in English translation.
[46] Hastings, *Wiriyamu,* 32.
[47] ibid.
[48] PT/TT/PIDE/D-F/001/00023, August 22, 1973.
[49] Lucinda Canelas and Isabel Salema, "Relatório militar revela que tropas portuguesa participaram decapitações," *Público,* December 18, 2012, 4–7; and Isabel Salema, "O império colonial em questão?," *Público,* December 16, 2012, 8–9.
[50] The Bibliography lists several situational reports in the PIDE archives for the period of 1970–1973.
[51] General Hama Tai, interview, 1994 and 1995.
[52] Ferrando, interview, 1995; and Alfonso Valverde de Lion, interview by author, Madrid, 1995.

Aroni confessed to the "crime," and was promptly shot dead. As he was hastily buried in a shallow grave, his three wives returned to the abandoned village to retrieve his body and give him a proper burial. Halfway through the disinterment, they fled again, upon being informed that a colonial unit, accompanied by DGS agents, was on its way to eliminate the entire village.[53]

Portuguese troops accompanied by the DGS then swooped on that and three other villages, Catacha, Kapinga and Mahanda. Fourteen people died following torture in that operation in the first two villages, and seven more had perished in a similar operation in Mahanda.[54] Having eliminated what they considered FRELIMO collaborators, the same colonial unit spread out to the north and targeted António, a known FRELIMO stronghold. FRELIMO attacks interrupted the final stages of the mission, forcing the Portuguese unit to abandon four victims.[55] One had died of three bullet wounds to the head, one from a bullet to the chest, and the third from an exploding blast close to the face. The fourth victim had been disemboweled. "We shall never forget the terrible scene."[56]

Conescence, Aroni's daughter, gave a lengthier account of this event two years after the death of her own father in this operation:

> The Portuguese came to the shamba where my father was cultivating, and by the time I took notice they had encircled him. They approached my mother and me and told us: "we are taking Aroni and he will not come back. You will never hear him again." They tied my father's hands and took him away in a car. My mother tried to follow on foot, but was left behind. Then she ran to the PIDE office, but they refused to let her in and she came back home. Later we learned that my father had been killed. We were told details. The Portuguese asked him: "Do you know why we are going to kill you?" He said he did not, and they told him: "we are going to kill you because your sons went to FRELIMO. He is a FRELIMO official. FRELIMO is killing us so we are going to kill you." My father answered: "you may kill me. My life is nothing—and my son is where he must be. Yes, it is true that he went to FRELIMO." The Portuguese gave my father a shovel and told him to dig a hole. He dug for a while and asked if it was enough. They told him to try to get into the hole. He got in. The Portuguese officer aimed at him but the gun got stuck. It fired on the second attempt. My father died immediately . . .[57]

The news of Aroni's death reached Valverde de Lion and Hernandez Robles three days later, on Friday, May 7. Aroni was well known and liked at the mission and a faithful parishioner. They dashed to retrieve his badly decomposed body lying in the middle of the hut, risking getting caught in crossfire perilously near between FRELIMO and its opponents. "We gave him a decent burial."

[53] "After the Massacre of Mukumbura: A Victim's Relatives Join the Struggle," *Mozambique Revolution*, 50 (1972): 8–9.
[54] The seven killed at Mahanda were: Chimuchamo, Ringuinoti, Pensura, Wacheni, Joane, Gomo, and Saimoni.
[55] Chief Januario, Cheredzera, Kaswaswaira, and Chirega.
[56] Ferrando, interview, 1995; Valverde, interview, 1995.
[57] *Mozambique Revolution*, 50 (1972): 8–9.

Valverde de Lion and Hernandez Robles found out about the António killings on Sunday May 9, as they waited for parishioners to arrive for mass. Not a soul stirred in António. A goatherd eventually appeared at the chapel to inform them of the killings and the subsequent exodus. Valverde de Lion went back to pick up some sheets and returned to bury the dead. He watched sorrowfully, he said, as the region emptied of people from António, Mahanda, Kapinga, Catacha, and Daque. Goats, gazelles, and rodents preyed on abandoned harvests. "We have to do something about this," he said repeatedly to himself. Without people in and around Mucumbura, they might as well pack up and go home. Perhaps they could help the colonial army and the DGS better understand the plight of the people of Mucumbura and propel them to ease off on the overwhelming use of terror to combat FRELIMO. They talked to the DGS, whose combative responses derailed their attempt at reconciliation. The local colonial unit, on the other hand, simply denied having interrogated parishioners as suspects.

In the face of these denials, Valverde de Lion and Hernandez Robles sought to compile systematic evidence. They were cautious about accepting at face value unconfirmed reports and sought eyewitnesses to the killings at Catacha, Kapinga, and Mahanda. Four came forward. One was a survivor who, having been forced to dig a communal shallow grave for the fourteen dead, managed to escape at three in the morning. He supplied the names of five or six victims whom he knew personally from the first two villages. The others he did not know by name. The people in the village of Mahanda who had escaped the carnage identified the others.[58] As for the names of the dead at Mahanda, the priests were told to connect with the wife of a victim named Ensure who, once in contact, identified them. Her evidence was corroborated by a returnee from Salisbury who happened to be in the village but who was later released unharmed as he managed to convince his interrogators that he did not know FRELIMO's whereabouts as he had just arrived from Rhodesia.

To ensure the veracity of eyewitness reports, Valverde de Lion and Hernandez Robles took a survivor to verify the burial site near the margins of the River Daque. "Some twenty feet from the grave we found a human head with hardly any flesh on the bones, ribs, legs and parts of the hands.... some ... had not been shot to death but beaten, tortured and cut up. He (the survivor) showed us big sticks thick with blood with which the victims must have been beaten." He knew then that he had incontrovertible proof to confront the DGS chief, who had earlier denied ever having visited Mahanda, let alone Kapinga and Catacha. Valverde de Lion pointed out that he had seen empty tins of army rations strewn near the skull. The DGS chief shrugged off Valverde de Lion's evidence as fiction. He was told to stay away from politics.

In the meantime, Father Hernandez Robles and a member of staff went to see Tete's bishop in an attempt to resolve "*los últimos problemas de Mucumbura.*"[59] The bishop would not come out to publicly oppose the killings. He was, though, willing to raise the

---

[58] The fourteen dead were: Guidibo, Miriamo, Grizi, Zeze, Kenia, Caropora, Fungurani, Pitroce, Maizi, Kenete, Matias, Diquissoni, Languisse, and Jona.
[59] Letter, Padre Alfonso Valverde de Lion to Padre Alberto Font Castellá.

matter with Tete's military, which sent an officer from the army's department of military justice to investigate. He arrived on June 7, 1971. During a private meeting, the Burgos Fathers laid out their evidence backed by eyewitness accounts supported with data collected during the personal visits to the burial site.

"Well," said the officer, "if you Fathers only reached the scene of death the following day, I can no longer believe what you tell me." "Your information comes from the blacks and by nature they are deceitful and full of lies." In other words, unless Valverde de Lion and Hernandez Robles had evidence from a non-black, the officer would be returning to Nampula empty-handed and with no reason to press charges. Besides, he added, the killings could well have been the work of FRELIMO to "harm us and to destroy the prestige of the Portuguese army ..." It had happened before at Buxo and elsewhere, suggested the officer.[60] Valverde de Lion and Hernandez Robles replied they could easily dismiss that contention. Why didn't the officer accompany them to visit the burial site to see for himself the forensic truth behind the killings? The officer, however, was satisfied with the inquest he had undertaken by speaking with the two priests and would be returning to Nampula with nothing significant to report.[61]

As a parting shot, he advised the priests to stick to preaching the Gospel to "these wretches." Really, "they are no brothers. You know very well that there are still tribes of savages among the blacks." He knew the situation well in these parts of Africa. After all, he too was like them, the priests that is, a civilized, practising Christian and fully conversant with the teachings of the Bible. After his return, Valverde de Lion and Hernandez Roble informed Tete's bishop and governor of the meeting with the officer and received in return renewed assurances that the leading perpetrators would be dealt with. They never were. Instead, the DGS and military officers in charge were relocated, and in one case promoted to a higher salary and rank.[62]

It was clear to Valverde de Lion and Hernandez Robles that the Tete bishopric had shifted its position. While continuing to silently support the state,[63] it was now willing to work behind the scenes with the Portuguese military to raise matters afflicting the missionaries. The DGS, as quoted by Brandão's study, had a different take on him. They thought Ribeiro a value-neutral prelate, supportive of neither the radicalized clergy below him nor the Portuguese military police complex in Tete.[64] The position of the Portuguese army on mass violence, remained as entrenched as before, as a political imperative threatening unbridled counter-insurgency, and not as a serious violation of human rights under war conditions. In the meantime, Portuguese operational forces would continue as before to view data from blacks as inherently flawed. What about photographs? Would these constitute third-party evidence sufficiently robust for the empire's judicial process?

---

[60] Ferrando, interview, 1995; and Valverde, interview, 1995.
[61] ibid.
[62] ibid.
[63] Ferrando, interview, 1995; and Ferrão, interview, 1995.
[64] See Brandão, *A Igreja Católica*.

Portuguese reprisals

A month after the officer's departure, Mucumbura saw its third bout of reprisals. FRELIMO guerrillas had crossed the border to kidnap Chief Bauren, a Rhodesian informant who had consistently betrayed FRELIMO positions with information garnered through his extensive social networks on both sides of the frontier. They failed to nab him. Alerted by his informants, Bauren had escaped, leaving his possessions behind, from which FRELIMO guerrillas took an item of value as their calling card. In the eyes of FRELIMO, he was a marked man and his Rhodesian protectors knew what to do next. They launched two operations, one to look for an "informant" who had betrayed Bauren's role in Rhodesian counter-insurgent intelligence, who was subsequently found, killed, his feet and hands cut off. He had been left on a hillock near Deveteve as a deterrent to others from his village.

The Christian community in the village rallied to give him a proper burial with the Burgos priests in attendance, who then found the perpetrators after a brief search. Confronting them with the facts, the priests stressed that the deceased, named David, was an upstanding member of the local community, married with four children, and came from a long family of community-minded civic leaders, and decidedly not a FRELIMO member or politically connected with Rhodesian insurgents.[65] "A very unfortunate thing, Father. Sorry, we thought he was a terrorist."[66]

Five days later, another unit of Rhodesian troops, having committed a similar error of judgment in Singe, attempted a cover-up by burning the bodies of eight civilian victims.[67] Villagers found the charred remains the next day and informed Valverde de Lion and Hernandez Robles. This time, they took a camera to the site guided by two children who had dodged bullets during the crossfire. They found the remains which they photographed and sent to the bishop of Tete. Would the bishop now do something about this? An officer arrived two days later at the mission demanding the Burgos hand over any additional photographs in their possession. "We informed him that we had already given everything we had to the bishop in Tete," who unbeknown to them had already sent the film to Lourenço Marques to be developed. Tete's bishop, who was duly informed of the meeting with the military, now feared he would not get back the offending images, which the Burgos had hoped could be used as admissible evidence to initiate legal proceedings over mass violence in Mucumbura.[68]

Now that the evidence was presumed to be in the hands of the secret police, it was fair to assume that the two priests were persons of great interest to the authorities.[69] It was only a matter of time before they, too, were hauled in for interrogation. Almost immediately after this incident, thirty-one Tete missionaries met to draft a note urging

---

[65] "After the Massacre of Mukumbura," 8–9.
[66] ibid.
[67] The victims were: the chief of Singa, his ten-year-old son, his married and pregnant daughter Ronica, his three daughters-in-law, namely, Matiguiri, Rotina, and Ester, and two babies, one the son of Matiguiti and the other of Ester.
[68] Ferrando, interview, 1995; and Valverde, interview, 1995.
[69] PT/TT/PIDE/D-F/001/00013, December 1, 1972. See also Brandão, *A Igreja Católica*.

Tete's bishop to speak up against mass violence; it was signed by thirty-six named priests and delivered on July 1, 1972.

In the meantime, the Burgos of Mucumbura watched helplessly as their mission unraveled before their eyes. "We had to speak for them . . . Many were our parishioners. Some we knew as fathers and mothers. We had baptized some at the mission. We had shared hours and hours with them, listening to them, helping them achieve something of value in life. They were here one day and gone the next. It was painful. It was '*doloroso*'—sad."[70]

Thereafter, the pace of military operations accelerated towards a terminal crescendo. By November, the joint DGS–military action had successfully targeted six specific villages believed to be FRELIMO strongholds, five of which were around Mucumbura and one located near the Estima Catholic mission.[71] Valverde de Lion and Hernandez Robles once again compiled a list of the dead, and where appropriate, annotating qualitative data to illustrate methods used in deploying mass violence, with supporting evidence where available.[72]

On Tuesday, November 2, 1971, an officer arrived at the Mucumbura mission to inform the priests that the civil and military authorities of the colony planned to clean up Buxo. "Now is the time to burn and exterminate that area." Thus began the fourth and final phase of the Mucumbura massacres. Two days later, helicopter-borne troops descended, wiping out everything between Mahanda and António. Valverde de Lion and Hernandez Robles witnessed, "more than fifty huts burn. Among them were our schools in António and the house of the teacher."[73] On that Saturday, the two priests assessed the carnage. They could not determine the exact death toll beyond the Buxo and António villages. To this day, what transpired there remains a mystery, as does the final death toll.[74]

On their visits to bury the dead, eyewitness accounts suggested a tiered killing spree, entailing the use of grenades to save bullets, followed by destruction of livestock and food granaries. In Buxo, the killings centered on two huts. In one, sixteen women and children were found dead, burned alive with grenades acting as incendiary devices thrown in the hut with all its doors slammed shut from the outside. The other hut contained the charred remains of three, of which only one could be identified.[75] One

---

[70] Enrique Ferrando, interview by author, Madrid, 1995; and Valverde, interview, 1995.
[71] The villages were: Guvanseve, Kampemberumbe, Karuvi, Traquino, Chicoa and Mague. Traquino was in the Estima mission. Chicoa and Mague suffered the most in terms of torture. Eleven suspects were apprehended and taken to the DGS prison for information retrieval using torture. They were Nejamin, a teacher at Baque, Linguitoni, Guidini, Kesissi, Andresoni, Bande, Kapemberumbe, Romeo, Chibunza, Baira and Masasa.
[72] The list of the dead included: Damian Gonga, Asami, Chabwedzeka, Bikico, Tauseni, Petro, Raice, Sami, Waite, Macaju, Chasica, Mabanda, Tadeo, Lingirani, Bicause, Tembo, Majana and Chamana. Damian Gonga was a school teacher. The DGS found on him a letter from one of the guerrillas. He was tortured in front of his pregnant wife and two very young children. He died at four in the afternoon of torture wounds. Evidence was provided by his wife. Majana was burned alive in her hut by a grenade.
[73] Hastings, *Wiriyamu*, 43–46.
[74] Hastings, *Wiriyamu*, 45.
[75] He was an old man of seventy, named Haidi, according to an informant.

woman who had escaped with half a shoulder missing gave the priests the names of ten victims in the first hut. Some of them were children as young as seven months old, and the rest were all women; one happened to be the widow of the late chief Buxo.[76]

Areas in and near António exhibited a similar carnage. Given the area as a FRELIMO stronghold, its cadres from a nearby base helped the two priests bury the dead, one a child of two or three, and two identified as ex-prisoners taken earlier for questioning at the local DGS office.[77]

The clean-up put an end to Mucumbura as a viable Catholic mission—Valverde de Lion and Hernandez Robles' *raison d'être* to be in the area ceased. Rather than give up, they tried one more time to put a stop to the killings by penning their fourth and final report "without any commentary," recording the deaths of eighty-one fully identified African villagers killed over a period of seven months between April and November 1971. This report attested to torture, flaying, death by dismemberment, vengeful killing, lynching, unbridled bigotry leading to death, and death by burning. "I got onto my motor-bike and travelled 700 kilometers (435 miles) to Tete . . . arrived and gave the report to the Bishop. He read it . . . and said: 'I am going to the governor immediately'. . . We both were interviewed by Governor Rocha Simões."

The bishop had also spoken to the governor on the previous day, and he read the report and said: "Father, if you say these things happened, I believe you, because we are having problems with the commandos here in the outskirts of Tete" . . . "Governor," I said, "we are tired of pretty words . . . I can no longer believe in pretty words . . . and Governor, excuse me. I must say what I think. After four massacres I have had enough and I am persuaded to tell the truth, that the most natural place for a Christian in these times is prison." "Calm down, Father, we'll see what we can do."[78] With that assurance from the governor, the meeting ended. On their part, the two priests left the bishop and the governor with a not-so-veiled threat of what they were likely to do next—seek help to end the bloodshed, from outside the Church if necessary.

They returned to the mission convinced more than ever that what they had witnessed was "only the beginning of an unending chain of injustices," the governor's assurances notwithstanding—and in that, they were proved right. Soon after the Mucumbura massacres, the colonial army began a similar clean-up of Marara, 64.5 miles northwest of Wiriyamu on the way to the Cahora Bassa dam. A Portuguese priest, Padre Luís Afonso da Costa, belonging to a congregation for missionary work in Africa established in 1867 by Daniele Comboni, Central Africa's first bishop, followed Valverde de Lion and Hernandez Robles' methodology to produce a similar record of victims of this clean-up, which was to last nearly five months, until May 1972. With Marara cleaned of suspected FRELIMO activists, the colonial army headed northeast towards Wiriyamu before moving southbound in the direction of Inhaminga, both

---

[76] For the record, the ten identified as dead were: Helena, widow of Buxo; her ten-year-old daughter, Margareta, aged eight; Maria, seven months old; Dzudzay, a twenty-year-old married woman; Rorosi, a two-year-old child; Majozi, a sixty-five-year old woman; Rute Chidekinde, a married woman; Kufa, the year-old daughter of Rute Chidekinde; and Massa, a seven-month-old baby.

[77] Their remains were identified as Julay and his nephew. Hastings, *Wiriyamu*, 44–47.

[78] Untitled typed transcript. Hastings' private papers, later reproduced with minor modifications in Hastings, *Wiriyamu*, 45.

sites of separate massacres, of which Wiriyamu came to occupy a central place in the annals of Portugal's imperial infamy.

In the meantime, Valverde de Lion and Hernandez Robles waited one last time for the hierarchy to make a public stand on the killings. Why are they so "scared to talk about all this in the Synod?" they asked. "We have sent all these reports to all the dioceses and to the Archbishop in Lourenço Marques. Why do they continue gagging us?"[79] It was time for action, they wrote. "We are grown men. They can't gag us. We must speak and risk all. We must obey God before men."[80]

This time, they tried to see if Tete priests could force a debate in the Synod. On November 28, Valverde de Lion, Hernandez Robles and three sisters at Mucumbura signed the report they had prepared before sending several copies to members of the Presbyteral Council in Tete. "Let us discuss it at our meeting," for January 11, 1972. Among the recipients was Father Jesus Camba.[81] The DGS on the alert rounded up sixteen missionary personnel for questioning.[82] Included among them was Camba who was frisked and found to have several copies of the report, which he had a right to have since he was to lead the discussion at the Synod. By then, a copy of the said document was already on its way to Madrid intended for publication in the Spanish press. In the meantime, Valverde de Lion and Hernandez Robles had crossed the border with a signed copy of the report in their pockets. They were headed to visit fellow priests at a nearby mission. It was New Year's Eve. Presumably alerted by the DGS, the Rhodesian police apprehended them, according to Hastings, on January 2, 1972,[83] took them to Salisbury for preliminary interrogation and then handed them over to the DGS, who shipped them to Tete's Matundo airport, to be transferred to Lourenço Marques's Machava prison.

That very week, three clerical pronouncements rattled Lisbon's political timbers. The first came from the metropolitan bishops who published a pastoral letter on the anniversary of "Pacem in Terris" encyclical, openly defending a litany of causes: basic human rights, political and social participation, pluralism, fairness in the political process, civic citizenship, and peace and justice.[84] Their message to the regime was clear. The Portuguese Church was calling for Portugal to realign to match the new Vatican II teachings.

Taking a similar cue, to celebrate World Peace Day, Father Joaquim Teles Sampaio in charge of Macúti Parish in Beira, and his curate Fernando Mendes, both Portuguese born, openly opposed the war from the pulpit, denouncing the massacres as inhumane

---

[79] Hastings, *Wiriyamu*, 45.
[80] ibid.
[81] Berenguer, interview, 1994 and 1995; Ferrando, interview, 1995; and Valverde, interview, 1995.
[82] They were: Manuel dos Anjos Martins, José Villa Lobo, Luis Afonso da Costa, Leonel Bettini, Renato Rosanelli, Domingo Camano, and Valentin Benigna of the Verona Congregation. Among the Burgos targeted for questioning were Padre Berenguer, Padre Mateus Carbonell, Padre Martin Hernandez Robles, and Padre Afonso Valverde de Lion. Padre Domingo Ferrão was alone among the diocesan priests in Tete. Sisters selected for questioning included Maria D. Vasquez Rodriguez, Maria Cemades Prada Rodrigues, and Maria Gaudenzia M. Talma. Data culled from several oral sources: Father Adrian Hastings, Miguel Buendia, Padre Domingo Ferrão, Padre Vicente Berenguer, and Padre José Sangalo.
[83] Hastings, *Wiriyamu*, 33.
[84] Manuel Braga da Cruz, "A Igreja na transição democrática portuguesa" *Lusitania Sacra: Revista do cengtro de estudos de história religiosa* viii/ix, 2 (1996/1997): 519–537.

and a basic violation of human dignity. In doing so, they had come out in clear support of their colleagues Valverde de Lion and Hernandez Robles, now languishing in solitary confinement awaiting trial, where they stayed for nearly twenty-three months, until November 16, 1973. Amnestied on that day, they were escorted to a plane bound for Spain.[85] Sampaio and Mendes on the other hand, had gone to trial in a military court eleven months earlier. Their court proceedings proved remarkably fair, with the now former bishop of Tete testifying for the defense, which eventually held sway in court. Both priests were given minor sentences and ordered to leave the colony immediately. They flew home to Portugal.[86]

In early February, forty priests from Tete urged the apostolic nuncio in Lisbon to help them put a stop to incarcerations and arrests of priests, before such measures of the Portuguese State unraveled the Church itself.[87]

> The Church is subordinate to the interests of the State; conditions are imposed and accepted which make it impossible to spread the Gospel courageously and realistically—and also to denounce the injustices committed against a people to whom human rights are, in practice, denied. If there is not, without delay, a grasp of the position ... on the part of the ecclesiastical institutions, we foresee grave consequences for the church itself.

Mucumbura priests are sent to prison

In apprehending the four priests, Portugal had breached a sacrosanct wall separating Church and State, bringing ecclesiastical discontent to a boil. In essence, Lisbon had signaled its hierarchy that it would no longer consider the Church immune from prosecution should it fail to rein in recalcitrants, or should priests and, for that matter, even prelates threaten what it considered the security of the State. To drive the point home, Lisbon mounted a smear campaign in print and film media against Tete's new bishop and the Burgos.[88]

In the face of this threat, the Church turned openly defiant. At the January 11 meeting, Tete's Presbyteral Council unanimously appointed Father da Costa to publicize widely what was happening in Tete.[89] With that choice for a spokesman, the Church below the prelates turned overtly political.

Da Costa began his assigned mission with an open letter to Caetano documenting the massacres at Mucumbura and Marara. Two papers then published this letter, one Spanish and the other French. We do not know how the Spanish journal *Vida Nueva* got hold of it. Their timing was unfortunate as it coincided with Valverde de Lion's and

---

[85] Ferrando, interview, 1995; Alfonso Valverde de Lion, interview by author, Madrid, 1995; and Buendia, interview, 1994 and 1995.
[86] "Mozambique: Translation of the trial report on the 'Macúti Fathers,'" *Archives of the International Secretariat of Amnesty International*, Inventory No. 442–446, File, 1531/51, AI Index, AFR 41/73.
[87] "Secret Plan to Protect 'Massacre' Survivors," *Sunday Times*, August 12, 1973, 7.
[88] Buendia, interview, 1994 and 1995.
[89] PT/TT/D-F/001/00002, January 1, 1971.

Hernandez Robles' incarceration under solitary confinement at the Machava prison. The French publication appeared in the Paris-based *Jeune Afrique*, which ran the story on January 22, 1972. By the end of January, the DGS, fearing an increase in this type of international publicity, informed Tete's bishop of their intention to apprehend priests threating the security of "the Portuguese nation." They identified da Costa to be at the top of the list. Da Costa had two choices, voluntary exile, or stay and desist from "engaging in politics."[90] In the meantime, Ferrando, Valverde de Lion and Hernandez Robles' temporary replacement at Mucumbura was prohibited from traveling east of Mucumbura, putting paid to parish work in the region. A similar order was issued to Father Renato Rosanelli of the Estima mission in the Chicoa region.[91] Later that month, the bishop of Tete had to decide on the future of the Mucumbara mission. He saw no point in continuing to operate it under such draconian conditions and ordered it to be closed for good, with instructions for the priests to hand over the keys to the mission to the local fiscal authorities.[92]

One prelate had quietly watched this drama unfold, Bishop Vieira. He had followed two sets of events, the massacres at Mucumbura and the escalation of mass violence in another area, Zóbuè and Capiri Janje, both of which deeply troubled him, as did the position that his colleagues and his superior, the colony's cardinal, had taken on Portugal's war.[93] Although Vieira had signed the letter drafted by the hierarchy critical of the White Fathers' decision to quit Mozambique, he became openly critical subsequently of the unhealthy relationship that had developed between the Church and the Portuguese State. He voiced his sentiments on the matter and more openly soon after the Portuguese coup, in this way:

> The Church has been in active collaboration with the colonial regime in that it has helped to spread Portuguese culture, has publicly associated itself with colonial leaders, and has preached a gospel of docile obedience to authority. It has also collaborated passively in that it has allowed itself to be used by the colonial power. It has tolerated the repression practiced by the regime, and from fear of prudence has been silent about the crimes and injustices of colonialism—particularly the war of repression and the reprisals which violated the fundamental rights of the people of Mozambique.[94]

Vieira added: "We prefer a Church that is persecuted but alive to a Church that is generously subsidized but at the price of damaging connivance at the behavior of the temporal powers."[95]

---

[90] Berenguer, interview, 1994 and 1995; Ferrando, interview, 1995; and Valverde, interview, 1995.
[91] Ferrando, interview, 1995.
[92] PT/TT/PIDE/D-F/001/00013, December 1, 1972, and, PT/TT/PIDE/D-F/001/00014, January 18, 1973.
[93] Cesar Bertulli, *Croce e Spada in Mozambico* (Rome: Coines, 1974).
[94] Bishop Manuel Pinto Vieira, quoted in Piero Gheddo, "A New Church is Born," *Biblical Studies*, accessed December 26, 2013, http://www.biblicalstudies.org.uk/pdf/rcl/10-2_156.pdf.
[95] Thomas C. Bruneau, "Church and State in Portugal: Crisis of Cross and Sword," *Journal of Church and State*, 18, 3 (1976): 481–491.

Vieira saw no alternative but to openly defy his superiors and the State. During a bilateral meeting with da Costa he encouraged him to get out of Mozambique, head to Europe, and publicize the massacres documented by the priests in Tete. *"Fale, denuncie, diga ao mundo o que se está a passar aqui!!!"*—"Speak up, denounce, tell the world what is happening here!" And Padre da Costa did just that![96] He went into exile. On his way out, he took with him data on the massacres, which the DGS failed to detect as he boarded the plane, enabling him subsequently to use it to pen a tightly woven document for a Catholic paper in Rome, which subsequently published it in May 1972. The first half of this Italian document retold the Valverde de Lion/Hernandez Robles story, chronologically arranging it as a list of the dead at Mucumbura and Marara. The second half provided details of human right abuses inflicted on Portuguese and foreign-born missionaries critical of the Portuguese colonial war in Mozambique.[97]

Da Costa's revelations failed to mitigate the use of mass violence in Portugal's war in Tete. If anything, it led to an increase in incarceration of dissident priests, a practice that continued for the remaining years of Caetanist Portugal. Recalcitrant white prelates and white foreign missionaries however, were dealt differently; they were exiled or expelled. Neither measure proved effective. On the contrary, it incendiated the Church's opposition to mass violence, which then gathered momentum after 1972, leading to more arrests and protests. By June 1972, colonial authorities had rounded up two hundred black Presbyterian, Congregationalist, Wesleyan, Adventist and Pentecostal Church leaders for allegedly inciting unrest. They were all sent to Machava, where they fared worse than their four white brethren languishing in the same prison. The arrest of the Presbyterian Synod president, Zedequias Manganhela, followed suit and proved most tragic. His stay in Machava was cut short six months after his arrival at the prison when he was found hung in his cell under mysterious circumstances.

The following year, Lisbon witnessed perhaps the most dramatic episode of resistance against the colonial wars, culminating in the arrest of two priests on the premises of Capela do Rato itself, a chapel of some fame in Lisbon.[98]

A month before Manganhela's untimely death, and five days before the Wiriyamu massacre, Angolan bishops joined the chorus. In a pastoral letter drafted after their Episcopal Conference, December 11, 1972, they reminded Lisbon of how they viewed the Church as something more than an instrument of State. Their understanding was that the Church did "not encourage a peace based on the dominion of one class over another, but a peace based on justice and consequently on a balanced distribution of goods and responsibilities, economic, social, political, without excluding any particular group."[99]

By then, the cerebrally inclined Bishop Vieira threw caution to the wind, openly engaging the state in a battle of wits over the Portuguese Church, which he viewed as

---

[96] Brandão, *A Igreja Católica*, 187.
[97] Hastings, interviews, 1977, 1978, 1979, 1981, 1995, 1996.
[98] João Miguel Almeida, *A oposição católica ao Estado Novo, 1958–1974* (Lisbon: Edições Nelson de Matos, 2008); Jorge Wemans, "Um grito contra a guerra," *Agencia Ecclesia*, accessed January 11, 2014, http://www.agencia.ecclesia.pt/cgi-bin/noticia.pl?id=8406, and Carlos Eduardo Machado Sangreman Proença and Francisco Salgado Zenha, *O Caso da Capela do Rato no Supremo Tribunal Administrativo* (Lisboa: Afrontamento, 1973), 1–98. See also Não apaguem a Memória!, accessed January 10, 2014, http://naoapaguemamemoria2.blogspot.com.
[99] "Angolan Bishops' Pastoral on Justice," *Catholic Herald*, November 3, 1972, 8.

ossified under the weight of a dated concordat. The Vatican had moved on since the days of Pius XXII, and so should Portugal's Church. In April 1974, Lisbon swooped down on Nampula and ejected him into exile, along with eleven Italian Verona Fathers under his care.[100]

Meanwhile, da Costa and the White Fathers' European publicity had not fared all that well—for a number of reasons. The revelations reached only small audiences among the converted. One set of the converted included subscribers of Church-related newspapers from Italy and Spain whose joint total readership comprised 80 million Catholics.[101] The other set was some 20,000 subscribers of the Tanzanian-based *Standard*, and readers of the London-based *Observer*.[102] Both sets of subscribers left out a swath of European readers, both secular and religious, uninformed of mass violence in Portugal's African colonies. In fact, from a strategic point of view, the revelations proved counter-productive in that they alerted Lisbon needlessly, thereby giving it time to prepare counter-measures. As we saw above, one such measure sent Bishop Vieira into pre-emptive exile, and another led to a mass expulsion of the Veronas under Vieira's pastoral care.

Further, the timeframe of the Mucumbura massacres suggested an extended period of "low-intensity mass violence" interspersed with short-lived killings, which Lisbon viewed as a counter-insurgency norm—at least, that is how Kaúlza de Arriaga viewed the casualties, "within the normal range of operations."[103] Each reprisal, cruel though it was, was a response to FRELIMO action or presence as detected by a network of local informants. This line of argument strengthened the position of the Portuguese apologists, weakening in the process "the human rights violation argument" of innocent civilians. Portugal therefore remained by and large "emotionally" untroubled by the revelations of its bloody conduct in Tete published in papers with limited circulation.[104]

The priests in Mozambique and those exiled in Spain discussed why their publicity campaign had failed to garner the attention of the broader public and how could they compel Portugal to publicly account for its violent conduct. Generally, we saw no way out said Padre Sangalo—not until two crucial changes occurred in Tete, one military and the other ecclesiastic.[105] Colonel Armindo Videira replaced Rocha Simões, as

---

[100] These observations benefited from discussions with José Capela, Father Adrian Hastings, and Miguel Buendia. See also Hastings, "Reflections," and Adrian Hastings, "Portugal's Other Rebellion," *The Observer*, April 21, 1974.
[101] *Nationmaster.com*, accessed January 2, 2014, http://www.nationmaster.com/index.php.
[102] In 1970, *The Standard* had a criculation of 20,000 readers. Martin Sturmer, *The Media History of Tanzania* (Ndanda Mission Press, 1998). "Tanzania: Government Takes Over 'The Standard' Newspaper," *ITN Source: Footage That Sets Your Story Apart*, accessed February 1, 2014. Circulation figures for *The Observer* for 1970 proved difficult to obtain. The history of that paper for the period suggests the paper's circulation was in decline in the face of aggressive marketing from two stables, *The Daily Telegraph* and the Roy Thompson-led *The Times*.
[103] Kaúlza de Arriaga in an interview with Michael Knipe, as quoted to the author by Knipe. Michael Knipe, interview by author, London, 1996.
[104] Hastings, interviews, 1977, 1978, 1979, 1981, 1995, 1996.
[105] Berenguer, interview, 1994 and 1995; Miguel Buendia, interview by author, Maputo, 1994 and 1995; Ferrando, interview, 1995; Alfonso Valverde de Lion, interview by author, Madrid, 1995; and Hastings, interviews, 1977, 1978, 1979, 1981, 1995, 1996.

military governor, and Dom Augusto Cesar Ferreira de Silva replaced Tete's founding bishop Félix Niza Ribeiro. With their respective installations, a new and final phase of mass violence was unleashed in Tete—Wiriyamu.

Wiriyamu was a massacre five times the size of Mucumbura, compressed into half a day with a three-day clean-up. It entailed deaths of innocent civilians, and a clearly defined and deliberately focused elimination of a triangle reputedly infested with FRELIMO. What Wiriyamu clearly lacked was a timely revelation with detailed evidence compelling Portugal to have to respond in real time. In other words, what was needed was for the material forces of history to dictate a course of events to reveal Wiriyamu. In the meantime, the work of constructing the Wiriyamu narrative began.

7

The Wiriyamu Narrative: Genesis and Revelation

The origins of the Wiriyamu story

The genesis of the Wiriyamu narrative began on the very night of December 16, 1972. That Saturday afternoon, two independent observers noticed Portuguese Air Force jets flying towards Wiriyamu. One observer in the triangle saw the actual bombardment: he neared the site after the jets left and hid behind reeds to witness the slaughter.[1]

The other observer was Padre Domingo Ferrão of Missão São Pedro. On that day, another seemingly unrelated event occurred. Domingo Kansande, a former student of Padre Vicente Berenguer, was on a mission—to visit the love of his life. She was expecting with his child. He knew abstinence was a requirement, and according to him, he had been expelled from the seminary for violating this rule. "What could I do? I was in love. But I wanted to be a teacher, a good one!" Kansande felt they had been harsh on him. Padre Ferrão saw him in a different light though, not as a disappointment but someone with a future as a teacher, perhaps a slightly tarnished character. Kansande was drawn closer to Padre Ferrão as his more charitably inclined mentor.[2]

Padre Ferrão was a trusted priest in the community. Bishop Resende had singled him out among his peers during his visit to the Tete diocese and encouraged him to study for the priesthood. Padre Ferrão, though, was an activist at heart and was promptly jailed for engaging in politics. Released from the notorious Machava correctional facility in the colonial capital, Lourenço Marques, he was allowed to return to Tete as a diocesan priest on one strict condition—eschew politics.

Prison changed him and his ministry. At face value, he stuck to his side of the bargain, devoting most of his spare time to produce a comprehensive lexicography of the Nyungwe, a language spoken in Chaworha and Wiriyamu. In reality, he transformed the ministry in Tete. "I could not engage in politics. That is not what priests do, I was told." "But I must help my people. Their suffering is mine. We have a culture and history here and I cannot let this culture and history disappear." "Yet I did not want to go to prison again," he added.

---

[1] He confirmed the massacre as an eyewitness to Peter Pringle who investigated the events.
[2] Domingo Kansande, interview by author, near Cantina Raul, 1995. Additional information provided by Padre Berenguer and Padre Sangalo.

Photo 3 Domingo Kansande, Cantina Raul, 1995

Missão São Pedro itself became a social and spiritual center for the local community in Tete, holding regular mass, and hosting weekly socials and dances on church premises. Weekend nights in Tete were filled with the sound of music and drumbeats. On hot and humid evenings, the occasional breeze would carry the music and the drumbeats in waves to soothe nearby villages enveloped in pitch darkness. "I was comforted by the sound of music from the dance halls. It would come and go like the Zambezi winds. It gave us hope and connected us to each other and to my brothers and sisters in other parts of Africa," said Karimu, a respondent interviewed at Wiriyamu.

These events proved ideal for FRELIMO activists to recruit new members, gather intelligence, and plan and execute insurgent attacks on the Portuguese military. The converse proved true. DGS agents also saw the socials as an opportunity to infiltrate FRELIMO, recruit informants among students, seminaries, and the Tete's youth swarming the dance floor.[3]

Kansande flourished under Padre Ferrão. "I liked him. I respected him. I believed in him. He was black and not like the white colonial Portuguese priests." Under him, Kansande developed a strong sense of self, as an individual as well as a member of a community committed to upholding its roots and heritage. Just before or at noon on

[3] Karimu, interview, 1995; and Ferrão, interview, 1995.

Photo 4 Padre Domingo Ferrão, Tete, 1995

December 16, 1972, Kansande left Tete's parish for the triangle, expecting to reach his destination just after sunset. He was looking forward to sharing a meal with his "*enamorada*" and her family and then head back the next day. For the first part of his journey, he hugged the dry creek and skirted around the DGS complex, crossing the road in the distance, to head south of the strategically fortified village of Mpharhamadwe. "Once I got there, I avoided the main road then and took the back way '*que os colonos não tinha [sic] conhecimento*'—unknown to the authorities."

By sunset, he had reached the southern perimeter of the triangle along the margins on the Zambezi, near the Luenha tributary. "The sun had gone down and that is when I met people I knew who had escaped the massacre. We talked and talked in the dark and asked each other who had died and who had escaped or might have escaped." As the number of dead increased, Kansande could not keep the tally in his head. "I had to make a list so I could remember who died and who was alive so we could tell them of the dead." "Yes on that night I used bits of butcher paper we kept for rolling cigarettes and a borrowed pencil to record the names of those killed. There was no light. We kept a fire going to help me write the list," said Kansande later, "(...) and we were so afraid to be caught and killed that night, by '*as tropas dos colonos*' the colonial soldiers."[4] "We watched each other's backs." In the end, they watched in silence as the fire died.

Elsewhere in the triangle, António Mixone and his brother had escaped a funeral pyre at Chaworha. "Mixone came to me completely agitated, talking, talking, talking breathlessly about guns, and bodies, and fire, and killings. He did not make any sense to me. Clearly the poor boy was traumatized," said Irmã Lúcia during the interview at her residence.[5] "Calm down and tell me slowly from the beginning. We cleaned his wounds and bandaged them and sent him to see Padre Ferrão. I sent many wounded and survivor victims to him on that day and the days that followed it." Irmã Lúcia had worked closely with Padre Ferrão during this period, occasionally donating medical supplies to him, "for what purpose, I did not wish to know. I was helping people who needed medical attention. That was my mission. The details of what he did with the supplies was his business. I was not interested."

By Sunday, reports began filtering in of people fleeing the triangle. Some reportedly headed towards Raimundo's FRELIMO base. That trickle came to an abrupt halt after FRELIMO placed draconian measures on movements of new refugees near its permanent and mobile base camps to foil enemy infiltration. "People had to go and visit relatives and they could not do now," said one informant.[6]

Some headed towards Changara, flooding the neighborhood near the mission, which was alerted of this influx during Sunday mass, when several students prayed aloud in unison for those who "had perished at Wiriyamu." It is uncertain if Padre Berenguer was at that prayer meeting, though he became aware of Wiriyamu on that Sunday as he rode the bus to Tete.[7] Bedraggled and destitute refugees clustered the bus stop at the Eighteenth Crossing on the main road that led to the triangle, all wanting to get away from the site. The bus driver insisted on charging the required fare. Several pleaded to be let on the bus, revealing what they had been through. Padre Berenguer witnessed the exchange and alerted fellow missionaries and priests once in Tete. "Something has got to be done about this," said Padre Berenguer to himself.[8]

Those fearing the presence of troops on the main road took the dirt tracks to Tete "to blend with others like us,"[9] meaning to be with friends and distant relatives claiming the latter's homes as their place of residence. A sizable portion of those who survived elected to be in Mpharhamadwe, which by the middle of that week was overflowing with people. Some sought refuge under makeshift shelters near baobab and tamarind trees dotting the periphery of the strategically fortified village. Mixone came to settle eventually under one such baobab perilously close to the main road before being taken away by Padre Sangalo to pre-empt his capture by the DGS.[10]

According to Kansande, he returned on late Sunday and sought out Padre Ferrão, who by then had "interviewed" several survivors from the hospital and the neighborhood

---

[4] Kansande, interview, 1995.
[5] Saez de Ugarte, interview, 1995.
[6] Zambezi, interview, 1995.
[7] "Mystery of priests' return from tour," *The Times*, August 17, 1974, 4.
[8] Berenguer, interview, 1994 and 1995.
[9] Kaniveti, interview, 1995.
[10] Ferrão, interview, 1995; Sangalo, interview, 1995.

near the mission to compile a list of the dead. Kansande gave Padre Ferrão his preliminary list, which covered only the dead for that day. Padre Ferrão subsequently expanded the list to include details of those killed during the three days that followed the initial carnage. To this end, he repeatedly sent Kansande into the Wiriyamu triangle, which was now the scene of an extensive manhunt for insurgents, specifically the chief of Wiriyamu and his family, who the Portuguese military considered responsible for welcoming FRELIMO in the triangle.

Using the Mucumbura report as a model, Padre Ferrão produced two lists of the dead to which qualitative data describing instances of mass violence were added. Together, they came to form the seeds for the two reports that were first published in Italy before it was eventually brought to London and aired in *The Times*.[11] The two reports, one on Chaworha and one on Wiriyamu, cataloged the names, ages, gender, marital status, and progeny of 178 killed—*not* 135, as previously recorded in an earlier text.[12] Neither Padre Ferrão nor Kansande exaggerated the near-definitive accuracy of the numbers of dead at Wiriyamu and its vicinity. "At times," said Kansande, "we knew who the person was who had been killed but we could not recall their names nor could we find the relatives to tell us the name."[13] Both knew the risk they were taking. Padre Ferrão in particular took great pains to protect his sources while keeping his records as transparent and as close to the truth as he could. "After all, I was a man of God, I had been tortured, and was terrified of going back to prison."[14]

The Chaworha report was concluded three days after the massacre on Tuesday, December 19, 1972, and included data from anonymous sources and five self-identified eyewitnesses, led by Mixone mentioned earlier.[15] In its first four paragraphs, the Chaworha report outlined, albeit impressionistically, the massacre. It then gave a detailed list of the names of forty-two men, women, girls, and boys killed, ending with short paragraphs proclaiming Chaworha a victim of a needless atrocity.[16]

"The purpose of the Chaworha list and the list on Wiriyamu was to produce a record of the dead," said Padre Ferrão. "*É pá. Era uma lista, só uma lista. Nada mais*" he said; "look, it was a list. Just a list. Nothing more. I was not interested in the history of what happened there. I wanted to name the people who died there. With such proof the Portuguese could not deny what they had done."[17] In other words, Padre Ferrão proved, quite understandably, uninterested in the narrative anatomy of the massacre at Chaworha on December 16, 1972. To undertake such a task would have required an on-site reconstruction with the aid of survivors and eyewitnesses, which at the time would have been well-nigh impossible for Padre Ferrão given the war conditions, and his mortal fear of being re-incarcerated.

---

[11] Hastings, interviews, 1977, 1978, 1979, 1981, 1995, 1996.
[12] Dhada, "The Wiriyamu Massacre of 1972."
[13] Kansande, interview, 1995.
[14] Ferrão, interview, 1995.
[15] Mixone, interview, 1995.
[16] Ferrão, interview, 1995.
[17] ibid.

Unlike the Chaworha text, Padre Ferrão's seven-page list of those killed at Wiriyamu used a much wider pool of informants. Completed on Saturday, January 6, twenty-one days after the event, it included data culled from several sources: the young seminarians and churchgoers who had alerted priests at Sunday mass on the 17th at the mission church in Changara;[18] villagers from several locations near Wiriyamu on the western banks of the Zambezi River contacted by Kansande; black and white soldiers who, horrified by the events, came forward with information on the killings; and survivors variously located in the triangle. Using the Mucumbura report as a model, the Wiriyamu report appeared as a list identifying the names, ages, gender, marital status, and progeny of 136 out of nearly 400 killed. Graphic details of atrocities interspersed the report, depicting an impromptu soccer match played with decapitated heads and head bashing against (what transpired later to be the nearby tamarind and baobab) trees. A pregnant woman was said to have been ripped open, while in another instance a child obediently sucked on a muzzle while a soldier pulled the trigger.

The first draft of the Wiriyamu report identified informants by name; these were later excised to protect them from reprisals. Padre Sangalo could not lay his hands on the first edition of this report for the purposes of verification for this narrative. "*Isto aconteceu á muintos anos atraz.*"[19] This happened long ago. I could not keep the list on me. I would have gone back to jail." He was under twenty-four-hour surveillance from secret police agents ensconced in a bunker-like structure across from his parish. He could not afford to go back to Machava prison. "I had a lot to do here in my parish." Padre Ferrão, however, reiterated that they had replaced the excised portion of the text identifying informants: "Despite difficulties—some of them imposed on us, others circumstantial—in drawing up a full list of the names of the victims of the massacre of the populations of Wiriyamu and Juwau, the sources of the detailed information we have collected give us the right to maintain the affirmation that more than 400 victims fell—probably around 500."[20]

Subsequently, twenty-six stenciled copies of the second edition of the report were produced. All the bishops in the colony received a copy, as did the heads of the various missionary congregations in the colony.

While the reports were being written into history, the newly appointed bishop of Tete was away on holiday. The Burgos priests in Tete briefed him on the massacre upon his return with a request to raise the matter with the Tete's military governor. "While we wait for a reply from him, the church should investigate," said the group to the bishop, recalls Padre Sangalo. The new bishop "*correu para ver o Governador* . . . dashed to see the Governor," who assured him the matter would receive appropriate attention. Unhappy with the results of the meeting, Dom Augusto de Silva raised his concerns during a legal briefing in Lourenço Marques with the lawyers handling the case of the incarcerated Macúti priests.

---

[18] Berenguer, interview, 1994 and 1995.
[19] Ferrão, interview, 1995.
[20] ibid.

At a stopover in Beira during a meeting of the Synod, he privately confided in Júlio Moure how unhappy he was about the situation, knowing of the dead left unburied in the triangle. They deserved a decent burial, he was reported to have said.[21] Besides, so many bodies exposed to the elements were a public health hazard. On Friday, January 5, the delegation of priests that had originally met the bishop in Tete got what they had asked for, in a manner of speaking. Dr José da Paz and two nurses, Irmã Lúcia and Irmã Fonseca, flew over Wiriyamu to see for themselves what had been put in writing in the two reports. Indeed, it was true, said Irmã Lúcia. "Bodies everywhere. We hovered. We did not land. But I could see a lot of dead bodies. Some appeared eaten by vultures with stray dogs roaming everywhere. Ughhh! My spine shivered. Thank God we got back safely. I did not want to be there on the ground."

The Church in Tete, indeed in Mozambique, waited to hear from Tete's military governor; no response was forthcoming. The Church then took the most momentous decision in this conflict. On March 31, 1973, the entire prelate, backed by the majority of priests and missionaries, lodged a formal letter of complaint to the governor-general of the colony:

> Having heard of details, which are being circulated, of the events which took place within the Chief Gandali [sic] regions, not far from the city of Tete, during the month of December last—events according to which hundreds of people, some of them absolutely innocent, might have lost their lives through the action of the armed forces . . . we cannot but express our most vehement indignation and protest.[22]

The protest letter elicited a curt response: the military is undertaking appropriate enquiries into the matter. The Church in Tete, along with the foreign missionaries operating in the colony, took that response as a sign to voice their concern outside the Church. The fight to publicize Portuguese mass violence was now official—a battle that Bishop Vieira had advocated for over a year. He was now joined by the entire hierarchy, except for the archbishop, who appeared resolutely opposed to the new move.

A month earlier, the Burgos priests had arrived at a similar conclusion—and taken the matter into their own hands. They had watched mass violence at close quarters, said Padre Sangalo, been promised a curb on such excesses, and experienced at first hand "a clear violation of the sanctity of the church," with the incarceration of priests. They had exhausted their good faith efforts hoping for an honest response and now had no option but to seek help outside the Church. But how? Given constant surveillance and postal censorship, where to start? "Why not smuggle the document?" asked several Burgos priests stationed in Changara and Chimoio. Once out, publicizing its details could begin. Hopefully, this time it would have an impact forceful enough for Portugal to change its ways of war. This opportunity to smuggle the narrative came in February, a month before the prelates' letter of protest.

---

[21] Berenguer, interview, 1994 and 1995.
[22] Hastings, *Wiriyamu*, 84.

Wiriyamu travels overseas

After January 1972, two figures in the Burgos congregation had risen to prominence: Miguel Buendia and Padre Júlio Padre Moure. Miguel Buendia, a recent arrival to Mozambique, was stationed briefly at the Muraça mission left vacant by the White Fathers before his subsequent secondment as an itinerant priest at Shamba and Lundo. Moure headed the congregation in Mozambique. Miguel Buendia's strongly held views aligned with Vatican II thinkers on the socially transformative role of the Church in developing societies. He thought the colonial hierarchy's silence in the face of mass violence unconscionable and elected to fight it intramurally, at the synodal meetings.

Buendia was a priest of action. He and Padre Moure defended priests and in particular fellow Burgos under attack from colonial authorities. Both took great pains not to needlessly antagonize the authorities so they could continue working towards getting fellow priests out of the Machava prison, while deflecting DGS aggression towards the clergy.[23]

Their campaign to free jailed priests was clearly a thorn in the colonial flesh. By insisting on due process, they had entangled the colony in a glacially paced judicial process. Such a process trammeled the colonial authorities' instinctive response—expel them outright after a brief period of incarceration—something that had been done in the past to good effect. The problem here was that the case of the Burgos priests became commingled with that of the Macúti priests, both Portuguese nationals. Where could they extradite the latter? Exile was out of the question since they were not prelates under Curial supervision. Further, once Amnesty International became involved in the judicial proceedings as observers, the cases of the Macúti and Burgos Fathers were "internationalized" as cases of human rights violations.

Were both Miguel Buendia and Padre Moure to continue their tenure in the colony, therefore, the authorities saw no end to problems, particularly in the event of victory for the defense. They could only guess how such an outcome would encourage Miguel Buendia and others like him to press for similar justice for the remainder, which included the 200-plus incarcerated priests and Church leaders. Clearly, they had no option but to expel them and thus rid themselves of two more recalcitrants among the clergy.

In early January 1972, Buendia received the first inkling that he, Padre Moure, and possibly Padre Berenguer were likely candidates for expulsion. During a visit to the colonial capital to see the attorney for the defense of his two colleagues, he was given access to a "highly secret dossier presenting the case for the defense for the Macúti priests." "They did not want me to see the dossier"[24] but the defense lawyer convincingly argued that the information should be shared to prepare a credible and soundly argued case, for which, he said, he needed well-informed and well-briefed character- and eyewitnesses. "So I read the dossier under strict security." What he discovered about the Burgos proved troubling—the DGS's extensive dossier viewed the entire Burgos congregation in the

---

[23] Miguel Buendia, interview by author, Maputo, 1994 and 1995, and Father Joseph, interview, 1994 and 1995.
[24] ibid.

colony as seditiously infected by "the communist bug." Padre Berenguer's journey to "sleep with the enemy" was cited as categorical proof of a strong alliance between the Burgos and FRELIMO. Miguel Buendia returned from Lourenço Marques on Tuesday 26, and soon thereafter informed the Changara-based Padre Berenguer of his findings and advised him that he could be the next target for expulsion.

Miguel Buendia and Padre Moure's own orders to leave the colony arrived on February 6—they had two weeks to pack and go. Both did just that and headed to the Burgos house in Beira before their prospective departure the next day. On Tuesday, February 20, at noon, they were ready to head for the airport. Just then, a Jeep drove to the house, with Father José Camba, a fellow Burgos who had driven 124 miles from his mission house in Chimoio ostensibly to say good-bye. In reality, he had come to hand him a sealed envelope containing the Wiriyamu report. "Miguel, take this to Spain. It is about Wiriyamu. Don't lose it. Keep it in a safe place." He was instructed to deliver the package to the director of Pamplona, Father Artazcoz in Madrid. The report, however, was incomplete, as it excluded the list of those killed at Chaworha—why the packet omitted the other reports remains a mystery. Neither Padre Moure, now in Mexico City, or José Camba could be reached to address this question. Haste and a last-minute opportunity may well have dictated smuggling out the heftier of the two reports.

Both arrived at the airport to find several colleagues waiting to bid farewell. DGS agents blocked them from seeing Miguel Buendia and Padre Moure despite their protests. They finally relented having sought approval from the colonial capital. In the meantime, a defense lawyer fighting the case for the Macúti fathers approached the two priests, warning them that they would be strip-searched. Airport officials were looking for illegal export of the colonial currency, which at that time could be exchanged for metropolitan escudos. Miguel Buendia worried the DGS would discover the packet on him. He had lost a lot of weight since his arrival in 1971, and the text could be seen bulging in his trouser pocket. "And it happened. They placed us in a room and opened the luggage." Miguel Buendia had left most of his clothes behind as he had lost so much weight. He was, though, carrying two books on liberation theology. The DGS and custom agents flipped through the pages, then looked at him straight in the eye and asked: "Do you have anything on you to declare? 'No', I said." Miguel Buendia rationalized later during the interview that he took the question to mean money and not a politically explosive text.

Miguel Buendia clutched the packet all the way to Lisbon on board the "TAP (Transportes Aéreos Portugueses) airplane, big, not a Jumbo," afraid to lose it. He did not dare to take a peek. He feared the DGS agents were on board the plane and waiting to pounce. They left Lourenço Marques that evening at 5:00 p.m., and arrived in Lisbon the next morning to transfer to a flight to Madrid, where they landed exhausted but glad to see Burgos colleagues waiting to welcome them home. They headed straight to a bed and breakfast for a prolonged rest, emerging occasionally to eat their meals prepared by the landlady. Once recovered, they read the contents of the packet. It was on Wiriyamu indeed, and they made haste to deliver it as instructed to the director of the Burgos congregation in Madrid.

In the meantime, Bertulli, who was in Rome, had received the two reports on Chaworha and Wiriyamu. How he came to acquire these documents is a mystery, but perhaps now that the Rome-based archives of the White Father's congregation are open, this mystery can be solved.[25] Bertulli felt that the matter deserved a transparent Portuguese response first. On May 12–13, he broached the matter with a high-ranking official of the Portuguese government present at a public meeting in Kamen, Germany. Portuguese response was disavowal. The reported massacres were "a work of FRELIMO," certainly not that of an imperial state of Portugal's standing. Bertulli felt stonewalled, and on Monday, June 4, 1973, *Cablo Press* published the texts in their entirety. Bertulli also forwarded a copy to Amnesty International, which received it on Monday, June 11.[26] In the end, the *Cablo* piece failed to make the splash that the Tete missionaries had expected, for exactly the same reasons that the earlier outing of the Mucumbura massacres had failed in garnering public attention—broader readership and front-page exposure forceful enough to compel a high-level response from imperial Portugal.[27]

Back in Madrid, Miguel Buendia and Padre Moure had enlisted the support of the Spanish foreign affairs ministry to pressure Lisbon to release the two Burgos missionaries, which was met with silence. The strongly worded letters failed to achieve the results they wanted. Miguel Buendia and Padre Moure, aware of the close ties between the secret police of the two states, pressed the matter no further lest they fall victim to incarceration by the secret police. Memories of complicity by Spanish secret police in the gruesome killing of Humberto Delgado were fresh in their minds.[28] There was little they could do so far away from their incarcerated colleagues. "We began to lose hope."[29]

They spent the next few weeks organizing the materials on the massacre and discussing strategies on how best to air the story. They examined multiple options. What they wanted was to attract international press coverage, and "get the United Nations involved."[30] That is when Hastings' entry into the narrative proved providential.

Some 1,192 miles from Madrid, Father Adrian Hastings was at the Selly Oak Colleges, Birmingham, busy preparing for a major tour of lectures at various dioceses in Rhodesia. Hastings had spent time in Uganda as a White Father missionary. As a historian of African Christianity, he had a fairly well-established network of colleagues engaged in missionary works in other parts of Africa, including Portuguese Mozambique. One such contact was Father van Asten, who had led that order's 1971 exit from the colony. Further, Hastings had penned several texts on the situation of the Church in the region and was therefore reasonably well versed with the challenges the Church was continuing to face in Mozambique.[31]

Hastings departed in April for the lecture tour, and while he was in Rhodesia, the Burgos Fathers informed him of the massacres. When probed for additional details,

---

[25] Miguel Buendia's testimony suggests the source to have been the Burgos in Madrid.
[26] Amnesty International, *Annual Report 1973–1974* (London: AI, 1974), 63–64.
[27] "Esclusivo: Massacri Nel Mozambico," *Cablo Press*, June 4, 1973, 5–11.
[28] "Portugal: Under the Eucalyptus Tree," *Time Magazine*, May 14, 1965; "1965—Assassinato de Humberto Delgado," accessed February 11, 2014, http://preview.tinyurl.com/lokkhb5.
[29] Buendia, interview, 1994 and 1995.
[30] ibid.
[31] Adrian Hastings and Ingrid Lowrie (eds.), *Christianity and the African Imagination: Essays in Honour of Adrian Hastings (Studies of Religion in Africa)* (Leiden: Brill Academic Publications, 2001).

they told him to get in touch with the Burgos' headquarters in Spain. This he did. He was scheduled to deliver a seminal paper on the Church's new thinking on ecumenical matters at an inter-communion conference in Salamanca in the middle of June and took the opportunity to raise the matter first with Father Artazcoz in Salamanca and then with Father Anaveros in Madrid.

The two meetings occurred the week of June 18. At the Madrid meeting, he was shown the documents that Miguel Buendia had smuggled out of Beira. Hastings felt that both the Burgos as churchmen and the document were genuinely worthy of deeper analysis.

> Studying the Wiriyamu report convinced me that here was something different. I had the greatest confidence in the reliability of the Burgos Fathers. They seemed to me, both those I had seen at work in Rhodesia and those I have met in Madrid, a fine and extremely disinterested group of men. They clearly take a mastery of African languages very seriously indeed. They are men who have committed themselves for life to the service of God and their fellow men, and have done so with obvious vigour, cheerfulness and simplicity of life.[32]

He asked Anaveros for a copy: they did not have a spare copy on hand but could send one on Wednesday, June 27. Hastings received the texts three days later. The Chaworha report was missing from the batch of two reports, one on Mucumbura and one on Wiriyamu.

The Mucumbura report, Hastings felt, had already been aired. It was too old to pique the interest of the wider readership in the news media. Aided by Spanish speakers, Hastings probed the text on Wiriyamu and was satisfied it was genuine front-page story. On Thursday, July 5, he cabled Madrid seeking their permission to publish. Anaveros replied the following day giving him the go-ahead. By then, Hastings had already decided on which paper to contact for the story—*The Times*. "They were a paper of repute, established, and with an intelligent readership," said Hastings. "They had an international reputation still worth something, you know."[33]

The labyrinth behind the publication

What propelled *The Times* to publish the text so quickly, and why did it make such a splash? The answers are complex, textured, and nuanced, far more labyrinthine than suggested in a recent work.[34] More importantly, these answers demonstrate, intellectually at least, how confluences of forces, ideas, and events utterly unconnected to the Wiriyamu narrative, helped the dead speak an unadulterated truth to imperial power. They did so through handlers at *The Times* and *The Sunday Times* who themselves were of working-class origins and who saw an opportunity—and took it— to tell the world a truly human story aching with mass violence!

---

[32] Hastings, *Wiriyamu*, 87.
[33] Hastings, interviews, 1977, 1978, 1979, 1981, 1995, 1996.
[34] Reis and Oliveira, "Cutting Heads," 80–103.

One factor at play here were the long-standing problems, going as far back as 1967, threatening *The Times* with prospective extinction. Until 1967, *The Times* had shown a remarkable and steady growth and diversity of readership under its chief editor, William Haley.[35] His stewardship had brought positive changes, resulting in an increase in the paper's circulation from 220,716 in 1956, four years after his arrival, to 282,000 in 1966, a year before his departure.

During his fourteen years at the helm of *The Times*, Haley had gained a reputation as "an outstanding and fair-minded newspaperman," a promoter of talent, cautious and decisive where it eventually mattered, and a sensible judge of character, political personalities, and events. One talent that flourished under him and who eventually pulled the trigger to publish the Wiriyamu story was Louis Heren, a journalist skilled at unearthing stories of human interest laced with political skulduggery.[36]

Haley's editorial leadership had ensured the paper's reputation as globally-minded and vigorously committed to present one solid mission-centric voice behind which journalists wrote without bylines. They did so with complete confidence, their integrity assured, their work protected from unwarranted editorial intrusions, and their liberty secured as institutional writers for *The Times*. "*The London Times* was once again a great paper," said a reporter, echoing the sentiments of many who contributed to Haley's bibliographic entry in the Britannica.[37]

With Haley's departure, *The Times* changed. For complex reasons, materially unimportant to this narrative, the paper's fortunes had declined quite dramatically by the end of 1967, prompting the proprietors to sell it to a Canadian publishing group headed by Ray Thompson, who saw the paper as a social asset with which to leverage a peerage for himself.[38] To this end, the new owners were prepared to fund the paper's deficit and appointed William Rees-Mogg[39] as chief editor to succeed William Haley; four years later Marmaduke Hussey joined him as the managing director.

In appointing the duo, the new owners committed a cardinal error of judgment. Professionally, neither was experienced in leading a paper of this heft or negotiating with unions to modernize the paper's printing technology. Rees-Mogg lacked the breadth of journalistic experience needed to keep the paper vigorous, experience that his predecessors and some of their talented writers had in abundance. In the past, such

---

[35] United Newspapers PLC and Fleet Holdings PLC, Monopolies and Mergers Commission (1985), 5–16.
[36] Louis Heren, *Growing Up Poor in London* (London: Hamish Hamilton, 1973); Louis Heren, *Growing Up on "The London Times"* (London: Hamish Hamilton, 1978); Louis Heren, *Memories of Times Past* (London: Hamish Hamilton, 1988), 210–236; and Godfrey Hodgson, "Louis Heren: Obituaries," *The Independent*, January 28, 1995.
[37] Wolfgang Saxon, "William J. Haley, British Journalist, Dies at 86," *New York Times*, September 9, 1987; and *The Papers of Sir William John Haley, 1901–1987*, Knight, Journalist, Churchill Archives Centre, Churchill College, Cambridge, GBR/0014/HALY, HALY 15, 1955–1969, 11 folders and volumes.
[38] Pringle, interview, 2012.
[39] Roy Hattersley, "Private pleasure, but no public virtue: A visit to Charterhouse convinces Roy Hattersley that it is a superb, but ultimately damaging, institution," *The Guardian*, July 16, 2007; Peter Preston, "Memoirs by William Rees-Mogg—Review: William Rees-Mogg's memoirs have plenty to tell us about the phone-hacking scandal," *The Guardian*, July 13, 2011; William Rees-Mogg, *Memoirs* (London: Harper Press, 2011), 72; and Peter Lewis, "Turbulent times for a pillar of the establishment: Memoirs by William Rees-Mogg," *Mail Online*, August 19, 2011.

a pool of talent had raised the profile of *The Times* as a Thunderer—a great paper of international repute.

Thus, the paper's international news coverage atrophied as it struggled to keep pace with global changes, particularly on current affairs afflicting colonies and empires during the late 1960s and early 1970s. This proved particularly true concerning news on Portugal and its African colonies, about which the paper remained for the most part value-neutral until the fall of 1972, publishing just under 535 articles on the subject, an average of 177 a year or an item of news every eight days.[40] An occasional article or two did appear during this period which sided with Portugal against communism favoring Portuguese counter-insurgency in Africa.[41]

Haley had rigorously adhered to principles of impartiality as a chief editor while cultivating a culture of the "writers' collective" among journalists at the paper. Rees-Mogg changed all that. He did away with the "no byline" policy. While this measure promoted talent, it also fractured the paper as a single authoritative voice of truth contributed to by the labor of the unidentified many.

He also saw no need to protect the ideological integrity of the paper from self-promotion, prompting him on occasions to write advocacy-driven op-ed pieces. One such text of patrician condescension called for changes in the Tory leadership to replace Lord Hume with Edward Heath, whose union-bashing policies ultimately came to threaten the paper's very survival.[42]

Normally, such measures to promote this sort of professional elitism would not have mattered in a class-riddled Britain. However, in the political climate that threatened Britain's industrial democracy in the early 1970s, they proved lethally toxic for the paper, particularly after the Tories won the general election. Rees-Mogg's snobbery did not help here; neither did Hussey's tussles with the unions. The positions taken by both strengthened the resolve by *The Times*' unionized staff of typesetters to consider strike action in that summer of 1973. That is when the Wiriyamu text landed on Louis Heren's desk.

Perhaps the most important factor that tipped the balance in the narrative's favor as a printable piece was context. Just as the union turmoil engulfed Britain, the Tory government of Edward Heath,[43] backed by an influential clutch of Tory Members of Parliament, were about to host Caetano in London to celebrate the 600th anniversary of the Anglo–Portuguese Alliance.[44] Hastings was at the time serving as member of a committee of the board of the Catholic Institute of International Relations (CIIR).

---

[40] Figures compiled from the *Annual Index for The Times of London* for the years under review.
[41] See, for instance, Staff, "Terrorists from Tanganyika," *The Times*, October 12, 1964, 11e; and, David Leigh, "War against Frelimo 'like fight with IRA'," *The Times*, July 18, 1973, 9c.
[42] Victor Bogdanor, "Memoirs: Only a Lame Leg to Stand On," *New Statesman,* July, 2011.
[43] Adrian Hastings, private diary entries for the months of July and August, 1973; and Knipe, interview, London, 1996.
[44] See the following issues of *The Times*: March 16, 1973, 8a; May 17, 1973, 18h; and May 23, 1973, 6h. Additional information on the alliance and reactions to it are to be found in Staff, "Motions by Tory MPs support Caetano visit," *The Times*, July 12, 1973, 16a. The Foreign and Commonwealth Office archives contain approximately fifty documents on the commemorative aspect of this alliance. See Bibliography for details.

This committee had been established to organize a public discourse on the imperial alliance. CIIR wanted a substance-driven examination of the Anglo–Portuguese Imperial Alliance—and not a display of pap, pomp, and pageantry publicly pandering to the celebration of "empires and their endurance," said Hastings.[45]

The CIIR committee had asked Hastings to focus on the role of the Church in the alliance. Neither the committee nor Hastings could have envisaged what followed. The committee proved deeply reluctant to allow the narrative to dominate the CIIR proceedings. At one point, the CIIR secretary-general remarked to Hastings, "One more massacre, who will be interested in that anyway?"[46] Hastings disagreed. The story needed airing and on the front pages of *The Times*, no less!

Hastings called *The Times* on Friday, July 6, late afternoon. Fortuitously, William Rees-Mogg, the chief editor, was not in at that late hour; Louis Heren was in executive charge. Heren himself was by then highly skilled at nurturing stories of momentous human interest. Like Haley, he had risen through the ranks and had been head of the paper's foreign desk in Washington, DC, where he had seen the debacle of My Lai unfold. Heren had returned to London in 1970, first as foreign editor and then its sole deputy editor. To him, this story of Wiriyamu smacked of Portugal's own My Lai.

He asked Hastings to forward the texts, which he did on Saturday. Heren received the package on Monday, and his call to Hastings that evening proved ominously thunderous for the story's outing. "We have to run the story tomorrow," he said to Hastings. "The typesetters are threatening to go on strike and we do not know when we will be in print again!"[47] That prospective strike threatening to bury the story for good combined with a hunch to tell truth to the world persuaded Heren to publish Wiriyamu. On July 10, 1973, *The Times* ran the story, and five days later, *The Sunday Times*' Insight Team followed suit with an extensive background coverage on the massacre.[48] Back in Lisbon, Caetano was six days shy of a rather quiet rain-soaked landing at Heathrow, which was now heavily fortified with police[49] to protect him from what the *Sunday Times* called "an unwelcome visit."[50]

---

[45] Hastings, interviews, 1977, 1978, 1979, 1981, 1995, 1996.
[46] ibid.
[47] ibid.
[48] "Mozambique: The Priest's Fight," *Sunday Times*, July 15, 1973, 17.
[49] "Heavy police precautions as Dr. Caetano begins his visit to Britain today," *The Times*, July 16, 1973, 1.
[50] "An unwelcome visit." *Sunday Times*, July 15, 1973, 16.

8

Portuguese Reaction to the Public Narrative

Of denials and dismissals

Portugal's response underwent several distinct phases over the course of a year during which its position changed from outright denial, to recognition of some form of mass violence, to contesting aspects of the narrative as revealed, to admission of the Wiriyamu massacre as reported in *The Times*. The response began with an angry denial.[1] Reactions from other quarters were every bit as intense.[2] Other reactions were more derisive.[3] Denial and deconstruction of Wiriyamu continued unabated, however. Some of these contested the veracity of the mass killings.[4] Others questioned the pedigree of the massacre as Portugal's very own "My Lai." Heren and Hastings first drew the comparison between Wiriyamu and My Lai in two texts, which remain the only publicly documented accounts of the massacre detailing the names of the dead, their number and the context of the events that brought Wiriyamu to extinction.[5]

The Times stuck to its position like a limpet. The story it had published was true; the priests as handlers of the sources, and the sources it had relied upon to construct the news story were solid. "It's ridiculous," said Hastings, when discussing the Portuguese claim "that Wiriyamu and the Nyantawatawa River did not appear on the map."[6] *The Times* continued to cover faithfully rebuttals, reports, and subsequent disavowal of the initial denial and did so extensively in, give or take, 208 articles—all published within six months, beginning in July.[7]

Both the British and American[8] governments officially sided with Portugal. The Tory "Young Turks"[9] demanded the British Press Council investigate *The Times*'

---

[1] A. M. Rendel, "Embassy issues angry reply," *The Times*, July 11, 1973, 1.
[2] *The Times*, July 17, 1973, 1f.
[3] For a glimpse of this type of derision particularly aimed at the priests who brought the story to light, see *The Times*, July 11, 1973, 6a.
[4] Staff, "Massacre allegation not proved," *The Times*, July 26, 1973, 10e.
[5] See, Hastings, *Wiriyamu*.
[6] David Leigh, "Priest derides official denial," *The Times*, July 11, 1973.
[7] For details, see *The Times Annual Index(es)* for the period—a complete set of which was consulted at the British Library, Newspaper Collection, Colindale.
[8] National Archives, RG 59, *Central Files 1970–73, POL 19 PORT-GUIN. Confidential; No Foreign Dissem; Controlled Dissem*. Drafted by Heyniger, cleared by Summ, and released by Mark.
[9] They were formally known as Young Conservatives and had formed a pro-Portuguese nucleus called the "Ad Hoc Anglo–Portuguese Friendship Society."

ethical conduct in publishing the story and examine any aberrations in fact-checking procedures,[10] while leaders of Tory opposition led by Harold Wilson of the Labour Party called for the cancellation of the visit and an inquiry into the massacre.[11] The Press Council, for its part, rejected the complaints from this group over the report of the massacre.[12] Several other social and economic forces chimed in: Tory patricians tied to economic interests in Southern Africa;[13] Tory entrepreneurs intimately connected with British exports[14] and import and manufacture of Portuguese Port wines;[15] the majority of the Tory cabinet ministers in the government hosting Caetano in Britain;[16] and the conservative flank in the Foreign and Commonwealth Office.[17]

The American pro-Portuguese position was complicated by their Azores Bases Agreement, much needed for American logistics for the war effort in Vietnam.[18] In one early instance, State department officials had overtly strengthened Portugal's case by publicly voicing their doubts over the story.[19]

Portugal drew strength from the British and American official positions and mounted a counter-narrative,[20] engaging a public relations firm to discredit the story while buttressing Caetano's reputation as a respectable dignified academic[21] and not, as one placard had suggested, a "butcher" and an "assassin."[22] This was not the first time that Portugal had engaged a public relations firm. As early as 1964, Lisbon had hired one such firm to combat its detractors in Washington and in Europe, spending millions on counter-propaganda generated by journalists on junkets to Mozambique who wrote stories to prove the veracity of its "Lusotropicalist" project.[23]

---

[10] "Press Council is asked to investigate," *The Times*, July 17, 1973.
[11] "No inquiry – No welcome," *The Times*, July 11, 1973, 17; House of Commons, "Mr. Wilson demands cancellation of visit by Portuguese leader," *The Times*, July 11, 1973, 7.
[12] "Press council rejects complaints over report of massacre," *The Times*, February 12, 1974, 9.
[13] A. M. Rendel, "Whitehall plays it by ear in Africa," *The Times*, July 19, 1973.
[14] "We have very considerable trade with Portugal. The value of our exports to Portugal in 1972 amounted to £114 million." Sir Alec Douglas-Home, *Hansard*, 860, July 17, 1973, cc.265–375.
[15] Douglas-Home's position is expressed in "Cancellation of Dr. Caetano's visit on the basis of articles in 'The London Times' would be to prejudge case against an old and loyal ally – Foreign Secretary," *The Times*, July 18, 1973.
[16] "Mr. Heath will not call off Portuguese state visit—Massacre denied by Lisbon," *The Times*, July 11, 1973, 1; Staff, "Motions by Tory MPs support Caetano visit," *The Times*, July 12, 1973, 16a; and, "Cancellation of Dr. Caetano's visit on basis of article in 'The London Times' would be to prejudge case against an old and loyal ally, Foreign State," *The Times*, July 18, 1973, 14.
[17] Norrie MacQueen and Pedro Aires Oliveira, "'Grocer Meets Butcher,' Marcello Caetano's London Visit of 1973 and the Last Days of Portugal's Estado Novo," *Cold War History*, 10, 1 (2010): 29–50.
[18] National Archives, *RG 59, Central Files 1970–73, POL 19 PORT-GUIN. Confidential; No Foreign Dissem; Controlled Dissem.* Drafted by Heyniger, cleared by Summ, and released by Mark.
[19] Robin Freedberg, "London Protesters Fail to Block Caetano Visit," *The Harvard Crimson*, July 17, 1973.
[20] "Portuguese 'butchery condemned," *The Times*, July 11, 1973, 6.
[21] A. M. Rendel, "Embassy issues angry reply," *The Times*, July 11, 1973, 1; and Jerome Caminada, "A sea of turbulence awaits Dr. Caetano during London visit," *The Times*, July 16, 1973.
[22] "Dr. Caetano and Mr. Heath meet angry demonstrations at Greenwich after peaceful day," *The Times*, July 17, 1973, 1, 14.
[23] *Africa Report*, 5 (April 1964): 10.

This time, they paid 120 young men and women to distribute pro-Lisbon leaflets declaring "Portugal like Great Britain Loves Peace" and "Portugal is forced to fight for Freedom as Great Britain was."[24] They hired a rent-a-mob outfit "for sixty-five pence an hour" to drown out 5,000 protesters standing in the pouring rain vigorously chanting anti-Portuguese slogans. The rented protesters had their own display placards in bold lettering: "allegations have proved false," and "Portugal fights to preserve non-racialism against all racialists."[25]

With this public protest underway, the Caetano government dismissed *The Times*' story as "a mare's nest,"[26] cooked up by its enemies to undermine its national security in the "overseas provinces." It was nothing short of an international conspiracy against Portugal, Lisbon averred.[27] According to their maps, Wiriyamu did not exist.[28] Where was the proof that it did? Given their own intimate knowledge of Tete, they could state with categorical certainty that Wiriyamu was a priestly fabrication, and the massacre a fiction. If *The Times* had proof, they should produce it.[29]

Hastings and the Burgos Fathers stationed in Madrid responded quickly with rebuttals. They knew where Wiriyamu was. Some had visited the place, one in particular to do a rapid assessment to establish a school in the triangle as an outpost to be managed by them from their mission either in Changara or Tete itself.[30]

Did Portugal truly not know where Wiriyamu was? It did. The very last day of his stay in London, a DGS agent was filing his customary report on insurgency in Tete, identifying not only Wiriyamu's location but outlining reasons for its destruction, namely, to eliminate Raimundo Dalepa himself and allegedly, "his bases nearby."[31]

Meanwhile, Portugal had already prepared a small abandoned village with charred huts northwest of the triangle as an alternative to Wiriyamu to counter Hastings' claims. Tete did indeed have a place locally known as *Williamo*—perhaps the priests and Hastings were referring to this village; if so it was too small a place to be of cartographic significance and certainly not large enough to accommodate a freshly executed carnage of the magnitude claimed in *The Times*. Truth-seekers, Portugal added, were welcome to tour Williamo to check the facts for themselves. Should they find evidence of a massacre in the area, "we will immediately order an inquiry,"[32] said Portugal's London-based director of Information Service stationed at the Portuguese Embassy in charge of facilitating Caetano's visit.

---

[24] Christopher Walker and David Leigh, "Distribution of pro-Lisbon leaflets was arranged by Zanzibari," *The Times*, July 17, 1973. See also "Reggie/Rent a Crowd/Lead into Snow," *JISC Media Hub of London*, July 17, 1973.

[25] Christopher Walker and David Leigh, "5,000 in London protest march," *The Times*, July 17, 1973.

[26] Anonymous, *'Wiriyamu' or a Mare's Nest* (Lisbon: Ministry of Foreign Affairs, 1973).

[27] The story "had been 'arranged' to coincide with Dr. Caetano's visit. We cannot even locate the village of Wiriyamu," said a Portuguese official. "Portuguese 'butchery condemned," *The Times*, July 11, 1973, 6.

[28] Harry Derelius, "Wiriyamu 'is marked on Tete mission maps'," *The Times*, July 16, 1973, 1d.

[29] "Censura 16, Wiriyamu (*)," *Notícias da Amadora*, 618, July 21, 1973.

[30] Berenguer, interview, 1994 and 1995; Padre José Sangalo, interview by author, Madrid, Spain, 1995; Hastings, interviews, 1977, 1978, 1979, 1981, 1995, 1996.

[31] PT/TT/PIDE/D-F/001/00021, July 19, 1973.

[32] José Pedro Castanheira, "Declarações de Marcello Caetano à BBC-TV," *O Expresso*, July 11, 2008.

Journalists who took up the Portuguese offer to visit the fictional Williamo found nothing significant to report. Once in Tete, they had been shepherded to a carefully orchestrated tour arranged by a team of two, a local influential pro-Salazarist businessman, Jorge Jardim,[33] and Tete's chief of secret police, Joaquim Sabino. Padre Ferrão was instructed to be cooperative and on call. "I was told by Jardim to nod when they came to see me," he said, "... And I did. What else could I do? I did not lie, but I did not volunteer the truth. Remember, I had been in prison before. Besides these journalists spoke English and stayed for ten minutes or so."[34]

Of the journalists who returned from Tete, three proved crucial to the story. One was Bruce Loudon, who strengthened the Portuguese case; the other two, Michael Knipe and Peter Pringle, did not. Bruce Loudon was a stringer based in Lisbon, who, it later transpired, served two "masters": the *London Financial Times* and the *Daily Telegraph*, on one hand, and Portugal's Secretariat of State for Information and Tourism, on the other.[35] Texts obtained three years after *The Times* outed Wiriyamu reveal that Loudon had volunteered to help Caetano launch "effective counter campaigns" entailing "a daily flow of information from Mozambique to a central point in Lisbon" to key individuals and opinion-formers.[36] Upon his return, Loudon wrote two damning reports for the *Daily Telegraph* repudiating the Wiriyamu story.[37]

The Times was now on the defensive and forced to address Portugal's counter-narrative. Its editors and staff felt the urgent need to corroborate its story with primary sources in Tete or sources independent of *The Times* who had spoken to eyewitnesses. According to Hastings, to avoid charges of ethical misconduct under a pressing exigency, its editors opted to do both: send its own journalists to Tete *and* procure eyewitnesses to "testify." Michael Knipe and Peter Pringle of *The Sunday Times* headed for Tete, while Hastings procured sources with direct knowledge of the events and invited them to come to London for a de-briefing.

Twenty-three years later, Knipe recalls that despite rumors that he had been denied entry into Mozambique, he had not. He had arrived in Tete on July 18 on an old visa that was valid until August.[38] He spent three days there, where he was successfully escorted to the fictitious site of Williamo. Knipe filed his story suggesting just that—that he had found the place called Williamo to be small and insignificant, with little evidence of freshly discharged bullet casings.[39] He successfully interviewed de Arriaga for two hours in Lourenço Marques however, but failed to elicit any response from the bishop of Tete, who

---

[33] Jorge Jardim's role in this affair and Luso-Malawi diplomacy is given in Jorge Jardim, *Moçambique–Terra Queimada* (Lisbon: Intervenção, 1976).
[34] Ferrão, interview, 1995.
[35] James Sanders, *South Africa and the International Media*, 11–12.
[36] "Telegraphed Tales," *Time Out*, 308 (1976): 5.
[37] Bruce Loudon, "No Massacres, say Tete Tribesmen," *The London Daily Telegraph*, July 13, 1973; and Bruce Loudon, "Priests Do Not Know of Massacre," *The London Daily Telegraph*, July 14, 1973. For the impact that this type of reporting had on "weakening" the case, see James J. Kilpatric, "The Portuguese Atrocity that Didn't Happen," *National Review* (May 10, 1974): 525–527.
[38] Michael Knipe, "African civilians suffering heavily in Mozambique war," *The Times*, July 21, 1973, 1.
[39] Cable: 1973Lourenn00559_b, 1973, August 14, 14: 46 (Tuesday).

had previously raised serious concerns and who was now resolutely silent.[40] "He was probably muzzled by the authorities."[41] By this time, the secret police had intensified surveillance of Knipe as he sought out Tete's missionaries and nuns directly connected to the case.[42]

Before he could tap new sources for a follow-up story, the Portuguese swooped in. They ejected him from Tete "for [his] own protection mind you."[43] "They could not guarantee my safety anywhere in Mozambique," he said, "because of public protests against *The Times*."[44] It appears that right then, nearly 40,000 people had gathered in the colonial capital to protest against "what was called the international campaign against Portugal."[45] It is unknown if these were genuine advocates pulling for the Caetano-led empire.

Meanwhile, Hastings had left London for New York on July 19, 1973, to testify on Wiriyamu before the United Nations Special Committee of twenty-four on Decolonization.[46] The following day, Caetano too left London for Lisbon, vilified by the public as a butcher and an "assassin." In Lisbon, however, he was met with a warm reception from a crowd chanting in unison "Viva, viva" and "Down with *The London Times*."[47]

The response from *The London Times* and *The Sunday Times* group

With their departure from London, the Wiriyamu narrative marched from a contested terrain towards a verified certainty. Days after his departure from London, Peter Pringle followed Knipe to see if he could succeed where Knipe had failed. Pringle was a seasoned reporter, and formed part of the Insight Team at *The Sunday Times* established for the sole purpose of investigating in-depth stories of the day. Wiriyamu caught the team's attention. Here was a case of mass violence aching for truth-ferreting journalists. Pringle was a natural choice to lead the probe. He was widely traveled in the Middle East and Africa, and had been to neighboring Rhodesia. Unlike Knipe, Pringle was complex in character. Observant and yet warm and engaging, Pringle had a steel-trap scientific mind and was a ferociously persistent risk-taker who possessed an uncanny

---

[40] Michael Knipe, "Mozambique bishop maintains his silence on reports of Massacres," *The Times*, July 23, 1973, 1.
[41] Knipe, interview, London, 1996.
[42] Michael Knipe, "Mozambique secret police keep an eye on correspondent from *The London Times*," *The Times*, July 25, 1973, 1.
[43] Michael Knipe, "Times man in Tete ordered to leave," *The Times*, July 24, 1973, 1; and Michael Knipe, "Mozambique secret police keep an eye on correspondent from the Times," *The Times*, July 25, 1973, 1.
[44] Michael Knipe, "Bishop maintains his silence on reports of massacre," *The Times*, July 23, 1973.
[45] José Shercliff, "40,000 people demonstrate in Mozambique capital," *The Times*, July 17, 1972.
[46] David Wigg, "Priest gives massacre details to UN committee," *The Times*, July 21, 1973. FRELIMO representatives at the meeting included the party's ideologue, Marcelino dos Santos, who at one point during his delivery commended Hastings for his great contribution "to the movement against oppression." "We appreciate your courage," he added. "Portuguese converge on Lisbon to welcome Dr. Caetano back home," *The Times*, July 20, 1973.
[47] "Portuguese converge on Lisbon to welcome Dr. Caetano back home," *The Times*, July 20, 1973.

Photo 5 Peter Pringle, Tete, 1973

ability to hover over narratives while immersed in discourses with informants. He cut an imposing figure at six foot plus, a multi-tasker with camera and notepad in hand, on the ready to investigate for the Insight Team.

Given that the Portuguese had managed to steer earlier investigators away from the real Wiriyamu, and that they had ejected Knipe out of Tete before he could get to the evidence, Pringle knew it would be difficult to reach *and* interview informants without attracting the attention of the secret police. If he was to succeed, he needed a quick, targeted entry into Tete. To this end, he planned his trajectory with characteristic care. He went to Spain first. The Burgos Fathers and their network prepared him on how to outmaneuver the secret police.[48] "When you arrive in Beira, get in touch with Jesus Camba. He will send you to the right place."[49]

From there, Pringle went straight to Lisbon on his way to Mozambique via Beira. He then spent three days in Tete and quickly mined the appropriate sources, thereby establishing the veracity of the story—and its location:

---

[48] Berenguer, interview, 1994 and 1995; and Hastings, interviews, 1977, 1978, 1979, 1981, 1995, 1996.
[49] Buendia, interview, 1994 and 1995.

The PIDE was very alert and ready to catch anyone who got near the truth. Peter came to Missão São Pedro because that is where the father superior of the mission resided. Peter said that he simply wanted to contact with survivors and hear their stories. I was put in charge to get him the information. Padre Castro fetched António and brought him to Missão São Pedro in his Land Rover. Mr. Pringle interviewed him, recorded it, and took a picture with him. Pringle also took a picture with Podista and her son, who were also survivors. And I appeared in the picture as well.[50]

Armed with a trove of evidence, Pringle sprinted out of the Hotel Zambêzia where he was staying to interview Tete's bishop. "The place was crawling with agents."[51] Unfortunately, a vigilant secret police agent lay in wait for him to appear near the bishopric, opposite the secret police headquarters; Pringle was whisked away for interrogation. The chief of the secret police Joaquim Sabino and his associates were displeased with his inordinately long day-visits to Missão São Pedro. In the past, journalists had visited Missão São Pedro, they said, but none had spent so much time there. Most were done within ten minutes or so. Why was he taking so long? What had he uncovered? They took away his notes, recordings and photos, "for review, mind you," they said. They assured him he would get them back. He was then ordered to leave Tete. His materials would be delivered upon his departure from Mozambique. They were never returned.[52]

However, according to Padre Berenguer, during their interrogation, Joaquim Sabino's men had failed to confiscate a couple of photographs of António Mixone, one with Pringle by his side and one showing a bullet gash on António's body.[53] Clearly, the Portuguese had historical wounds to hide. Pringle's recollection is more nuanced and direct. While they were busy reviewing his materials, Pringle's nifty sleight of hand pushed a roll of film at the edge of the desk in his jacket pocket.[54]

Pringle returned to London and filed his story, first from the colonial capital,[55] with a follow-up which appeared in *The Sunday Times* on August 3, 1973, and was subsequently picked up by *The Times*. Portugal and pro-Portuguese detractors of the Wiriyamu narrative had lost a weapon, that of denial of Wiriyamu as a place.[56] Both *The Sunday Times* and *The Times'* procedural conduct in publishing the story had shown good faith in exercising due diligence and could comfortably stand by their narratives, which had now been verified against primary sources.[57] The evidence did exist; the place did exist, and would continue to exist as long as eyewitnesses and survivors remained alive and beyond the reach of the Portuguese secret police. With

[50] Sangalo, interview, 1995.
[51] Pringle, phone interview, 2012.
[52] Pringle, interview, 2012.
[53] Copies of both are in the author's possession.
[54] Pringle, interview, 2012.
[55] Peter Pringle, "Secret police seize my Mozambique tapes," *Sunday Times*, July 29, 1973, 1.
[56] J. K. Liddle, "Readers' Letters," *Sunday Times*, August 12, 1973, 13.
[57] Christopher Walker, "Call to UN over boy's Wiriyamu evidence," *The Times*, August 6, 1973, 4.

these revelations, the Burgos came to fear reprisals;[58] as did the Roman cardinalate. Holland's Cardinal Alfrink stepped in, calling on the Bishop of Tete to protect the Church and the survivors.[59] The Tete hierarchy responded, as it had before, with silence. The bishopric of Tete refused to "become involved in controversy."[60]

Portugal, on the other hand, resisted all demands for free access to the site and its survivors in an attempt to forestall deeper probes that might uncover additional details of the massacre's magnitude. Portugal did not keep track of who went where in the triangle, said Lisbon. Nor did it keep a record of movements to and from strategic hamlets in the triangle under their administrative care. In any case, the area was under counter-insurgency, and therefore too risky for unarmed civilians.[61]

One such unarmed civilian, a survivor, nearly didn't make it—António Mixone. After their filing, one of Pringle's stories was picked up by the BBC. Padre Sangalo was in Tete then at his one-room home in Matundo, and he picks up the story from here:

> I used to listen to the BBC World Service regularly. That night the reception was bad and I had the radio close to my ear when I heard how a certain foreign journalist had found a young survivor and had interviewed him. Oh, my God, that is Mixone, I said. They will kill him if they catch him.
>
> I must do something right away. I and the other padres secretly met at the Burgos mission house—we had to avoid detection from the secret police when in Tete. We were in a race against time. I do not remember who was at the meeting. We discussed what to do. We decided to send him into hiding. But where? Anywhere in Tete, he would be discovered, and in the end killed. The best thing was to hand him over to FRELIMO. He would be safest with them, since they were experienced in protecting themselves and others of value to them from the Portuguese authorities. But who would take him to them? And how would we engineer this?
>
> Padre Ferrão could not get involved. He was black. He had already been in prison for his political views; and in any case, the PIDE were watching him and the mission very closely. The only person who could do it and would not raise suspicion was me. I was in Matundo and far away from Tete City and Missão São Pedro. Also, I was in good standing still with Inspector Sabino, the chief of secret police. He believed in me, at least that is what I thought. Also it is true I had indirect contacts with FRELIMO but they were near Missão São Pedro and not in Matundo. No one associated with FRELIMO, came to visit me there. Matundo was surrounded by whites and it was risky to be seen fraternizing with suspected "*turras*." This was very funny and a bit ironic, "*na realidade!*"—really! Because FRELIMO transported their guns, little arms and other supplies and God knows what else behind the mission near the bridge where the Zambezi waters narrow. Eventually, that is where FRELIMO launched their assaults on Vila Pery, south of the Tete province.

[58] Richard Wigg, "Reprisal on Wiriyamu survivors feared," *The Times*, August 6, 1973, 5.
[59] "Cardinal makes plea to Mozambique bishop," *Sunday Times*, August 26, 1973, 7.
[60] "Bishop of Tete says his duty is not to become involved in controversy," *The Times*, July 17, 1973, 1; and "Secret plan to protect 'massacre' survivors," *Sunday Times*, August 12, 1973, 7.
[61] Cable: *1973Lourenn00559_b, 1973*, August 14, 46.

We also knew we could not get Missão São Pedro involved in any way. So my Tete contacts and those of Padre Ferrão were useless. We needed a place outside Tete and someone with FRELIMO contacts there to help us safely hand him over. After much discussion and thought, we found the ideal place—the Comboniani mission near Changara, 50 to 60 kilometers from Tete.

The next day, I woke up at 5 in the morning, took a shower and got ready. At 5:30, I left for Mpharhamadwe on my Suzuki motor-ped. I would have gone a bit later if I still had my other motor-ped, my 250 Cc Honda which could reach the speed of 60 kilometers per hour. But I sold it to someone in the Portuguese Air Force who unfortunately never paid me. Aghhh! What can you do, when someone says he now does not have the money and he and his family is broke because of some tragedy. I let it go.

I arrived in M'Phadwe an hour later at around 6:30. To get to M'Phadwe, I had to cross the bridge and go through Tete and hope not to be stopped by police or tailed by the secret service. That is why it took me an hour to get there. I looked for António and found him at the foot of the baobab tree. He was up and nearly ready. He knew I was coming because I had sent a message that I was coming to visit him that morning. I had not seen him since December 1972 during his stay in Tete hospital. He had grown and really looked to me more like a man than a small boy. Also I liked that he was dressed discreetly, not to attract attention.

I spoke to his people, near and dear to him, his family, and explained why he was being taken. I couldn't just take him away without telling them why. After all, he still had family members around him who had survived the Chaworha massacre. So I spoke to them about the danger António was in and that the PIDE was looking to kill him. I felt it necessary to say that because that was the truth and his family needed to know the real truth, the real story. Otherwise, it would have been a long morning with discussions and more discussions and more weighing ins and more "let us not do anything hasty and leave him with us" kind of thinking. He would have been surely dead within days if not hours. In less than one hour, they could be there. Of course, his relatives didn't want the boy to die having survived the massacre; so they hurriedly organized his small bundle of clothes and we left at 7:30—and just in time.[62]

He transported Mixone on his motor-ped to a neutral point of contact for FRELIMO to take him away to safety and returned to find Sabino's men on a manhunt for him. By then, Mixone had crossed the border into Zambia on his way to Tanzania to be debriefed by FRELIMO. In August, the DGS apprehended Padre Sangalo on charges of sedition. The Bishop of Tete was informed of these changes but failed to intervene. Padre Sangalo was interrogated in the presence of informers and subsequently put on a plane bound for Lisbon and then Madrid.[63]

---

[62] Sangalo, interview, 1995.
[63] Peter Pringle, Father Jose Sangalo, and Burgos Fathers, "My ordeal with the secret police—and my bishop," *Sunday Times*, December 9, 1973, 9; and, PT/TT/PIDE/D-F/001/00023, August 22, 1973.

Although Pringle's texts strengthened the Wiriyamu narrative, *The Times* sought additional corroborative evidence to address critics questioning Pringle's powers of recall as a journalist. On August 6, 1973, two priests arrived at the offices of *The Times*: Padre Vicente Berenguer and Padre Júlio Moure. Both said they knew exactly where Wiriyamu was. As mentioned earlier, Padre Berenguer was on a bus at the Eighteenth Crossing near Wiriyamu when he had seen survivors trying to board the bus on which he was traveling.[64] Both corroborated the core of *The Times*' Wiriyamu narrative. Both named five survivors who saw the massacre.[65] "In fact, Wiriyamu has a huge baobab tree with its name tattooed on its trunk," recalled Padre Berenguer. Another source quoting German engineers working in Cahora Bassa dam backed Pringle's findings.

Understanding the Portuguese volte-face

In the face of mounting evidence of a veritable bloodbath in the triangle, Caetano secretly ordered a judicial inquiry into Wiriyamu. Given Portugal's public denials and its expulsion of missionaries, the Roman Catholic Church secretly planned to ensure the safety of five known survivors in Tete.[66] Lisbon's "rigorous inquiry," on the other hand, revealed "a total absence of the alleged facts in the places alleged by the accusers," though the inquiry revealed, "isolated forces had disobeyed orders and have committed at least one 'retaliatory act,' but not at the place alleged by Spanish priests."[67] This was a blatant lie. By this time, Wiriyamu had undergone several such investigations, two of which had been headed by Portuguese medics.[68] The office of the military justice had carried out the third "perhaps in January" of 1973, according to de Arriaga.[69] The present order at Caetano's behest was Lisbon's fourth, fifth if a dissident probe into the affair headed by Jorge Jardim is included, and sixth if the Church hierarchy's airborne visit over the site is tallied.[70]

Irmã Lúcia, a sister involved in the first investigation led by de Arriaga, recalls the events to have taken place soon after de Arriaga's return from Lisbon in late December, and not early January as reported by the general. "I remember it well. One day, a military official stood at my front door. *Eu não sei mesmo qual dia mas lembro-me parece que era antes do Natal.* I do not recall which day but I remember that perhaps it was before Christmas" of 1973.[71] He asked her to pack her bags and get ready to head for Nampula on a military plane. On board, she saw Dr Paz, with whom she had hovered over a small

---

[64] Harry Debelius, "Priest says he spoke to survivors," *The Times*, July 18, 1973.
[65] "Onus on Portugal," *Sunday Times*, August 5, 1973, 12; Peter Pringle, "I survived the Mozambique Massacre," *Sunday Times*, August 5, 1973, 13; and Richard Wigg, "Missionary names five survivors who saw Mozambique massacre," *The Times*, August 6, 1973, 1, 4.
[66] "Secret plan to protect 'massacre' survivors," *Sunday Times*, August 12, 1973, 7.
[67] "Lisbon inquiry rejects massacre story," *The Times*, August 20, 1973, 1.
[68] Adrian Hastings, "The three inquiries: The missionaries, the Bishops, and the Army," *The Times*, August 2, 1973, 14.
[69] Michael Knipe, "Portuguese Army chief defends policy in Mozambique," *The Times*, July 30, 1972.
[70] As quoted in Jack Andersen, "Richard Allen and '73 Massacre in Mozambique," *Washington Post*, December 12, 1972.
[71] De Arriaga's own testimony suggests it was indeed before Christmas. General Kaúlza de Arriaga, *Wiriyamu: Síntese*, accessed March 19, 2010, http://cidadevirtual.pt/k-arriaga/Wiriamu.html.

roadside portion of the Wiriyamu where bodies lay baking in the sun. He looked very pale and withdrawn. Neither said much. Irmã Lúcia said she began to furiously roll her rosary beads. "Oh, what will they do to me?" Once in Nampula, military officials debriefed them. "I told them everything I saw. I did not hold back. I told them we had hovered over parts of the massacre site near the main road." She returned to her parish. "I never saw Dr Paz again!" she said.[72]

De Arriaga's investigation entailed oral interviews but not on-site inspection.[73] By then, the point was moot—the dead had been largely incinerated or buried in communal graves. Some of the remaining informants, who could have participated in the inquiry but were not approached were too terrified to speak for fear of reprisal. Others who had in the meantime been expelled from Mozambique[74] converged in October 1973 to testify before the UN's Commission of Inquiry on the Reported Massacres in Mozambique.[75]

De Arriaga subsequently communicated his findings to Lisbon in a secret memorandum: civilian casualties were involved during Operation Entrapment, but such collateral damage was to be expected in counter-insurgency. The persons responsible were being dealt with appropriately, he added.[76] Meanwhile, he continued as before, pursuing an uncompromisingly aggressive strategy of attrition in Tete, which led to two post-Wiriyamu massacres, one at Kateme and one in Inhaminga, both documented by foreign missionaries, and both outside the scope of this narrative.[77]

Two factors propelled de Arriaga to resist an inquiry: political rivalry between him and his equally ambitious peer leading a similar war in Portugese Guinea, and loyalty to his commanding officers, whose support he could count on when needed. At the time of Operation Marosca, he was in Lisbon,[78] partly to shore up his political fortune. By late 1972, he was facing the meteoric rise of a rival, a formidable cavalry General, later Field Marshall, the charismatic António de Spínola.[79] Unlike him, Spínola was winning the military aspect of the war in Portuguese Guinea,[80] and was gunning for change in the Caetano-led empire.[81] De Arriaga—ideologically opposed to a post-Salazarist Portugal stripped of its colonies—was secretly advocating Caetano's removal.[82] To this

---

[72] Saez de Ugarte, interview, 1995.
[73] ibid.
[74] Among them, twenty-eight were priests and nuns, of whom twelve were based in Madrid, and twelve in Rome. For details, see UN public archives of documents under A/AC.165/PV series: PV.6, PV7, PV.8, PV.9, PV.10, PV.11; PV.12; PV.13; PV.14; PV.15; and PV.16.
[75] General Assembly, *Report of the Commission of Inquiry on the Reported Massacres in Mozambique, Official Records: Twenty-Ninth Session, Supplement*, 21, A/9621 (1974), 1–41.
[76] "Memorando enviado por Kaúlza de Arriaga a Pimentel dos Santos," n.d.
[77] Fathers J. Martens, A. Verdaasdonk, J. van Rijen, A. van Kampen, and J. Tielemans, "Diary of Inhaminga," *Issue: A Journal of Opinion*, 4, 2 (1974): 62–73.
[78] De Arriaga, *Wiriyamu: Síntese*.
[79] PT/TT/PIDE/D-F/001/00029, January 18, 1974.
[80] Dhada, *Warriors at Work*, 37–45.
[81] António de Spínola, *Portugal e o Futuro* (Lisbon: Arcadia, 1974). Additional materials on this work are to be found on the Cavaleiros do Norte blog, accessed March 14, 2010, http://cavaleirosdonorte. blogspot.com/2010/02/portugal-e-o-futuro-de-António-spinola.html.
[82] Coronel Manuel Amaro Bernardo, "Entrevista do General Kaúlza de Arriaga," carried out in 1997, accessed March 19, 2010, http://macua.blogs.com/moambique_para_todos/wiriamu/. De Arriaga's views on the loss of the empire was later fully developed in a collaborative text three years after the end of the Portuguese empire, in Joaquim da Luz Cunha, Kaúlza de Arriaga, Bethencourt Rodrigues, and Silvino Silvério Marques, *África: A Vitória Traída* (Braga, Lisbon: Editorial Inervenção, 1977).

end, he had began assembling influential allies to challenge Caetano.[83] One key convert to his camp was Jorge Jardim, the influential Salazarist masterminding Caetano's damage-control strategy in Tete.[84]

De Arriaga *had* to resist a Wiriyamu inquiry to protect his chosen subordinate protégé Videira who could rally the troops under his command to back his political move against Caetano. The alternative was to commit political *hara-kiri*, which would have removed him as a contestant to António Spinola, leaving the latter unopposed to tackle Caetano.

Lisbon got wind of these machinations and relieved him of his command, thereby ending his power-base to launch his political career. Videira had already been called to Lisbon.[85] Defiant and unrepentant, de Arriaga had the last say as he departed the colonial capital, declaring his work unfinished but proud of his soldiers and their heroic performance in battle for the glory of the nation. In other words, Wiriyamu was in essence an inevitable civilian casualty of counter-insurgency and not a blot on Portugal's imperial history.[86] Publicly, he continued to maintain this absolute denial of the Portuguese massacre of Wiriyamu, as Caetano had done until 2009. Nothing unwarranted had occurred at Wiriyamu:[87] "*Não ocorreu nada em Wiriamu. Não houve nenhum crime em Wiriamu.*"[88] No crime was committed. Five years later, he changed the text slightly, admitting that approximately sixty died, among them terrorists and civilians.[89] This is how the Wiriyamu whitewash, if we can call it that, helped to ruin de Arriaga's nascent political career as he lunged at Caetano's leadership, which came to naught.

The Caetano regime was now on the defensive in the face of de Arriaga's findings that essentially confirmed the basic outline of *The Times*' narrative to be true. By August 20, 1973, even Bruce Loudon, who had backed Lisbon in the denial, admitted in an *apologia pro vita sua* that the colonial army had engaged in carnage but he rationalized it by explaining how and why it had taken place.

By mid-August, Portugal came out and admitted: "some killings of innocent civilians may well have taken place, but this was only to be expected in guerrilla war."[90] In other words, while it could no longer deny the existence of Wiriyamu, it still could deny the magnitude of the killings, and did so somewhat indefensibly while Caetano remained in power.[91]

However, the preponderance of evidence suggested that *The Times*' Wiriyamu report narrating the massacre of 400 or more was indeed true at the location as revealed—and had been true all along. The truth of that story could have been told

---

[83] Eduardo de Sousa Ferreira, "An Analysis of the 'Spinola Affair,'" *Africa Today*, 21, 2 (1974): 69–73.
[84] Jardim's views are given in Jorge Jardim, *Moçambique–Terra Queimada* (Lisbon: Intervenção, 1976).
[85] "Portuguese commander leaves Tete," *The Times*, September 10, 1973, 4.
[86] For de Arriaga's side of the story, explore his Wiriyamu-related documents, accessed March 19, 2010, http://cidadevirtual.pt/k-arriaga/Wiriamu.html.
[87] "Censura 16, "Wiriyamu (tape recording)," *Notícias da Amadora*, 618, July 21, 1973.
[88] Paulo Oliveira, "Kaúlza de Arriaga e o 'Peso de Wiriamu,'" *Público*, February 4, 2004.
[89] João Paulo Guerra, *Descolonização Portuguesa: O Regresso das Caravelas* (Lisbon: Oficina dos Livros, 2009), 61.
[90] *Cable: 1973Lourenn00559_b, 1973,* August 14, 14: 46.
[91] "Lisbon inquiry rejects massacre story," *The Times*, August 20, 1973, 1.

with greater depth and detail, perhaps, but for Portugal's obduracy in obstructing access to primary sources. On balance, Portugal's conduct after the revelations exacerbated the tragedy, said Hastings.[92] It shifted the burden of proof on Portugal to furnish the evidence needed to support their contentions.

More bad news followed that exposed Portugal's duplicity—claiming denial while clearly knowing the real truth. Nearly a month after Loudon's piece appeared in *The Daily Telegraph*, *The Times* published the letter from the bishops of Mozambique, mentioned earlier in this text, that had been sent to the colonial governor-general well before *The Times* revelation, in which they discussed the massacre while protesting over the colonial army's excessive use of violence in counter-insurgency. Five days after the publication of this letter, the Johannesburg *Star* of September 25, 1973, confirmed that according to their Portuguese primary sources, the story of Wiriyamu as revealed in *The Times* was true.[93] Following demands from fourteen countries for an international commission of inquiry,[94] the United Nations formed a tri-continental commission three months later to investigate the massacre.

In the meantime, the changes in Portugal's positions had riddled its counter-narrative with untenable contradictions. The US State Department's private view was less charitable. Portugal had bungled the handling with reversals lacking in credibility.[95] While admitting publicly to having engaged in a probable case of mass violence, its military continued denying the story, except for a pro-Spinola faction of the Portuguese armed forces which considered the colonial wars politically lost. This faction, it was revealed later in the papers had already confirmed privately the veracity of the massacre, which the Caetanist regime quashed as a rumor.[96] The state, meanwhile, persecuted anyone in its empire, including priests, seditiously connected with the story. In some instances, torture was used on victims to extort information, leading to arrests on treasonous charges.[97]

In engaging in quibbles over a place of carnage, and over numbers killed, Portugal dismissed a graver gut-wrenching moral argument: acts of inhumanity against innocent civilians. These quibbles, though, proved inconsequential. The revelations of the Wiriyamu massacre had the effect FRELIMO most wanted—shatter the silence enveloping Portugal's wars in Africa,[98] opening fissures of discontent in the empire. The revelations demoralized the army in Tete, allowing Raimundo Dalepa to besiege the city of Tete, while FRELIMO cadres advanced deeper into Mozambique's Manica-e-Sofala midriff. Six months after the revelations, Caetano's regime fell. The Portuguese-armed forces toppled it in a bloodless coup, declaring the war in the colonies as politically unwinnable.[99]

---

[92] Hastings, interviews, 1977, 1978, 1979, 1981, 1995, 1996.
[93] Michael Knipe, "S. African newspaper gives new details of Portuguese massacre at Wiriyamu," *The Times*, September 26, 1973, 1.
[94] "14 Countries call for inquiry on massacre," *The Times*, November 8, 1973, 10.
[95] US Department of State, "More on Alleged Mozambique Massacre," *Cable: 1973Lourenn00559_b, 1973* August 14, 14: 46.
[96] "Army report confirms Wiriyamu massacre," *The Times*, April 24, 1974, 8.
[97] Harry Debelius, "Portuguese accused of torture by priests," *The Times*, November 20, [n.year].
[98] Marcello Caetano, *Depoimento* (Rio de Janeiro: Distribuidora Record, 1974), 182.
[99] António de Spínola, *Portugal e o Futuro: Análise da Conjuntura Nacional* (Lisbon: Editora Arcádia, 1974), 247.

Democracy was ushered into Portugal with tumultuous fragility. Mozambique too was set free at last. In this sense, Wiriyamu became part of a wider narrative that collectively helped Portugal usher in pluralism and grant negotiated independence for the colonized fighting its empire in Africa. In fact, you could be forgiven to think, Wiriyamu liberated Portugal from the shackles of imperial fascism.

The new regime, once established, acknowledged fully the veracity of *The Times*' narrative *in carne et sanguine*.[100] By then, the United Nations had already documented the story on its own by cataloging the evidence,[101] which it then published as a report seven months after the coup, on November 22, 1974.[102] That is how the Wiriyamu narrative was revealed, dismissed, denied in parts, and contested with counter-narratives, and how it came finally to rest as a commonly agreed text—until 2012.

---

[100] Foreign Staff, "Army report confirms Wiriyamu Massacre," *The Times*, April 24, 1974, 8.
[101] Tim Jones, "UN hearing on Portuguese atrocity reports begins," *The Times*, May 15, 1974, 5.
[102] "UN report accuses Portugal of atrocities," *The Times*, December 10, 1974, 1.

9

Wiriyamu before the Massacre

In 2012, the Birmingham-based journal *Civil Wars* published an article on Wiriyamu. As discussed earlier in this book, the article suggested, the lacuna in affirmative narratives on Wiriyamu was sufficiently strong to question its overall veracity. Seven key weaknesses in the story, the article imputed, undermined Wiriyamu's integrity: its identity, location, the fact that Portuguese maps do not mention it; where the massacres occurred; transiency of the wiped-out villages; identity of the killers; uncertainty of what happened on that day of December 16, 1972; and the exact numbers killed.

It makes little sense to rehash the methods the article deployed to support all these claims—we have tackled our response to them in this book's earlier chapters. What remains to be done here and in the rest of the book is to tackle questions I left unaddressed in my two responses to the article, of which one was published in that same journal.[1]

Wiriyamu and the destroyers

Where was Wiriyamu and who destroyed it? Several independent sources confirm Wiriyamu's existence. It was clearly named in Tete's mission maps,[2] which *The Times* of London subsequently confirmed.[3] It was recorded on a Portuguese map drawn on tracing paper, which this author viewed recently.[4] Apart from the 216 families interviewed who are familiar with the sites of the massacre,[5] several can identify the villages in the Wiriyamu triangle.[6] Of these, at least forty-seven knew of Wiriyamu. Forty-five could attest to it as a place on the map. Only five denied the place existed as reported, without having paid a visit to the site to back their claims. Fifteen lived in or near Wiriyamu before the massacre, fourteen were there during the massacre, eleven visited it almost immediately after the

---

[1] Dhada, "The Wiriyamu Massacre of 1972: Response to Reis and Oliveira": 551–558; and Dhada, "The Wiriyamu Massacre of 1972: Its Context, Genesis, and Revelation": 1–31.
[2] Harry Derelius, "Wiriyamu 'is marked on Tete mission maps," *The Times*, July 16, 1973, 1d.
[3] ibid.
[4] Access to view this map was granted on two conditions, not to reveal its provenance and not to provide its precise location. However, assiduous efforts are underway to ferret it out of its closely guarded archival shell.
[5] See Table 3, Djemusse population census, 1972 estimates; Table 4, Wiriyamu population census, 1972 estimates; Table 5, Juawu population census, 1972 estimates; Table 6, Riachu population census, 1972 estimates; and Table 7, Chaworha population census, 1972 estimates.
[6] See Table 1, Attesters to Wiriyamu.

massacre, and two spent time at the site decades later to piece together life before Wiriyamu's destruction or reconstruct the destruction itself.

Of the numbers cited here, six were priests and a nun, one a medical doctor, seven were survivors, two were helicopter pilots, one took an inspection team to hover over the site, twenty were army and DGS personnel or persons associated with the colonial apparatus, three were civilians, two associated with FRELIMO, and two are—Cabrita and myself. One corpulent sentinel who had borne witness to everyday life at Wiriyamu, stood immovably grounded, watching the carnage unfold, helpless, and bereft of tears. It was a baobab—its silky girth tattooed with "Wiriyamu." The tree reportedly "died" in the early 1990s.

Two groups were directly responsible for the massacre: the DGS and the Portuguese colonial armed forces. Both groups were exceptionally well trained for Operation Marosca, as we shall see in a moment. The DGS contingent was headed by Chico, and Johnny, both familiar with the area. Both were skilled in torture, extortion, and had recruited many paid informants at sponsored football matches and dance events sponsored by the Tete diocese. Both acted at the instructional behest of the DGS.

The other component was important too, namely, soldiers of the Sixth Company of Commandos, trained to be pathologically efficient in executing missions akin to Marosca; the B. Caç 17 logistic support unit; and the Portuguese Air Force.

The Sixth Company of commandos was established in January 1972, after undergoing rigorous formative training first at the battalion headquarters for Mozambique-based commandos in Nampula, and then advanced three-month-long counter-insurgency preparation. On August 9, 1972, 150 of the company's 204 members were selected to form the Sixth Company of commandos, supported by medics, logistics, communication, radio and telegraph transmissions, transportation personnel.[7]

This contingent split subsequently into six groups, each comprising of five highly mobile alpha sub-units. Except for a brief interlude of twenty-eight days between October 20 and November 17, 1972, the C group of the Sixth Company began operating in Tete upon arrival on August 23, 1972, where it remained until January 1973. Once the war had intensified south of Tete, the Company was pulled out, given a month's rest before new deployment, and dispatched to Inhaminga on February 22, 1973, to stem FRELIMO's advance towards Beira. There the unit stayed for thirteen months, during which time it destroyed 300 homes in a series of sixteen three-day missions in an effort to capture FRELIMO combatants.

According to its commander, dated intelligence underpinned his unit's failure to capture them. "By the time we got there, the trail had run cold, and the enemy was nowhere to be seen."[8] Without captured enemy combatants, the men in his unit had no fresh intelligence to stem FRELIMO's southern march. On June 1, 1974, the unit made one final month-long push against FRELIMO in Inhaminga, during which time it carried out thirteen three-day operations engaging direct enemy fire. This offensive

---

[7] 6ª Companhia de Commandos de Moçambique, *História da Unidade: Primeiro Fascículo* (Montepuez: CCM, 1992).
[8] Melo, interview, 1995 and 2014.

was operationally perhaps the most intense in the history of this company and similar commando units operating in the region. In the end, they had little to show for it, the exception being a post-Wiriyamu massacre at Inhaminga—Portugal's last bloodbath before its exit a year later—in which 200 villagers died, some hung by their feet during interrogation, others subjected to torture.[9]

Wiriyamu's killers acted as plenipotentiaries for Portugal's African empire in colonial Mozambique. They were not killers on a binge. Oral evidence from survivors corroborate first-hand accounts by a military commander that this massacre was planned and executed as intended. Further, the massacre was not as interpreted on the pages of *The Times* as Portugal's My Lai, that is to say, unauthorized by military high command.[10] Luis Heren of *The Times* made that analogy partly because he was a journalist committed to publish stories of human interest, and partly because he had been exposed to My Lai revelations during his stay in Washington as foreign editor. It is not surprising that the DGS's archives under the PIDE nomenclature appear to single out Chico as one of several architects of the massacre, thereby allowing interpretative room, to view the massacre an act of unauthorized mass violence.[11] The responsibility conclusively rested, and still rests, on Portugal's blood-soaked shoulders.

The Wiriyamu triangle in structural perspective

Wiriyamu began life at the turn of the last century "*mas não estamos certos quando*," but we are not so sure when. "What we know is that Sanganembo, the founder, came from the south near the Luenha River..." after the Tawara rebellion of 1917[12] "to this place where we are standing," said my informants. "He came accompanied by our ancestors." "What do you mean ancestors?" "*Assim como falamos*," just as we said. Pressed to explain the riddle, they added, "he did not come alone but the spirits of our ancestors told him to place roots here." The neighboring village of Chaworha had a similar genesis, though very little is known of its prosopographic origins. The little we know suggests the village to have had a succession of leaders, the last of whom was said to have been the savviest.

If what was said of Wiriyamu's founding was true, then they had chosen well. Protected by mountains on all three sides, Wiriyamu was cobwebbed with streams, creeks and puddles. It was set in a forest, helpful for making coal and for the spirit world to nurture the emerging villages. Fifty years after its foundation, Wiriyamu and the surrounding communities blossomed to play an important role in the colonial cattle-raising economy. Leading the pack were 325 families from the four villages living in the Wiriyamu complex, and the village of Chaworha, which together generated over

---

[9] Special Correspondence, "Portuguese commander denies massacres," *Catholic Herald*, May 24, 1974; and Martens et al., "Diary of Inhaminga," 62–73.
[10] Melo, interview, 1995 and 2014.
[11] PT/TT/PIDE/D-F/001/00023.
[12] For a discussion on the tradition of resistance to colonial rule in the region, see Allen F. Isaacman, *The Tradition of Resistance in Mozambique: The Zambesi Valley, 1850–1921* (Berkeley: University of California Press, 1976), 163–177.

half a million Portuguese escudos in total assets, the majority held in cattle stock.[13] Excluded from this equation were the villages of Trabuco and Kongorhogondo, of which we know very little, but which form an important part of this story.

Wiriyamu was located in Tete, a colonial district of 37,999 square miles with a population of 488,668 in 1970, spread across 1,390 villages and cities. According to the 1997 census, Tete's population doubled to 1,144,604, increasing again ten years later to reach 1,783,967.[14] The population of Wiriyamu and the surrounding communities in 1970 was estimated at 13,264 spread over 40 villages, the largest of which was Inhacumba, just north of Chaworha. After the massacre, it came to accommodate 2,500 people, some of whom were Chaworha survivors. The smallest hamlet was Capese, again near the Zambezi, off the Luenha tributary in the southernmost tip of the triangle.[15]

There are no reliable figures on the triangle's population in the census records after 1970. The 2007 census suggests a drop, provided that the triangle's population is combined with the rest of the Changara region, which declined because of resettlement and social upheavals brought on by the Cahora Bassa dam.[16]

Wiriyamu's surrounding geography was distinct. Wedged at the uppermost part of a triangle south of the mighty Zambezi, its apex pointed to Tete, the district capital. It was surrounded on three sides by five mountains: Coroeira to the north, Nhanguiro to the west, with Nhadimba, Jaque and Pamaboe bordering the adjoining colonial district in the south, Manica-e-Sofala. A highway to its left built in the 1970s connected Changara to the city of Tete, 15.5 miles from Wiriyamu. Changara, originally named after a descendant of the Mutapa dynasty circa 1759–1785,[17] was a small colonial outpost 50 miles south of Tete. The Luenha River, also known as the Mavuzi or M'vuzi, a tributary of the River Zambezi, ran along Wiriyamu's southern base. The Luenha, the north–south road from Tete, and the River Zambezi as it bent southbound away from Tete city, cradled Wiriyamu and Chaworha (see Map 3, of the triangle).

Wiriyamu sat perched on the chin of a massive rock shaped like a seahorse bent at its neck, which later came to acquire a deeply etched north–south footpath studded with baobabs. It shared with Chaworha a large clearing used as a football field and cattle market located between Cravina and Cambalame. A switchback dirt track later cleaved the rock on which Wiriyamu sat. At the eastern end of the track stood the aforementioned baobab tree. Years later, that tree acquired a tattoo spelling the words "Wiriyamu." Before Wiriyamu's destruction seventy years later, the track was approximately 6.5 miles long, and ran east–west. That same track etched the margins of a seasonal creek connecting the banks of the River Zambezi to the main thoroughfare,

---

[13] Information calculated from retail pricing of cows, chickens, and goats provided by informants.
[14] See Mustafah Dhada, "Table, Tete Villages and Estimated Population, 1970–2007," accessed May 18, 2014, http://preview.tinyurl.com/q4yn52t.
[15] See Table 2, Wiriyamu triangle, population census, 1970–2007; and Map 3 of the Wiriyamu triangle.
[16] Instituto nacional de Estatística, *Geohive, Mozambique, General Information*, accessed October 12, 2014, http://www.geohive.com/cntry/mozambique.aspx.
[17] D. N. Beach, "The Mutapa Dynasty: A Comparison of Documentary and Traditional Evidence," *History in Africa*, 3 (1976): 10.

which later was developed into a highway at a T junction called "Cruzmanento 18," the Eighteenth Crossing.[18]

Of the forty villages in the triangle, five (not three) were affected by the massacre: Wiriyamu, Djemusse, Riachu, Juawu and Chaworha. Wiriyamu's thirty families lived in forty-three homes; Djemusse's thirty-five families were in forty-three houses; Riachu's fourteen families nested in thirty-six thatched mud-huts; Juawu was led by thirty families living in forty-three houses; and Chaworha, the largest village, had 107 families living in 128 houses.[19]

After the massacre, the villages of Juawu, Djemusse, Riachu and Chaworha disappeared. Given that none of the dead had been given a timely and proper burial, a return would have invited the spirits of the departed to haunt the living.[20] When pressed to explain, "Why wake up the dead?" they responded. If parallel studies among the Shona are any indication, it would be safe to assume that the people of Wiriyamu subscribed to a type of Ngozi and Chikwambo, two spirits from the dead, one requiring specific restitutions to avenge the wronged and the other beyond healing, destined to inhabit the living, causing behavioral and social dissonance from the inside out.[21]

Some of the returning survivors reconstituted the villages of Juawu and Wiriyamu at a location nearby. Others congregated along the Pata and the Eighteenth Crossing to form several new villages, the largest of which were Cuevo, Cambalame, Lami and Chinhome. One batch of survivors regrouped to form the village of Nicompe, under the shadow of Chaworha's rocky outcrop. "Wasn't that risky, to be so near the former village?" "But we are Christians and protected from such visitations... *eles não podem visitar-nos*, they cannot visit us," murmured Mixone. The chapel he helped build near the site stood, in his view, as an expiatory sentinel to protect the living from the haunting dead.

The village of Djemusse lay 0.93 miles east of Juawu and was perilously close to the Cahora Bassa power lines at Mepinga Triangulation Station.[22] Very little is known about its structure and physical geography before erasure, except for the two baobab trees framing its top and tail. The village itself was spread on a flat surface offering a clear view of the horizon. The village ended in a drop, below which lay the semi-circular gulch nesting Riachu. Djemusse's one baobab was located 692 adult footsteps from the chief Wiriyamu's compound. Its snarly root-knuckles guarded bone remnants of victims that fell at this massacre site.

Diagonal from Djemusse lay Riachu. Nestled under large boulders some seven to ten feet below Wiriyamu, it was twenty-three adult paces northeast of Bulachu's hut. The latter stood at the mouth of the village and was near a tamarind tree close to the

---

[18] See Map 3 of the Wiriyamu triangle.
[19] See Table 2, Wiriyamu triangle, population census, 1970–2007, which incidentally excludes the census for Ratinho which, for reasons unknown, eluded the census-takers in 1997.
[20] For an useful study on haunting and spirit possession, see Victor Igreja, Beatrice Dias-Lambranca, Douglas A. Hershey, Limore Racin, Annemiek Richters, and Ria Reis, "The Epidemiology of Spirit Possession in the Aftermath of Mass Political Violence in Mozambique," *Social Science and Medicine*, 71 (2010): 592–599.
[21] Heike Schmidt, "Healing the Wounds of War: Memories of Violence and the Making of History in Zimbabwe's Most Recent Past," *Journal of Southern African Studies*, 23, 2 (June 1997): 301–310.
[22] Igreja, Dias-Lambranca, Hearchey, Racin, Richters, and Reis, "The Epidemology of Spirit Possession," 592–599.

Riachu gulch. Riachu was difficult to detect from Wiriyamu's central village, which saved some of its people during Operation Entrapment; those who perished happened to be visiting other affected villages. A seasonal stream cut through the village, making the soil rich for pasture and suitable for small agricultural plots.[23]

The village of Juawu was 4.9 miles from the Eighteenth Crossing. Its western edge dropped into a ravine studded with trees bereft of trunks, branches and foliage, their stumps left alive to grow again. The trees supplied much needed "*lenha,*" wood for domestic consumption, and wood for making coal. The village maintained a makeshift brewery and butchery and an open-air space that served as a watering hole during social gatherings. Juawu also had an adobe platform on its eastern edge used by spirit mediums in the triangle.

A three-mile-long windy footpath connected these villages with Chaworha, which was nearly one mile away to the northwest as the crow flies. This village was located 446 feet above sea level. Headed by its chief, the village of Chaworha nestled behind an elevated set of boulders shaped like a crocodile looped around mud-huts. Chaworha stretched itself flat against the dry creek, the southern margins of which rose to accommodate a windy footpath towards Riachu. Weeks before its destruction, Chaworha had acquired a well dug by the colonial authorities to provide a steady supply of water to the village.

After its foundation, the Wiriyamu triangle went through three historical periods. The first period of rapid economic growth, lasting for forty years, was driven by easy access to water; followed by a dramatic rise in social inequality. In the last period, Wiriyamu faced two threats to its survival: one from the chieftaincy of Kongorhogondo; and the other from a DGS mole. One lonely voice stood helplessly outside these threats, warning the villages of an apocalypse, "one of these days and very soon, you are going to see '*fogo, fogo*.'" By that, he meant the place was rife for burning—or that is how my informants interpreted it in retrospect. But they added, he was a bit touched, unhinged… "*ele era loco, um pouco parafuzado*," an outcast dismissed as a fool!

Creeks, rivers, and puddles

Water was central to the Wiriyamu triangle's first historical period. Its people viewed water as an ecological resource and as a gift from the spirit world. As an ecological resource, they shared water with the wild flora and fauna, the latter occupying the lion's share in the nearby Zambezi River, leaving the people an exclusive access to water "*no terreno, e la em baixo*" both on and in the ground (i.e. in creeks, streams, river, puddles, and wells).

Fauna-dominated water was shared as a communal resource. The norm for bathing in the river followed a simple cautionary ritual. Before wading into the river, bathers would throw a rock where crocodiles were spotted. Any splash or sudden movement

---

[23] As we saw earlier, the Zambezi patriarch had the largest number of goats in the village, an important fact that played a crucial role in the events that brought FRELIMO to the Wiriyamu village.

that ensued would confirm their presence and the spot was avoided. There were times when villagers would bathe in the exact spot vacated by them. On such instances, several would stand as sentinels to alert them of the approaching tailed marauders. Crocodiles assumed another significance outside ecology, characterizing malevolence in the context of the spirit world;[24] as did lions when turned predators. Here, they signified aberrant conduct calling for remedial rituals and restitution.

Hippopotamuses were a different matter. Here, there appeared to have been few effective tools to displace them, particularly when fishing in canoes. There were incidents in the triangle when whole canoes would capsize, thrown up in the air by the sudden rise of a submerged hippo.

Four creeks and a major river, a tributary of the mighty Zambezi, supplied water to the triangle. Matacamtuira fed the village of Nicompo, which was wedged between Chaworha and Wiriyamu. The Nhaticona creek supplied water to three villages: Wiriyamu, Cabuiro, and Cambalane. The Pata creek, which faced a boulder blocking the neck of the Zambezi, hugged the periphery of the Mapara village, the smallest in this nook, and as it approached the 488-feet-high rocky outcrop north of Wiriyamu, it bifurcated into two creeks, Chirodue, which followed the northern contours of the Wiriyamu outcrops near the village of Riachu, and Nhaticona, which squiggled towards the main road, passing through the village of Juawu, where it ran nearly dry. Both the creek and the sparsely populated village of Mapara were later used to transport FRELIMO arms and ammunition. The Chirodue creek connecting Pata with Matucamtuira descended into a pool used by Riachu during rainy season.

The boulder blocking the mouth of Pata engorged the Zambezi upstream, enough to feed a widely etched gash formed by the Cuiro River, north of Pata. This river fed the seasonal creeks downstream, while supplying water for both Wiriyamu and occasionally Chaworha's southern neighbor, Nicompo. This river also formed a clear "border" between Chaworha and Wiriyamu.

The other major river, the Luenha, had a much grander style. While the creeks at the apex of the triangle were somewhat unpredictable as water suppliers, the Luenha slithered along the base of the triangle, snaking through the Changara highway on its way south. The supply of steady and abundant water here nurtured the second most populous set of six villages in the triangle, all clustered around Mandie.[25]

Between October and May, the triangle relied exclusively on rainfall, while surplus rain water replenished the creeks and streams, which then served the needs of the triangle between May and September, by which time the creeks and seasonal streams ran dry in time for the rainy seasons to fill them up. Dry creeks, though, helped demarcate villages. Watering holes dug during the rainy seasons as offshoots from creeks met the needs of grazing animals after the month of May. Occasionally, watery creeks were an opportunity for children and young adults to learn to fish.

---

[24] Kyed and Buur, "New Sites of Citizenship," 579.
[25] ibid.

The spirit world and the rainmakers

From the viewpoint of the spirit world, rainmaking, and celebrating its downpour, was central for a balanced relationship between the heavens above holding water, "*a água lá no céu*," the people of Wiriyamu needing water, and the spirit of the ancestors facilitating the downpour.

At the center of rainmaking stood *mphondorho*, also referred to in the written literature on a similar entity among the Shona as *mhondoro*, the lion spirit, a benevolent spirit hovering over the living, embodying ancestors (here Wiriyamu's past chieftaincies). There is now considerable literature on the spirit world, secret forests, sorcery,[26] witchcraft,[27] and spirit mediums covering Malawi, the Zambezi,[28] present-day Zimbabwe among the Shona people and northwest Zimbabwe in general,[29] and the Ndau,[30] though very little exists on Tete's Nyungwe living in the triangle. While this body of works informs the narrative here, its focus lies elsewhere, specifically, how informants viewed the lion spirit as a rainmaker.

Briefly, the chiefs of Wiriyamu and Chaworha "*controlava tudo isto que está ver*" controlled everything that you see here. They led the people, governed their affairs, and acted as arbitrators of personal conflicts, contests over land use, domestic disputes, and disputes related to animal husbandry.

For matters of visionary importance, the well-being and prosperity of the community as a whole, or for matters outside their comprehension or immediate competence, the chiefs accessed the greater power of the spirit world. To this end, a designated envoy of the chief tapped specially qualified persons, spirit mediums; through whom the *mphondorho* would speak, and in the case of rainmaking instruct them what to do next.

---

[26] Harry G. West, "Sorcery of Construction and Socialist Modernization: Ways of Understanding Power in Postcolonial Mozambique," *American Ethnologist*, 28, 1 (February 2001): 119–150; and Harry G. West, "Creative Destruction and Sorcery of Construction: Power, Hope and Suspicion in Post-War Mozambique," *Cahiers d'Études Africaines*, 37, 147 (1997): 675–698.

[27] Kingsley Garbett, "Contrasting Realities: Changing Perceptions of Shona Witch Beliefs and Practices," *Social Analysis: The International Journal of Social and Cultural Practice*, 42, 2 (July 1998): 24–47; Paolo Israel, "The War of Lions: Witch-Hunts, Occult Idioms and Post-Socialism in Northern Mozambique," *Journal of Southern African Studies*, 35, 1 (March 2009): 155–174.

[28] C. S. Lancaster, "The Zambesi Goba Ancestral Cult," *Africa: Journal of the International African Institute*, 47, 3 (1977): 229–241.

[29] David Auret, "The Mhondoro Spirits of Supernatural Significance in the Culture of the Shona," *African Studies*, 41, 2 (1982): 173–187; Terrence Ranger, "Territorial Cults in the History of Central Africa," *The Journal of African History*, 14, 4 (1973): 581–597; Jocelyn Alexander and Terence Ranger, "Competition and Integration in the Religious History of North-Western Zimbabwe," *Journal of Religion in Africa*, 28, 1 (February 1988): 3–31; and David Lan, *Guns and Rain: Guerrillas and Spirit Mediums in Zimbabwe* (Berkeley: University of California Press, 1995), 31–39, 61–68, 139–153, 157–174, 210–215, and 219–222. Lan's text is critically reviewed in M. F. C. Bourbillon, "Guns and Rain: Taking Structural Analysis Too Far," *Africa: Journal of the International African Institute*, 57, 2 (1987): 263–274.

[30] Victor Igreja, Béatrice Dias-Lambranca and Annemiek Richters, "Gamba Spirits, Gender Relations, and Healing in Post-Civil War Gorongosa, Mozambique," *The Journal of the Royal Anthropological Institute*, 14, 2 (June 2008): 353–371.

The role of the spirit medium extended to expiating demons, neutralizing curses, and reining in malevolent spirits unleashed by design or begging to be healed. As a hovering spirit, the *mphondorho* was ever present as an umbilical continuum linking the people to their collective past, while communing with them in the present. To be inattentive to it and its power, seen always for the good, led to chaos and calamity. When it appeared, invoked or uninvited, specific rituals via the spirit medium facilitated contact, which, once established, allowed the people to seek its help.

The triangle had two such spirit mediums. One was Senhor Soda. The name of the other escaped my informants. "He was not that good," they added. "Oh, what made him not so good but the good good or very good?" I asked. "But there was also a third one." "Who?" I interjected. "Oh, not that one!" said one informant to Bulachu Pensadu Zambezi, ignoring the rest of us. "Nah, he went mad." "But who?" I insisted, "who?" "The one who said *fogo, fogo*," they replied. One informant arched his eyebrow, pitying my clear inability to second guess where the text was heading.

Spirit mediums excelling at what they did, exhibited an aversion to modernity, had undergone rigorously long apprenticeships and were seen by the community as persons of integrity. An elusive itinerant lifestyle allowed them to remain detached from local politics. This contextual independence afforded maximum transparency for the lion spirit to speak through flesh and blood. In the case of Senhor Soda, where he lived is to this day unclear. "He lived over there," said a member of the Tenente Valeta household, pointing towards the mountains guarding the Luenha River. "But where exactly? Can you take me there to talk to him?" "Well, I don't know I can. He might not be there, or he might. He moves."[31]

But what ensured the *mphondorho* an unrefracted communion with the people of Wiriyamu was the spirit medium's view that because their body allowed *mphondorho* to vocalize, it justly deserved protection from external forces inimical to the spirit world. Avoiding modernity at all costs was seen as paramount, such as eschewing the use of perfumed substances, proximity to blood, substances contaminated with blood, and excessive contacts with the symbols of colonial power and their representatives. This allowed the lion spirit to be close to the spirit medium's etherial jugular. In this regard, the spirit mediums in the triangle shared a similar lifestyle with their counterparts south of the border among the Shona.[32]

Very little information was forthcoming on the formative and prolonged training of the spirit mediums, except that "We can't tell you more about this. He can. Senhor Soda can. What we know is that it takes years for them to mature." Additional discussion with informants suggested the process entailed a long period of increasing success with a gradual acceptance by the community of a given spirit medium as an effective professional.

Here an advocate proved crucial in lubricating the professionalization process. His role—he was always a male—was to negotiate between the chiefs who designated him as a mediator, and the spirit medium. In this way, the advocate parleyed his power-base

---

[31] Vasco Valeta, interview, 1995.
[32] Lan, *Guns and Rain*, 31–39, 61–68, 139–153, 157–174, 210–215, and 219–222.

on which a spirit medium built his practice in the field. This process was as much symbiotically intuitive as culture-of-evidence driven.

To illustrate how important the advocate was in mediating the needs of the village while promoting a spirit medium, the case of Mr "Fogo Fogo" is instructive. He was an apprentice in the field but had repeatedly failed as a rainmaker. Lack of *savoir-faire* did not help in procuring an advocate with diplomatic skills to advance his professional narrative.

Without the soft skills, he was left at the margins, still able to channel some form of intuitive understanding of the rapidly changing political landscape sweeping the triangle, and convey these with a genuine intent to win back his standing in the community. Given that he worked for a cattle buyer based in a neighboring village, he may well have overheard his employer and his white friends talk about the triangle. Additional inquiries on this front failed to produce concrete evidence on whether he was indeed inspired by the *mphondorho* to speak on an event about to occur or was simply conveying what he had overheard.

The ritual for rainmaking began with a change of clothes. "They had to be cotton," not synthetic. Senhor Soda then headed towards Juawu, walking staff in hand, to the adobe platform. While seated, he cleansed himself and the air of impurities with tobacco smoke for the *mphondorho* to enter. Senhor Soda then went into a trance. "But isn't tobacco smelly?" I asked. "No. You are not listening carefully here... *vocé não está ouvir bem aquí.*" The tobacco smoke created a vaporous shroud to throw a veil around the lion spirit as it entered the spirit medium. Thus transfused into his flesh, and therefore under human embodiment, the *mphondorho* instructed Senhor Soda what to do next to address the needs of the supplicants.

The *mphondorho* could prescribe more serious rituals to resolve cases of severe drought or cases needing expiation of deeply embedded curses. These rituals might include a pilgrimage to the sacred forest—here, my research trail went cold, except to note that the triangle had several such sacred forests, which, no one knew where or if they knew where, were unwilling to reveal its location.[33] Normally, Senhor Soda led the procession, staff in hand, followed by vestal virgins. "Why virgins?" "Because they are not tampered by men. They are pure," was the reply. It is not known what transpired once the procession entered the sacred forest. Similar studies elsewhere indicate its importance in expiation rituals and conservation of the local ecology.[34]

Village life

Access to water allowed a reasonably well-settled existence, details of which are worthy of note here, if only to dispel the transiency thesis. What follows is a post-mortem portrait of village life in the triangle re-created without a time frame. It is

---

[33] Zambezi, interview, 1995; Kaniveti, interview, 1995; António Cachavi, interview by author, Tete, 1995; Vasco Valeta, interview, 1995; Podista Mchenga, interview by author, Tete and Wiriyamu, 1995; Mixone, interview, 1995; a member of the Xavieri household, interview by author, Riachu, 1995; and Tomas Pita Cebola, Facebook interview, 2014 and 2015.

[34] Bruce A. Byers, Robert N. Cunliffe, and Andrew T. Hudak, "Linking the Conservation of Culture and Nature: A Case Study of Sacred Forests in Zimbabwe," *Human Ecology*, 29, 2 (June 2001): 187–218.

indeed as denuded of textured depth as Landeg White's *Magomero* is not.[35] Nevertheless, its brevity accomplishes two objectives: to lift the curtain on Wiriyamu's biography before its destruction without intentionally inviting it to be viewed as a rural idyl, and to lay the groundwork for what was about to happen on the morning of December, 16—the subject of the next chapter.

Outside cattle raising, the five villages came to rely heavily on subsistence agriculture. Households with more than one female spouse had that number of "*machambas*"— horticultural plots. Men were known to gather around *machambas* to discuss important "affairs of the state," socialize, and drink.

The chief of Wiriyamu was known for this practice, as was Tenente Valeta, the elder. Both were to be found, steeped in a conference *à deux*, when the Portuguese troops descended on their village. The fact that an individual possessed several *machambas* was a sign of wealth. While grain silos protected their contents from rodents, their capacity and ornamental look was indicative of their owners' wealth and power.

The staple diet consisted of "*tchima*" made of "*mapira*," shogun flour, "*mexoeira*," pearl millet, cassava plant, beans, vegetables, and occasionally, meat. Cow, but not goat, milk was consumed. Baobab leaves and fruits were consumed when food was scarce.[36] Machambas relied on the rain for the most part. Those located near creeks and streams fared better during periods of drought. "Slash and burn" cleared and fertilized land for *machambas*. This practice had one added benefit: grilled rats, an important source of protein during food shortage.

Cooking was done with kindling. Any surplus food was usually stored or sold. As indicated earlier, more robust wood was turned into coal and sold to generate extra revenue. Respondents offered conflicting reports on who collected kindling. Men promptly claimed the task as theirs, while the women chuckled at their response.[37] Informants south of the triangle suggested the women were normally in charge of kindling for domestic use, with children assigned to help on occasions, while the men gathered wood for brewing beer and distilling spirits. Two locations appeared to have been harvested extensively for wood, near Juawu, mentioned earlier, and south of Djemusse near a footpath leading to the River Luenha.

Children were generally allowed to play and help siblings with animal husbandry. Girls were generally socialized early to tend to their mothers' *machambas*, collect kindling, and where appropriate, help with de-husking grains, pounding maniocs, and doing assigned domestic chores.

Older male children herded goats and other animals, and when of age were given "seed" animals to begin their own herd. Older women had a special role and function in mentoring younger females in the ways of the village. Women fetched water from the several creeks and streams. Younger men did too—in fact, boys

---

[35] Landeg White, *Magomero: Portrait of an African Village* (Cambridge: Cambridge University Press, 1989).
[36] Kaniveti, interview, 1995.
[37] Zambezi, interview, 1995; Kaniveti, interview, 1995; Vasco Valeta, interview, 1995; Podista Mchenga, interview by author, Tete and Wiriyamu, 1995; Mixone, interview, 1995; and a member of Xavieri household, interview by author, Riachu, 1995.

were sometimes assigned to help. Football was a popular sport and was played in the football field.

All successful rainmaking events normally ended with celebrations, which are worthy of a brief note here since one such celebration was planned for that fateful Saturday to welcome the downpour weeks earlier. The preparation for the celebration had begun a few days beforehand by brewing "*pombe*" and "*cachaço*." "*Pombe* is easy to make and not as strong," meaning intoxicating, said Kalifornia Kaniveti. "*Cachaço* is a lot of work." It involved repeated distillation of *pombe* to yield a higher alcohol content. The two chief ingredients were flour and sugar, with "*malambe*," the hard-shelled baobab fruit, as a fermenting agent. The distillation process required copious amount of wood and prolonged tending of the fire in the makeshift furnace. "The mixture of flour and sugar had to be '*balançado*,' just right," explained Kalifornia Kaniveti. These tasks were shared among men, who took the opportunity to gather around the distillery, gossip, talk about the rain, taste the previous batch, and test the new brew as it neared completion. Surplus alcohol was bartered and sometimes sold. Several in the community had gained the reputation as master distillers. The Kanivetis from Juawu, and the Tenente Valetas from Wiriyamu, were two such masters. The identity of brewers and distillers in Chaworha could not be traced.

The seed money to buy raw materials for beer had come from the local makeshift butcher's shop. As a family with resources, the Kanivetis from Juawu dominated the field as brewers. In addition, Juawu was ideally located to attract foot traffic, as it was nearest to the main road, near a crossroads leading to Chaworha, Wiriyamu and beyond. There is little evidence to suggest that the Xavieris from Riachu who had the resources to fund a similar brewery, did so, at least not on that fateful Saturday. Where the Tenente Valetas obtained the financing for their brewing enterprise in the last few months of Wiriyamu's life is unclear. Given their close relationship with the wealthy chief of Wiriyamu, he would have been the logical choice as their financial backer. Because of the role they played in keeping the socializing wheels in motion, meat sellers, brewers and distillers were held in high esteem.[38]

In addition to celebrating rain, the people of the triangle also danced to welcome visitors, petition deities to relieve hardships, eulogize the recently departed, commemorate the dead, and celebrate births, weddings and coming of age. Informants mentioned several forms of dancing for each occasion. The words and rhythm of the songs usually matched the context of the occasion. Five forms were highlighted by informants. "Xiwere" and "Valimba" were danced by couples, not necessarily married. The "Mafue" and the "Njole" were reserved for women and young girls, with the men accompanying on drums. The "Nyau" was a favorite among young men, accompanied by women singers. This dance gave adults a chance to see their offspring perform in public, while the women identified prospective sons-in-laws. Dances moved to the rhythm of "*batuques*" or "Ngoma," drums draped in goat skin.[39]

---

[38] Karimu, interview, 1995; and Elídio, interview, 1995.
[39] Informants from the following households: Kaniveti, Pentad Zambezi, Mixone, Chamambica, Ghandali, Culheri and Folocone. Additional information provided by Tomas Pita Cebola, Facebook interview correspondence, 2014 and 2015.

After Wiriyamu's destruction, no evidence was voluntarily provided on dancing to memorialize the massacre. For that matter, nothing materially significant was discovered to suggest spirit mediums engaged in expiation rituals to lay to rest the dead left to putrefy.

Cattle barons and the poor

Wiriyamu entered its second historical period after Sanganembo's death in the late 1950s or early 1960s. His eldest son was appointed successor—oral sources are hazy on the exact succession procedure. Chaworha too saw a change in leadership. Committed to rapid economic expansion, the new chief Wiriyamu set his sights on increasing cattle production. Chaworha's chief elected to stick predominantly to goats, with cattle-raising as a revenue booster. By the late 1960s, both Wiriyamu and Chaworha dominated the center of the triangle as animal producers. Eighty percent of cattle sold in the local colonial market came from the Wiriyamu complex of four villages, with Riachu and Juawu leading the pack. Chaworha continued as the main supplier of goats for wholesale consumers (see Tables 2 to 7).

Wiriyamu's economic strategy was grazing-intensive and failed to take account of climate change. For several years now, temperatures in the region had increased and there had been a steady decline in rainfall,[40] putting pressure on water usage. Wiriyamu felt this pressure most. Chaworha was unaffected because it had a readier access to water from both ends of the village: the tributary of the Zambezi from the east, and an equally well-supplied water creek from the west, and a recently acquired water-well. Given that it mostly bred goats, Chaworha could downsize its holdings more easily to access available water.

Partly to address this water-based challenge, Wiriyamu restructured into four task-dominant villages. Sub-chiefs oversaw each village in the group under Wiriyamu's titular chieftaincy. Because of its deeply hewn creeks below Wiriyamu, Riachu became the main cattle-raising node for the complex. Juawu became a gateway for selling cattle for wholesalers and retailers near the Eighteenth Crossing off the main highway. Djemusse in the meantime bucked the trend, focusing on goat-rearing and poultry, largely because its rocky surface was too poor for cattle-grazing. The nearest pasture proved too steep for ready access to it. Goats were easier to sell to retailers and therefore less risky. The downside to this equation was that Djemusse had to work ten times harder to generate the same revenue.

While this re-organization in devolutionary capitalism maximized the resources at hand, it encouraged a dramatic rise in cattle baronies, the super rich, and a broader increase of social inequality. The Xavieris from Riachu, the Kanivetis from Juawu and the chief Wiriyamu himself owned 40 percent of the entire wealth of the five villages in the triangle. Chaworha had one super rich cattle baron, the Kabutris.

---

[40] M. McSweeney, M. New, and G. Lizcano, *Mozambique: UNDP Climate Change Country Profiles* (Oxford: Oxford University School of Geography and Environment), accessed January 19, 2015, http://preview.tinyurl.com/qd6439p.

Taking the five villages as an aggregate, twenty-four out of 216 families virtually controlled its economic wealth, with the Xaviris of Riachu holding 25 percent of the market share. Using wealth in animal husbandry as a crude indicator of socio-economic fitness, 50 percent of people in Juawu and Wiriyamu had nothing to their name. Djemusse had 31 percent of people without domestic animals. Riachu had the least number of poor, 7 percent—but that figure is deceptive, as we shall see in a moment. While Chaworha's 38 percent of inhabitants could be considered as poor, its wealth was more evenly spread among the top 62 percent.

Wiriyamu's measure had one additional side effect, which was felt most acutely in Riachu. Here, women outnumbered men and constituted 69 percent of the total population in the village. Given that Riachu ranked second among its five peers as a supplier of cattle and goats to the colonial economy,[41] did this mean women led the triangle? There is little evidence to suggest that. Polygamy played a role here, as did the dominant number of female offspring. Of Riachu's fourteen families, only six were monogamous. The rest served as variable capital to underpin the economic success led by the most powerful patriarchy in the triangle. As a family, the Xavieris maintained close ties with the Wiriyamus, and that family's plenipotentiaries in Juawu, on whose good will they depended to broker the wholesale of cows and goats. They kept the retail business firmly in their hands, as did the other two super-rich families.[42] Women here played a subaltern role, and an important one, social networking, managing herds, and commissioning transportation and sale of animals.

The final days

Wiriyamu entered its final historical period in the early 1970s. As we have seen, its leadership differed in significant ways from Chaworha's. Wiriyamu embraced "the magicalities of modernity," to borrow Jean and John Comaroff's phrase. Promoting unbridled development, he simply enhanced his power, deriving its strengths from traditional sources inspired by occult cosmologies.[43] Before the massacre, he courted foreign missionaries, somewhat unsuccessfully at first, to bring to his community schools and possibly an infirmary. He also courted the colony's volunteer force for public works to dig a well. Spartan evidence casts doubt on whether he would have been open to conversion, given this open disposition to welcome new experiences. Those close to him thought differently. In their view, chief Wiriyamu was and remained to his dying day rooted to traditional belief systems. Padre Sangalo thought time and missionary efforts were on their side. Perhaps because of this, his colleagues did a feasibility study to establish a missionary presence during a visit to the area—but nothing came of it. "We waited to see how things developed," said Padre Sangalo. Just before the Portuguese discovery of FRELIMO presence in the area, Wiriyamu people heard rumors they were now in line for a government-sponsored well.

---

[41] See Table 6, Riachu population census, 1972 estimates.
[42] ibid.
[43] Jean Comaroff and John Comaroff (eds.), *Modernity and Its Malcontents: Ritual and Power in Postcolonial Africa* (Chicago: Chicago University Press, 1993), xxx.

Chief Wiriyamu was a savvy problem-solver. To this end, he built alliances with fellow chiefs to enhance his power base, and cultivated mutually beneficial trading contacts with the world outside: retailers, veterinarians, cattle brokers, and shopkeepers. From these beneficial links, and the exposure to the world outside, he clearly understood the threat that rejections of FRELIMO's courtship presented to him were he to spurn these advances during the first meeting at his home that fall. He was also careful not to antagonize the Portuguese authorities. His tactful handling of Portuguese cattle traders' encounters with FRELIMO cadres was one of many examples of his diplomatic tendencies.

He also liked to ruminate, to avoid conflict and to compromise. Rarely did he seek to impose his will on the people, informants averred. His concern was to see the villages under him advance freely, with little interference. Clearly, he stood to gain the most from this *laissez-faire* approach. "He believed in letting people be and allowing time to heal wounds," said one of the Tenente Valetas.[44] Bulachu concurred, and so did members of the Kaniveti and Xavieri families, whose views were also clearly biased to favor the oligarchy.

He had been raised that way, they said, with the knowledge that someday he would assume the mantle of leadership from his father. Once in power, he acted decisively. He changed the governance structure, devolving power to his lieutenants over daily matters under his jurisdiction. With this devolution, Djemusse expanded to several households. Riachu blossomed. Juawu emerged to be prominent in a number of fields, from retail goat trading to distilleries. The new chief, though, retained "*o poder de bater o batuque*"—the power to beat the drum, that is, to call the people to an assembly.

Like Wiriyamu, the chief of Chaworha promoted economic growth but under a controlled setting, ensuring everyone who needed and wanted access to water and grazing land had it to develop family enterprises. Giving equal opportunity to everyone helped the village to attain a flatter wealth pyramid led by a group of seven economically powerful families. From the viewpoint of governance, the chief had a much harder task at hand than Wiriyamu. Devolution would not have worked here to rein in the political and economic interests of the powerful seven, while ensuring the bottom 30 percent of the village had a fair chance to prosper.

His, then, was a socially progressive agenda under a centralized executive leadership. Lack of frequent communication with neighboring Wiriyamu helped, as did its geography, to insulate it from outside influences, enabling him to develop a village worthy of praise by his ancestors, one proud of its culture, and intensely aware of its valuable but fragile social stability. This stability, as we saw earlier, had come to rest on natural resources, access to the cattle market for trade, and now additional supply of water from the well nearby. It is understandable, therefore, that when approached by the Portuguese authorities to move the village to M'phadwe, he resisted. Why should he? The place was a goat pen, without access to water for domestic animals, no land for grazing, and above all, fenced in. He was reportedly to have said to the authorities that he had seen M'phadwe, and it was a prison camp, rootless—dead.

Like Wiriyamu, Chaworha's chief too developed links with like-minded chieftaincies in the region. Chief Matambo became particularly close, paying frequent visits to

---

[44] Vasco Valeta, interview, 1995.

Chaworha. The relationship was cemented with intermarriages between prominent houses in the two chieftencies.

Chaworha and Wiriyamu, though physically isolated from one another, shared two enemies: Chief Kongorhogondo and a mole working for the DGS, Chico Cachavi. Local information on the Kongorhogondos and his village proved hard to come by. What we know is fractured. Nearly a decade after Sanganembo led the way in founding Wiriyamu, Portugal had acquired a new chief, some 4,695 miles away in Lisbon, António de Oliveira Salazar. His 1930s Colonial Act subsequently instituted a three-tiered structure for local administration. *Regedorias* territorial units headed by a colonially appointed *régulo*, chief, headed two lesser demographic units, *grupos de povoações* and *povoações* both led by their respective chiefs. This arrangement brought the triangle under three chieftancies: Matambo, Gandar and Rego. Chaworha and Wiriyamu were under the titular jurisdiction of Gandar. Juawu, Djemusse, Riachu became *povoações*, which as a group fell under Wiriyamu's authority.

The chieftaincy of Kongorhogondo remained as is, effectively on a par with the chief of Gandar, who eventually proved too weak to promote villages under his jurisdiction, allowing Kongorhogondo to muscle in on his turf. Kongorhogondo was ambitious, tenacious, had a network of supporters and was a known quantity among the Portuguese. In the early 1970s, animosity intensified over two issues: conflict over perspectives on modernity, and failure to reach a diplomatic solution on two marital discords affecting the families of the three chieftaincies.

Kongorhogondo viewed the people of the five villages from two angles: ethnic and ideological. He considered them beneath him. "*Nos éramos inferiores que eles,*" "we were inferior than them," said Kalifornia Kaniveti, Bulachu Zambezi, and one member of the Juawu family when pressed to elaborate on this point. "We were not considered true Nyungwe." "But you both spoke the same language, no? Are you not of the same ethnic group?" "Yes, we did. We are." "So how can you be inferior to them?" I asked. "We were not as pure as them?" "In what way?" I asked? "They were powerful and dark" was the best reply I got. "He practised ancient religion, witchcraft and sorcery and that sort of thing. We stayed clear of him and his folk."

In other words, he viewed Wiriyamu's modernist tendencies as a betrayal of traditional values, implying thereby that they had ceased to rely exclusively on traditional healing, demonic expiations, and use of curses as social deterrents; electing instead to consider using Tete's infirmary and hospital for healing purposes and courting missionaries to provide education in the community. We now know from studies on occult cosmologies[45] that Kongorhogondo's response was normal as resistance to modernity threatening the traditional exercise of power. "I know what you do. One day, this black magic thing will be the death of you," said Padre Sangalo during one of his meetings with him.[46]

---

[45] Jean Comaroff, *Body of Power, Spirit of Resistance: The Culture and History of South African People* (Chicago: Chicago University Press, 1985); June Nash, *We Eat the Mines and the Mines Eat Us: Dependency and Exploitation in Bolivian Tin Mines* (New York: Columbia University Press, 1979); and Aihiwa Ong, *Spirits of Resistance and Capitalist Discipline: Factory Women in Malaysia* (Albany: State University of New York Press, 1987).
[46] Sangalo, interview, 1995.

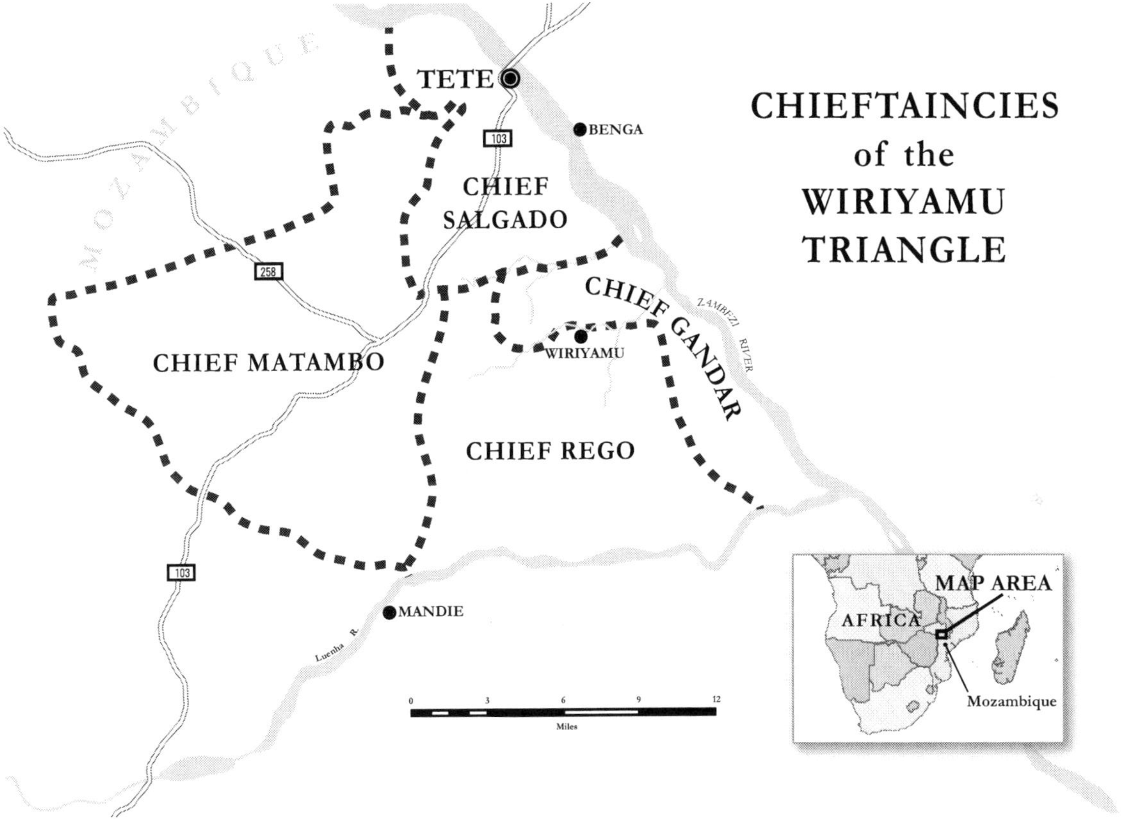

Map 2 Chieftaincies of the Wiriyamu triangle.

Kongorhogondo, on the other hand, saw little use for Padre Sangalo's religion. He had everything he needed to live a traditional life and lead his people accordingly. How Kongorhogondo squared this traditionalism with the career choices his two sons had made remained unexplained. One, Tai, had elected to join the Portuguese militia. The other, Johnny, had embedded deeper into the Portuguese administrative flesh, having joined the DGS no less, as Chico Cachavi's lieutenant. Perhaps he did not see their career choice as ideologically problematic, but an advantage, in that he now had two sons with colonial clout to threaten his adversaries.

The chiefs of Wiriyamu and Chaworha sought to defuse the situation through marriage, one between chief Wiriyamu's daughter Nonika to Kongorhogondo's son Tai and the other between Tai's brother Johnny to an outsider adopted by the Chaworha elders as their own. The latter couple was subsequently welcomed into Chaworha and given the right to adopt the chief as its grandfather.

The two chiefs' objectives, however, were undermined by domestic violence. As we saw earlier, Nonika sought refuge at her parents' place, which led Tai to go after her—a fatal move that led to the premature discovery of FRELIMO's logistics brigade behind the Wiriyamu village. The other marriage was fraught with violence, and ended in divorce. Both spouses moved out of Chaworha: Johnny headed for Tete, and his former spouse settled in Mpharhamadwe. Consonbera Marizane had watched the couple with keen interest as they settled in Chaworha. Something about Johnny's wife caught his eye and eventually his heart. Upon their divorce and departure, Consonbera headed to Mpharhamadwe. The courtship blossomed and she returned to Chaworha, where she had been happiest in her life, as the new wife of Mr Marizane. On hearing the news, Johnny was apoplectic. "Consonbera! Consonbera! Consonbera!" he kept repeating himself. "How could she do that! But Consonbera is nothing," he exclaimed. This rancor, as we shall see in a moment, played a fatal role in initiating Chaworha's first death.

The two chiefs found Chico Cachavi more difficult to tackle. Aided by Johnny, he was the eyes and ears of the DGS in the triangle. Both were illiterate. Both had been recruited for their familiarity with the local customs and culture. Chico was initially welcomed into the community, given his passion for playing the drums, "*tocar Ngoma*." "When he played the drums, he was in another world," claimed his younger brother during an interview. That is not because he was drunk. "No, he did not drink. He hated alcohol. He said it messed up his drumming," his brother added.[47]

The Wiriyamu and Chaworha leaders had another reason to allow Chico in their midst. Chico was passionate about football. Even though he did not play it himself, he was known to sponsor teams, paying for football kits and accessories that cost more than his salary. Senhor Elídio suspected the funds to be from the DGS. Why would the DGS fund such a venture? Football was and remained an ideal venue to mobilize anti-colonial recruits in most of Luso-Africa. The most documented case was in Guinea-Bissau, where the Portuguese had been initially taken by surprise.[48] The DGS had

---

[47] António Cachavi, interview by author, Tete, 1995.
[48] See Dhada, *Warriors at Work*, 2, 146.

learned their lesson and had turned the tables on the nationalists, by sponsoring football venues in Tete to recruit paid informants. What better way to keep tabs on the triangle than football? Wiriyamu and Chaworha leaders, on the other hand, saw this as an opportunity for their young to bond, socialize, and let off steam.

The arrangement did not last. Chico's other debilitating habits got in the way. Extortion was one; according to two informants, Elídio and Chico's brother, unbridled sexual appetite was another, which riled most people in the triangle. "*Ele levava tudo que queria, galihas, mulheres, filhas de outro e não sei mais o qué,*"—"he took what he wanted, chicken, women, others' daughters, and I don't know what else." By late 1972, he had overstayed his welcome. His access to the village's resources diminished, as did his predatory raids on women.

On Thursday, December 14, 1972, Mr Fogo Fogo appeared at the cattle market. He was there to help his employer load up cows on his truck. He was overheard muttering as he looked left and right, "... *vocês vão ver fogo fogo*"—"you are going to witness fires." Did he intend the mutterings to be heard as a warning? Who exactly was near him to hear clearly the text? No one could tell. Those who heard him from a distance dismissed him as a raving lunatic.

The following day, the Kalifornia household woke up early to prepare for the party to be held on Saturday. The plan was to slaughter a cow, drum up customers to buy meat, and with the seed money begin brewing beer and stronger spirits the next day. By late afternoon, Kalifornia was ready to set up his stall for the next day. He went to bed early, he said, but could not sleep. The dogs were barking relentlessly. "My heart was going thump, thump." "Excitement?" I probed. "Hmmmm, after what happened, it was a sign..." "You mean an omen?" "Yes, those dogs barking.... something was different." "You mean they were disturbed?" "Yes. But I tried to go to sleep..."

By that Friday night, Chico and Johnny's bitter resentment towards the triangle had already seeped into the lethal cocktail of information that the Portuguese were brewing to launch their assault on Chaworha and Wiriyamu. They pounced on the triangle the next day. Thus ensued Operation Entrapment—Marosca.

10

The Anatomy of the Wiriyamu Massacre

On December 16, 1972, Chaworha woke up to a normal day. No one appeared to have stirred in the chief's household. His neighbors, the Mixones, had woken up early. Their sons, António and his young brother, were itching to go down to the river. The goats needed an early start at grazing before the cows monopolized the watering holes and the adjacent pasture. They had one pregnant goat. She could deliver anytime now, and they had quite a bit to do before that kid arrived. Elsewhere nothing stirred. Chaworha was quiet.

Not Wiriyamu. A few weeks earlier, a senior spirit medium had been summoned to "make rain happen."[1] The ceremony was long and intense. No rains came. The Wiriyamus called Senhor Soda then. Perhaps he could coax the skies to open up their bounty. He came through. It rained. The ground was wet and smelled of fresh earth. People in Wiriyamu woke up early to celebrate. The Kanivetis had slaughtered an animal to sell the meat, and prepared their brewing equipment. The men assembled outside to talk of rain and how much meat they had to sell to buy the appropriate amount of sugar and flour for brewing. Kalifornia Kaniveti had his back to the wood-culling fields in the distant west of the village. Others were clustered in Juawu's social gathering space.

By this time, the Tenente Valeta's home in Wiriyamu had come to life. Visitors from Riachu arrived early to meet and greet. One of Tenente's daughters had traveled from another village quite a distance away to visit her parents. Children gathered elsewhere, playing nearby between the two trees, one near the Tenente Valeta's and one on the edge of the village near Bulachu Zambezi's house overlooking Riachu. Among the older children playing was Vasco Tenente Valetta.

Chief Wiriyamu and his *aide-de-camp* Tenente Valeta, the elder, were seen heading to the former's *machamba* to "talk business," over *pombe*. It is not clear if they had *cachaço* with them. If they did, they would have been too inebriated by noon to react with alacrity to any emergency in the village, given *cachaço*'s potency. There they stayed that whole afternoon.

Little is known of events of the day in Riachu and Djemusse. Some of Riachu's womenfolk were in Wiriyamu. Riachu's men were nowhere to be seen. As far as it can be ascertained, Djemusse's women and men had stayed put. Like in Chaworha,

[1] Vasco Valeta, interview, 1995.

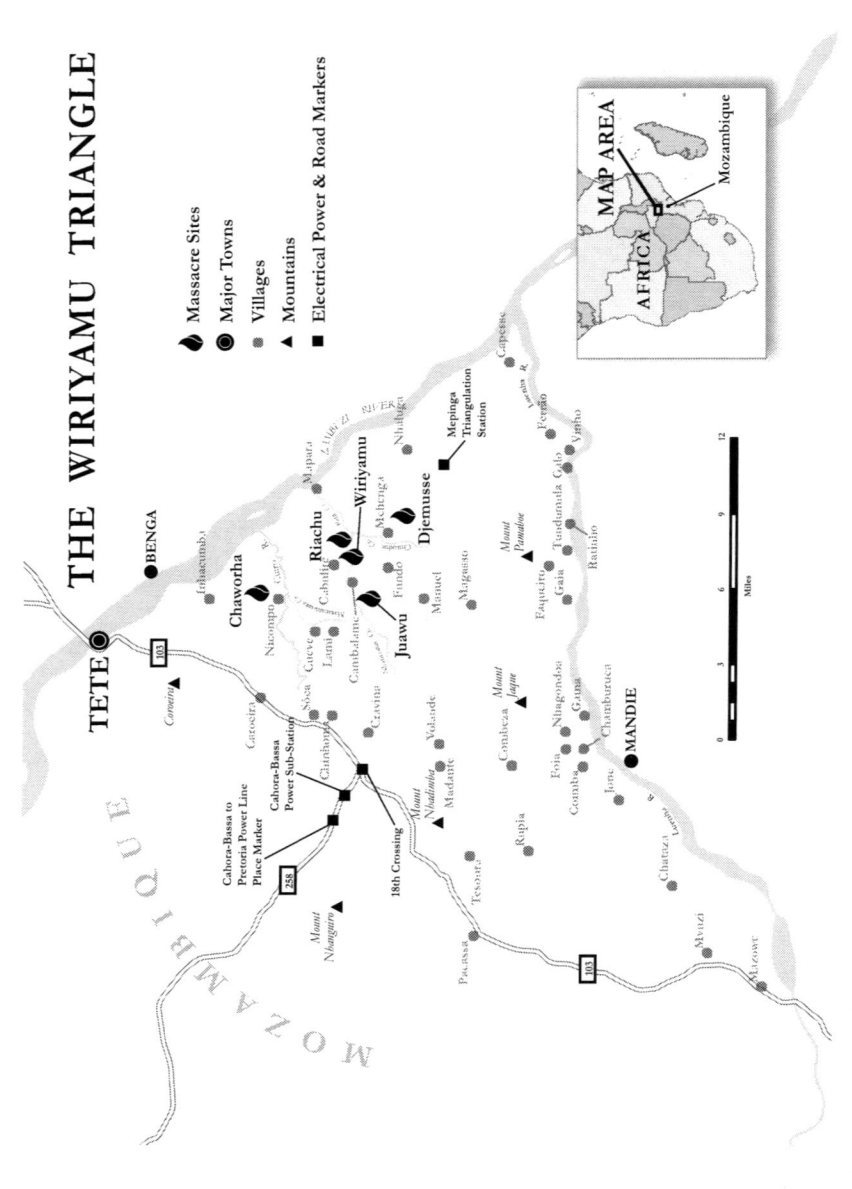

Map 3 The Wiriyamu triangle

everything was quiet there—except for a respondent whose identity was lost among other data, due to the deterioration of poorly conserved paper records during fieldwork. He was visiting Chaworha where he stayed until noon, moments after the Portuguese arrived.

Fifteen-and-a-half miles to the north, Portugal's strategists gathered early at Tete's regional military headquarters—Zona Operacional de Tete (ZOT). That morning at about 6:30, Antonino Melo, the commander of the Sixth Commando Unit, was ordered to be at the headquarters. He was not meant to lead the unit, but its commander had fallen ill with appendicitis. Melo was next in line. He assumed unit command. He arrived on time and was ushered in to the conference room. He stood to attention facing an oval table, saluted, and was put at ease. Seated facing him were high-ranking officials. They were above his pay grade, he said. He could not identify who was who. He understood his orders: "go to Wiriyamu and clean it up." The order did not surprise him. He had carried out numerous such operations. Indeed, his company's operational log confirms this. Many of these entailed clean-ups. Melo could not recall how many.

"But what did these orders mean?" Melo was asked during the interviews.[2] "Normally," said Melo, "we would go into the area... *e nós limpava tudo isso*, we cleaned everything," erased everything. It was that simple. "To save bullets, we shoved people into huts, threw unpinned grenades, shut the door and boom!" The thatched roof would lift up, expel hot air, suck in fresh oxygen, and come down igniting. Those not killed by the blast died from the fire. They then destroyed granaries, other foodstuffs and livestock, time permitting. "You see we moved fast. We did not want to get embroiled in FRELIMO crossfire, not if we could help it," added Melo.

He was also informed that the DGS would accompany his unit. He found this odd. He had never participated in a joint operation, even though these had been in place in the south during the massacres at Mucumbura and Estima. Just before noon, a logistics support unit encircled the villages and planted red flags around the outer perimeter. At first, the flags went undetected. Mrs Mixone was in her "quintal," fenced-in yard, in Chaworha. She saw her young son arrive cradling the pregnant goat, which he did not want to see die and thereby lose the race to his brother to own his own herd. "Mama, she is delivering and I am hungry," recalls António's brother, of the conversation. The goat was made comfortable as she fetched food for her young son. She then noticed the flag and wondered what it meant. "What is that?" she asked her son. "I don't know, Mama." Instinct told her it was a bad omen. By then, António too had returned home, having followed his brother.

Padre Domingo Ferrão of Missão São Pedro had just finished having his lunch and, as was his habit, headed with a book in hand towards the mission school's tree to lean against, read, and take a nap. "Suddenly, I heard this roar and saw metal arrows, fighter jets, heading towards the triangle." Funny, he mumbled to himself, "I don't see these things often. I wonder what they are up to?" He leaned back against the tree and dozed off. He could not tell if the staff of the hospital relatively close by had heard the jets roaring.[3]

---

[2] Melo, interview, 1995 and 2014.
[3] Ferrão, interview, 1995.

In the meantime, Portuguese Air Force pilots bombed the perimeter of the five villages. One gauntlet left open diagonal to Juawu formed a tunnel to catch anyone fleeing towards Mpharhamadwe. Five helicopters reportedly arrived thereafter. Three can be accounted for. One near Chaworha disgorged DGS agents in full uniform headed by Chico Cachavi and Johnny Kongorhogondo. Two hovered, one near Juawu and the other near Djemusse. Neither landed. The ankle-deep tree stumps stood in the way. "The helicopters would normally hover and we would jump, land, and run," recalls Melo. "But I am a bit vague on this point. I think that is what happened," added Melo. Someone called Kalifornia Kaniveti's attention to the hovering noise "down there." "What is that noise?" "Ah, probably nothing. *São os militários... dor de cabeça...*," "they are the military... headache..."

"But did you not see this coming?" he was asked during the interview; "this" here implying the war. Bulachu sat close by listening to the interview. Kalifornia Kaniveti was silent. Bulachu retrieved the silence from unrecorded history. "You see we knew there was war there in the distance. We never thought it would come to us." They were fighting each other and it had nothing to do with us," he added in not so many words. Bulachu ignored, or perhaps chose to ignore, that he had by then joined FRELIMO after the first round of talks at Dalepa's base camp. When this was pointed out to him on the final day of exit interviews, Bulachu shrugged his shoulders. "War is war. They are all the same." Did he mean he was disillusioned with FRELIMO?" He was not asked that question. After a short pause, he retrieved his ambiguity. "We first suffered '*contra os colonos*,' against the colonialists. Then we had another war. War, war, war. We people suffered. We continue to suffer. Look at us. What do we have for all this war!"[4]

Sadism and fire at Chaworha

The first helicopter arrived at Chaworha. It carried both DGS agents and the third unit of the Sixth Company of commandos; informants could not confirm this. Chico and Johnny summoned everyone to assemble near the chief's "quintal." "We stood here, no, here," said António pointing to a spot. "Here exactly?" he was asked. "Are you sure?" "Yes, here, right here. I stood here... and my brother was behind me. All this was clear of growth then, flat," pointing to a spot sixty-nine steps from the tree that partly shaded the chief's quintal. The immediate sequence of the events after this is unclear. People then assembled gradually as uniformed men ferreted them out of their homes. That is how the Mixone brothers were found out as they prepared to flee. Chico asked the Djemusse visitor to run back to the Wiriyamu village with a message. "Tell the chief to call the people to assemble, *bater o batuque*." He said, he made a dash for it. He had seen enough. He knew he had narrowly escaped death. He got to the Wiriyamu village and told someone, he is not sure who, that "they were coming" and they should assemble. With that message delivered, he ran to Djemusse to alert them of what he had just seen, and what he thought was about to happen. He eventually escaped from

---

[4] Zambezi, interview, 1995.

The Anatomy of the Wiriyamu Massacre 163

Photo 6 The reconstruction of the Chaworha massacre, 1995, with Mixone showing where he stood as he watched Consembera, the first victim of the massacre, fall where Abidu Karimu stands in the image

Djemusse. Years later, he went blind, for undisclosed reasons. He recalled the events of the day visionless but with clarity no less, as he arrived, walking stick in hand, to be interviewed at Djemusse.

Back in Chaworha, the gathering grew. Johnny stood beside Chico. Why had they refused to move to Mpharhamadwe as they were told? Chief Chaworha replied that they had done no such thing; they were waiting a response reassuring them access to water and grazing land for their animals. Chaworha's request was reasonable. The *aldeamentos* were notoriously ill-equipped for pastoral existence—even the Portuguese authorities admitted as much. Several chiefs had migrated to neighboring territories rather than move into them.[5]

In front lay perhaps the most famous marker of all—the tree casting a soothing shadow opposite Chaworha's first death row. Just then, Consonbera was seen walking at a leisurely pace towards the tree. He had come from the dense cluster of homes of one of the seven well-to-do families at the margins of the dry creek near the football field. He appeared oblivious to what was happening near the quintal, at least according to António. As he neared the tree, Johnny Kongorhogondo spotted him and fired. Consonbera fell, dead.

Chaworha's destruction began. The assembled were asked to clap their hands and told—this was it. They were about to die. They should prepare to meet their Maker.

---

[5] PT/TT/PIDE/D-F/001/00025, October 4, 1973; and PT-TT-PIDE-D-F-001-00006, February 9, 1972.

Pandemonium ensued once shooting began. Fifty-three among the assembled near chief Chaworha's yard fell.[6] As the rest ran to escape, Chico bellowed, "Aphani Wense! Aphani Wense! Kill Them All. Leave no one alive. No witnesses." The armed men in uniform split in two. One group gathered the bodies in a pile. Aided by "*capim*," grass, the pile was set on fire. The other group formed a semi-circle within shooting range to kill escapees and anyone rising to escape from the pile. António was on the edge of the pile of bodies, as was his brother, he said. Both had fallen, unconscious but unhurt. António regained consciousness as the heat of burning flesh reached him. He made a dash for it, as did his youngest brother, four-year-old Domingo. Four others escaped this pile.[7] The Portuguese armed men, "black and white" said António, fired in their direction. "I ran fast. Did not look back." One bullet hit him on the shoulder. Ignoring the wound, he continued to run until he was safe.

By then, he had reached chief Matambo's village. "We were related." He told him what had happened. His other younger brother Zeca was already there. "I then went down the river" to clean up. He returned and stayed there until morning. The next day, a close relative in the Portuguese militia arrived in full uniform so he would not be stopped both ways by Portuguese armed men on the prowl for survivors. He took António to Tete's hospital where Irmã Lúcia worked, to have his wound looked at. António jumped on the back of the bicycle. The whereabouts of António's younger brother is uncertain from this point onwards.

In the meantime, Chief Matambo had ordered his people to vacate the village, just in case they were next on the list. Days later, Chief Trabuco, Chaworha's neighbor, visited the scene of the carnage. He counted up to 300 dead. Thereafter he stopped. That is what he reportedly told Padre Ferrão via an intermediary, whose identity is still a mystery, but could well have been Kansande. Padre Ferrão could not confirm this. Kansande could not recall this to be true.

Juawu's swift disappearance

The killings at Juawu and Wiriyamu were less sadistic. We know a little of Juawu's destruction. The commandos hit the ground running to clean up the scene, just as the helicopter rose up to leave. Evidence on how they killed appears spartan. One eyewitness, hidden behind a clump of tall reeds in a gulch nearby, and who could not be traced for this study, saw Melo's men from the first unit of the Sixth Company of Commandos throw grenades into huts packed with people, while others fired on escapees.[8] Assuming the grenade-throwing tactics described by Melo earlier, it would be safe to conclude this eyewitness account to be the unexaggerated truth. Juawu's destruction, in other words, was assuredly swift, clinical, concise, and cold; of that we can be certain.

---

[6] Ferrão, interview, 1995.
[7] They were: Serina, aged thirteen, daughter of Irisone; Tembo, aged five, son of Batista; Manuel, aged thirteen, son of Mantrujare; and Podista, wife of Mchenga.
[8] Information provided by Padre Ferrão.

The other eyewitness was Kalifornia Kaniveti, perhaps the most alert among the men gathered in the socializing space at Juawu. He ran as the carnage got underway. He slung a goat on the back of his neck and two infants in each arm and descended the mound, crossing the road that led to the Eighteenth Crossing. He then heard rotors following from behind. He stooped low to "avoid the blades," he said, but kept running until he could not. He fell and dropped his precious cargo. "I looked at the sky." Like a dragonfly, the helicopter above stopped too, hovering nearly motionless. He saw the pilot direct him to Mpharhamadwe. He got up and ran and kept running, only to stop again, this time to drink some water from a stream before he crossed it. The helicopter then left him there. Kaniveti ended his testimony with, "that pilot saved my life," implying him to be a bird of mercy delivering a new lease of life. There is little reason to doubt Kaniveti's evidence crediting the Portuguese with an uncorroborated act of mercy. Perhaps the pilot intended to save him, or perhaps he attempted to funnel him into the arms of a commando unit. As we saw earlier, this unit had engaged in helping Melo's men with logistics support, and was on the prowl looking for escapees in the area. Kaniveti was to return to the site a few days later. "I was starving and needed food," he said. He found the place deserted. Hyenas were already picking on the bodies. He did not dare go to the Wiriyamu village. "I took two goats with me," he said and returned to Mpharhamadwe "where I settled down." "I never returned."

Wiriyamu's demise and Melo's act of mercy

Before the arrival of Melo and his men, someone had been sent to inform chief Wiriyamu to call people to assemble. He and Tenente Valeta questioned the messenger for additional details. Normally, such requests would have followed direct contact with a colonial administrator to discuss the purpose of the assembly. He probed a bit further and may well have surmised this to be a trap. He and Tenente Valeta left the scene of carnage about to unfold. It is unclear where Tenente Valeta went. Chief Wiriyamu, however, sought refuge with Dalepa's men, who placed him under protection.

The killings at Wiriyamu were equally swift but a bit more nuanced. While others ignited huts brimming with people, Melo himself directed the shoving of people into Tenente Valeta's hut, one of the largest in the village. The task proved easy since many were already there for the social gathering. At one point, Melo felt a grip on his leg. He looked down and his eyes met hers. A young girl aged below ten held him tightly, refusing to budge. He could not pry himself free. Melo ordered his men to retrieve her mother from the hut and told them both to flee. Twenty-three years later, upon being told that Melo would be interviewed for the project, the young girl, now a full-grown woman, requested to convey her thanks to Melo for saving her life. When told this, Melo went quiet but sat erect and composed. For reasons of tact, he was not asked what propelled him to act this way.

With several unpinned grenades thrown in, the hut was slammed shut. Inside were Vasco and her sister. "*Wkenewkene gente.. não podia respirar*" said Vasco in Nyungwe patois, loosely translated as "we were too many... it was difficult to breathe." His sister was nearest to the back door, which she pushed open. Melo's men had not noticed the hut had a back door, said Melo. Vasco and her sister made a run for it just as the grenades blasted to lift up the thatched roof. There ended the largest carnage of Wiriyamu. With a swift clean-up complete just before sunset, Melo and his men headed to set up camp quite a distance from the site, hunting escapees on the way.

Melo later revealed with humbling understatement and great delicacy that he had protected another girl from being raped by his men as they marched to set up camp. The men under his command were warned of dire consequences, or words to that effect. The girl was safely delivered to someone or told to seek refuge with "her own people."

Chief Wiriyamu, though, suffered a tragic death at the southern end of the triangle. Dalepa's men proved careless, leaving their charge unprotected. Once word of this got out, Wiriyamu was an easy target for a Portuguese-armed manhunt. He died leaving several offspring, one of whom, a member of FRELIMO, returned after the war to reconstitute a new Wiriyamu, some distance from the original site.

One could be forgiven for judging chief Wiriyamu's conduct as cowardly, given that in the end his escape brought him only a temporary reprieve. Dying with his people as their leader would have been more becoming, even heroic, and certainly worthy of an heir to Sanganembo, the founder.

In his defense, though, chief Wiriyamu could not have behaved any differently. Embracing the Portuguese would have assured his instant death, sparing the village perhaps—witness the case of chief Buxo near Mucumbura. Siding with FRELIMO in the open would have cost him his life and Wiriyamu's destruction expectedly sooner; that is exactly how the village of António and its chief in Mucumbura met their end once they were discovered. Deemed "*turras*," terrorists, they were promptly eliminated.

The only option chief Wiriyamu knew was diplomacy: keep both parties satisfied but discreetly at bay. What he did not account for was a tangle of factors: the premature discovery of FRELIMO's logistic route behind the village, FRELIMO's brazen lack of foresight for the region's public security once discovered by cattle traders and various Portuguese personnel, domestic violence by the Kongorhogondo offspring, Kongorhogondo's continuing animosity towards the two chiefs, Chico's predilections, Portugal's tenuous understanding of the triangle, and inaccurate intelligence. Chief Wiriyamu had played his cards right, except for the last one—to walk away from his chieftaincy into the arms of Dalepa, the man who he thought could protect his life until he returned to rebuild Wiriyamu, perhaps as its chief. He died, carrying a burden of tragic defeat that few would have chosen to undertake willingly in history.

Djemusse in flames before dark

Djemusse's clean-up took longer. Chico and Johnny formed part of the violent interrogation. Where were they hiding FRELIMO? Did they know their bases? "Reveal what you know or die," they were told. At some point, a helicopter arrived but hovered above ground on the left of the baobab tree that framed Djemusse's entrance to pick up a handful of "confessors" for in-depth interrogations at the DGS headquarters.

Photo 7 Reconstruction of the final gauntlet that faced the people of Charowha, with Abidu Karimu leading the discussion, 1995

One informant, Senhor Elídio, later reported to have heard cries from torture victims emanating from the blood-splattered walls of the DGS cells. "No, please, no more. Please stop. I don't know. *Para, para Chico, por amor de Deus.* Stop, stop Chico, for the love of God."[9]

By sundown, the interrogations had outlived their usefulness. There were no more "confessions" to be had. The uniformed armed men split in two; one formed a wide gauntlet, while the other group stood in a semi-circle to cull escapees for the final kill. Upon instruction, Djemusse's people formed a line facing their smoldering homes. Chico was leaning against the aforementioned baobab tree as people got in line. Just then, he moved forward and picked for himself two women from the file. This study omits the family identity and names of the two victims, which was provided by three informants. Both successfully reconstructed their lives after August 1973. Alive during the period of the fieldwork, they were left alone for ethical reasons.

The armed men ordered the assembled to run for their lives, which they did. It is unclear how many escaped. One informant remembers zigzagging straight into a smoke-filled burning hut. He did not feel the heat, he said, and the smoke probably saved his life.

The helicopter departed with its human cargo. The soldiers, on the other hand, joined their unit command for the overnight camping to prepare for the next three days' manhunt, which according to information provided to Padre Ferrão spread to as far as Luis, Corneta, Gama, and smaller villages under the chieftaincy of Rego. Data on the three-day manhunt is practically non-existent except for fragments suggesting an indeterminate number of casualties.[10]

The whereabouts of Chico and Johnny immediately after the killings are uncertain until after sunset on that Saturday when Chico was spotted at Cantina Raul's retail shop south of Djemusse interrogating customers he suspected to be inimical to the state.[11] FRELIMO assassinated Chico shortly after Wiriyamu's outing in *The Times of London*, ostensibly to pay for his wrongful incarceration of a close relative of a FRELIMO cadre whom the DGS had captured, tortured and executed.[12]

In reality, FRELIMO sources interviewed here suggest Chico's death was planned and executed by FRELIMO's female detachment unit,[13] to signal to others involved in the massacre that they would be next.[14] Chico was in the shower preparing to go out for the evening when he heard three female voices outside the bathroom window inviting him to join them at a local party. Never one to miss an opportunity for quick assignations,[15] "*ele gostava demazaido de mulheres...* he liked women," Chico asked

---

[9] Elídio, interview, 1995.
[10] Ferrando, interview, 1995; Kansande, interview, 1995; and Berenguer, interview, 1994 and 1995.
[11] Kansande, interview, 1995.
[12] PT/TT/PIDE/D-F/001/00023.
[13] A brief history of this unit is given in Harry G. West, "Girls with Guns: Narrating the Experience of War of Frelimo's 'Female Detachment'," *Anthropological Quarterly*, 73, 4 (2000): 180–194.
[14] General Hama Tai, interview, 1994 and 1995; Ferrão, interview, 1995; and Elídio, interview, 1995.
[15] Elídio, interview, 1995.

them to wait, which is exactly what the voices outside needed to hear, namely, Chico's exact location in the house. An unpinned grenade hit him standing in the confined space of the small bath cubicle. DGS inquiries led to arrests, further interrogations, and revenge killings.[16]

His brother António was on his way home on his bicycle, having taken off early from work at the local ironmongers, when he heard a boom as he neared the house. He rushed to see his brother slumped with a hole in his upper chest. "Blood splattered" all over him, and "I could hear him breathing *como um peixe fora de agua*... like fish out of water." Someone went to inform the DGS office, which sent a Land Rover to take him to the hospital, but he was dead on arrival.[17]

Following pressure from the Church hierarchy and colonial medics, Tete's regional high command ordered Melo and his men to return to the massacre site and dispose of the bodies. Melo was instructed to take shovels and leave behind his guns, but he was reluctant: a FRELIMO ambush while they buried the dead would have sealed their own fate. Just as well that he ignored the orders, he said. Transported by helicopter, he was told to be at a rendezvous after they had finished disposing of the bodies, which had lain exposed to the sun, and had been picked on by animals and vultures. He shielded his mouth and nose with a neck scarf soaked in Old Spice and organized communal graves for bodies that could be buried. As for the rest, "we burned what we could." "To this day, I cannot stand the smell of that aftershave."[18]

Melo's men headed to the rendezvous to avoid being there after sunset. The helicopter failed to pick them up. Melo, fearing an ambush, ordered his men to head for the main road towards the Eighteenth Crossing. It is not clear if it was at this point that they exchanged fire with a FRELIMO unit nearby. Once on the main road, Melo and his men hitched a ride to Tete's airport, where fellow commandos were poised to leave for Nampula. Melo never got a satisfactory answer about the army's failure to pick them up. He is still perplexed to this day. Was the high command's failure to pick them up intentional?[19]

A tally of the numbers killed

Two entities provide us with estimates on the numbers killed at Wiriyamu. Portuguese sources pegged it to circa 200 or perhaps fewer. The methods used to arrive at this figure are unclear, though they can be surmised with relative ease, given this text's earlier discussion of how the publicized narrative was constructed. One was a set of interviews with medics and two nuns who undertook visual scans over a selected area

---

[16] PT/TT/PIDE/D-F/001/00023, three issues: September 4, 1973; August 24, 1973; and, August 6, 1973.
[17] António Cachavi, interview by author, Tete, 1995.
[18] Melo, interview, 1995 and 2014.
[19] ibid.

from helicopters soon after the massacre; the other was data from military personnel and Church hierarchy familiar with aspects of the massacre.[20]

Both sets are methodologically flawed. When interviewed in 1975, Irmã Lúcia Saez de Ugarte insisted her visit to the site covered the carnage nearest to the main road, implying Juawu. "It was quick. We did not want to be shot down. We wanted some proof to tell the authorities it was a public health hazard,"[21] and the bodies needed to be buried.

As far as can be ascertained, none of the perpetrators were brought in for in-depth questioning. The commanding officer on the ground, Melo, does not recall undergoing such a process. "At any rate, we were moving fast," and it was difficult to know what was happening where and who was doing what.[22] Melo is right. The only way one could understand the anatomy of this carnage was to treat it as a jigsaw puzzle and solve it one piece at a time with oral micro-data from perpetrators, primary Church informants, priests, survivors and their families. Cabrita's treatment of the massacre as a theater of blood-soaked chaos therefore does make sense here, in that it echoes Melo's view expressed during his interview with this author.[23] While it is true that emotions ran high at Chaworha and at the final countdown in Djemusse, this text suggests, Operation Marosca was sanctioned from above as an act of miasmic destruction.

But what about the evidentiary materials that the Church hierarchy shared with the Portuguese authorities? Why did the authorities not consider these valid to determine their estimate of the dead? After all, the Bishop of Tete, horrified at the carnage, which he believed to include around 500 casualties, had raised the matter with the Tete's military high command. We know this because he confided these concerns to the Italian diplomatic personnel in Beira as he returned from the colonial capital where he had testified on behalf of the incarcerated Macúti fathers.[24]

Three explanations clarify Portugal's minimal figures: military, moral and racial. The high command had a vested interest in lowering the figures to project it as an inevitable collateral in a counter-insurgency. The lower figure served an additional purpose. It weakened Portugal's moral responsibility with the "it was only an atrocity, certainly not as grave as a massacre" argument.

Furthermore, the hierarchy's figures relied on Padre Ferrão's list, which instantly rendered it worthless in the eyes of some elements of the colonial administration. An earlier precedence during the Mucumbura massacres showed how a certain military officer of the Portuguese judiciary viewed evidence from black informants—patent lies.[25] This prejudice could well have been shared among elements in the colonial armed forces, prompting "a small number of casualties" thesis during Lisbon's post-denial and doubt phases over Wiriyamu.

---

[20] Dhada, "The Wiriyamu Massacre of 1972," 1–31.
[21] Saez de Ugarte, interview, 1995.
[22] Melo, interview, 1995 and 2014.
[23] ibid.
[24] Hastings, interviews, 1977, 1978, 1979, 1981, and 1996; and Ferrão, interview, 1995.
[25] Ferrando, interview, 1995.

Padre Ferrão led the other entity. His list of the dead benefited from verifiable and primary source data, which initially suggested nearly 500 dead. As stated earlier, Padre Ferrão's list documents 178 dead, and how they died. Of the fifty-three bodies that fell in the second round of shootings after Consembera's death, forty-two victims came from Chaworha's eighteen families. The chief of Chaworha's family lost three members; the Mixones, three; the Irisonis, nine; the Remadis, three; the Akimos, two; the Birifis, four; the Batistas, four; the Mdekas, three; the Mchengas, two; and the Kunesas, two.[26] The list identifies an additional eighty-six who fell as they ran through a gauntlet. They are identified by first names, with nine bearing first and last names.

Padre Ferrão's list is graphic in specifying the methods used to kill. The largest number, thirty-one, were killed by hand grenades tossed into huts whose doors were then slammed shut. An additional ten died from being thrashed and kicked repeatedly. One died from having to suck a muzzle of a gun before it was triggered. Four were killed after being raped. Two were pregnant women ripped open to die, fetuses exposed. Three were delivered a *coup de grâce* after repeated beatings failed to elicit useful intelligence on FRELIMO.

Although Padre Ferrão's list is vague on who died where, field research suggests that of the 178 killed, forty-two were from Chaworha, twenty-seven from Juawu, seven from Wiriyamu, thirty-six from Djemusse, one from Riachu, and the location of the remaining sixty-six could not be determined. Gender composition identified 102 men, seventy-five women, and two fetuses.

Fieldwork suggests that Padre Ferrão's list is incomplete. The total tally is 385 *named* dead (please refer to the revelant tables at the end of this text). This tally excludes the following: casualties during the three days' manhunt, Jane and John Does untraceable due to memory loss, and victims brought to the DGS headquarters for in-depth interrogation. Of the 385, 118 died in Chaworha, fifty-five in Juawu, forty-one in Wiriyamu, 104 in Djemusse, and one in Riachu. The location of the rest cannot be specified.

Seventy males, forty-six females, and two in the womb died in Chaworha. Thirty-two males and twenty-three females died in Juawu. Wiriyamu lost sixteen males and twenty-five females—the large casualty of females here reflects their social gathering at Tenente Valeta senior's home. Djemusse lost fifty-four males and fifty females. In Riachu, only one female could be identified—Aqueria Tenente. The names and identifying particulars of each of the 385 are given in the accompanying tables.

The massacre wiped out 30 percent of Chaworha's population. Djemusse suffered the second heaviest casualties, followed by Juawu. Djemusse's demographic erasure stood at 27 percent and that of Juawu at 14.29 percent. Wiriyamu suffered the lightest casualties, followed by Riachu. Eighty-nine percent of Wiriyamu survived the onslaught. Riachu's near intact escape is deceptive in that its casualties are likely to remain buried in the list for the fallen at unspecified locations. That list of casualties constitutes 27 percent of the total number killed.

---

[26] Information provided by Padre Ferrão. Also see Hastings, *Wiriyamu*, 72–83.

The Portuguese massacre of Wiriyamu in colonial Mozambique wiped out 28.52 percent of the total population of the five affected villages. It was equivalent in percentage terms, though evidently not in magnitude, to killing 2,461,276 out of 8.63 million living souls in Portugal in 1972.[27] Regardless of the exact demographic details of the deceased, Wiriyamu was a massacre. Whitewashing it will not erase the culture of evidence presented here.

---

[27] "Portugal Population, Actual Value, Historical Data," *Worldbank 2014 Trading Economics*, accessed May 1, 2014, www.tradingeconomics.com/portugal/population

11

Conclusion

The Wiriyamu massacre was a case of structurally determined mass violence in Portugal's colonial wars, not unlike similar massacres during wars of suppression by colonial and white settler powers in Africa.[1] While singular factors governed each unique case, three immediate factors framed the case of Wiriyamu: Portugal's obduracy to free Mozambique constitutionally, FRELIMO's armed nationalism, and the two chiefs' diplomacy. Portugal could not have acted any differently; it could not give what its own could not have in the metropolis. As an imperial nation with African colonies, it was firmly gripped by a toxic trifecta: an authoritarian government, a mission to civilize its African subjugated, and Cold War rhetoric. Salazarist ideology incarcerated Portugal's nationalist and imperial narratives, drawing its strength from the secret police to enforce a socially disengaged civil society. Economic nationalism channeled development under corporatist ideology.[2] In this sense, Salazar was eminently qualified as an authoritarian to rule 8.5 million people silenced to submission. Gifted in balancing the nation's books, he was equally talented in envisioning glacially insular life for himself, and for his nation and its empire, protected from and resistant to change.

The colonies, too, mirrored Portugal's political soul as a sleepy hollow laced with micro-aggression, with a few exceptions. While tax revenues helped balance the books, forced labor helped generate cotton and cash crops, and facilitate corporations with long-term leases to exploit natural resources. This formula worked to its advantage, in that commercial enterprises did the work for the imperial state, while the state profited by taxing the corporations, the labor force, and the mineworkers sent to South Africa. This form of corporatist colonialism came with a price tag—structured violence, which eventually bubbled into eruptive discontent. Salazar's reign was not unique in wielding such a silent killer of the colonized.

Portugal's civilizing mission, on the other hand, aimed to inspire a shared sociocultural commons for its overseas colonies. In reality, this imagined landscape failed to develop beyond rhetoric, because Portugal lacked the personnel to cultivate mentoring

---

[1] Wiriyamu was "written in tears and blood right across southern Africa," said Bishop Colin Winter of Namibia. "Britain 'has betrayed Africa at the UN'," *The Times*, December 17, 1973, 6.

[2] Howard J. Wiarda, *Corporatism and Development: The Portuguese Experience* (Amherst: The University of Massachusetts Press, 1977).

partnerships between citizen emissaries and colonized subjects. As a result, rural Mozambique's demographic tapestry remained unaffected by this rhetorical artifact, except in the cities where people were freer to interact across race and ethnic lines, and assimilate across cultural and social divides. Of course, this is not to suggest that forced labor and migration did not have an impact; it did, adversely.

The regime expected the Church in Tete to Portugalize the "natives." That did not happen as intended. Instead, foreign missionaries and secular priests hired to fill the shortage of Portuguese clergy carved their own de-Portugalizing furrows. By the 1970s, their work germinated critical thinkers for a socially engaged civil society, one that questioned the colonial narrative.

Portugal viewed FRELIMO in the context of the Cold War. Accordingly, FRELIMO's threat to its empire and state transcended insurgent nationalism. As a nationalist movement, Portugal maintained, FRELIMO threatened not only that nation but also its allies, and ultimately Western Christian civilization. Obduracy, therefore, was the only logical choice to opt for. Portugal had to stand its ground and fight the communist-inspired "menace." Mass violence formed part of that anti-insurgent narrative.

FRELIMO too had to resort to fight to free Mozambique! While its formation was a sum of many organizational parts brought together by Tanzanian leaders, the struggle to oust Portugal from the colony developed in stages. It was only after the change in leadership that ushered in Samora Machel's Presidency that the fight intensified. What had so far been a battle of wits with a little weaponry turned into a full-scale insurgency, and with it FRELIMO too entered its own portals of internecine violence strewn with summary executions in the name of ideological rectitude. In this, local authorities suffered the most, contributing in the end to the rise of discontent against post-independence FRELIMO fueled by external powers in the region.

The Portuguese side too saw changes of leadership, changes in economic investment policies, and changes in strategy. The PIDE-intensive raids in two places, the colonial capital and the migrant enclaves in neighboring territories, gave way to serious operational offensives. The armed forces were transformed from fighting forces with arms and ammunition dating back to the Second World War into NATO-equipped forces, with specialized counter-insurgent units ready for battle.

Portugal's imperial troops in Mozambique had an advantage over their Vietnam-based American counterparts, who were accountable to voters indirectly and more directly to the free press. Without such constraints, imperial troops in the newly formed theater of war in Tete could act with impunity. FRELIMO knew this and acted accordingly.

No two individuals understood this contest better than Armindo Videira and Raimundo Dalepa. Both locked horns in the triangle over two issues: FRELIMO logistics to supply forces near Inhaminga and Portuguese defense vulnerability surrounding the Cahora Bassa Dam. In the middle stood two venerable chiefs. Both were seasoned village elders, one more inclined to follow devolutionary politics than the other. While Chief Wiriyamu could be viewed as a *laissez-faire* modernist, chief Chaworha was a socially progressive conservative, hesitant to entertain new ideas unless these strengthened the village's broad economic and socially distributive base.

Both, however, viewed diplomacy as a tool to diffuse, pre-empt, or neutralize conflict. Both sought to compromise in the face of contumacy while seeking to preserve the integrity of their respective rulership. Both saw no option but to act as they did: keep the parties in conflict at bay and keep them satisfied at a reasonable cost. In the end, diplomacy proved too vitreous to secure the survival of the five villages in the triangle. Hence the massacre.

There is no single, simple role of the Church in the Wiriyamu massacre. One factor was the rise of a sentient leadership willing to be forged by the heat of lived-in experiences. The new Bishop Resende changed the tenor of Tete's church. Mercifully, Portugal's shortage of priests helped him choose priests he thought fit for Tete's needs under his episcopacy. The result was a richly diverse, highly eclectic group of imported priests who took their mission seriously and understood their isolation in remote corners of Tete to be an asset with which to envision a socially vibrant community of believers. The White Fathers and the Burgos excelled in this kind of work: the White Fathers because of their African-based ministries, and the Burgos because of their formative training in poverty-stricken parishes in Franco's Spain and their individual personalities.

Padre Castellá artfully exploited both sides to serve his Church. Enrique Ferrando wielded his pen, recording instances of mass violence, while advocating for the rights of the poor. Alfonso Valverde de Lion would not desist until he unearthed what he thought was the unvarnished truth. Miguel Buendia was adept at pushing colleagues inclined to sit on the fence off the ledge with calibrated arguments passionately delivered. Wedged between fear and faith, Padre Ferrão recorded each victim as a number in his list of the dead, while dreading incarceration. Among them was Padre Berenguer. His magic tricks won the loyalty of young men as parishioners. His patrician calmness kept the story consistent as detractors sought to derail its veracity. Perhaps the most colorful priest here was Padre Sangalo, the son of a bullfighter, and a speed-demon on a Suzuki. His knack to befriend officials deep in enemy territory saved his life and that of an eyewitness, which ultimately turned the tables on Portugal's counter-narrative.

Above them hovered Rome. Now undergoing a dramatic doctrinal shift, it offered solace to the socially transformative ministries at ground level, catapulting Lisbon into a war of words with Rome.

Wiriyamu's genesis and revelation was equally strewn with remarkable talent, each uniquely placed to contribute to the narrative. While Kansande labored to record victims perched on a boulder with a borrowed pencil on scraps of paper in the thick of the triangle on the very night of the massacre, others worked on verifying the story. Pringle, returning empty-handed from the DGS office, filed his story on memory recall, knowing well how the vultures of counter-narrative would pounce on his text and on his integrity as an investigative journalist.

Of the other personalities involved in this part of the story, two are worthy of note: Heren and Hastings. Heren was a natural newshound with a knack for publishing historically significant texts. Washington had refined this talent while exposing him to the My Lai debacle. Had his phlegmatic superior been in the office on the day *The Times* received the story, Wiriyamu's fate as a narrative would have been uncertain. The fact that he habitually kept bankers' hours, leaving early for sundowners, meant Heren

Photo 8 Father Adrian Hastings, Leeds, 1996

was in executive charge. That serendipity, and the threat of the paper's closure, funneled Wiriyamu to land on the pages of *The Times*.

Hastings stood up to Portugal. Its attacks on him as a "mad scarecrow and lying agitator,"[3] came to naught. While the monograph excluded the blow-by-blow account

---

[3] "Lisbon paper attacks Wiriyamu priest," *The Times*, January 28, 1974, 5.

of this offensive, suffice to say that Hastings spent the better part of that and the following year nursing the story. Wiriyamu changed Hastings, leading him in later years to engage in similar works on the atrocities in Bosnia and Herzegovina.

There is little point in rehashing the text's treatment on the Portuguese lies, denials and counter-rebuttals, except to reiterate that they were a tragic expression of Portugal's Caetanist dictatorship; more so than a genuine discourse to examine lacuna in the narrative that could render the story fictional. Portugal's denial was to be expected, given its incarceration in Salazar's ideological cage. The Wiriyamu narrative rattled this cage. So did many others, including the military officers who assailed the regime's portals to liberate Portugal. Hastings stood poised, as it were, to hand over the new rulers of a freed Portugal the text of a truth denied.

Contesting Wiriyamu's location and details forty years after the revelation is truly tilting at windmills. Nevertheless, absence of a response could tempt revisionists to strip previously unassailable truths about the triangle, and thereby reverse-engineer self-forgetting, "*oubli de réserve*," or "back-up forgetting," to quote Paul Ricouer again.[4] As this text indicates, the place existed as a reasonably well-rooted set of five villages, alive with culture. It had a unique identity. It was a society asymmetrically rich in mirth and merriment, filled with love, pain, fisticuffs and marital discord, characters with endearing names, people with nicknames to signify flaws in their character, strong beer and spirits, goats, chickens, cows, pigs, crocodiles, sorcerers, hippos, mambas, edible rats, toads, rivers, creeks, boulders, and puddles, men and women, young and old, babies and kids, football fields, goat pens, trees, mountains, breweries, butchers, horticultural plots, artisan coal-makers, granaries, musicians, vocalists, drummers, herbalists and healers, cattle brokers, courtship rituals, dance traditions, spirit mediums, rainmakers, a cattle market, lion-spirit kings, and more.

The villages also had a social, economic and governance structure, with cattle barons and the poor, and a well-established network of alliances and alignments. Their leaders knew how to deal with neighbors, missionaries, cattle-buyers, Portuguese officials, police spies and moles, and people in the world outside. They recognized the world of the spirits and dealt with them as respectfully as they could. They could act with tact and diplomacy, though not always successfully.

The massacre destroyed all this. The biography of Wiriyamu's destruction tells us how 385 individuals with names, identities, and souls worth cherishing perished, with many more unaccounted for. That part of the narrative, while heartrending, is laced with spite, ambiguous valor, retrieval of human souls about to perish in adobe ovens, and more. In re-reading this portion of the text, I wonder how professional history must treat executioners and texts erasing or obfuscating an incontrovertible though fragile and fractured truth; for that matter, how should an empire engage in transparency to deal with what it has done forty years ago? Should Portugal just file and forget it? Should it apologize for the mass violence during its colonial wars? Should it offer reparations? How should Portugal heal its own wounds as perpetrator of a violent

---

[4] Ricouer, *Memory, History, Forgetting*, 414.

colonial past? Does one man's act of impetuous mercy redeem an empire's structured pursuit of mass violence? Juridical and moral judgments aside, what epistemic rubric for evil must one devise to evaluate troughs of systematic killings mixed with acts of mercy, inadvertent or intentional, under colonialism? These questions haunt me in the depths of many nights, aching for answers—in vain. All I hear in response are deafening sounds of blood-curdling silence. Truly, with massacres like these, who needs a conscience?

Tables

Table 1 Attesters to Wiriyamu

Name	Did not visit Wiriyamu	Saw Wiriyamu	Lived in/near Wiriyamu	Individuals at the massacre	Visitors immediately after the massacre	Visitors long after the massacre
Authors:						
Felícia Cabrita	0	1	0	0	0	1
Mustafah Dhada	0	1	0	0	0	1
Colonial personnel:						
A paramilitary water well driller	0	1	0	0	0	0
Maicoro, a Portuguese military intelligence personnel accompanying the cattle buyer	0	1	0	0	0	0
Antonino Melo	0	1	0	1	1	1
Armindo Vieira	1	0	0	0	0	0
Chico Cachavi	0	1	0	1	0	0
Helicopter pilot who saved Kalifornia Kaniveti's life	0	1	0	0	0	0
Helicopter pilot flying Dr Paz and Lúcia	0	1	0	0	1	0
Informant working with Chico Cachavi	0	1	0	0	0	0
Johnny Kongorhogondo	0	1	1	1	0	0
Jorge Jardim	1	0	0	0	0	0
Kaúlza de Arriaga	1	0	0	0	0	0
Members of Military Justice Inquiry No. 1	1	0	0	0	0	0
Members of Military Justice Inquiry No. 2	1	0	0	0	0	0
Six Portuguese cattle buyers: Gonçalves, Miranda, Aguiar, Raul de Zambeze, Telia and Melo	0	6	0	0	0	0
Tai Kongorhogondo	0	1	1	0	0	0

(*Continued*)

Table 1 (Continued)

Name	Did not visit Wiriyamu	Saw Wiriyamu	Lived in/near Wiriyamu	Individuals at the massacre	Visitors immediately after the massacre	Visitors long after the massacre
Civilians:						
Abidu Karimu	0	1	0	0	0	1
António Cachavi	0	1	0	0	0	0
Nonika Wiriyamu Sanganembo	0	1	0	1	0	0
Senhor Elídio	0	1	0	0	0	1
FRELIMO:						
FRELIMO cadre responsible for the first contact with the triangle	0	1	1	0	0	0
FRELIMO Regional Commander, Dalepa	0	1	1	0	0	0
Acquainted with life at Wiriyamu:						
Bulachu Pensadu Zambezi	0	1	1	0	0	1
Domingo Kansande	0	1	1	0	1	1
Chief Matambo	0	1	1	1	1	0
Chief Trabuco	0	1	1	1	1	0
Medic:						
Dr Paz	0	1	0	0	1	0
Priests and nuns:						
Assistant to Irmã Lúcia Saez de Ugarte	0	1			1	
Bishop of Tete	0	0	0	0	0	0
Irmã Lúcia Saez de Ugarte	0	1	0	0	1	0
Padre José Sangalo	0	0	0	0	0	0
Padre Júlio Moure	0	1	0	0	0	0
Padre Vicente Berenguer	0	1	0	0	1	1
Survivors:						
António Mixone	0	1	1	1	0	1
Brother of António Mixone	0	1	1	1	0	1
Chamambique	0	1	1	1	0	0
Inéria Tenente Valeta	0	1	1	1	0	1
Kalifornia Kaniveti	0	1	1	1	1	1
Podista Mchenga	0	1	1	1	0	1
The Baobab Tree	0	1	1	1	1	1
Vasco Tenente Valeta	0	1	1	1	0	1
Total	**5**	**40**	**15**	**14**	**11**	**14**

Table 2 Wiriyamu triangle, population census, 1970–2007

Name	Lat	Long	Elev ft.	Ranking: large to small Villages	Estimated Population in 1970	Estimated Population in 1997	Estimated Population in 2007
Aldeia Mvuzi	−16.5	33.41	531	29	132.73	310.90	484.56
Aldeia Nhagondoa	−16.42	33.54	505	7	908.12	2127.08	3315.25
Aldeia Pacassa	−16.37	33.42	1102	18	143.92	337.11	525.41
Aldeia Wiriamo *	−16.3	33.65	488	17	149.88	351.06	547.15
Cabulire	−16.29	33.64	501	16	160.26	375.38	585.06
Cambalame	−16.3	33.63	567	15	162.03	379.53	591.53
Capesse	−16.39	33.76	331	39	62.22	145.74	227.15
Caroeira	−16.25	33.56	1020	13	178.69	418.55	652.35
Chamburuca	−16.43	33.53	410	3	1128.67	2643.68	4120.40
Chataza	−16.48	33.45	577	8	261.68	612.94	955.32
Chinhoma	−16.29	33.55	1122	19	143.92	337.11	525.41
Coimba	−16.43	33.52	623	4	1070.71	2507.93	3908.83
Combeza	−16.39	33.52	574	9	219.10	513.20	799.87
Cravina	−16.31	33.54	1030	20	143.92	337.11	525.41
Cueve	−16.28	33.6	813	12	180.46	422.70	658.82
Faquero	−16.41	33.64	531	33	92.33	216.25	337.05
Ferrão	−16.41	33.72	337	34	83.87	196.46	306.19
Foia	−16.42	33.53	551	6	955.85	2238.89	3489.50
Fundo	−16.32	33.64	853	21	143.92	337.11	525.41
Gaia	−16.42	33.62	413	35	82.99	194.38	302.96
Galo	−16.42	33.7	357	37	66.89	156.67	244.19
Gama	−16.43	33.55	413	2	1140.10	2670.45	4162.13
Inhancumba	−16.22	33.62	334	1	2564.58	6007.00	9362.44
Jone	−16.45	33.5	623	5	1021.94	2393.68	3730.75
Lami	−16.29	33.6	813	14	163.00	381.79	595.05
Madante	−16.35	33.52	866	22	143.92	337.11	525.41
Magasso	−16.34	33.62	1036	23	143.92	337.11	525.41
Manuel	−16.21	33.46	967	10	199.78	467.95	729.34
Mapara	−16.28	33.69	488	32	109.55	256.60	399.93
Mazowe	−16.53	33.39	492	30	131.69	308.45	480.74
Mchenga	−16.32	33.66	718	28	142.96	334.84	521.88
Nhaluga	−16.33	33.71	354	31	115.10	269.61	420.21
Nicompo	−16.26	33.62	446	11	196.97	461.35	719.06
Rupia	−16.4	33.47	984	24	143.92	337.11	525.41
Sóca	−16.28	33.55	928	25	143.92	337.11	525.41
Tesoura	−16.38	33.48	905	26	143.92	337.11	525.41
Tundumula	−16.42	33.65	410	36	79.69	186.65	290.91
Vinho	−16.42	33.71	633	38	63.27	148.19	230.97
Volande	−16.34	33.54	1131	27	143.92	337.11	525.41
Total					13264.32	31068.95	48423.70

Note: The author's census suggests a population of 165 people (87 adult males and 78 adult females). The figures above omit figures for Chaworha, Juawu, Riachu and Djemusse. In part, this is reflective of poor colonial cartography for the region, and in part because the population never returned to the affected sites, opting to cluster around Inhacumba, Gama, Chamburuca, and Coimba.

Sources: Instituto Nacional de Estatística, *Apresentação dos resultados definitivos e de indicadores sócio demográficos do censo 2007*, accessed March 1, 2014, http://www.tete.gov.mz/informacao/estatistica/resultados_censo_2007.pdf; Falling Rain Genomiocs, Inc., The Worldwide Index, accessed March 1, 2014, http://www.fallingrain.com/world/MZ/08/; and, http://www.geohive.com/cntry/mozambique.aspx.

Table 3 Djemusse population census, 1972 estimates

Family ID	Last name	First name	Middle name	Wives	Houses	Sons	Daughters	Cows	Goats	Pigs	Chickens
D1	Nhangamira	Djemusse		1	1	1		8			11
D2	Gandari	Cinturawu		3	3	4	5	9			20
D3	Gandali	Chuchupica		2	2	7	3	6	19		11
D4	Gandali	Pacanate		1	1	5	2	6			10
D5	Gandar	Barra		1	1	2	2				
D6	Gandali	Thuma	Chuchupica	2	2		1		30	2	10
D7	Gandali	Chico	Chuchupica	1	1	2	1			1	15
D8	Gandali	Pita	Chuchupica	2	2	5	2			2	5
D9	Pacanate	Vinte		1	1	2	2			1	
D10	Juawu	Ntsimbu		1	1	2	2		20	1	8
D11	Juawu	Sankhalane		1	1	4	1		12	2	16
D12	Juawu	Cheucane	Ntsimbu	1	1	2	5			2	7
D13	Juawu	Luis	Ntsimbu	1		1					
D14	Juawu	Guezane		1	1	1					
D15	Juawu	Panganane		1		1					17
D16	Tropa	Cussamba	Dausse	1	1	1	2				
D17	Tropa	Salimawu	Dausse	1	1	2	1			2	
D18	Cathoia	Filipe			1	1	2				12
D19	Cathoia	Buerezane	Filipe	1	1		1		12	1	
D20	Cathoia	Thangueladzulo	Felipe	1	1		1				14
D21	Folocone	Cudanguirana		3	3	4	1	18	24	3	10
D22	Folocone	Horacio	Cudanguirana	2	2	4	1				
D23	Folocone	Vinta	Cudanguirana	1	1		1				
D24	Tesoura	Folocone		1	1	1	3				9
D25	Juawu	Curewanao	Sankhalane	1	1	3	2		5	1	12
D26	Tropa	Dausse		1	1	1	3			2	
D27	Tropa	Laqui		1	1	1	1			2	10
D28	Macajo	Cufuniwa		1	1	1	2		6	1	16
D29	Tropa	Dequerane	Dausse	1	1	2	1		11	1	
D30	Folocone	Culinga		1	1	1	2			1	10
D31	Cathoia	Buundzirani	Filipe	1	1	2	2				7
D32	Cuchipira	Juawu		1	1	3	2				10
D33	N'tsimbre	N'change		1	1	3	1			2	
D34	Folocone	Chadzatambi			1						
D35	Folocone	Madomingo			1						
Total				41	43	69	54	47	139	27	230

Table 4 Wiriyamu population census, 1972 estimates

Family ID	Last name	First name	Middle name	Wives	Houses	Sons	Daughters	Cows	Goats	Pigs
W1	Sanganembo	Wiriyamu		3	3	5	4	67	45	3
W2	Valeta	Tenente		2	2	3	4	9	30	1
W3	Zambezi	Pensadu		1	1			29	49	1
W4	Zambezi	Bulachu	Pensadu	2	2	2	1		29	2
W5	Sanganembo	Lasquene	Wiriyamu	2	2	6	1	18	9	2
W6	Sanganembo	Luis	Wiriyamu	2	2	6	1	18	9	2
W7	Sanganembo	Afonso	Wiriyamu	1	1	3	2			1
W8	Baute	Cupitiwa			1					
W9	Culheri	Chuva		2	2	5	3			2
W10	Baulene	Arnaldu		1	1	1				1
W11	Fote	Massquene		2	2	1	2	6		2
W12	Fote	Lendissawu		1	1	1	1			1
W13	Sanganembo	Punguzani	Wiriyamu	1	1	2	2	6		1
W14	Fote	Salacuchipa		2	2	2	4	8	30	2
W15	Valeta	Avelinu	Tenente	2	2	1	1		4	1
W16	Valeta	Khaniaweni	Tenente	1	1		2			1
W17	Campute	Fugueti		1	1			9		1
W18	Luis	Inalio		3	3	6	1		4	2
W19	Inaciu	Denja		1	1	1	1			1
W20	Campute	Chenguitani		1	1	1	1			1
W21	Valeta	Kiripene	Tenente	1	1	3			3	1
W22	Matope	Sianani		1	1	1				
W23	Maibequi	Zeninu		1	1					1
W24	Maibequi	Limbicani		1	1	1	1			1
W25	Aranace	Maniju		2	2	3	1			2
W26	Magassu	Simbulani	Tanque	1	1					1
W27	Magassu	Tanque		1	1			6	25	1
W28	Zeze	Sinoia		1	1	2				1
W29	Xukussi	Macaju		1	1	1		6	25	1
W30	Macaju	Tembo		1	1	1				1
Total				43	43	57	35	182	262	39

Table 5 Juawu population census, 1972 estimates

Family ID	Last name	First name	Middle name	Wives	Houses	Sons	Daughters	Cows	Goats	Pigs	Chickens
J1	Kaniveti	Jembo		1	1		1	150	30		
J2	Kaniveti	Marfes		1	1	5		16			
J3	Kaniveti	Maningue		1	1	2	3		16		
J4	Kaniveti	Sinate		2	1	2	8				
J5	Juawu	Antoniu		2	2	6	4	5	20	2	
J6	Simoco	Jon		2	2	4	1	40	20		
J7	Changambica	Saize		1		3	2	20	10		
J8	Changambica	Mitivo	Saize	2	2	4	2				
J9	Kaniveti	Kalifornia		2	2	8	7	12	15	2	
J10	Changambica	Mualeka	Saize	1	1	1	2				
J11	Campande	Greia		2	2	1	6	8			
J12	Capena	Chapuca		3	3	6				1	
J13	Capena	Jantar		1	1	4				1	
J14	Capena	Manejo		1	1	5	2				
J15	Capena	Daquinani		1	1	2					
J16	Jantar	Oitenta		1	1	1					
J17	Jantar	Languirone		1	1	1					
J18	Capena	Cupensar		1	1	2	1	5			
J19	Juawu	Manuel		2	2	4	1		15		
J20	Juawu	Antoniu		1	1	5	4				
J21	Juawu	Bernardu		1	1	1	1				
J22	Juawu	Vanolo		1	1	2	1				
J23	Joque	Alfonso		1	2	2					
J24	Zacarias	Escrivawu		3	3	8	4	50	39	2	
J25	Zacarias	Comandar	Escrivawu	1	1	2			3		
J26	Zacarias	Binossi		2	2	4	5	34	25	1	
J27	Zacarias	Tove	Escrivawu	1	1	2	2			1	
J28	Viola	Magaio		2	2	6	1		15	1	
J29	Viola	Cado		1	1	1	2			1	
J30	Manjiricao	Djindja		1	1	1	2			1	
Total				43	43	95	62	340	205	17	

Table 6 Riachu population census, 1972 estimates

Family ID	Last name	First name	Middle name	Wives	Houses	Sons	Daughters	Cows	Goats	Pigs	Chickens
R1	Chimbadzu	Xavieri		2	2			17	50		
R2	Xavieri	Juawu		2	2	6	6	250	500	4	
R3	Xavieri	Simone		1	1		2		30		
R4	Xavieri	Davidi		2	3	3	5	7	10		
R5	Xavieri	Jdero		2	4	2	5	20	30	5	
R6	Juawu	Ernestu		1	1		3		25		
R7	Juawu	Trabalhau		1	2	1	7		17		
R8	Solar	Baulene		3	7	12	6	27	40	12	
R9	Solar	Joze	Baulene	1	1	1	3		20		
R10	Solar	Alfredu	Baulene	1	2	2	3	5	10		
R11	Solar	Horacio	Baulene	1	2	1	3		15		
R12	Solar	Sondadi	Baulene	1	2		4		7		
R13	Xavieri	Kussirira			1						
R14	Solar	Tome	Baulene	2	3	2	3	17			
Total				20	33	30	50	343	754	21	

Table 7 Chaworha population census, 1972 estimates

Family ID	Last name	First name	Middle name	Houses	Wives	Sons	Daughters	Cows	Goats	Pigs	Chickens
C7	Chamambica	Mantrujari		2	2	7	3	10	50	2	
C7a	Chamambica	Rui	Mantrujari	1	1	1					
C7b	Chamambica	Juawu	Mantrujari								
C8	Chamambica	Mauricio	Mantrujari	**2**	2	5	1	20	25	2	
C9	Marizane	Consembera		2	2	3	1	3		2	
C9a	Marizane	Marco		2	2	5	1		30	2	
C10	Xavier	Fulicane		**2**	2	1	2			2	
C11	Chaworha	Hagimo		2	2	5	4		35	2	
C12	Chaworha	Briefe		2	2	1	2		30	2	
C14	Marizane	Fernando		2	2	2	1		15	2	
C15	Marizane	Batista		2	2	4	2	5	30	2	
C16	Supinho	Nideka			2	6	3	0	75	2	
C17	Xavier	Bernardo		1	1	2			6	1	
C18	Mantrujare	Manuel		1	1	2			4	1	
C19	Mixone	Luis		1	1				7		
C20	Wirhisone	Alberto		1	1				20	1	
C21	Marizane	N'chenga		2	2	3	1		8	1	
C22	Chamambicca	Jo		1	1	1	1		7	1	
C23	Xavier	Alberto		1	1	2	1			1	
C24	Puebve	T'rabuco	Trabuco	2	2	1	3	9	20	2	
C25	Puebve	Mangisani	Trabuco	2	2	4	5	7	4	2	
C26	Puebve	Ciko		1	1	1	1		6	2	
C27	Puebve	Carlito	Mangisani Trabuco	1	1	1	3		7	2	
C28	Sabote	Quelimane		2	2	1	2		50	2	
C29	Puebve	Sabote		2	2	3	4		12	1	
C30	Sabote	Conekera		1	1	3	2		30	4	
C31	Puebve	Ficha		1	1	3	1			2	
C32	Chateta	Tembo		1	1	1	6		50	2	
C33	Puebve	Peratu		1	1	5					

(*Continued*)

Table 7 (Continued)

Family ID	Last name	First name	Middle name	Houses	Wives	Sons	Daughters	Cows	Goats	Pigs	Chickens
C34	Djasse	Marcelino		2	2	5	1	3	3	2	
C35	Djasse	Luiz		1	1	2	2			2	
C36	Djasse	Francisco		1	1	1	3			4	
C37	Djasse	Nataku		2	2	6			12	2	
C38	Alberto	Manteiga		1	1	8	4	15	12	1	
C39	Alberto	Luiz (Mayayah)	Manteiga	1	1	4	2	7	8	1	
C40	Chabvurura	Thauru		2	2	1	3	12	30	2	
C41	Chabvurura	Manuel	Thauru	2	2	2	3		3	2	
C42	Carvalho	George		1	1	5	1		6	1	
C43	Marizane	Domingos		1	1	2	2		5	1	
C44	Tsembera	Pedro	Marco	1	1	1	1			1	
C45	Tsembera	Juawu		1	1		1			1	
C46	Mauricio	Fugatu		3	3	3	4		10	3	
C47	Mantrujare	Joaquim		1	1	2	3		3	1	
C48	Xavier	Ze	Guizado	1	1	2	1			1	
C49	Xavier	Guizado									
C50	Wirhisone	António		1	1	2	2		4	2	
C51	Chaworha	Armindo	Hagimo	2	2	3	3	5		2	
C52	Xavier	Manuel	Guizado	1	1	1	2			1	
C53	Alberto	Simawu	Manteiga	1	1	2	2		6	1	
C54	Alberto	Sisito	Manteiga	1	1	1	3			1	
C55	Alberto	Ernesto	Manteiga	1	1	2	1		6	1	
C56	Manteiga	Necreto		1	1	1	2			1	
C57	Manteiga	Eusebio		1	1	1	1			1	
C58	Manteiga	Juawu		1	1		1			1	
C59	Tembo	Miguel		1	1		3			1	
C60	Rapozo	Arnado		1	1	3	3		16	1	
C61	Rapozo	Abirio		1	1		4			1	
C62	Marizane	Funani		1	1	2	2		10	1	

(Continued)

Table 7 (Continued)

Family ID	Last name	First name	Middle name	Houses	Wives	Sons	Daughters	Cows	Goats	Pigs	Chickens
C63	Kussai	Kurhanau		3	3	3	4		12	3	
C64	Kussai	Abirio		1	1	2	1			1	
C65	Kussai	António		2	2	2	2			2	
C66	Marizane	Kutungiwa		1	1	2	3		6	1	
C67	Chamambica	Jo		1			1		6	1	
C68	Kutungiwa	Luiz		1		1	1			1	
C69	Tembo	Mario		1		1				1	
C70	Tembo	Raimundu		1		1			3	1	
C71	Wirhisone	Armando		1	1	2			4	1	
C72	Mixone	Zeca		2	2	4	4	35	45	2	
C73	Tembo	Basiliu		1	1		1			1	
C74	Mantrujare	Eusebio		1		1		1	3	1	
C75	Guizado	Vicente		1			2				
C76	Mauricio	Castro		1			1				
C77	Mauricio	Ze		1		1					
C78	Tembo	Enrique		1			2			1	
C79	Tembo	Arnaldo		1		1	1			1	
C80	Batista	Manuel		1		1				1	
C81	Mangissane	Alberto		1		2				1	
C82	Mangissane	Arlindo		1			1				
C83	Pheratu	Abirio		1	1	2			6	1	
C84	Pheratu	Pintu		1	1	1				1	
C85	Pheratu	Buxa		1	1	1				1	
C86	Tembo	Mario "Fulucani"		1	1		1			1	
C87	Pheratu	Orlando		1	1		1		1	1	
C88	Sande	Jose	Commandai	1	1	2	1		5	1	
C89	Sande	Commandai		2	2	3	3		12	2	
C90	Sande	N'graze		1	1	2	2		4	1	
C91	Graze	Raimu		1	1				6	1	

(*Continued*)

Table 7 (Continued)

Family ID	Last name	First name	Middle name	Houses	Wives	Sons	Daughters	Cows	Goats	Pigs	Chickens
C92	Sabawu	Manuel		1	1	3	5	9	12	1	
C93	Sabawu	Rodrigue		1	1	5	4	12	20	1	
C94	Junta	Alfonso		1	1	4	2		12	1	
C95	Juawu	Peter		1	1	3	4		20	1	
C96	Juawu	Abirio	Peter	1	1	2			2	1	
C97	Arroz	Jose		1	1	2	3			1	
C98	Virrimbo	Evaristo		1	1	3	4		12	1	
C99	Virrimbo	Cutepa		1	1	3	4		16	1	
C100	Farraz	Tchalani		1	1	2	4			1	
C101	Virrimbo	Contente		1	1	3	2			1	
C102	Domingo	Luis		1	1		1			1	
C103	Luiz	Jose		1	1	1	2		5	1	
C104	Sande	Bera		1	1	1	2		6	1	
C105	Sande	Kusandurhica	(Vira Costa)	1	1	2	2		12	1	
C106	Khamba	Kutcheza		1	1	2	2		12	1	
C107	Khamba	Carlos	Kutcheza	1	1		2			1	
C108	Khamba	M'zaluanu	Kutcheza	1	1	2	1			1	
C109	Kabutiri	Shapasuka		1	1	4	6	56	30	1	
C110	Maucinal	George		2	2	3	3		12	2	
C112	Mauricio	Djeepe									
Total				130	132	215	197	209	939	139	

Table 8 List of the dead in Djemusse, December 16, 1972

Last name/ only name known	First name	Middle name	Husbands/ adult males	Wives/ adult females	Sons/ young males (age 1 month to 15 years)	Daughters/ young females (age 1 month to 15 years)	In the womb (1 to 9 months)
Dzedzereke			1	1	1		
Lekerani			1	1	1		
Nguiniya				1			
Firipi			1	1	3		
Zerista				1			
Bwezani			1				
Khapitoni			1	2	4		
Liyanla				1			
Djemusse			1				
Julia				1			
Djipi					1		
Alista				1			
Mtsimpho	Juawu		1				
Nsemberembe					1		
Thomasi			1				
Artencia						1	
Duwalinya				1			
Sadista				1			
Florinda				1			
Aesta						1	
Eduardo					1		
Tembo					1		
Panganane		Juawu	1				
Ntsimbu		Juawu	1		2	1	
Cheucane	Ntsimbu	Juawu	1	1			
Luis	Ntsimbu	Juawu	1	1			
Filipe		Cathoia	1	1		1	
Cinturawu		Gandari	1	1		2	
Cudanguirana		Folocone	1	3	1	1	
Horacio	Cudanguirana	Folocone	1	1			
Vinta	Cudanguirana	Folocone	1	1			
Folocone		Tesoura	1	1	1	1	
Dausse		Tropa	1	1			
Laqui		Tropa	1	1	1		
Cufuniwa		Macajo	1	1	1	2	
Dequerane	Dausse	Tropa	1	1	2	1	
Chuchupica		Gandali	1	2	2		
Culinga		Folocone	1	1	1	2	
Buundzirani	Filipe	Cathoia	1	1	2	2	
N'change		N'tsimbre	1	1	1	1	
Thuma	Chuchupica	Gandali	1	2			
			27	34	27	16	0

Sources: Padre Ferrão's list of the dead, and the author's fieldwork interviews, 1994–1995.

Table 9 List of the dead in Wiriyamu, December 16, 1972

Last name/ only name known	First name	Middle name	Husbands/ adult males	Wives/ adult females	Sons/ young males (age 1 month to 15 years)	Daughters/ young females (age 1 month to 15 years)	In the womb (1 to 9 months)
Vira				1			
Dinho						1	
Hortencia				1			
Chuva			1	1			
Vaina				1		1	
Macaju	Tembo		1	1	1		
Valeta	Khaniiaweni	Tenente	1	1		2	
Xukussi	Macaju		1	1			
Campute	Chenguitani		1		1		
Matope	Sianani		1		1		
Campute	Fugueti		1				
Luis	Inacio			1	2	1	
Valeta	Avelinu	Tenente		2	1	1	
Culheri	Chuva			2	1	2	
Valeta	Tenente			2	1	3	
Sanganembo	Wiriyamu				1		
Total			**7**	**14**	**9**	**11**	**0**

Sources: Padre Ferrão's list of the dead, and the author's fieldwork interviews, 1994–1995.

Table 10 List of the dead in Juawu, December 16, 1972

Last name/only name known	First name	Middle name	Husbands/ adult males	Wives/ adult females	Sons/ young males (age 1 month to 15 years)	Daughters/ young females (age 1 month to 15 years)	In the womb (1 to 9 months)
Biritsta				1			
Luwo					1		
Siria				1			
Saizi			1	2	1	2	
Gwaninifuwa			1				
Kachigamba					1		
Kuxupika	Ghandali		1	2	1	1	
Luwina				1			
Aluviyana				1			
Kuitanti			1				
Caetano					1		
Kuchepa					1		
Biyuzeyani					1		
Djinja			1				
Alufinati			1				
Mbiriyandende			1				
Chintheya						1	
Zeca					1		
Changambica	Mualeka	Saize	1	1	3	2	
Capena	Chapuca		1		1	2	
Capena	Jantar		1	3	4		
Capena	Daquinani		1	1	2		
Jantar	Oitenta		1	1	2	1	
Total			**12**	**14**	**20**	**9**	**0**

Sources: Padre Ferrão's list of the dead, and the author's fieldwork interviews, 1994–1995.

Table 11 List of the dead in Chaworha, December 16, 1972

Last name/ only name known	First name	Middle name	Husbands/ adult males	Wives/ adult females	Sons/ young males (age 1 month to 15 years)	Daughters/ young females (age 1 month to 15 years)	In the womb (1 to 9 months)
Chaworha	Chief		1	1			
Chaworha	Xavieri		1				
Mixone			1	1	1	1	
Irisoni			1	2	3	2	
Irisoni	Ramadi		1	1	1		
Akimu			1	1			
Birifi			1	1	2		
Batista			1	1	2		
Mdeka			1	1			
Mchenga			1	1			
Kunesa			1	1			
Marko			1				
Consenbera			1				
Pita			1				
Alberto	Manteiga		1				
Alberto	Simawu	Manteiga	1			2	
Chabvurura	Thauru		1	2	1	3	
Chamambica	Jo		1	1			
Chaworha	Hagimo		1	2	5	3	
Chaworha	Briefe		1	2	2		
Manzane	Consembera		1		2		
Marizane	Batista		1	2	2	2	
Marizane	N'chenga		1	1	3	1	
Mauricio	Djeepe		1				
Mixone	Luis		1	1	1		1
Puebve	T'rabuco		1	1	1	3	
Puebve	Sabote		1	1			
Puebve	Ficha		1				
Puebve	Peratu		1				
Supinho	Nideka		1	2	6	2	
Wirhisone	Alberto		1	1	1		1
Xavier	Bernardo		1				
Pinto					1		
Mayeza					1		
Mundani					1		
Djipi					1		
Chamambica	Mauricio	Mantrujari			1		
Total			**32**	**27**	**38**	**19**	**2**

Sources: Padre Ferrão's list of the dead, and the author's fieldwork interviews, 1994–1995.

Table 12 List of the dead in the triangle, unspecified locations, December 16, 1972

Last name/ only name known	First name	Middle name	Husbands/ adult males	Wives/ adult females	Sons/ young males (age 1 month to 15 years)	Daughters/ young females (age 1 month to 15 years)	In the womb (1 to 9 months)
Olinda						1	
Lainya				1			
Zabere						1	
Rosa						1	
Zaberia						1	
Alista						1	
Guideria				1			
Khembo			1				
Kamuzi					1		
Sunturu			1				
Dziwani					1		
Magreta				1			
Mario						1	
Fuguete			1				
Rita						1	
Chakupendeka			1	1			
Kulinga			1	1	1	1	
Keresiya				1	3		
Massalambani					1		
Chinai					1		
Domingos					1		
Mboy						1	
Chiposi					1		
Augusto					1		
Farau					1		
António					1		
Anguina				1			
Jantar			1				
Luisa						1	
Matias					1		
Nkhonde					1		
Xanu					1		
Djoni			1				
Chawene					1		
Lodiya						1	
Mario					1		
Fostina				1			
Rosa						1	
Maria					1		
Boy							
Zostina				1			1
Domingos					1		
Xanu					1		
Kuwela					1		
Chipiri					1		
Chuma						1	

(*Continued*)

Table 12 (Continued)

Last name/ only name known	First name	Middle name	Husbands/ adult males	Wives/ adult females	Sons/ young males (age 1 month to 15 years)	Daughters/ young females (age 1 month to 15 years)	In the womb (1 to 9 months)
Makonda					1		
Marko					1		
Luisa					1		
Mario					1		
Raul					1		
Duzeria				1			
Cecilia				1			
Faliosa				1			
Domina				1			
Chintheya						1	
Kupensar			1				
Chaphuka			1				
Djoni			1				
Total			**10**	**13**	**28**	**14**	**1**

Sources: Padre Ferrão's list of the dead, and the author's fieldwork interviews, 1994–1995.

Bibliography

Portuguese manuscript collection: Torre do Tombo

"Situação no distrito de Tete." PT/TT/D-F/001/0000. May 29, 1970.
"Relatório da situação no Distrito de Tete de 16 a 31 de Março de 1971."
    PT/TT/D-F/001/00001, April 7, 1971.
"Situação no distrito de Tete." PT/TT/D-F/001/00001, April 7, 1971.
"Relatório da situação no Distrito de Tete de 1 a 15 de Abril de 1971."
    PT/TT/D-F/001/00001, April 27, 1971.
"Relatório da situação no Distrito de Tete de 16 a 30 de Abril de 1971."
    PT/TT/D-F/001/00001, May 11, 1971.
"Relatório da situação no Distrito de Tete de 01 a 15 de Maio de 1971."
    PT/TT/D-F/001/00001, May 28, 1971.
"Relatório de situação no 12/73 [de Tete], 16 a 30 de Junho de 1973."
    PT/TT/PIDE/D-F/001/00020, September 24, 1971.
"Situação no período de 1 a 15 de Setembro de 1971 em Tete."
    PT/TT/PIDE/D-F/001/00003, September 24, 1971.
"Situação referida ao período de 16 a 30 de Setembro de 1971 em Tete."
    PT/TT/PIDE/D-F/001/00003, October 11, 1971.
"Situação em Tete no período de 1 a 15 de Novembro de 1971." PT/TT/D-F/001/00004,
    November 24, 1971.
"Situação em Tete no período de 16 a 30 de Novembro de 1971." PT/TT/D-F/001/00004,
    December 10, 1971.
"Relatório de situação interna no 7/71." PT/TT/D-F/001/00005, December 26, 1971.
"Situação no período de 1 a 15 de Dezembro de 1971 em Tete." PT/TT/D-F/001/00005,
    December 30, 1971.
"Situação no período de 1 a 15 de Janeiro de 1972 em Tete." PT/TT/D-F/001/00005,
    January 12, 1972.
"Situação no período de 16 a 31 de Dezembro de 1971 em Tete." PT/TT/D-F/001/00005,
    January 12, 1972.
"Situação no distrito de Tete no período de 1 a 15 de Janeiro de 1972."
    PT/TT/D-F/001/00005, January 31, 1972.
"Relatório de situação de 16 a 31 de Janeiro de 1972 em Tete." PT-TT-PIDE-
    D-F-001-00006, February 9, 1972.
"Situação no período de 1 a 15 de Janeiro de 1972 em Tete." PT-TT-PIDE-D-F-001-00006,
    February 25, 1972.
"Relatório Periódico de Informações-Grupo III: Tete." PT-TT-PIDE-D-F-001-00006,
    February 28, 1972.
"Situação no período de 16 a 29 de Fevereiro de 1972 em Tete." PT-TT-PIDE-
    D-F-001-00006, March 9, 1972.
"Situação no distrito de Tete na segunda quinzena de Fevereiro de 1972." PT-TT-PIDE-
    D-F-001-00006, March 15, 1972.

"Situação em Tete no período de 1 a 15 de Abril de 1972." PT/TT/PIDE/D-F/001/00007, April 26, 1972.
"[Relatório resumido da] Situação no distrito de Tete, de 1 a 15 de Maio de 1972." PT/TT/PIDE/D-F/001/00008, May 3, 1972.
"Relatório de Situação [de Tete], 16 a 30 de Abril de 1972." PT/TT/PIDE/D-F/001/00007, May 11, 1972.
"[Resumo] do Relatório de Situação de Tete no período de 1 a 15 de Outubro de 1972." PT/TT/PIDE/D-F/001/00011, May 25, 1972.
"Relatório [completo] da situação em Tete no período de 1 a 15 de Maio de 1972." PT/TT/PIDE/D-F/001/00008, May 30, 1972.
"Relatório de situação [no distrito de Tete], 16 a 31 de Maio de 1972 Geral." PT/TT/PIDE/D-F/001/00008, June 13, 1972.
"Situação no distrito de Tete, 16 a 31 de Maio de 1972 Resumo." PT/TT/PIDE/D-F/001/00008, June 13, 1972.
"Relatório de situação no 11/72 [de Tete], 1 a 15 de Junho de 1972." PT/TT/PIDE/D-F/001/00008, June 17, 1972.
"Relatório de situação no 12/72 [de Tete], 16 a 30 de Junho de 1972." PT/TT/PIDE/D-F/001/00008, July 3, 1972.
"Relatório de Situação no 13/72 [de Tete], de 1 a 15 de Julho de 1972." PT/TT/PIDE/D-F/001/00009, July 17, 1972.
"Relatório de Situação no 14/72 em Tete, de16 a 31 de Julho de 1972." PT/TT/D-F/001/00009, August 2, 1972.
"Relatório de Situação no 15/72 de Tete, 1 a 15 de Agosto de 1972." PT/TT/PIDE/D-F/001/00010, August 16, 1972.
"Relatório de Situação no 17/72 de Tete;de 1 a 15 de Setembro de 1972." PT/TT/PIDE/D-F/001/00010, September 18, 1972.
"Relatório de Situação no 11/73 [de Tete], 1 a 15 de Junho de 1973." PT/TT/PIDE/D-F/001/00019, September 18, 1972.
"Relatório de Situação no 19/72 em Tete, no período de 1 a 15 de Outubro de 1972." PT/TT/PIDE/D-F/001/00011, October 16, 1972.
"Relatório de Situação no 20/72 [de Tete], no período de 16 a 31 de Outubro de 1972." PT/TT/D-F/001/00012, November 2, 1972.
"Relatório de Situação no 22/72 [de Tete], 16 a 30 de Novembro de 1972." PT/TT/PIDE/D-F/001/00013, December 1, 1972.
"Relatório de situação no 3/73 [de Tete], 1 a 15 de Fevereiro de 1973." PT/TT/PIDE/D-F/001/00015, February 19, 1973.
"Relatório de situação nº 6/73 [de Tete], 15 a 31 de Março de 1973." PT/TT/D-F/001/00017. April 3, 1973.
"Acontecimentos ocorridos na povoação de Wiriyamo Tete." PT/TT/PIDE/D-F/001/00021, July 16, 1973.
"Situação no eixo Changara-Tete-Matundo." PT/TT/PIDE/D-F/001/00022, August 11, 1973.
"Relatório de Situação no 16/73 [de Tete], 16 a 31 de Agosto de 1973." PT/TT/D-F/001/00023, September 4, 1973.
"Relatório de Situação no 17/73 [de Tete], 1 a 15 de Setembro de 1973." PT/TT/PIDE/D-F/001/00024, September 19, 1973.
"Relatório de situação no 18/73 [de Tete], 16 a 30 de Setembro de 1973." PT/TT/PIDE/D-F/001/00025, October 4, 1973.
"Relatório Extraordinário da Situação de Moçambique." PT/TT/PIDE/D-F/001/00026, October 20, 1973.

"Situação em Tete no período de 1 a 15 de Outubro de 1971." PT-TT-PIDE-D-F-001-000003, October 26, 1973.
"Relatório de situação no 23/73 de Tete, 1 a 15 de Dezembro de 1973." PT/TT/PIDE/D-F/001/00028, December 19, 1973.

British manuscript collection: Foreign and Commonwealth Office

600th anniversary of Anglo-Portuguese Treaty of Alliance. FCO 9/1587, 1972.
600th anniversary of Anglo-Portuguese Treaty of Alliance. FCO 9/1586, 1972.
600th anniversary of Anglo-Portuguese Treaty of Alliance. FCO 9/1585, 1972.
600th anniversary of the first treaty of Anglo-Portuguese Alliance: general items. FCO 9/1805, 1973.
600th anniversary of the first treaty of Anglo-Portuguese Alliance: general items. FCO 9/1807, 1973.
600th anniversary of the first treaty of Anglo-Portuguese Alliance: general items. FCO 9/1806, 1973.
600th anniversary of the first treaty of Anglo-Portuguese Alliance: information aspects. FCO 9/1802, 1973.
600th anniversary of the first treaty of Anglo-Portuguese Alliance: visit by Professor Caetano, Prime Minister.... 56. FCO 9/1798, 1973.
600th anniversary of the first treaty of Anglo-Portuguese Alliance: visit by Professor Caetano, Prime Minister.... FCO 9/1799, 1973.
600th anniversary of the first treaty of Anglo-Portuguese Alliance: visit by Professor Caetano, Prime Minister.... FCO 9/1795, 1973.
600th anniversary of the first treaty of Anglo-Portuguese Alliance: visit by Professor Caetano, Prime Minister.... FCO 9/1796, 1973.
600th anniversary of the first treaty of Anglo-Portuguese Alliance: visit by Professor Caetano, Prime Minister.... FCO 9/1797, 1973.
600th anniversary of the first treaty of Anglo-Portuguese Alliance: visit by Professor Caetano, Prime Minister.... FCO 9/1801, 1973.
600th anniversary of the first treaty of Anglo-Portuguese Alliance: visit by Professor Caetano, Prime Minister.... FCO 9/1800, 1973.
600th anniversary of the first treaty of Anglo-Portuguese Alliance: visit of HRH Prince Philip to.... FCO 9/1803, 1973.
600th anniversary of the first treaty of Anglo-Portuguese Alliance: visit of HRH Prince Philip to.... FCO 9/1804, 1973.
Allegations concerning involvement of Rhodesian Forces in massacres in Tete province of Mozambique. FCO 36/1491, 1973.
Criticism of celebrations marking 600th anniversary of the first treaty of Anglo-Portuguese Alliance. FCO 9/1791, 1973.
Criticism of celebrations marking 600th anniversary of the first treaty of Anglo-Portuguese Alliance. FCO 9/1792, 1973.
Head of State correspondence regarding 600th Anniversary of Anglo-Portuguese Alliance. FCO 57/512, 1973.
Military situation in Mozambique: alleged massacres by Portuguese troops. FCO 45/1312, 1973.
Military situation in Mozambique: alleged massacres by Portuguese troops. FCO 45/1310, 1973.

Military situation in Mozambique: alleged massacres by Portuguese troops. FCO 45/1313, 1973.
Military situation in Mozambique: alleged massacres by Portuguese troops. FCO 45/1315, 1973.
Military situation in Mozambique: alleged massacres by Portuguese troops. FCO 45/1311, 1973.
Military situation in Mozambique: alleged massacres by Portuguese troops. FCO 45/1314, 1973.
Publicity on 600th anniversary of Anglo–Portuguese Treaty of Alliance. FCO 26/935, 1972.
United Nations General Assembly's Commission of Inquiry into the Reported Massacres in Mozambique. FCO 58/798, 1974.
Visit by Dr Marcello Caetano, Portuguese Prime Minister, July 1973, to coincide with 600th anniversary.... PREM 15/1826, 1970–1974.
Visits to Mozambique by members of HM Diplomatic Service in Portugal. FCO 45/1316, 1973.

FRELIMO ephemera and Maputo-based oral sources

Mozambique Revolution (New York Edition) 1, 1 (1964).
Mozambique Revolution (New York Edition) 1, 2 (1963?).
Mozambique Revolution (New York Edition) 1, 3 (1963?).
Mozambique Revolution (New York Edition) 1, 4 (March 24, 1965).
Mozambique Revolution (New York Edition) 1, 5 (June 1965).
Mozambique Revolution 01 (December 1963).
Mozambique Revolution 02 (January 1964).
Mozambique Revolution 03 (February 1964).
Mozambique Revolution 04 (March 1964).
Mozambique Revolution 05 (April 1964).
Mozambique Revolution 06 (May 1964).
Mozambique Revolution 07 (June 1964).
Mozambique Revolution 08 (July 1964).
Mozambique Revolution 09 (August 1964).
Mozambique Revolution 10 (September 1964).
Mozambique Revolution 11 (October 1964).
Mozambique Revolution 12 (November 1964).
Mozambique Revolution 13 (December 1964).
Mozambique Revolution 15 (February 1965).
Mozambique Revolution 16 (March 1965).
Mozambique Revolution 17 (April 1965).
Mozambique Revolution 18 (May 1965).
Mozambique Revolution 19 (June 1965).
Mozambique Revolution 20 (August 1965).
Mozambique Revolution 21 (September 1965).
Mozambique Revolution 22 (November 1965).
Mozambique Revolution 23 (February 1966).
Mozambique Revolution 24 (May 1966).
Mozambique Revolution 25 (July 1966).
Mozambique Revolution 26 (September 1966).

Mozambique Revolution 27 (December 1966).
Mozambique Revolution 28 (May 1967).
Mozambique Revolution 29 (July 1967).
Mozambique Revolution 30 (September 1967).
Mozambique Revolution 31 (November 1967).
Mozambique Revolution 32 (January 1968).
Mozambique Revolution 33 (March 1968).
Mozambique Revolution 34 (May 1968).
Mozambique Revolution 35 (September 1968).
Mozambique Revolution 36 (December 1968).
Mozambique Revolution 37 (February 1969).
Mozambique Revolution 38 (April 1969).
Mozambique Revolution 39 (July 1969).
Mozambique Revolution 40 (September 1969).
Mozambique Revolution 41 (December 1969).
Mozambique Revolution 42 (March 1969).
Mozambique Revolution 43 (June 1970).
Mozambique Revolution 44 (September 1970).
Mozambique Revolution 45 (December 1970).
Mozambique Revolution 46 (April 1971).
Mozambique Revolution 47 (June 1971).
Mozambique Revolution 48 (September 1917).
Mozambique Revolution 49 (December 1971).
Mozambique Revolution 50 (March 1971).
Mozambique Revolution 51 (June 1972).
Mozambique Revolution 52 (September 1972).
Mozambique Revolution 53 (December 1972).
Mozambique Revolution 54 (March 1973).
Mozambique Revolution 55 (June 1973).
Mozambique Revolution 56 (September 1973).
Mozambique Revolution 57 (December 1973).
Mozambique Revolution 58 (March 1974).
Mozambique Revolution 59 (June 1974).
Mozambique Revolution 60 (September 1974).
Mozambique Revolution 61 (June 1974).
Mozambique Revolution 14 (January 1965).

New York Edition of Mozambique Revolution 1, 2 (1964).
New York Edition of Mozambique Revolution 1, 4 (1964).
New York Edition of Mozambique Revolution 1, 5 (1964).

Voz da Revolução (April 1966).
Voz da Revolução 01 (June 1965).
Voz da Revolução 06 (September 1966).
Voz da Revolução 07 (January 1967).
Voz da Revolução 07? (January/February 1972).
Voz da Revolução 08 (March 1973).
Voz da Revolução 08 May 1968 (February 1969).
Voz da Revolução 08(a) May 1968 (May 1968).

Voz da Revolução 09 (April/May 1972).
Voz da Revolução 10 (June 1972).
Voz da Revolução 11 (July/August 1972).
Voz da Revolução 12 (August/September 1972).
Voz da Revolução 12 (September 1972).
Voz da Revolução 14 (December 1972).
Voz da Revolução 16 (March 1973).
Voz da Revolução 17 (April/May 1973).
Voz da Revolução 20 (October/December 1973).
Voz da Revolução 22 (May/July 1974).

"Celebration of the third anniversary of the Mozambique revolution, August 23, 1967 *Boletim de Informação* 5 (February 1964).
Bulletin d'information 5 (March 1964).
Chilcote, Ronald H., *Emerging Nationalism in Portuguese Africa: Documents* (Stanford: Hoover Institution Press, 1972), 1–709.
Communiqué Mozambique Revolution: Resolutions of the Central Committee, 2nd Congress, September 25, 1968.
Comrade Jose Monteiro, "FRELIMO representative in Algeria, answers questions on the Mozambique Revolution." *Mozambique Revolution* (September 1968).
Chilcote, Ronald H., *Emerging Nationalism in Portuguese Africa: A Bibliography of Documentary Ephemera through 1965* (Stanford: Hoover Institution Press, 1969), 1–134.
Révolution Africaine 19 (1963).
The Mozambican Woman in the Revolution (1969).

Chipande, Joaquim. Interview by Sol de Carvalho. Tape recording. Samora Machel Documentation Center, Maputo, 2003.
Ferreira, João. Interview by Sol de Carvalho. Tape recording. Samora Machel Documentation Center, Maputo, 2003.
Manave, Aurélio. Interview by Sol de Carvalho. Tape recording. Samora Machel Documentation Center, Maputo, 2003.
Neves, José Branco. Interview by Sol de Carvalho. Recorded transcript, 17 pages. Samora Machel Documentation Center, Maputo, 2003.

Missionary ephemera, IEME: Instituto Español de Misiones Extranjeras, Madrid

"!Si el cartero supiera lo que va repartiendo!" *ID.* . . (Feb. 1960): 32–33.
"?Monje y Fanatico Por Africa: Volveras a Mozambique?" *ID.* . . (Apr. 1962): 29.
"Confidencias al Caer la Tarde." *ID.* . . (Apr. 1961): 13–14.
"Dia a dia en Mukumbura." *ID.* . . (Feb. 1966): 24–26.
"Dia a dia en Mukumbura." *ID.* . . (Mar. 1966): 14–15.
"Dia a dia en Mukumbura." *ID.* . . (Mar. 1966): 20–21.
"Dia a dia en Mukumbura." *ID.* . . (Jun. 1966): 29–32.
"Dia a dia en Mukumbura." *ID.* . . (Oct. 1966): 28–30.
"Dia a dia en Mukumbura." *ID.* . . (Nov. 1966): 29–31.
"Dia a dia en Mukumbura." *ID.* . . (Jan. 1967): 22–23.
"Dia a dia en Mukumbura." *ID.* . . (Mar. 1967): 28–29.

"Dia a dia en Mukumbura." *ID*... (Apr. 1967): 26–27.
"Dia a dia eu Mukumbura." *ID*... (Dec. 1965): 9–10.
"El Mal Humor de los misioneros." *ID*... (Dec. 1964): n.p.
"El PadreFerrando se nos marcha otra vez a Mozambique." *ID*... (May 1965): 26–28.
"Fiesta Doble de Primera Clase, con Octava a Perpetua." *ID*... (Feb. 1961): 8–9.
"Instituto Espanol de san Francisco Javier para Misiones Extranjeras." *ID*... (Dec. 1965): 9.
"La Vuelta del Misionero." *ID*... (Oct. 1965): 12.
"Los Chy-Nhanjas tienen mas Corazon." *ID*... (May 1968): 14–15.
"Notas de un Viaje." *ID*... (Oct. 1967): 29–30.
"Notas de un Viaje." *ID*... (Nov. 1967): 30–31.
"Notas de un Viaje." *ID*... (Dec. 1962): 17–20.
"Otra vez el Congo." *ID*... (Jan. 1965): 18–21.
"Tambien los padres de los misioneros." *ID*... (Jun. 1965): 34–37.
"Terezinha." *ID*... (Mar. 1964): 20–21.
"Tortilla Espanola en Mozambique." *ID*... (Jan. 1961): 14–15, 24–25.
"Un Cura Misionero Entrevista a un Medico Misionero." *ID*... (Mar. 1963): 14–15.
"Un dia en Mukumbura (con el Dr. Sansebastian)." *ID*... (May 1967): 14.
"Un Mozambicano en Navarra." *ID*... (Nov. 1964): 12–13.

Interviews, fieldnotes, and tape recordings

Alberto household. Interview by author. Fieldnotes. Chaworha, 1995.
Aranace household. Interview by author. Fieldnotes. Wiriyamu, 1995.
Batista household. Interview by author. Fieldnotes. Chaworha, 1995.
Baulene household. Interview by author. Fieldnotes. Wiriyamu, 1995.
Baute household. Interview by author. Fieldnotes. Wiriyamu, 1995.
Buendia, Miguel. Interview by author. Tape recording. Maputo, 1994 and 1995.
Cabrita, Felícia. Phone interview by author. Lisbon, 1995.
Cachavi, António. Interview by author. Tape recording. Tete, 1995.
Campande household. Interview by author. Fieldnotes. Juawu, 1995.
Campute household. Interview by author. Fieldnotes. Wiriyamu, 1995.
Capela, José. Interview by author. Fieldnotes. Maputo, 1994 and 1995.
Capena household. Interview by author. Fieldnotes. Juawu, 1995.
Carvalho household. Interview by author. Fieldnotes. Chaworha, 1995.
Castellá, Padre Alberto Font. Interview by author. Tape recording. Changara, Tete, 1995.
Cathoia household. Interview by author. Fieldnotes. Djemusse, 1995.
Cebola, Tomas Pita. Facebook interview by author. Changara, 2014 and 2015.
Chabvurura household. Interview by author. Fieldnotes. Chaworha, 1995.
Chamambica household. Interview by author. Fieldnotes. Chaworha, 1995.
Changambica household. Interview by author. Fieldnotes. Juawu, 1995.
Chateta household. Interview by author. Fieldnotes. Chaworha, 1995.
Chaworha household. Interview by author. Fieldnotes. Chaworha, 1995.
Chimbadzu household. Interview by author. Fieldnotes. Riachu, 1995.
Chuva, António. Interview by author. Tape recording. Wiriyamu, Riachu, and Djemusse, 1995.
Cuchipira household. Interview by author. Fieldnotes. Djemusse, 1995.
Culheri household. Interview by author. Fieldnotes. Wiriyamu, 1995.

Bibliography

Djasse household. Interview by author. Fieldnotes. Chaworha, 1995.
Domingo household. Interview by author. Fieldnotes. Chaworha, 1995.
Elídio, Senhor. Interview by author. Fieldnotes. Wiriyamu, Chaworha, Cantina Raul, and Matundo, Tete, 1995.
Farraz household. Interview by author. Fieldnotes. Chaworha, 1995.
Ferrando, Enrique. Interview by author. Tape recording. Madrid, Spain, 1995.
Ferrão, Padre Domingo. Interview by author. Tape recording. Tete Diocese, 1995.
Folocone household. Interview by author. Fieldnotes. Djemusse, 1995.
Fote household. Interview by author. Fieldnotes. Wiriyamu, 1995.
Gandali household. Interview by author. Fieldnotes. Djemusse, 1995.
Gandari household. Interview by author. Fieldnotes. Djemusse, 1995.
Graze household. Interview by author. Fieldnotes. Chaworha, 1995.
Grouveta, General António Bonifácio. Interview by author. Fieldnotes. Maputo, 1994 and 1995.
Guizado household. Interview by author. Fieldnotes. Chaworha, 1995.
Hastings, Father Adrian. Interview by author. Fieldnotes. Oxford, London, and Leeds, 1977, 1978, 1979, and 1981.
Hastings, Father Adrian. Interview by author. Tape recording. Leeds, 1996.
Inaciu household. Interview by author. Fieldnotes. Wiriyamu, 1995.
Jantar household. Interview by author. Fieldnotes. Juawu, 1995.
Joque household. Interview by author. Fieldnotes. Juawu, 1995.
Joseph, White Father, formerly of Zóbuè Seminary. Interview by author. Fieldnotes. Seminário Maior, Maputo, 1994 and 1995.
Juawu household in Chaworha. Interview by author. Fieldnotes. Chaworha, 1995.
Juawu household in Djemuuse. Interview by author. Fieldnotes. Djemusse, 1995.
Juawu household in Juawu. Interview by author. Fieldnotes. Juawu, 1995.
Juawu household in Riachu. Interview by author. Fieldnotes. Riachu, 1995.
Junta household. Interview by author. Fieldnotes. Chaworha, 1995.
Kaniveti, Kalifornia. Interview by author. Fieldnotes. Wiriyamu and Juawu, 1995.
Kansande, Domingo. Interview by author. Tape recording. Near Cantina Raul, 1995.
Karimu, Abidu. Interview by author. Fieldnotes. Tete, 1995.
Khamba household. Interview by author. Fieldnotes. Chaworha, 1995.
Knipe, Michael. Interview by author. Tape recording. London, 1996.
Kussai household. Interview by author. Fieldnotes. Chaworha, 1995.
Kutungiwa household. Interview by author. Fieldnotes. Chaworha, 1995.
Llopis, Padre Vicente Berenguer. Interview by author. Tape recording. Maputo, 1994 and 1995.
Luis household. Interview by author. Fieldnotes. Wiriyamu, 1995.
Macajo household. Interview by author. Fieldnotes. Djemusse, 1995.
Macaju household. Interview by author. Fieldnotes. Wiriyamu, 1995.
Magassu household. Interview by author. Fieldnotes. Wiriyamu, 1995.
Maibequi household. Interview by author. Fieldnotes. Wiriyamu, 1995.
Mangissane household. Interview by author. Fieldnotes. Chaworha, 1995.
Manjiricao household. Interview by author. Fieldnotes. Juawu, 1995.
Manteiga household. Interview by author. Fieldnotes. Chaworha, 1995.
Mantrujare household. Interview by author. Fieldnotes. Chaworha, 1995.
Marizane household. Interview by author. Fieldnotes. Chaworha, 1995.
Marrão, Isaías. Interview by author. Fieldnotes. Chaworha, 1995.
Matope household. Interview by author. Fieldnotes. Wiriyamu, 1995.

Matsinha, Mariano de Araújo. Interview by author. Fieldnotes. Maputo, 1994 and 1995.
Mauncial household. Interview by author. Fieldnotes. Chaworha, 1995.
Mauricio household. Interview by author. Fieldnotes. Chaworha, 1995.
Mchenga, Podista. Interview by author. Fieldnotes. Tete and Wiriyamu, 1995.
Melo, Antonino. Interview by author. Tape recording. Near Lisbon, Portugal, 1995 and 2014.
Mixone household. Interview by author. Fieldnotes. Chaworha, 1995.
Mixone, António. Interview by author. Tape recording. Tete and Chaworha, 1995.
N'tsimbre household. Interview by author. Fieldnotes. Djemusse, 1995.
Nhangamira household. Interview by author. Fieldnotes. Djemusse, 1995.
Pacanate household. Interview by author. Fieldnotes. Djemusse, 1995.
Pheratu household. Interview by author. Fieldnotes. Chaworha, 1995.
Pringle, Peter. Interview by author. Tape recording. New York, 2013 and 2015.
Puedve household. Interview by author. Fieldnotes. Chaworha, 1995.
Rapozo household. Interview by author. Fieldnotes. Chaworha, 1995.
Raul, Cantineiro. Interview by author. Fieldnotes. Cantina Raul, 1995.
Sabawu household. Interview by author. Fieldnotes. Chaworha, 1995.
Sabote household. Interview by author. Fieldnotes. Chaworha, 1995.
Saez de Ugarte, Irmã Lúcia. Interview by author. Tape recording. Tete, 1995.
Sande household. Interview by author. Fieldnotes. Chaworha, 1995.
Sangalo, Padre José. Interview by author. Tape recording. Madrid, Spain, 1995.
Sanganembo household. Interview by author. Fieldnotes. Wiriyamu, 1995.
Simoco household. Interview by author. Fieldnotes. Juawu, 1995.
Solar household. Interview by author. Fieldnotes. Riachu, 1995.
Supinho household. Interview by author. Fieldnotes. Chaworha, 1995.
Tai, General Hama. Interview by author. Fieldnotes. Maputo, 1994 and 1995.
Tembo household. Interview by author. Fieldnotes. Chaworha, 1995.
Tesoura household. Interview by author. Fieldnotes. Djemusse, 1995.
Tropa household. Interview by author. Fieldnotes. Djemusse, 1995.
Tsembera household. Interview by author. Fieldnotes. Chaworha, 1995.
Valeta household. Interview by author. Fieldnotes. Wiriyamu, 1995.
Valeta, Enéria Tenente. Interview by author. Tape recording. Wiriyamu and Riachu, 1995.
Valeta, Vasco Tenente. Interview by author. Tape recording. Wiriyamu, Tete, 1995.
Valverde de Lion, Alfonso. Interview by author. Tape recording. Madrid, 1995.
Viola household. Interview by author. Fieldnotes. Juawu, 1995.
Virimbo household. Interview by author. Fieldnotes. Chaworha, 1995.
Wain, Christopher. Interview by author. Fieldnotes. London, 1996.
Wirhisone household. Interview by author. Fieldnotes. Chaworha, 1995.
Xavier household. Interview by author. Fieldnotes. Chaworha, 1995.
Xavier, João. Interview by author. Fieldnotes. Riachu, 1995.
Xavieri household. Interview by author. Fieldnotes. Riachu, 1995.
Xukussi household. Interview by author. Fieldnotes. Wiriyamu, 1995.
Zacarias household. Interview by author. Fieldnotes. Juawu, 1995.
Zambezi, Bulachu Pensadu. Interview by author. Fieldnotes. Tete and Wiriyamu, 1995.
Zeze household. Interview by author. Fieldnotes. Wiriyamu, 1995.

Articles, *The London Times*

Akinyemi, A. Bolaji, "Withdrawal of the White Fathers from Mozambique." *The Times*, July 21, 1973, 13e.
"All the Africans in Tete know where massacre took place, ousted missionary says in Madrid." *The Times*, July 13, 1973, 4.
Ashford, Nicholas, "Guerrillas accused of killing 12 Africans in Mozambique." *The Times*, January 11, 1974, 6a.
Baird, Tom, "Other reported massacres in Africa (Letter to the editor)." *The Times*, July 20, 1973, 17e.
Barridge, Dr Dorothy, "A Mozambique inquiry." *The Times*, August 13, 1973, 11d.
"Bishop of Tete says his duty is not to become involved in controversy." *The Times*, July 17, 1973, 6.
Bovey, D., "Withdrawal of the White Fathers from Mozambique." *The Times*, July 21, 1973, 13d.
"Britain 'has betrayed Africa at the UN'." *The Times*. December 17, 1973, 6.
Calvert, Michael. "Policy of authorities in Mozambique (Letter to the editor)." *The Times*, August 9, 1973, 13.
Caminada, Jerome, "A sea of turbulence awaits Dr. Caetano during London visit." *The Times*, July 16, 1973, 12a.
Caminada, Jerome, "The interrogation of Father Hastings." *The Times*, July 12, 1973, 6b.
Clark, George, "Labour demand for inquiry at massacre scene." *The Times*, July 16, 1973, 4e.
Clarke, Kenneth, "Attitude to race in Mozambique (Letter to the editor)." *The Times*, July 19, 1973, 19e.
Correspondent, "Rally of Liberal elements in Lisbon planned." *The Times*, July 7, 1973, 6c.
Debelius, Harry, "Portuguese accused of torture by priests." *The Times*, November 27, 1973, 5h.
Debelius, Harry, "Priest says he spoke to survivors." *The Times*, July 18, 1973, 1d.
Debelius, Harry, "Spanish priest confirms atrocities report." *The Times*, July 12, 1973, 1a.
Debelius, Harry, "Wiriyamu 'is marked on Tete mission maps'." *The Times*, July 16, 1973, 1d.
Editorial, "The weapon of counter terror." *The Times*, July 18, 1973, 17a.
Edwards, Rev. Francis, "A Mozambique inquiry (Letter to the editor)." *The Times*, August 17, 1973, 15f.
Elstoh, Peter, "Attitude to race in Mozambique (Letter to the editor)." *The Times*, July 19, 1973, 19e.
Fitzgerald, J. P. A., "A Mozambique inquiry." *The Times*, August 15, 1973, 15d.
Foot, Sir Dingle, "Portugal as ally (Letter to the editor)." *The Times*, July 28, 1973, 13.
France-Presse, Agence, "Bishop urges Portugal to end colonial wars." *The Times*, March 23, 1974, 4d.
France-Presse, Agence, "Bomb attacks in Lisbon." *The Times*, July 12, 1973, 6b.
France-Presse, Agence, "Burgos Order must leave by New Year." *The Times*, August 23, 1973, 8a.
France-Presse, Agence, "Criticism of Portugal as inquiry ends." *The Times*, June 15, 1974, 6d.
France-Presse, Agence, "Frelimo report issued on massacre by Portuguese." *The Times*, October 8, 1973, 4f.
France-Presse, Agence, "Missionaries tell of new killing in Mozambique." *The Times*, May 16, 1974, 6f.

Bibliography

France-Presse, Agence, "New massacres alleged by nun in Mozambique." *The Times*, March 22, 1974, 9a.
France-Presse, Agence, "Portuguese army chief criticizes wars in Africa." *The Times*, February 23, 1974, 5e.
France-Presse, Agence, "Support for Frelimo from Brandt party." *The Times*, August 7, 1973, 1h.
France-Presse, Agence, "Survivors describe Frelimo raid on village." *The Times*, January 14, 1974, 5d.
France-Presse, Agence, "UN inquiry 'confirms massacre'." *The Times*, June 18, 1974, 1g.
France-Presse, Agence, "Villagers tell of atrocities by Portuguese." *The Times*, June 6, 1974, 6f.
Gale, Dr G. W., "Britain and Portugal." *The Times*, July 26, 1973, 7f.
Galvin, D. G., "Massacre allegations (Letter to the editor)." *The Times*, August 4, 1973, 13d.
Harvey, Robert, "Other reported massacres in Africa (Letter to the editor)." *The Times*, July 20, 1973, 17e.
Hastings, Adrian, "Policy of authorities in Mozambique." *The Times*, August 9, 1973, 13.
Hastings, Adrian, "Portuguese massacre reported by priest." *The Times*, July 10, 1973, 1h.
"Heavy police precautions as Dr. Caetano begins his visit to Britain today." *The Times*, July 16, 1973, 1.
Heren, Louis, "Church inquiry confirmed massacres in Mozambique." *The Times*, September 21, 1973, 1d.
Heren, Louis, "More massacre evidence by priests." *The Times*, July 13, 1973, 1e.
Holden, David, "Portuguese paradoxes." *The Times*, July 15, 1973, 2c.
Hollis, Christopher, "A Mozambique inquiry." *The Times*, August 23, 1973, 15d.
Huckerby, Martin, "Missionary tells of beatings in prison." *The Times*, April 19, 1974, 6h.
Ibekwe, S. D., "Withdrawal of the White Fathers from Mozambique." *The Times*, July 21, 1973, 13d.
International, United Press, "Missionaries say they were not expelled." *The Times*, April 20, 1974, 4g.
James, J. C., "Other reported massacres in Africa (Letter to the editor)." *The Times*, July 20, 1973, 17e.
Jones, Tim, "British journalist appeals to UN commission." *The Times*, May 16, 1974, 6g.
Jones, Tim, "UN hearing on Portuguese atrocity reports begins." *The Times*, May 15, 1974, 5a.
Keating, D., "Mozambique (Letter to the editor)." *The Times*, July 18, 1973, 17d.
Kennan, George F., "Double standards over Mozambique (Letter to the editor)." *The Times*, July 25, 1973, 17d.
Knipe, Michael, "Mozambique secret police keep an eye on correspondent from the *Times*." *The Times*, July 25, 1973, 1.
Knipe, Michael, "S. African newspaper gives new details of Portuguese massacre at Wiriyamu." *The Times*, September 26, 1973.
Knipe, Michael, "African civilians suffering heavily in Mozambique war." *The Times*, July 21, 1973, 1d.
Knipe, Michael, "Bishop of Nampula and six priests pushed, kicked, punched." *The Times*, March 22, 1974, 9a.
Knipe, Michael, "Mozambique bishop maintains his silence on massacres." *The Times*, July 23, 1973, 1c.
Knipe, Michael, "New group calls for Wiriyamu inquiry." *The Times*, May 3, 1974, 6f.
Knipe, Michael, "No sign of Burgos priests at airport." *The Times*, November 24, 1973, 7h.

Knipe, Michael, "Portuguese Army chief defends policy in Mozambique." *The Times*, July 30, 1973, 1c.
Knipe, Michael, "Times man in Tete is ordered to leave." *The Times*, July 24, 1973, 1d.
Leigh, David, and Chris Walker, "Distribution of pro-Lisbon leaflets was arranged by Zanzibari." *The Times*, July 17, 1973, 1f.
Leigh, David, "Dr Caetano begins visit to Britain today." *The Times*, July 16, 1973, 1a.
Leigh, David, "Priest derides official denial." *The Times*, July 11, 1973, 6a.
Leigh, David, "War against Frelimo 'like fight with IRA'." *The Times*, July 18, 1973, 9c.
Lindley, Robert, "Banned priest speaks out on killings in Mozambique." *The Times*, July 15, 1973, 1e.
"Lisbon inquiry rejects massacre story." *The Times*, August 20, 1973.
Longley, Clifford, "An accusing finger in the wake of Wiriyamu." *The Times*, January 7, 1974, 7g.
Longley, Clifford, "Missionaries denounce Mozambique Church." *The Times*, April 17, 1974, 5b.
Lord Colyton, "The Church in Mozambique (Letter to the editor)." *The Times*, August 7, 1973, 13d.
Lord Gifford, "Frelimo activities (Letter to the editor)." *The Times*, February 13, 1974, 15a.
MacCallum Scott, J. H., "Withdrawal of the White Fathers from Mozambique." *The Times*, July 21, 1973, 13d.
Moore, Richard, "Other reported massacres in Africa (Letter to the editor)." *The Times*, July 20, 1973, 17e.
Mortimor, Edward, "How Portugal has clung to her African empire." *The Times*, July 11, 1973, 16d.
Nichols, Peter, "Appeal to the Pope over Portuguese repressions." *The Times*, October 11, 1973, 7c.
Nichols, Peter, "Vatican-Lisbon links strained by expulsions." *The Times*, April 15, 1974, 3g.
"Nine arrested during protest outside Buckingham Palace." *The Times*, July 18, 1973, 1.
"No inquiry, No welcome." *The Times,* July 11, 1973.
Noyes, Hugh, "Sir Alec quotes the past at Mr Wilson." *The Times*, July 18, 1973, 1a.
Oestreicher, Paul, "Blood on whose hands in Mozambique?" *The Times*, July 14, 1973, 14e.
Oestreicher, Paul, "Mozambique (Letter to the editor)." *The Times*, July 18, 1973, 17d.
Our Correspondent, "Amnesty hope for priests." *The Times*, November 19, 1973, 5f.
Our Correspondent, "Archbishop refutes massacre criticism." *The Times*, December 14, 1974, 10c.
Our Correspondent, "Bishops deplore incidents in Mozambique." *The Times*, March 27, 1974, 7d.
Our Correspondent, "Burgos priests are brought back to Madrid." *The Times*, November 26, 1973, 4c.
Our Correspondent, "Chiefs of Portugal's armed forces dismissed, military on alert." *The Times*, March 15, 1974, 1b.
Our Correspondent, "Churches urge junta to free colonies." *The Times*, May 7, 1974, 5h.
Our Correspondent, "Dr Caetano attacks world climate in which dissidents thrive." *The Times*, February 18, 1974, 6a.
Our Correspondent, "Dr Caetano clips wings of Portugal's Opposition." *The Times*, September 13, 1973, 5d.
Our Correspondent, "Junta inquiry into reports of Mozambique massacres." *The Times*, May 13, 1974, 4d.

Our Correspondent, "Le monde says Africans' silence is surprising." *The Times*, July 19, 1973, 7e.
Our Correspondent, "Lisbon offers to help inquiry into Mozambique killings." *The Times*, June 1, 1974, 6a.
Our Correspondent, "Lisbon paper attacks Wiriyamu priest." *The Times*, January 28, 1974, 5c.
Our Correspondent, "Missionaries say it was wise to quit Mozambique." *The Times*, April 22, 1974, 5a.
Our Correspondent, "Mozambique prelate criticizes officials." *The Times*, December 21, 1973, 5f.
Our Correspondent, "Nuncio helps bishops settle their differences." *The Times*, April 6, 1974, 4h.
Our Correspondent, "Portuguese bishops praise Mozambique colleagues." *The Times*, October 4, 1973, 8g.
Our Correspondent, "Portuguese claim nun had links with guerrillas." *The Times*, March 25, 1974, 5a.
Our Correspondent, "Portuguese liberals debate plans for reform." *The Times*, July 30, 1973, 4c.
Our Correspondent, "Priest sent recruits to Frelimo." *The Times*, June 13, 1974, 7b.
Our Correspondent, "Priests denounce role of Church in Mozambique." *The Times*, March 29, 1974, 7a.
Our Correspondent, "Rebels blamed for deaths in Mozambique." *The Times*, January 4, 1974, 5a.
Our Correspondent, "Wiriyamu investigator on mission to Lisbon." *The Times*, May 25, 1974, 6d.
Our Correspondent, "World churches give $450,000 to fight racism." *The Times*, February 21, 1974, 6g.
Our Diplomatic Correspondent, "New Mozambique massacre reported." *The Times*, May 11, 1974, 1b.
Our Foreign News Staff, "More British embassy targets." *The Times*, September 18, 1973, 1c.
Our Foreign Staff, "Army report confirms Wiriyamu massacre." *The Times*, April 24, 1974, 8h.
Our Own Correspondent, "14 countries call for inquiry on 'massacre'." *The Times*, November 8, 1973, 10c.
Our Own Correspondent, "Bishop of Tete briefs the Pope on Mozambique." *The Times*, September 14, 1973, 6f.
Our Own Correspondent, "*Le Monde* says Africans' silence is surprising." *The Times*, July 19, 1973, 7h.
Our Own Correspondent, "UN ignored Portugal's requests for observers." *The Times*, July 12, 1973, 6a.
Our Own Correspondent, "UN to hold inquiry on Portuguese 'atrocities'." *The Times*, December 14, 1973, 1g.
Palmer, M. W., "Other reported massacres in Africa (Letter to the editor)." *The Times*, July 20, 1973, 17e.
Paul, Rev. John, "Attitude to race in Mozambique (Letter to the editor)." *The Times*, July 19, 1973, 19e.
Paul, Rev. John, "The Church in Mozambique." *The Times*, August 7, 1973, 13d.
"Portuguese 'butchery' condemned." *The Times*, July 11, 1973, 6.
"Portuguese commander leaves Tete." *The Times*, September 10, 1973, 4.

"Portuguese converge on Lisbon to welcome Dr. Caetano back home." *The Times,* July 20, 1973.
"Press Council is asked to investigate." *The Times,* July 17, 1973.
Press, Associated, "Portuguese expel bishop from Mozambique." *The Times,* April 16, 1974, 1a.
Rendel, A. M., "Dr Caetano rules out UN inquiry into massacre allegations." *The Times,* July 19, 1973, 1g.
Rendel, A. M., "Embassy issues angry reply." *The Times,* July 11, 1973, 1a.
Rendel, A. M., "Lord Mayor offers an apology to Portuguese leader." *The Times,* July 18, 1973, 9a.
Rendel, A.M., "Whitehall plays it by ear in Africa." *The Times,* July 19, 1973.
Reuter, "British journalist tells UN of Portuguese 'massacre'." *The Times,* March 6, 1974, 5e.
Reuter, "Dr Patricio answers critics of Portugal." *The Times,* August 13, 1973, 4f.
Reuter, "Frelimo official tells of Mozambique massacres." *The Times,* June 4, 1974, 6a.
Reuter, "Jurists press Portugal to try priests held two years." *The Times,* November 15, 1973, 9g.
Reuter, "Mystery of priests' return from tour." *The Times,* August 17, 1973, 4f.
Reuter, "Opposition pick candidates for Portuguese poll." *The Times,* September 18, 1973, 6e.
Reuter, "Portuguese order expulsion of six missionaries." *The Times,* March 23, 1974, 4e.
Reuter, "Priests escape after riots in Mozambique." *The Times,* April 13, 1974, 5f.
Reuter, "Sweden to double its aid to Frelimo." *The Times,* July 16, 1973, 1d.
Reuter, "Sweden triples its aid to Frelimo fighters." *The Times,* March 26, 1974, 5c.
Reuter, "UN report accuses Portugal of atrocities." *The Times,* December 10, 1974, 1f.
Robinson, Oliver. "Withdrawal of the White Fathers from Mozambique." *The Times,* July 21, 1973, 13e.
Rosenberg, David S., "Withdrawal of the White Fathers from Mozambique." *The Times,* July 21, 1973, 13d.
Shercliff, Jose, "40,000 people demonstrate in Mozambique capital." *The Times,* July 17, 1973, 6a.
Shercliff, Jose, "Close friend of dismissed general and other officers arrested." *The Times,* March 18, 1974, 6a.
Shercliff, Jose, "Historic move by Portugal speeds decolonization." *The Times,* July 29, 1974, 4a.
Shercliff, Jose, "Portugal to launch an investigation." *The Times,* July 12, 1973, 1c.
Shercliff, Jose, "Portuguese report on Wiriyamu events." *The Times,* November 1, 1973, 8c.
Shercliff, Jose, "Sad last chapter to a general's book." *The Times,* March 16, 1974, 4e.
Staff Reporter, "Mr Wilson wants Portugal out of Nato." *The Times,* July 14, 1973, 4a.
Staff Reporter, "New Portuguese envoy to Britain named." *The Times,* October 1, 1973, 6e.
Staff Reporters, "Dr Caetano and Mr Heath meet angry demonstrators." *The Times,* July 17, 1973, 1f.
Staff, "Bishops condemn Tete massacre." *The Times,* September 13, 1973, 6h.
Staff, "Britain 'has betrayed Africa at UN'." *The Times,* December 17, 1973, 6g.
Staff, "Burgos fathers are charged with treason." *The Times,* July 27, 1973, 1a.
Staff, "Cancellation of visit on basis of article." *The Times,* July 18, 1973, 14b.
Staff, "Canon urges Christian backing for violence." *The Times,* May 14, 1974, 7f.
Staff, "Churches to help deserters from Portuguese forces." *The Times,* August 28, 1973, 6b.
Staff, "Government have no facts to substantiate allegations." *The Times,* July 11, 1973, 8a
Staff, "Massacre allegation not proved." *The Times,* July 26, 1973, 10e.

Staff, "Misssionary work viewed in Mozambique as subversive." *The Times*, August 3, 1973, 6f.
Staff, "Monument to Wiriyamu dead." *The Times*, May 19, 1975, 1e.
Staff, "Motions by Tory MPs support Caetano visit." *The Times*, July 12, 1973, 16a.
Staff, "Mozambique priests arrive." *The Times*, April 23, 1974, 4e.
Staff, "Mozambique: the priests' fight." *The Times*, July 15, 1973, 17a.
Staff, "Portugal alliance criticized." *The Times*, July 7, 1973, 3.
Staff, "Portugal sets a precedent (Editorial)." *The Times*, July 29, 1974, 13a.
Staff, "Portugal's aims in Mozambique explained." *The Times*, July 30, 1973, 4e.
Staff, "Portugal's turbulent Priests (Editorial)." *The Times*, April 19, 1974, 17a.
Staff, "Press council rejects complaints over report of massacre." *The Times*, February 12, 1974, 9a.
Staff, "Priest describes aftermath of massacre." *The Times*, August 6, 1973, 4e.
Staff, "Protests likely during visit by Dr Caetano." *The Times*, July 9, 1973, 4e.
Staff, "The three inquiries: the Missionaries, Bishops, and Army." *The Times*, August 2, 1973, 14a.
Staff, "UN body votes for massacre inquiry." *The Times*, November 10, 1973, 1a.
Staff, "Violence in Tete is deplored by Patriarch." *The Times*, September 20, 1973, 1h.
Staff, "Wilson demands cancellation of visit." *The Times*, July 11, 1973, 7a.
Stanhope, Henry, "Africans share burden of fighting Frelimo." *The Times*, July 12, 1973, 6a.
Stanton, Hannah, "Mozambique (Letter to the Editor)." *The Times*, July 18, 1973, 17d.
Strafford, Peter, "UN diplomatic snub to Portugal." *The Times*, December 19, 1973, 7b.
Sweeney, Christopher, "Emigres accuse Special Branch." *The Times*, July 12, 1973, 16b.
Tereshchuk, David, "Mozambique (Letter to the Editor)." *The Times*, July 18, 1973, 17d.
Thomas, Donald H., "Withdrawal of the White Fathers from Mozambique." *The Times*, July 21, 1973, 13d.
Walker, Christopher, and David Leigh, "5,000 in London protest march." *The Times*, July 17, 1973.
Walker, Christopher, and David Leigh, "Distribution of pro-Lisbon leaflets was arranged by Zanzibari." *The Times*, July 17, 1973.
Walker, Christopher, "300 police ring Caetano reception." *The Times*, July 19, 1973, 7e.
Walker, Christopher, "Call to UN over Wiriyamu evidence." *The Times*, August 6, 1973, 4d.
Walker, Christopher, "More people join in protests over Caetano visit." *The Times*, July 18, 1973, 9d.
Warrender, Anthony, "Portuguese in Africa (Letter to the Editor)." *The Times*, August 2, 1973, 15e.
West, S. George, "Britain and Portugal." *The Times*, July 26, 1973, 17e.
Wigg, David, "Priest gives massacre details to UN committee." *The Times*, July 21, 1973, 5a.
Wigg, Richard, "Missionary names five survivors who saw massacre." *The Times*, August 6, 1973, 1c.
Wigg, Richard, "Reprisal on Wiriyamu survivors feared." *The Times*, August 7, 1973, 5f.
"Wiriyamu village located." *The Times*, July 13, 1973, 4.
Wood, David, "Heath will not call off Portuguese state visit." *The Times*, July 11, 1973, 1a.
"Yelling and jeers as Commons debate visit of Dr Caetano." *The Times*, July 18, 1973, 1.

Articles, *The London Sunday Times*

"An unwelcome visit." *Sunday Times*, July 15, 1973, 16.
"Cardinal makes plea to Mozambique bishop." *Sunday Times*, August 26, 1973, 7.

"Confusion over Mozambique toll." *Sunday Times*, January 31, 1971, 1.
Da Fonseca, Jose, "Wiriyamu—Rome's duty." *Sunday Times*, August 12, 1973, 13.
Golledge, Dr N. H., "Vicious attack on oldest ally." *Sunday Times*, July 22, 1973, 18.
Holden, David, "After 500 years, Portugal begins Africa pull-out." *Sunday Times*, May 19, 1974, 11.
Liddle, J. K., "Readers' Letters." *Sunday Times*, August 12, 1973, 13.
Lindley, Robert, "Banned priest speaks out on killings in Mozambique." *Sunday Times*, July 15, 1973, 1.
Meredith, Martin, "Frelimo will be allowed to form political party." *Sunday Times*, May 5, 1974, 6.
Meredith, Martin, "Portugal's weary army pulls back." *Sunday Times*, July 28, 1974, 9.
"Mozambique—The priest's fight." *Sunday Times*, July 15, 1973, 17.
"My ordeal with the secret police—and my bishop." *Sunday Times*, December 9, 1973, 9.
"Onus on Portugal." *Sunday Times*, August 5, 1973, 12.
Perrott, Roy, "What Prince Philip will find in Portugal after 600 years of its special—and peculiar—relationship with Britain." *Sunday Times*, June 3, 1973, 9.
Pogrund, Benjamin, "Atrocity claim in Mozambique." *Sunday Times*, January 14, 1973, 6.
Pringle, Peter, Father Jose Sangalo, and Burgos Fathers, "My ordeal with the secret police—and my bishop." *Sunday Times*, 9 December 9, 1973, 9.
Pringle, Peter, "Guerrila army fights on." *Sunday Times*, July 14, 1974, 11.
Pringle, Peter, "I survived the Mozambique massacre." *Sunday Times*, August 5, 1973, 13.
Pringle, Peter, "Secret police seize my Mozambique tapes." *Sunday Times*, July 29, 1973, 1.
Pringle, Peter, "Priest raps Pope over Mozambique." *Sunday Times*, January 6, 1974, 6.
Pringle, Peter, "Troops mutiny in Angola then tell why on secret tape." *Sunday Times*, June 30, 1974, 9.
Reuter, "Missionaries expelled." *Sunday Times*, April 14, 1974, 1.
Schirmer, Peter, "'Torture' trial this week." *Sunday Times*, October 27, 1968, 9.
"Secret plan to protect 'massacre' survivors." *Sunday Times*, August 12, 1973, 7.
"Secret police seize my Mozambique tapes." *Sunday Times*, July 29, 1973, 1.
"Sect alleges brutality in Mozambique." *Sunday Times*, December 28, 1975, 5.
Shercliff, Jose, "Portugal starts to free colonies." *Sunday Times*, July 28, 1974, 1.
"Somebody listen before it's too late." *Sunday Times*, December 2, 1973, 28.
Sunday Times Reporter, "UN hears new version of massacre." *Sunday Times*, March 10, 1974, 10.
"Tete massacre report backed up." *Sunday Times*, September 30, 1973, 10.
"The fire and the pity—two faces of the war in Mozambique." *Sunday Times*, July 22, 1973, 5.
"Troops refuse to fight Frelimo." *Sunday Times*, July 21, 1974, 1.
Weiss, Ruth, "A war Portugal cannot afford." *Sunday Times*, July 28, 1974, 50.

Articles, *Africa Report*

Aarback, Gunnel, "Debate on the Interpellation, March 30 1967." *Africa Report*, 13, 7 (1968): 67–68, 71–72.
"Africa Day By Day: December 17–January 18." *Africa Report*, 17, 2 (1972): 6.
"Africa Day By Day: February 23–March 22." *Africa Report*, 17, 4 (1972): 11.
"Africa Day By Day: January 20–February 22." *Africa Report*, 17, 3 (1972): 6.
"Africa Day By Day: June 8–June 18. *Africa Report*, 17, 7 (1972): 24.

"Africa Day By Day: OAU Summit." *Africa Report*, 17, 7 (1972): 35.
"Africa Day By Day: September 29–October 31." *Africa Report*, 17, 9 (1972): 28.
"Africa Day By Day." *Africa Report*, 17, 6 (1972): 11.
"Africa Report Fact Sheet Series." *Africa Report*, 9, 6 (1964).
"African Political Parties of Portuguese Africa—Angola Mozambique and Portuguese Guinea." *Africa Report*, 12, 8 (1967): 15.
Christie, Iain, "Mozambique: Frelimo's New Struggle." *Africa Report*, 20, 3 (1975): 36.
Christie, Iain, "Mozambique: Portrait of President Machel." *Africa Report*, 20, 3 (1975): 15–17.
"Dar es Salaam." *Africa Report*, 8, 7 (1963): 35.
Davidson, Basil, "Arms and the Portuguese—What Kinds of Aid Does Portugal Get from its Nato Allies and What is its Role in the Colonial Wars?" *Africa Report*, 15, 5 (1970): 36.
Degnan, Michael, and Virgilio De Lemos, "Two Views of Wiriyamu." *Africa Report*, 5, 18 (1973): 36.
Degnan, Michael, "The Three Wars of Mozambique." *Africa Report*, 18, 5 (1973): 6–10, 12–13.
Delemos, Virgilio, "Mozambique: The Businesses are Edgy." *Africa Report*, 18, 4 (1973): 65.
Diamond, Robert A., and David Fouquet, "Portugal and the United States: Atlantic Islands and European Strategy as Pawns in African Wars." *Africa Report*, 15, 5 (1970): 15–17.
Diggs Jr., Charles C., "US and Portugal: We are on the Wrong Side." *Africa Report*, 18, 3 (1973): 34–35.
Dodson, James M., "Dynamics of Insurgency in Mozambique." *Africa Report*, 12, 8 (1967): 52–55.
Hachten, William A., "Newspapers in Africa: Change or Decay? Government Intervention is Drastically Altering the Press's Role while Basic Problems Remain." *Africa Report*, 15, 9 (1970): 25–28.
Hance, William A., "Three Economies." *Africa Report*, 12, 8 (1967): 23–30.
Hance, Williams A., "Cahora [Sic] Bassa Hydro Project: Portugal and South Africa Seek Political and Economic Gains from Joint Investment." *Africa Report*, 115, 5 (1970): 20–21.
Howe, Marvine, "Portugal at War: Hawks Doves and Owls, How Long Can Portugal Hold Out in Africa and at Home?" *Africa Report*, 14, 7 (1969): 16–21.
Huth, Arno, "A Report from the United Nations." *Africa Report*, 7, 9 (1962): 31–32.
"III. Politics of the Revolt." *Africa Report*, 7, 10 (1962): 9.
"Labor Reforms Planned in Portuguese Africa." *Africa Report*, 7, 8 (1962): 20.
Loucheim, Donald H., "The OAU Assembly in Accra." *Africa Report*, 10, 11 (1965): 35–36.
Marcum, John A., "A Martyr for Mozambique." *Africa Report*, 14, 8 (1969): 35.
Marcum, John A., "Three Revolutions." *Africa Report*, 12, 8 (1967): 36.
Martin, David, "Portugal: The Real Structure of Power." *Africa Report*, 19, 3 (1974): 35.
Mondlane, Eduardo Chitlangu Chivambo, "Conversation with Eduardo Mondlane by Helen Kitchen." *Africa Report*, 12, 8 (1967): 31–32, 49–51.
"Mozambique—Carriers Serving Mozambique. *Africa Report*, 10, 2 (1965): 29.
"News in Brief: African Bishops Unite at Vatican Council." *Africa Report*, 7, 10 (1962): 18–19.
"News in Brief: Angola (November 18–November 29), Mozambique (November 16–November 26), Portuguese Guinea (November 29–December 3)." *Africa Report*, 11, 1 (1966): 29.

"News in Brief: East Africa (June 11–July 1), French-Speaking Africa (June 13–July 3), Organization of African Unity (June 10–July 7), Portuguese Africa (June 10–July 6)." *Africa Report*, 10, 8 (1965): 36.

"News in Brief: East Africa (May 11–June 10), Maghreb (May 25–27), OCAM (May 25–26), Organization of African Unity (May 25–June 10), Portuguese Africa (May 13–May 19), United Nations (May 25–June 10)." *Africa Report*, 10, 7 (1965): 34.

"News in Brief: Governor-General Resigns in Mozambique. *Africa Report*, 7, 11 (1962): 22.

"News in Brief: Indians in Mozambique Ordered to Move On." *Africa Report*, 7, 7 (1962): 12.

"News in Brief: January 11–February 10: Organization of African Unity and East Africa." *Africa Report*, 11, 3 (1966): 21; 25–26; 29–30.

"News in Brief: Liberia (July 26–August 16), Libya (July 13–August 31), Malagasy Republic (July 15–August 28), Malawi (July 12–August 29), Mali (July 3–September 1), Muaritania (July 16–September 3), Mauritus (September 7), Morocco (July 14–August 5)." *Africa Report*, 10, 9 (1969): 48–49.

"News in Brief: Malawi (June 14–July 4), Mozambique (June 22–July 8). » *Africa Report*, 10, 8 (1965): 28–29.

"News in Brief: Malawi, Rwanda, Zambia, North Africa, Portuguese Africa, Spanish Africa, Southern Africa." *Africa Report*, 11, 4 (1966): 30–31, 33.

"News in Brief: Malawi, Rwanda, Zambia, Sudan, Tunisia, United Arab Republic, Portuguese Africa, Mozambique, Portuguese Guinea, Southern Africa." *Africa Report*, 11, 9 (1966): 26, 29–30, 34.

"News in Brief: Mauritania (October 26–November 9), Morocco (October 17–November 10), Mozambique (October 11–November 8), East Africa (November 5), Maghreb (October 21), Organization of African Unity (October 11–November 6)." *Africa Report*, 10, 11 (1965): 25, 33–34.

"News in Brief: May 1–August 31: East and Central Africa Education, European Economic Community, Organization of African Unity, Refugees, East Africa, Northern Africa, Portuguese Africa, Southern Africa." *Africa Report*, 13, 7 (1968): 25–26, 36, 41–42, 45–46.

"News in Brief: Middle Africa, Northern Africa, Portuguese Africa, Southern Africa." *Africa Report*, 13, 4 (1968): 25–26, 29–30.

"News in Brief: Mondlane Departs for Dar-es-Salaam." *Africa Report*, 8, 2 (1963): 20.

"News in Brief: Mozambique, December 24–January 7." *Africa Report*, 10, 2 (1965): 48.

"News in Brief: Mozambique, February 23–February 26." *Africa Report*, 10, 4 (1965): 32.

"News in Brief: Mozambique, January 12–January 29." *Africa Report*, 10, 3 (1965): 38.

"News in Brief: Mozambique, March 12–March 27." *Africa Report*, 10, 5 (1965): 36.

"News in Brief: Mozambique, May 27–June 7." *Africa Report*, 10, 7 (1965): 27–28, 32.

"News in Brief: Mozambique, May 3–May 5." *Africa Report*, 10, 6 (1965): 31–32.

"News in Brief: Mozambique, November 15–December 4." *Africa Report*, 10, 1 (1965): 29.

"News in Brief: Mozambique, October 11–November 11." *Africa Report*, 9, 11 (1964): 23.

"News in Brief: Mozambique, July 1." *Africa Report*, 9, 8 (1964): 20.

"News in Brief: Mozambique, July 23–August 27." *Africa Report*, 9, 9 (1964): 26.

"News in Brief: Mozambique, October 5–10." *Africa Report*, 9, 10 (1964): 24.

"News in Brief: Mozambique." *Africa Report*, 8, 10 (1963): 31.

"News in Brief: Namibia Portuguese Territories." *Africa Report*, 19, 2 (1974): 32–33.

"News in Brief: November 26–December 11." *Africa Report*, 10, 1 (1965): 32.

"News in Brief: Organization of African Unity (July 20–August 24), OCAM Portuguese Africa (July 14–September 1), United Nations (July 27–August 9)." *Africa Report*, 10, 9 (1965): 60.

"News in Brief: Portuguese Africa (December 12–January 1), Angola (December 1–December 15), Mozambique (December 20–January 1), Portuguese Guinea (December 15–December 27), Southern Africa (December 13–23)." *Africa Report*, 11, 2 (1966): 30–31.
"News in Brief: Portuguese Africa, Mozambique, Portuguese Guinea, Southern Africa." *Africa Report*, 11, 7 (1966): 41–43.
"News in Brief: Portuguese Africa, Mozambique, Spanish Africa." *Africa Report*, 11, 6 (1966): 37.
"News in Brief: Portuguese Africa, Southern Africa, Mozambique." *Africa Report*, 14, 2 (1969): 32, 40.
"News in Brief: Portuguese Africa, Southern Africa, South Africa." *Africa Report*, 11, 5 (1966): 36–38.
"News in Brief: Portuguese Africa, Southern Africa." *Africa Report*, 12, 3 (1967): 30.
"News in Brief: Portuguese Africa, Southern Africa." *Africa Report*, 12, 4 (1967): 29–30.
"News in Brief: Portuguese Africa, Southern Africa." *Africa Report*, 13, 5 (1968): 33–34.
"News in Brief: Portuguese Africa, Southern Africa." *Africa Report*, 13, 6 (1968): 34.
"News in Brief: Portuguese Africa, Southern Africa." *Africa Report*, 14, 5/6 (1969): 47–48.
"News in Brief: Portuguese Africa." *Africa Report*, 14, 1 (1969): 29.
"News in Brief: Portuguese Africa." *Africa Report*, 9, 1 (1964): 16.
"News in Brief: Rwanda, Portuguese Africa, Southern Africa." *Africa Report*, 13, 1 (1968): 29, 35.
"News in Brief: September 1–30, Belgium and Africa Francophone Organization of African Unity World Bank Group, East Africa, Portuguese Africa, Southern Africa." *Africa Report*, 13, 8 (1968): 21–22, 29–30.
"News in Brief: Seychelles, Tanzania, Uganda, Equatorial Africa, Portuguese Africa, Mozambique." *Africa Report*, 12, 2 (1967): 23, 30.
"News in Brief: Tanzania, October 9–November 11." *Africa Report*, 9, 11 (1964): 27–28.
"News in Brief: The Portuguese Territories." *Africa Report*, 19, 1 (1974): 30–31.
"News in Brief: Three FRELIMO Officials Form Rival Party." *Africa Report*, 8, 6 (1963): 23–24.
"News in Brief: Tunisia, Portuguese Africa." *Africa Report*, 11, 8 (1966): 33.
"News in Brief: UN Scores Portugal for African Policies." *Africa Report*, 7, 1 (1962): 11.
"News in Brief: Zambia, September 12–October 10." *Africa Report*, 9, 10 (1964): 28–29.
Nogueira, Dr Alberto Franco, "The View from Lisbon." *Africa Report*, 12, 8 (1967): 56–57.
Oudes, Bruce, "Guerilla Chic and the Perfect Martini." *Africa Report*, 17, 7 (1972): 40–44.
Oudes, Bruce, "Portugal's Coup: Good Fortune for the US." *Africa Report*, 19, 3 (1974): 44–47.
"Out of Africa: Mozambique" *Africa Report*, 17, 7 (1972): 4.
"Out of Africa: Southern Africa." *Africa Report*, 17, 4 (1972): 35.
Sanger, Clyde, "Nyasaland Becomes Malawi: An Assessment." *Africa Report*, 9, 8 (1964): 8–9, 11.
Segal, Aaron, "Havana's Tricontinental Conference." *Africa Report*, 11, 4 (1966): 51.
"The OAU's Operation Liberation: Status Report." *Africa Report*, 8, 8 (1963): 16–18.
"The USSR and Africa in 1965." *Africa Report*, 10, 10 (1965): 30–32.
University, Syracuse, "Eduardo Mondlane Memorial Fund." *Africa Report*, 16, 3 (1971).
Walshe, A. P., "Rhodesia: Backdrop to Crisis." *Africa Report*, 9, 10 (1964): 36.
Whitaker, Paul M., "Arms and the Nationalists: Where and on What Terms Do They Obtain Their Support and How Important is External Aid to Their Revolution?" *Africa Report*, 15, 5 (1970): 36.

Books, miscellaneous articles, periodicals, and reports

Adam, Yussuf, "Samora Machel e o desenvolvimento de Moçambique," in António Soupa (ed.), *Samora: Homem em Povo*. Maputo: Maguezo Editores, 2001.
Adam, Yussuf, and Hilário Alumasse Dyuti, "Entrevista: o massacre de Mueda—falam testemunhas." *Arquivo*, 14 (1993): 117–128.
Alexander, Jocelyn, and Terence Ranger, "Competition and Integration in the Religious History of North-Western Zimbabwe." *Journal of Religion in Africa*, 28, 1 (Feb. 1988): 3–31.
Allina, Eric, *Slavery by Any Other Name: African Life under Company Rule in Colonial Mozambique*. Charlottesville: University of Virginia Press, 2012.
Almeida, João Miguel, *A oposição católica ao Estado Novo, 1958–1974*. Lisbon: Edições Nelson de Matos, 2008.
"Américo Tomás Em Moçambique, 1964," accessed December 11, 2013, https://www.youtube.com/watch?v=9rS46Ptd0Z0.
Amnesty International, *Annual Report 1973–1974*. London: Amnesty International, 1974.
Andersen, Jack, "Richard Allen and '73 Massacre in Mozambique." *Washington Post*, December 12, 1972.
Andrade, Mário de, "Literature and Nationalism in Angola." *Presénce Africaine*, 13, 41 (1962): 115–122.
Andrade, Mário de, "Poesia Africana de Expressão Portugusa, Breve Notas Explicativas." *Presénce Africaine*, 80, 58 (1966): 433–500.
"Angolan Bishops' Pastoral on Justice." *Catholic Herald*, November 3, 1972.
Ankersmit, Frank, "Reply to Professor Zagorin." *History and Theory*, xxix (1990): 275–296.
Antunes, António Lobo, *Os Cus de Judas*. Lisboa: Objetiva, 1979.
Antunes, António Lobo, *The Land at the End of the World*. New York: W. W. Norton, 2012.
Antunes, José Freire, *A Guera de África, 1961–1974, Volume I and Volume II*. Lisbon: Temas e Debates, 1996.
Arriaga, General Kaúlza de, *História das Tropas Pára-quedistas Portuguesas*, vol. III, BCP 21, CTP.1, accessed January 1, 2010, http://preview.tinyurl.com/qzeovqb.
Arriaga, General Kaúlza de, *Wiriyamu: Síntese*, accessed March 19, 2010, http://cidadevirtual.pt/k-arriaga/Wiriamu.html.
Asten, Father Theodore van, "Notes" (December 1974): 1–2, Father Adrian Hastings Archive, Borthwick Institute, Box WIR2: B4/1.
"Atrocities and Massacres, 1960–1977: Wiriyamu, Mueda and Others, Dossier MZ-0354." *Mozambique History Net*, accessed July 15, 2012, http://www.mozambiquehistory.net/massacres.html.
Auret, David, "The Mhondoro Spirits of Supernatural Significance in the Culture of the Shona." *African Studies*, 41, 2 (1982): 173–187.
Azedevo, Carlos A. Moreira, "Perfil biographic de D. Sebastião Soares de Resende." *Lusitania Sacra*, 2, 6 (1994).
Azevedo, Carlos, Manuel Marques Novo, José A. Correia Pereira, and America Montes Moreira, *Franciscans em Mozambique, cem anos de missão, 1898–1998*. Barga: Editorial Franciscana, 2000.
Baritussio, Arnaldo, *Mozambique, 50 anni id persons die missionary combonian*. Bologna: Editrice Missionaria Italiana, 1997.
Barnhill, John, *DSM-5 Clinical Cases*. Arlington, Virginia: American Psychiatric Association, 2013.
Barraclough, Geoffrey, "History, Morals and Politics." *International Affairs*, 34, 1 (1958): 1–15.

Barraclough, Geoffrey, "Scientific Method and the Work of the Historian." *Studies in Logic and the Foundations of Mathematics*, 44 (1966): 584-594.

Barraclough, Geoffrey, "The Social Dimensions of Crisis," in *Germany 1919-1932: The Weimar Culture, Social Research*, 39, 2 (1972): 341-359.

Bastos, Susana Pereira, "Ambivalence and Phantasm in the Portuguese Colonial Discursive Production on Indians (Mozambique)." *Lusotopie*, 15, 1 (2008): 77-95.

Beckett, I., "The Portuguese Army: The Campaign in Mozambique 1964-74," in *Armed Forces and Modern Counter-Insurgency*, eds. I. Beckett and J. Pimlott. London: Croon Helm, 1977, 136-162.

Bender, Gerald J., *Angola under the Portuguese: The Myth and the Reality*. Berkeley: University of California Press, 1978.

Bernardo Coronel, Manuel Amaro, "Entrevista do General Kaúlza de Arriaga," accessed March 19, 2010, http://macua.blogs.com/moambique_para_todos/wiriamu/.

Bertulli, Cesar, *A Cruz e a Espada em Moçambique*. Lisbon: Portugalia Editora, 1974.

Bjerk, Paul, "African Files in Portuguese Archives." *History in Africa*, 31 (2004): 463-468.

Bogdanor, Victor, "Memoirs: Only a Lame Leg to Stand On." *New Statesman*, July, 2011. Accessed July 8, 2012.

Borges, Anselmo (ed.), *D Manuel Vieira Pinto. Arcebispo de Nampula. Cristianismo: Política e Mística*. Lisbon: Edições ASA, 1992.

Borges, Anselmo, "Massacres de Wiriyamu e visita de Marcello Caetano a Londres," accessed January 10, 2014, http://www.guerracolonial.org/index.php?content=2087.

Bourbillon, M. F. C., "Guns and Rain: Taking Structural Analysis Too Far." *Africa: Journal of the International African Institute*, 57, 2 (1987): 263-274.

Bragança, Aquino de, and Immanuel Wallerstein (eds.), *The African Liberation Reader: Documents of the National Liberation Movements, Volume 2*. London: Zed Press, 1982.

Bragança, Aquino de, and Jacques Depelchin, "From Idealization of Frelimo to the Understanding of Mozambique Recent History." *Review (Fernand Braudel Center)* 11, 1 (1988): 95-117.

Brandão, Arnaldo Baritussio, *Mozambique, 50 anni id persons die missionary combonian*. Bologna: Editrice Missionaria Italiana, 1997.

Brandão, Pedro Ramos, *A Igreja Católica e o Estado Novo em Moçambique, 1960/1974*. Lisbon: Editorial Notícias, 2004.

Bruneau, Thomas C., "Church and State in Portugal: The Crisis of Cross and Sword." *Journal of Church and State*, 18, 3 (1976).

Bullington, J. R., "Assessing Pacification in Vietnam: We Won the Counterinsurgency War!" *Small Wars Journal* (March 23, 2012).

Buur, Lars, and Maria Helene Kyed, "Contested Sources of Authority: Re-Claiming State Sovereignty by Formalizing Traditional Authority in Mozambique." *Development and Change*, 37, 4 (2006): 847-869.

Byers, Bruce A., Robert N. Cunliffe, and Andrew T. Hudak, "Linking the Conservation of Culture and Nature: A Case Study of Sacred Forests in Zimbabwe." *Human Ecology*, 29, 2 (June 2001): 187-218.

Cabaço, José Luís, *Moçambique: Identidade, Colonialismo e Libertação*, preface by Omar Ribeiro Tomaz. São Paulo: Editora Unesp/ANPOCS, 2009.

Cabecinhas, Rosa, and João Feijó, "Collective Memories of Portuguese Colonial Action in Africa: Representations of the Colonial Past among Mozambicans and Portuguese Youths." *International Journal of Conflict and Violence*, 4, 1 (2010): 28-44.

Cabrita, Felícia, and Paulo Camacho, *Regresso a Wiriyamu*. Portugal, Sociedade Independente de Comunicação, 1998.
Cabrita, Felícia, "Os Mortos Não Sofrem." *Revista Expresso*, December 5, 1992.
Cabrita, Felícia, "Wiriyamu, Viagem ao Fundo do Terror." *Revista Expresso*, November 21, 1998.
Cabrita, Felícia, *Massacres em África*. Lisbon: A Esfera dos Livros, 2008.
Cabrita, João M., *Mozambique: The Tortuous Road to Democracy*. Basingstoke: Palgrave Macmillan, 2001.
Caetano, Marcello, *Depoimento*. Rio de Janeiro: Distribuidora Record, 1974.
Cahen, Michel, "L'État Nouveau e la Diversification Religieuse au Mozambique, 1930-1974. I. Le Résistible essor de la Portugalisation Catholique (1930-1961)." *Cahiers d'Études Africaine*, xl-2 (2000).
Calvão, Guilherme Almor De Alpoím, Comandante da Marinha reformado e ex-combatente na Guerra Colonial, "Quantos Morreram em Mueda?" *Jornal Público*, June 16, 2002.
Canelas, Lucinda, and Esabel Salema, "Relatório Militar revela que tropas portuguesas participaram em decapitações." *O Público*, December 16, 2012, 4.
Capela, José, "Para a História do Diário de Moçambique." *Arquivo. Boletim do Arquivo Histórico de Moçambique*, 6 (1989).
Cardoso, Margarida, *A Costa dos Murmúrios*, DVD. Lisbon: Filmes do Tejo, 2004.
Carlos Eduardo Machado Sangreman Proença and Francisco Salgado Zenha, *O Caso da Capela do Rato no Supremo Tribunal Administrativo*. Lisboa: Afrontamento, 1973.
Carr, E. H., *What Is History?* London: Vintage, 1967.
Carvalho, Susana Maria Correia Poças de, "Dois olhares sobre uma guerra: A Costa dos Murmúrios." MA thesis, The Open University, Lisbon, 2008.
Castanheira, José Pedro, "Declarações de Marcello Caetano à BBC-TV." *O Expresso*, July 11, 2008.
"Censura 16, "Wiriyamu (*)." *Notícias da Amadora*, July 21, 1973.
Chipande, Alberto Joaquim, "The Massacre of Mueda." *Mozambique Revolution*, 43 (1970): 12-14.
Christian Geffray, *La cause des Armes: Anthropologie de la guerre civile au Mozambique*. Paris: Karthala, 1990.
Christie, Ian, *Samora Machel: A Biography*. London: Zed Press, 1989.
Coelho, João Paulo Borges, *O Início da Luta Armada Em Tete, 1968-1969*. Maputo: Archivo Histórico de Moçambique, 1989.
Coelho, Jorge Borges, "Protected Villages and Communal Villages in the Mozambican Province of Tete, 1968-1982." PhD thesis, University of Bradford, 1993.
Coelho, Jorge Borges, "Sa Violência Ordenada à Ordem Pós-Colonial Violenta." *Lusotopie* (2003): 175-193.
Cohen, David William, "In a Nation of White Cars... One White-Car, or 'A White Car' Becomes a Truth," in Luise White, Stephan F. Meischer, and David William Cohen (eds.), *African Words, African Voices: Critical Practices in Oral History*. Bloomington: Indiana University Press, 2001, 264-280.
Cohen, David William, "The Undefining of Oral Traditions." *Ethnohistory*, 36, 1 (Winter 1986): 9-18.
Collingwood, Robin George, *The Idea of History*. Oxford: Oxford University Press, 1994.
Comaroff, Jean, *Body of Power, Spirit of Resistance: The Culture and History of South African People*. Chicago: Chicago University Press, 1985.

Comaroff, Jean, and John Comaroff (eds.), *Modernity and Its Malcontents: Ritual and Power in Postcolonial Africa*. Chicago: Chicago University Press, 1993, xxx.

Comissão para o Estado das Campanhas de África, *Resenha histórico-militar da Campanhas de África: Dispositivo das nossas forças: Moçambique*. Lisbon: Estado-Maior do Exército, 1989.

Correia, M. Alves, *Missões Franciscanas Portuguesas de Mozambique e da Guiné*. Braga: Typography das Missões Franciscanas, 1934.

Costa, Ernesto Gonçalves, *A Obra Missionária em Moçambique e o Poder Político*. Braga: Editorial Franciscana, 1996.

Creemos 13TV, *Misioneros por el Mundo, Misioón Mozambique*, accessed June 1, 2013, http://www.youtube.com/watch?v=BXbt5pY8Mug.

Cruz, Manuel Braga da, "A Igreja na transição democrática portuguesa." *Lusitania Sacra: Revista do centro de estudos de história religiosa*, viii/ix, 2 (1996/1997).

Cunha, Joaquim da Luz, Kaúlza de Arriaga, Bethencourt Rodrigues, and Silvino Silvério Marques, *África: A Vitória Traída* (Braga, Lisbon: Editorial Inervenção, 1977).

Dhada, Mustafah, "Contesting Terrains Over a Massacre: The Case of Wiriyamu," in *Contesting Terrains and Constructed Categories: Critical Issues in Contemporary Africa*, eds. George Clement Bond and Niger C. Gibson. Boulder: Westview Press, 2001.

Dhada, Mustafah, "Frankly My Dear, We Should Give a Damn!" *Peace Review*, 12: 3 (2000): 457–462.

Dhada, Mustafah, "The Wiriyamu Massacre of 1972: Its Context, Genesis, and Revelation." *History in Africa* (June 2013).

Dhada, Mustafah, "The Wiriyamu Massacre of 1972: Response to Reis and Oliveira." *Civil Wars*, 15, 4 (2103): 551–558.

Dinerman, A., *Revolution, Counter-Revolution and Revisionism in Postcolonial Africa: The Case of Mozambique, 1974–1994*. London: Routledge, 2006.

Diocese de Tete, accessed December 23, 2013, http://www.diocesedetete.org.mz/diocese/features.html.

"Diocese of Tete, Mozambique," accessed December 22, 2013, http://www.gcatholic.org/dioceses/diocese/tete0.htm.

Diop, Alioune, "Niam n'qoura ou les raisons d'être de Présence Africaine." *Présence Africaine*, I (1947).

Diplomático, Arquivo Histórico, "D. Altino Ribeiro Santana, *Bispo da Beira*, 1973–1974." PT/AHD/MU/GM/GNP/RNP/0456/07052.

"Dispute with Vatican after Pope's Reception of Rebel Leaders from Portuguese Africa...." *Keesing's Contemporary Archives*, xvii (1970): 24147.

Douglas-Home, Sir Alec, *Hansard* 860 (1973): cc.265–375.

"Esclusivo: Massacri Nel Mozambico." *Cablo Press*, June 4, 1973, 5–11.

"Fact and Fiction in Mozambique: The Bishops' Communique." *The Tablet Archives*, accessed December 24, 2013, http://archive.thetablet.co.uk/article/26th-june-1971/19/documentation.

Farmer, Paul, "On Suffering and Structural Violence: A View from Below." *Daedalus*, 125, 1 (1996): 263.

"Fazem-se Casas e Casas, Sem Ruas: Isaías Marrão, um home, uma história." *Jornal Calowera*, March 22, 2010, 18–19.

Ferreira, Carolin Overhoff, "Decolonizing the Mind? The Representation of the African Colonial War in Portuguese Cinema." *Studies in European Cinema*, 2, 3 (2005): 227–239.

Ferreira, Eduardo de Sousa, "An Analysis of the 'Spinola Affair.'" *Africa Today*, 21, 2 (1974): 69–73.
Florêncio, Fernando, "Autoridads tradicionais vandal de Moçambique: o regress do indirect rule ou uma espécie de nep-direct rule?" *Análise Social*, 43, 187 (2008): 369–391.
Freedberg, Robin, "London Protesters Fail to Block Caetano Visit." *The Harvard Crimson*, July 17, 1973.
Funada-Classen, Sayaka, *The Origins of War in Mozambique*. Somerset West: African Minds, 2013.
Furtado, Joaquim, *A Guerra Colonial do Ultramar de Libertação*. Lisbon: Rádio e Televisão de Portugal, RTP, 2012.
Garbett, Kingsley, "Contrasting Realities: Changing Perceptions of Shona Witch Beliefs and Practices." *Social Analysis: The International Journal of Social and Cultural Practice*, 42, 2 (July 1998): 24–47.
Garcia, Francisco Miguel Gouveia Pinto Proença, "Análise global de uma guerra (Moçambique 1964–1974)." PhD Dissertation, Universidade Portucalense, 2001.
General Assembly, *Report of the Commission of Inquiry on the Reported Massacres in Mozambique, Official Records: Twenty-Ninth Session, Supplement*, 21, A/9621 (1974), 1–41.
Gheddo, Piero, "A New Church is Born." *Biblical Studies*, December 26, 2013.
Gheddo, Piero, "Una chiesa nuova nasce dalla persecuzione." *Mondo e missione*, 22 (2013).
Glick, Peter, and Elizabeth Levy Paluck, "The Aftermath of Genocide: History as a Proximal Cause." *Journal of Social Issues*, 69, 1 (March 2013): 200–208.
Gonçalves, Euclides, "Finding the Chief: Political Decentralisation and Traditional Authority in Mocumbi, Southern Mozambique." *Africa Insight*, 35, 3 (September 2005): 64–70.
Guerra, João Paulo, *Descolonização Portuguesa: O Regresso das Caravelas*. Lisbon: Oficina dos Livros, 2009.
Hall, Margaret, and Tom Young, *Confronting Leviathan: Mozambique since Independence*. Athens: Ohio University Press, 1997.
Hanlon, Joseph, *Mozambique: The Revolution Under Fire*. London: Zed Books, 1984.
Hastings, Adrian, and Ingrid Lowrie (eds.), *Christianity and the African Imagination: Essays in Honour of Adrian Hastings (Studies of Religion in Africa)*. Leiden: Brill Academic, 2001.
Hastings, Adrian, "Portugal's Other Rebellion." *The Observer*, April 21, 1974.
Hastings, Adrian, "Reflections upon the War in Mozambique." *African Affairs*, 292 (1974): 263–276.
Hastings, Adrian, private diary entries for the months of July and August, 1973.
Hastings, Adrian, *The Church in Africa: 1450–1950*. Oxford: Clarendon Press, 1994.
Hastings, Adrian, *Wiriyamu: My Lai in Mozambique*. London: Search Press, 1974.
Hedges, David, "Apontamento Sobre as Relações Entre Malawi e Moçambique, 1961–1987." *Cadernos de Historia*, 6 (1987).
Helgesson, Alf, *Church, State and People in Mozambique: A Historical Study with Special Emphasis on Methodist Developments in the Inhambane Region*. Uppsala: Studia Missionalia Upsaliensia, 1994.
Henderson, R., "Relations of Neighbourliness: Malawi and Portugal, 1964–74." *Journal of Modern African Studies*, 15, 3 (1977).
Henriksen, Thomas H., *Revolution and Counter-Revolution: Mozambique's War of Independence, 1964–1974*. Westport, Connecticut: Greenwood Press, 1983.
Heren, Louis, *Growing Up on "The London Times."* London: Hamish Hamilton, 1978.

Heren, Louis, *Growing Up Poor in London*. London: Hamish Hamilton, 1973.
Heren, Louis, *Memories of Times Past*. London: Hamish Hamilton, 1988.
Hodgson, Godfrey, "Heren, Louis: Obituaries." *The Independent*, January 28, 1995. See also, http://www.londonbooks.co.uk/affiliates/index.php?productID=544&a=londonistbooks.
Hussey, W., "The War in Tete a Threat to All in Southern Africa." *Johannesburg Star*, July 1, 1972.
IDAF, *Terror in Tete: A Documentary Report of Portuguese Atrocities in Tete District, Mozambique, 1971–1972*. London: IDAF, 1973.
Igreja, Victor, "The Effects of Traumatic Experiences on the Infant–Mother Relationship in the Former War Zones of Central Mozambique: The Case of Madzawe in Gorongoza." *Infant Mental Health Journal*, 24, 5 (2003): 469–494.
Igreja, Victor, "Frelimo's Political Ruling through Violence and Memory in Postcolonial Mozambique." *Journal of Southern African Studies*, 36, 4 (December 2010): 781.
Igreja, Victor, Béatrice Dias-Lambranca, and Annemiek Richters, "Gamba Spirits, Gender Relations, and Healing in Post-Civil War Gorongosa, Mozambique." *The Journal of the Royal Anthropological Institute*, 14, 2 (June 2008): 353–371.
Igreja, Victor, Beatrice Dias-Lambranca, Douglas A. Hershey, Limore Racin, Annemiek Richters, and Ria Reis, "The Epidemiology of Spirit Possession in the Aftermath of Mass Political Violence in Mozambique." *Social Science and Medicine*, 71 (2010): 592–599.
Igreja, Victor, Wim Kleijn, Beatrice Dias-Lambranca, Clara Calero, and Annemick Richters, "Agricultural Cycle and the Prevalence of Postraumatic Stress Disorder: A Longitudinal Community Study in Postwar Mozambique." *Journal of Traumatic Stress*, 22, 3 (June 2009): 172–179.
Isaacman, Allen F., *A Luta Continua: Creating a New Society in Mozambique*. Southern Africa Pamphlets, No. 1, State University of New York, 1978.
Isaacman, Allen F., and Barbara Isaacman, *Mozambique: From Colonialism to Revolution, 1900–1982*. Boulder: Westview Press, 1983.
Isaacman, Allen F., *Dams, Displacement and the Delusion of Development: Cahora Bassa and Its Legacies in Mozambique, 1965–2007*. Ohio: Ohio University Press, 2013.
Isaacman, Allen F., *The Tradition of Resistance in Mozambique: The Zambesi Valley, 1850–1921*. Berkeley: University of California Press, 1976.
Israel, Paolo, "A Loosening Grip: The Liberation Script in Mozambican History." *Kronos*, 39, 1 (January 2013): 1–9.
Israel, Paolo, "The Formulaic Revolution: Song and the 'Popular Memory' of the Mozambican Liberation Struggle." *Cahiers d'Études africaines*, L 1, 197 (2010): 181–216.
Israel, Paolo, "The War of Lions: Witch-Hunts, Occult Idioms and Post-Socialism in Northern Mozambique." *Journal of Southern African Studies*, 35, 1 (March 2009): 155–174.
Israel, Paolo, *In Step with the Times: Mapiko Masquerades of Mozambique*. Athens: Ohio University Press, 2014.
Jardim, Jorge, *Moçambique: Terra Queimada*. Lisbon: Intervenção, 1976.
"Joaquim Chissano: Há gente com tendência para desprezar e deturpar a história." (Saturday, August 18, 2012). accessed August 18, 2013, http://preview.tinyurl.com/ohvow5h.
Johnson, Jessica, "Agency-Level Interventions for Preventing and Treating Trauma: A Qualitative Study." Master of Social Work Clinical Research Papers, Paper 41, http://sophia.stkate.edu/msw_papers/41.

Jones, Griff, *Britain and Nyasaland: A Story of Inattention. Fitful Care, and Political Vacillation*. London: Allen and Unwin, 1964.
Jorge, Lídia, *A Costa dos Murmúrios*. Lisbon: Publicações Dom Quixote, 2008.
Jundanian, Brendan F., "Resettlement Programs: Counterinsurgency in Mozambique." *Comparative Politics*, 6 (1974): 519–540.
Karodia, Farida, *A Shattering of Silence*. Oxford: Heinemann, 1993.
Kienzler, Hanna, "Debating War Trauma and Post-Traumatic Stress Disorder (PTSD) in an Interdisciplinary Arena." *Social Science and Medicine*, 67 (2008): 218–227.
Kilpatric, James J., "The Portuguese Atrocity that Didn't Happen." *National Review*, May 10, 1974.
Klenman, Arthur, Veena Das, and Margaret M. Lock, *Social Suffering*. Berkeley: University of California Press, 1997.
Kyed, Helene Maria, and Lars Buur, "New Sites of Citizenship: Recognition of Traditional Authority and Group-Based Citizenship in Mozambique." *Journal of Southern African Studies*, 32, 3 (September 2006): 563–581.
LaCapra, Dominick, *Writing History, Writing Trauma*. Baltimore: The Johns Hopkins University Press, 2001.
Lan, David, *Guns and Rain: Guerrillas and Spirit Mediums in Zimbabwe*. Berkeley: University of California Press, 1995.
Lancaster, C. S., "The Zambesi Goba Ancestral Cult." *Africa: Journal of the International African Institute*, 47, 3 (1977): 229–241.
Larsen, Ingemai, "Silenced Voices: Colonial and Anti-Colonial Literature in Portuguese Literary History." *Lusotopie*, 13, 2 (2006): 59–69.
Laweki, Lawe, alias João Baptista Truzão, "A Outra Face dos Acontecimentos: Uma Resposta a Janet Mondlane," accessed August 12, 2013, http://macua.blogs.com/moambique_para_todos/2011/10/a-outra-face-dos-acontecimentos.html.
Leguèbe, J., "Mozambique Under Frelimo Rule," in W. Veenhoven and W. Ewing (eds.), *Case Studies on Human Rights and Fundamental Freedoms*. The Hague: Martinus Nijhoff, 1976.
Lima, A. Carlos, *Aspectos da Liberdate Religiosa. Caso do Bispo da Beira*. Lisbon/Braga: Diário do Minho, 1970.
Lima, A. Carlos, *Caso do Bispo da Beira, Documentos*. Porto: Civilização, 1990.
Lion, Alfonso Valverde de, and Martin Hernandez Robles, "Mucumbura 1971 and Human Rights Recognized by Portugal at the United Nations." Mss. Father Hastings Personal Archives.
Lloyd-Jones, Stewart, and António Costa Pinto (eds.), *The Last Empire: Thirty Years of Portuguese Decolonization*. Bristol: Intellect Books, 2003.
Lopes, Félix, *Missões Franciscanas em Moçambique, 1898–1970*. Braga: Editorial Franciscana, 1970.
Loudon, Bruce, "No Massacres, say Tete Tribesmen." *The London Daily Telegraph*, July 13, 1973.
Loudon, Bruce, "Priests Do Not Know of Massacre." *The London Daily Telegraph*, July 14, 1973.
Luzia, J., "A Igreja das Palhotas. Genese da Igreja em Moçambique, Entre o Colonialismo e a Independencia." *Cadernos de Estudos Africanos*, 4 (1989): 127.
MacQueen, Norrie, and Pedro Aires Oliveira, "'Grocer Meets Butcher,' Marcello Caetano's London Visit of 1973 and the Last Days of Portugal's Estado Novo." *Cold War History*, 10, 1 (2010): 29–50.
Maia, Angela, Teresa McIntyre, M. Graça Pereira, and Eugénia Ribeiro, "War Exposure and

Post-Traumatic Stress as Predictors of Portuguese Colonial War Veterans' Physical Health." *Anxiety, Stress, and Coping*, 24, 3 (May 2011): 309–325.

"Marcelino dos Santos, Vice President Frelimo, testifying before the Committee of 24 of the United Nations, 20 July, 1973." *ACOA Fact Sheets* (August 1973).

Marques, João Filipe, "Les Racistes, C'est Les Autres." *Lusotopie*, 14, 1 (2007): 88.

Martens, Fathers J. and A. Verdaasdonk, J. van Rijen, A. van Kampen, and J. Tielemans, "Diary of Inhaminga." *Issue: A Journal of Opinion*, 4, 2 (1974): 62–73.

"Massacre de Wiriyamu (01 de 07)." (no web title), accessed June 15, 2012, http://preview.tinyurl.com/pvvve8a.

"Massacres de Wiriyamu e visita de Marcello Caetano a Londres." *Gerracolonial.org*, accessed January 10, 2014, http://preview.tinyurl.com/ntxyqta.

Mata, María Eugénia, "Interracial Marriage in the Last Portuguese Colonial Empire." *E-Journal of Portuguese History*, 5, 1 (2007): 19.

McKenna, S. J. Joseph C., *Finding a Social Voice: The Church and Marxism in Africa*. New York: Fordham University Press, 1997.

McSweeney, M., M. New, and G. Lizcano, *Mozambique: UNDP Climate Change Country Profiles*. Oxford: Oxford University School of Geography and Environment, 2012.

Medeiros, Paulo de, "Hauntings, Memory, Fiction and the Portuguese Wars," in Timothy G. Ashplant (ed.), *The Politics of War Memory and Commemoration*. London: Routledge, 2000.

"Memorando enviado por Kaúlza de Arriaga a Pimentel dos Santos." n.d.

Meneses, Filipe Ribeiro de, "Parallel Diplomacy, Parallel War: The PIDE/DGS's Dealings with Rhodesia and South Africa, 1961–74." *Journal of Contemporary History*, 49, 2 (2014): 366–389.

Meneses, Filipe Ribeiro de, *Salazar: A Political Biography*. New York: Enigma Books, 2009.

Middlemas, Keith, *Cabora Bassa: Politics and Engineering in Southern Africa*. London: Weidenfeld and Nicolson, 1975.

Minter, William, *Portuguese Africa and the West*. New York: Monthly Review Press, 1972.

Minter, William, "Propaganda and Reality in Mozambique." *Africa Today*, 16, 2 (1969): 3.

Modlane, Janet, "Mozambique Institute: Ray of Hope for Refugees." *Toward Freedom*, 14, 11 (1965): np.

Mondlane, Eduardo C., "The Kitwe Papers: Race Relations and Portuguese Colonial Policy, With Special Reference to Mozambique." *Africa Today*, 15, 1 (1968).

Mondlane, Eduardo C., *The Struggle for Mozambique*. Harmondsworth: Penguin Books, 1970.

Mondlane, Eduardo, "Frelimo White Paper." *African Historical Studies*, 2: 2 (1969): 321.

Morier-Genoud, Eric, "The Catholic Church, Religious Orders and the Making of Politics in Colonial Mozambique: The Case of the Diocese of Beira, 1940–1974." PhD Dissertation, State University of New York, 2005.

Morris, Michael, *Terrorism: The First Full Account in Detail of Terrorism and Insurgency in Southern Africa*. Capetown: Howard Timmins, 1971.

Moutinho, Isabel, *The Colonial Wars in Contemporary Portuguese Fiction*. Suffolk, UK: Tamesis Books, 2008.

"Mozambique in London." *The Tablet Archives*, accessed December 24, 2013, http://archive.thetablet.co.uk/article/11th-august-1973/16/the-tablet-notebook.

"Mozambique: Translation of the Trial Report on the 'Macúti Fathers.'" *Archives of the International Secretariat of Amnesty International*, Inventory No. 442-446, File, 1531/51, AI Index, AFR 41/73.

"Mueda: memórias de um massacre." *Tempo*, 609, June 13, 1982, 24.
Munslow, Barry, *Mozambique: The Revolution and Its Origins*. Harlow: Longman, 1983.
Munslow, Barry, *Samora Machel: An African Revolutionary*. London: Zed Books, 1985.
Ncomo, Barnabé Lucas, *Uria Simango: Um homem, Uma causa*. Maputo: Edições Novafrica, 2003.
Newitt, Malyn, "Towards a History of Modern Moçambique." *Rhodesian History*, 7, 5 (1974).
Newitt, Maylin, *A History of Mozambique*. London: Hurst, 1995.
News, Oberlin Alumni Notes, "In Memory of Eduardo Chivambo Mondlane '53, 1920-1969, to be Honored at May Reunion." *Oberlin.edu*, accessed June 1, 2010, http://www.oberlin.edu/alummag/oampast/oam_spring98/Alum_n_n/eduardo.html.
Oliveira, Paulo, "Kaúlza de Arriaga e o 'Peso de Wiriamu.'" *Público*, February 4, 2004.
Opello Jr., Walter C., "Guerrilla War in Portuguese Africa: An Assessment of the Balance of Forces in Mozambique." *Issue: A Journal of Opinion*, 4, 2 (1974): 29-37.
Opello Jr., Walter C., "Pluralism and Elite Conflict in an Independence Movement: FRELIMO in the 1960s." *Journal of Southern African Studies*, 2, 1 (October 1975): 66-82.
Panaf Great Lives, Eduardo Mondlane. London: Panaf, 1972.
Parker, Kevin, "Wiriyamu and the War in Tete, 1971-1974." MA thesis, University of York, 1982.
Patel, N., and R. Hajat, "Foreign Policy and International Relations," in *Government and Politics in Malawi*, eds. N. Patel and L. Svasand. Zomba, Malawi: Kachere, 2007, 99-105.
Paul, John, *Mozambique: Memoirs of a Revolution*. Harmondsworth: Penguin Books, 1975.
Pereira, M. Graça, and Susana Pedras, "Vitimização Secundária nos Filhos Adultos de Veteranos da Guerra Colonial Portuguesa." *Psicologia: Reflexão e Crítica*, 24, 4 (2011): 702-709.
Pereira, M. Graça, Susana Pedras, and Cristina Lopes, "Post-Traumatic Stress, Psychological Morbidity, Pychopathology, Family Functioning, and Quality of Life in Portuguese War Veterans." *Traumatology*, 18 (2013): 49-58.
Pereira, Zélia, "Les Jésuites et la formation d'élites au Mozambique, 1961-1974." LFM, *Social Sciences and Missions*, 14 (July 2004): 75-116.
Pinto, António Costa, and Maria Inácia Rezola, "Political Catholicism, Crisis of Democracy and Salazar's New State in Portugal." *Totalitarian Movements and Political Religions*, 8, 2 (June 2007): 353-368.
Pinto, Nuno Tiago, *Dias de Coragem e de Amizade: 50 Histórias Sobre A Guerra Colonial*. Lisbon: A Esfera dos Livros, 2011.
Pitcher, Anne, "Forgetting from Above and Memory from Below: Strategies of Legitimation and Struggle in Postsocialist Mozambique." *Africa: Journal of the International African Institute*, 76, 1 (2006): 88-122.
Portugaise, Etudiants d'Afriques, "Situation des Etudiants Noirs Dans le Monde." *Presénce Africaine*, 13 (1952): 236.
"Portugal: Under the Eucalyptus Tree." *Time Magazine*, May 14, 1965.
"Portugal's Rule by Violence Exposed: Massacre in Mozambique." *ACOA Fact Sheet* (August 1973): 3-4.
"Priests 'give details of massacre.'" *The Catholic Herald*, October 8, 1971.
Proença, Carlos Eduardo Machado Sangreman, and Francisco Salgado Zenha, *O Caso da Capela do Rato no Supremo Tribunal Administrativo*. Lisbon: Afrontamento, 1973.
"Quantos Morreram Em Mueda." *Macua.org*, accessed December 16, 2011, http://www.Macua.Org/Quantos_Morreram_Em_Mueda.Htm.

Ramos, Pedro, *A Igreja Católica e o Estado Novo em Moçambique, 1960/1974*. Lisbon: Editorial Notícias, 2004.
Ranger, Terrence, "Territorial Cults in the History of Central Africa." *The Journal of African History*, 14, 4 (1973): 581–597.
Rees-Mogg, William, *Memoirs*. London: Harper Press, 2011.
"Reggie/Rent a Crowd/Lead into Snow." *JISC Media Hub of London*, July 17, 1973.
Reis, Bruno C., and Pedro A. Oliveira, "Cutting Heads or Winning Hearts: Late Colonial Portuguese Counterinsurgency and the Wiriyamu Massacre of 1972." *Civil Wars*, 14, 1 (2012): 80–103.
Reis, Bruno C., and Pedro A. Oliveira, "Reply to Mustafah Dhada." *Civil Wars*, 14, 4 (2013): 559–562.
Resende, Sebastião Soares de, *Os Grandes Relativos Humanos em Moçambique*. Porto: Livraria Nelita Editora, 1957.
Resende, Sebastião Soares de, *Problemas do Ensino Missionário*. Beira: Tip. E.A.O., 1962.
Resende, Sebastião Soares de, *Responsibilidades dos Leigos*. Porto: Oficinas Gráficas da Sociedade de Papelaria, 1957.
Resende, Sebastião Soares de, *Um Moçambique Melhor*. Lisbon: Livraria Morais Editora, 1963.
"Reunião de indígenas perturbada por agitadores estrangeiros que foram repelidos." *O Século*, June 19, 1960.
Ribeiro, António Sousa, *Terror em Tete: Relato Documental das Atrocidades dos Portugueses no Distrito de Tete, Moçambique, 1971–1972*. Porto: A. Regra do Jogo, 1974.
Ricouer, Paul, "The Model of the Text: Meaningful Action Considered as Text," in *From Text to Action*. Evanston: Northwestern University Press, 2007, 140–164.
Ricouer, Paul, *Memory, History, Forgetting*, Translated by K. Blamey and D. Pellauer. Chicago: Chicago University Press, 2006.
Saavedra, Ricardo de, *Os Dias Do Fim*. Lisbon: Editorial Notícias, 1995.
Sagawa, Mukuse Daniel, "Power Politics or Personality? Re-Visiting Malawi's Foreign Policy Conception and Strategy under Kamuzu Banda, 1964–1994." *Forum for Development Studies*, 38, 2 (2011).
Salema, Isabel, "O império colonial em questão?" *Público*, December 16, 2012.
Sanders, James, *South Africa and the International Media 1972–1979, A Struggle for Representation*. New York: Routledge, 2011.
Sandra, L. Bloom, "Caring for the Caregiver: Avoiding and Treating Vicarious Traumatization," in A. Giardino, E. Datner, and J. Asher (eds.), *In Sexual Assault, Victimization Across the Lifespan*. MO: G. W. Medical Publishing, 2003, 459–470.
Sansone, Livio, "Eduardo Mondlane and the Social Sciences." *Vibrant: Virtual Brazilian Anthropology*, 10, 2 (July–December 2013): 73–111.
Santos, José Rodrigues dos, *O Anjo Branco*. Lisbon: Gravida, 2010.
Santos, Marcelino dos, "Discurso: Proferido, Primeiro Congresso." CEA Pasta 967.5 25/I (Dar es Salam, 1962): 6–7.
Santos, Marcelino dos, "Nós não estamos arrependidos." Canal de Moçambique, May 17, 2006 Broadcast," accessed August 18, 2013, http://macua.blogs.com/moambique_para_todos/2006/05/retrospectiva_s.html.
Sassine, Williams, *Wirriyamu*. London: Heinemann, 1980.
Saul, John, and C. Leys, "Lubango and After." *Journal of South African Studies*, 29, 2 (2003): 334–353.
Saul, John, "Frelimo and the Mozambique Revolution." *Monthly Review*, 24, 10 (1973): 22–52.
Saul, John (ed.), *A Difficult Road: The Transition to Socialism in Mozambique*. New York: Monthly Review Press, 1985.

Saul, John, *Socialist Ideology and the Struggle for Southern Africa*. Trenton, New Jersey: Africa World Press, 1990.
Saxon, Wolfgang, "William J. Haley, British Journalist, Dies at 86." *New York Times*, September 9, 1987.
Schäuble, Michaela, "'Imagined suicide': Self-Sacrifice and the Making of Heroes in Post-War Croatia." *Anthropology Matters Journal*, 8, 1 (2006): 1-14.
Schmidt, Heike, "Healing the Wounds of War: Memories of Violence and the Making of History in Zimbabwe's Most Recent Past." *Journal of Southern African Studies*, 23, 2 (1997): 301-310.
Serapião, Luis B., "Mozambique Liberation Front (Frelimo) and Religion in Mozambique, 1962-1988." *Africa, Revista trimestrale di studi e documentazione dell'Instituto italiano per l'Africa e l'Oriente*, 48, 1 (March 1993).
Serapião, Luis B., "The Influence of the Catholic Church on Portuguese Colonial Policy." *Current Bibliography on African Affairs*, 7, 2 (1974).
Serapião, Luis B., "The Preaching of Portuguese Colonialism and the Protest of the White Fathers." *Issues: A Quarterly Journal of Africanist Opinion*, 2, 1 (1972).
Serapião, Luis B., "The Roman Catholic Church and the Principle of Self-Determination: A Case Study of Mozambique." *Journal of Church and State*, 23, 2 (1981).
Serra, C., *Novos Combates Pela Mentalidade Sociológica*. Maputo: Livraria Universitaria, UEM, 1997.
Shore, Herb, "Mondlane, Machel and Mozambique: From Rebellion to Revolution." *Africa Today*, 21, 1 (1974): 3-12.
Shore, Herbert, "Resistance and Revolution in the Life of Eduardo Mondlane," in E. Mondlane, *The Struggle for Mozambique*. London: Zed Press, 1983, xii-xxxi.
Shore, Herbert, Oberlin College Collection: Series 1. "Biographical Files, 1950s-2003" and Series 4. 1952-1966. Subseries 1, "Writings by Eduardo Mondlane, 1952-1968, nd," Box 1.
Shore, Herbert, Oberlin College Collection: Series 3. "Frelimo-Subject Files, 1958-1979, 1988, 1990, 1996-1997, nd."
Silva, Teresa Cruz e, "Igrejas Protestantes no Sul de Moçambique e nacionalismo: O Caso da 'Missão Suiça' (1940-1974)." *Estudos Moçambicanos*, 10 (1992).
Silva, Teresa Cruz e, *Protestant Churches and the Formation of Political Consciousness in Southern Mozambique (1930-1974)*. Basil: P. Schletwein, 2001.
Silva, Tony Simões da, "Raced Encounters, Sexed Transactions: 'Luso-Tropicalism' and the Portuguese Colonial Empire, Pretexts." *Literary and Cultural Studies*, 11,1 (2002): 27-39.
Simpson, Duncan A. H., *A Igreja Católica e o Estado Novo Salazarista*. Lisbon: Edições Almedina, 2014.
6ª Companhia de Commandos de Moçambique, *História da Unidade: Primeiro Fascículo*. Montepuez: CCM, 1992.
Sousa, José Augusto Alves de, and Francisco Augusto da Cuz Correia, *500 Anos de Evangelização em Moçambique (11 de Março de 1948 - 1 de Março de 1998)*. Maputo/Braga: Paulinas/Livraria A.I., 1998.
Sousa, José Augusto Alves de, *Os Jesuítas em Moçambique, 1541-1991. No Cinquentenário do Quarto Período da Nossa Missão*. Braga: Livraria Apostolado da Imprensa, 1991.
Special Correspondence, "Portuguese Commander Denies Massacres." *Catholic Herald*, May 24, 1974.
Stock, Robert, "Apologising for Colonial Violence: The Documentary Film *Regresso a Wriyamu*, Transitional Justice, and Portuguese-Mozambican Decolonization," in Brigit

Schwelling (ed.), *Reconciliation, Civil Society, and the Politics of Memory: Transnational Initiatives in the 20th and 21st Century*. Bielefeld: Verlag, 2012, 239–276.

Sturmer, Martin, *The Media History of Tanzania*. Ndanda: Ndanda Mission Press, 1998.

Tajú, Gulamo, "Dom Sebastião Soares de Resende, Primeiro Bispo da Beira: Notas Para Uma Cronologia." *Archivo, Boletim do Arquivo Histórico de Moçambique* (October 1989): 149–176.

"Tanzania: Government Takes Over 'The Standard' Newspaper." *ITN Source: Footage That Sets Your Story Apart*, accessed February 1, 2014.

Tavuyanago, Baxter, "Renamo: From Military Confrontation to Peaceful Democratic Engagement, 1976–2009." *African Journal of Political Science and International Relations*, 4, 1 (2011): 42–51.

"Telegraphed Tales." *Time Out*, 308 (1976): 5.

"The White Fathers' Testimony." *Mozambique Revolution*, 48 (July to September 1971): 21–22.

Thomas, Martin, *The French Colonial Mind, Volume 2: Violence, Military Encounters, and Colonialism*. Lincoln: University of Nebraska Press, 2012.

Thompson, Paul, *The Voice of the Past*. Oxford: Oxford University Press, 1988.

Tonimbeni, Corrado, "The State, Labour Migration and the Transnational Discourse: A Historical Perspective from Mozambique." *Stichproben. Wiener Zeitschrift fur kritische Africastudien*, 8 (2005): 5.

Toruillot, Michel-Rolph, *Silencing the Past: Power and the Production of History*. Boston: Beacon Press, 1995.

Vail, Leroy, and Landeg White, "Forms of Resistance: Songs and Perceptions of Power in Colonial Mozambique." *American Historical Review*, 88, 4 (1983): 883–919.

Vansena, Jan M., *Oral Tradition as History*. Madison: The University of Wisconsin Press, 1985.

"We have very considerable trade with Portugal. The value of our exports to Portugal in 1972 amounted to £114 million." Sir Alec Douglas-Home, *Hansard* 860, July 17, 1973, cc265-375.

Welensky, Roy, *Four Thousand Days*. London: Collins, 1964.

Wemans, Jorge, "Um grito contra a guerra." *Agência Ecclesia*, accessed January 11, 2014, http://www.agencia.ecclesia.pt/cgi-bin/noticia.pl?id=8406.

West, Harry G., "Creative Destruction and Sorcery of Construction: Power, Hope and Suspicion in Post-War Mozambique, *Cahiers d'Études Africaines*, 37, 147 (1997): 675–698.

West, Harry G., "Girls with Guns: Narrating the Experience of War of Frelimo's 'Female Detachment'." *Anthropological Quarterly*, 73, 4 (2000): 180–194.

West, Harry G., "Sorcery of Construction and Socialist Modernization: Ways of Understanding Power in Postcolonial Mozambique." *American Ethnologist*, 28, 1 (2001): 119–150.

West, Harry G., "This Neighbor is Not My Uncle!": Changing Relations of Power and Authority on the Mueda Plateau." *Journal of Southern African Studies*, 24, 1 (1998): 141–160.

West, Harry G., "Voices Twice Silenced: Betrayal and Mourning at Colonialism's End in Mozambique." *Anthropological Theory*, 3, 3 (2003): 343–365.

West, Harry G., and Scott Kloeck-Jenson, "Betwixt and Between: 'Traditional Authority' and Democratic Decentralization in Post-War Mozambique." *African Affairs*, 98, 393 (1988): 455–484.

West, Harry G., *Kupilikula: Governance and the Invisible Ream in Mozambique*. Chicago: Chicago University Press, 2005.
"White Fathers 'backed the rebels,'" *Catholic Herald UK,* June 11, 1971, 2.
White, Landeg, *Magomero: Portrait of an African Village*. Cambridge: Cambridge University Press, 1989.
Wiarda, Howard J., *Corporatism and Development: The Portuguese Experience*. Amherst: The University of Massachusetts Press, 1977.
"Wiriyamu." *Choppertech Blog*, accessed June 15, 2012, http://choppertech.blogspot.com/.
"Wiriyamu" or a Mare's Nest. Lisbon: Ministry of Foreign Affairs, 1973.
"Wiriyamu e Outras Polémicas" in Macua Blogs, accessed June 10, 2012, http://macua.blogs.com/.
"Wiriyamu...o que foi?" *Cuamba Blog*, accessed November 17, 2012, http://cuamba.blogspot.com/2010/01/wiriyamu-o-que-foi.html.

Index

Page numbers in *italics* refer to figures and tables.

act of mercy 165–6
African and Asian Studies (AFRAS), University of Sussex 13
Aldridge, Jr., Leo Clington 45
American government reaction 125–6, 137
arms procurement/supply routes, FRELIMO 46–7, 50–1, 59–60, 63, 64, 65–6, 67, 145

Banda, Kamuzu 48, 49
Barraclough, G. 8–9
Berenguer, Padre 87, 92, 114, 131, 134, 175
Bertulli, Father Cesare 24, 97, 119–20
Britain
    Caetano visit to 123, 124, 126–7, 129
    government reaction 125–6
    journalists and publications 121–34, 136–7, 141
Buendia, Miguel 90, 91, 118–21, 175
Burgos mission 74, 75–7, 175
    imprisonment of priests 106–10, 111, 118–19
    massacre and smuggled report 116–17, 118–21, 127
    Times journalist and secret police 130–3
    see also Mucumbura mission; Unkanha mission
Buxo, Chief of 90, 92–3, 98
Búzi 5–7

Cabral, A.L. 1–3
Cabrita, F. 22–3, 24–5
Cachavi, Chico 66–7, 140, 154, 156–7, 162, 162–4, 166–9

Caetano, Marcello 11, 12, 53, 134, 135–6, 137
    British visit 123, 124, 126–7, 129
Cahora Bassa dam 41, 56–7, 60, 67, 86
Carr, E.H. 9
Castellá, Padre Alberto Font 78–86, 87, 89, 175
Catholic Institute of International Relations (CIIR) 18–19, 123–4
cattle barons 151–2
cattle trader, Portuguese 66
Chaworha 143, 159–62, *167*
    Chief of 65, 153–4, 156–7, 174–5
    economy 151, 152, 153
    and FRELIMO 63, 67
    investigations/research 22, 35
    number of deaths 171, *193*
    population census (1972) estimates *186–9*
    report 115, 119–20, 121
    sadism and fire 162–4
    survivor (António Mixone) 6, 36, 114, 133, 159, 161, 162–3, 164
Church in Tete 69–71, 175
    and mass violence 87–90
    missionary protest against silence 93–7
    missions 2, 74–5
        see also Burgos mission; White Fathers; *specific missions*
    and nationalist struggle *see under* FRELIMO
    Portugalization 75–8, 174
    protest letter to governor-general 117
    records 18–20
    relations with State 69–70, 72
    shortage of priests 72–5, 174, 175
Conga, Apostle Daniel 87–8

da Costa, Padre Luis Afonso 104, 106–7, 108, 109
da Costa Gomes, General Francisco 53–4
Dalepa, Raimundo 60–1, 66, 67, 68, 86, 127, 166, 174
de Arriaga, General Kaúlza 54–5, 56, 58, 59, 134–6
de Lion, Valverde 88, 97, 99–100, 101, 103–4, 105–7, 108, 175
deaths
   FRELIMO
      assassination of Chico Cachavi 168–9
      leaders 50–1
   Wiriyamu massacre 169–72, *190–5*
denials and doubts 23–5, 125–9, 177
DGS *see* secret police (DGS/PIDE)
diplomacy
   exile politics and 1–5
   nationalist 46
   village chiefs 175
Djemusse
   economy 151, 152, 153
   massacre 143, 166–9
   number of deaths 171, *190*
   population census (1972) estimates *182*
dos Santos, Dr Rodrigues 24, 25–6, 27–8
dos Santos, Marcelino 8, 43–4, 45, 51–2

Elído, Senhor 35–6, 156–7
exile politics 1–5

Ferrando, Enrique 87, 88, 90, 91, 107, 175
Ferrão, Padre 111, 112–16, 161, 164, 170–1, 175
fictional works 26–8
Fogo Fogo, Mr 148, 157
food production, Wiriyamu triangle 149
food supply, FRELIMO 65–6, 67
FRELIMO 13–16, 174–5
   arms procurement/supply routes 46–7, 50–1, 59–60, 63, 64, 65–6, 67, 145
   assassination of Chico Cachavi 168–9
   and Church 77–86, 88–90
   accounts 24–5

   parish responses to liberation struggle 90–3
   self-determination goal 19, 45
   White Fathers mission, Zóbuè 96
formative leadership 42–6
and Mucumbura massacre 97–101, 102, 104–5
nationalist diplomacy, internal dissent and deaths 46–52
oral research 33
origins of Wiriyama story 112, 114, 115
and Portugese colonial armed forces (Sixth Company) 140–1
Portuguese counter-insurgency and change of guard 52–6
presence in Wiriyamu 152–3
protection of Mixone 133
revelations of massacre 137
role of water in Tete warfare 56–60
strategic importance of Wiriyamu 60–8

Geffray, C. 15–16
Graham, B. 13, 14
Gwenjere, Padre Mateus Pinho 45, 47, 49, 50

Hastings, Father Adrian 5, 176–7
   diaries/monograph 19, 21, 22, 24, 25, 26
   massacre report and publication 120–1, 123–4, 127, 128, 137
   My Lai comparison 125
   photographic evidence 28
   UN Special Committee 129
Heren, Louis 123, 124, 125, 141, 175–6

imprisonment of priests 106–10, 111, 118–19
Internation Defense and Aid Fund (IDAF) 20–1, 24, 25, 26

Juawu
   economy 151, 152, 153
   massacre 143, 164–5
   number of deaths 171, *192*

Index

population census (1972) estimates *184*
research 35
survivor (Kalifornia Kanivet) 36, 154, 157, 162, 165

Kaniveti, Kalifornia 36, 154, 157, 162, 165
Kansande, Domingo 111, 112–15, 116, 175
Karimu, Adibu 35, 39, *163*, *167*
Kaunda, Kenneth 49
Kavandame, Lázaro 44, 51
kidnappings 91–2
Kienzler, H. 36
Knipe, Michael 128–9, 130
Kongorhogondo, Chief 64–5, 154–6
Kongorhogondo, Johnny 66–7, 140, 156, 162, 166, 168

literature review 11–12, 28–9
   affirmative literature 20–1
   anti-affirmative literature 23–6
   Church and other public records 18–20
   fictional works 26–8
   Portuguese sources 16–18, 25–6
   two perspectives 21–3
   written sources and their limits 13–16
Loudon, Bruce 23, 128, 136
Lúcia, Irmã (nurse) 117, 134–5, 164
Lundo, Chief of 90–1

Machel, S. 13, 45, 51–2
Magaia, Samuel Filipe 43, 45, 47
Malawi (Nyasaland) 48–9, 50, 53
Marrãro, Isaías 34, 35
Matambo, Chief 91, 153–4, 164
Melo, Antonio (commander) 22, 23, 39, 161, 162, 164, 169, 170
   act of mercy 165–6
micro-aggression 7, 18
missions 2, 74–5
   see also specific missions
Mixone, António 6, 36, 114, 133, 159, 161, 162–3, 164
Mocumbi, Pascoal 43, 44, 51–2
Mondlane, Eduardo 1–3, 16, 43, 45, 46, 47, 49, 50–1

Mondlane, Janet 45, 46, 47, 51
Moure, Padre 118–21, 134
Mozambican National Resistance (Renamo) 14–15, 55
Mozambique Institute 45, 47, 49, 50
Mucumbura mission 77, 87–8, 89–90, 91–3
   and massacre 97–101, 102, 103–6
   imprisonment of priests 106–10
   reprisals 102–6
Mungwambe, José 43, 44
Mutaca, Lourenço 44
My Lai massacre, comparison 124, 125, 141

nationalist insurgency 41–2
   see also FRELIMO
Neto, A. 1–5
Nungo, Silvério 50–1

Oliveira, P.A. 23–4
Operation Gordian Knot 55
oral research
   consolidation 40
   fieldwork 37–9
   first phase methodology 31–4
   informants and team leaders 34–6
   interviews off site 39
   loss of data and vicarious trauma 39–40

Parker, K. 21–2
Paz, Dr José 117, 134–5
photographic evidence 28
police (DGS/PIDE) 51
   agents
      Mucumbura 98
      recruitment 96
      see also Cachavi, Chico; Kongorhogondo, Johnny
   and armed forces 56, 90, 99
   Djemusse massacre 166–8
   expulsion of Padre Berenduer 92
   and FRELIMO 59, 66, 85–6
   interrogation of Padre Castellã 80–1
   methods 18
   Mucumbura massacre and aftermath 99, 100, 101, 105, 107, 108

232 Index

Times journalist 130–3
Wiriyama massacre 140, 161, 162
   report 118–19, 127
Pope Paul VI 93, 96
Pope Pius XII 69
Portugalization 75–8, 174
Portuguese Air Force 111, 133, 140, 162
Portuguese colonial armed forces
   (Sixth Company) 140–1, 161, 162, 164, 165
   see also Melo, Antonio (commander)
Portuguese colonial rule 173–8
   Catholic Church
      Vatican 4, 69, 93, 96, 175
      see also Church in Tete; *specific missions*
   counter-insurgency and change of guard 52–6
   exile politics and diplomacy 1–5
   framing of narrative 5–10
   nationalist resistance *see* FRELIMO
   research *see* literature review
   see also specific premiers
Portuguese responses
   denials and doubts 23–5, 125–9, 177
   volte-face 134–8
priests
   imprisonment of 106–10, 111, 118–19
   shortage of 72–5, 174, 175
Pringle, Peter 39, 128, 129–32, 175
public records 18–20

Reis, B.C. 23–4
research *see* literature review; oral research
Resende, Bishop 72–5, 175
Rhodesia 48, 50, 89–90
Riachu 63, 143–4, 145, 150
   economy 150, 151
   population census (1972) estimates 185
Ribeiro, Bishop Félix Niza 74, 81, 101, 110
Robles, Hernandez 88 97, 99–101, 103–4, 105–7, 108

Salazar, António de Oliveira 42–3, 52, 53–4, 69, 72, 77, 173

Sangalo, Padre José 39, 87, 89, 90, 116–17, 132–3, 152, 154–6, 175
Sassine, W. 26, 27
secret police *see* police (DGS/PIDE)
self-determination 19, 45
Simango, Rev. Uria 43, 44, 45, 50, 51
Smith, Ian 89–90
Soda, Senhor 61, 64, 66, 147, 148
South Africa 48, 50
spirit mediums/rainmakers 146–8
   Senhor Elído 35–6, 156–7
   Senhor Soda 61, 64, 66, 147, 148

Tenente Valeta family 62, 147, 149, 150, 153, 159, 165
   survivors 36
testimonies
   attesters *179–80*
   types of 32
Tete *2*, 16, 41
   FRELIMO 49
   journalists and reports 128–9, 130–3, 136–7
   literature review 21–3
   oral research 33
   role of water in warfare 56–60
   see also Church in Tete; *specific villages*
Tete, Bishop of
   Mucumbura massacre 100–1, 102–3, 104, 106–7
   Wiriyamu massacre 116, 170
Thompson, P. 31
Times/Sunday Times 121–4, 125–6, 128, 129–34, 136–7, 141
Tomás, Américo 52, 53
traders/trading networks 66, 90

United Nations (UN) 46, 49, 57
   Commission of Inquiry 135
   reports 19, 138
   Special Committee 129
Unkanha mission 77
   Church–State relations 78–80
   conflict over burials 80–3
   and FRELIMO 83–6, 88–9

Vail, L. 17
Valeta siblings 36

Vatican 4, 69, 93, 96, 175
Videira, Colonel Armindo Martins 58–9, 60, 61, 67, 109–10, 136, 174
Vieira Pinto, Bishop Dom 71, 95, 107–9

water, role of 56–60, 144–5, 151
  see also spirit mediums/rainmakers
White Fathers 45, 74, 75, 76, 175
  Mucumbura massacre 97, 109
  protest and expulsion 93–6
  Wiriyamu massacre reports 120
White, L. 17
Wiriyamu, Chief of 64–6, 152–3, 154, 156–7, 159, 166, 174–5
Wiriyamu massacre
  anatomy of 159–72
  attesters *179–80*
  groups responsible for 139–41
  numbers killed 169–72, *190–5*
Wiriyamu report 115–16
  origins of 111–17
  smuggled overseas 118–21
  Times publication 121–4

Wiriyamu triangle 141–4, *160*, 177
  chieftancies *155*
  economic expansion and inequality 151–2
  final days 152–7
  population census (1970–2007) *181*
  spirit world *see* spirit mediums/rainmakers
  village life 148–51
  water 144–5, 148–9, 151
Wiriyamu village
  list of dead *191*
  population census estimates *183*

Xavier, Vasco 36

Zambeze, Avelino 87–8
Zambezi, Bulachu Pensadu 36, 61–8, 147, 154, 162
Zambezi River 41, 56–60
Zambia (Northern Rhodesia) 49, 59–60
Zóbuè, White Fathers mission 93–6

Made in the USA
Columbia, SC
27 June 2017